— Words at War —

— WORDS AT WAR —

The Civil War and American Journalism

Edited by
David B. Sachsman
S. Kittrell Rushing
Roy Morris Jr.

— Purdue University Press / West Lafayette, Indiana —

Library of Congress Cataloging-in-Publication Data

Words at war : the Civil War and American journalism / edited by David B.
Sachsman, S. Kittrell Rushing, and Roy Morris Jr.
  p. cm. — (The Civil War and the popular imagination)
  ISBN 978-1-55753-490-3
  1. United States—History—Civil War, 1861–1865—Press coverage. 2. United
States—History—Civil War, 1861–1865—Journalists. 3. Press and politics—
United States—History—19th century. 4. American newspapers—History—
19th century. 5. Journalism—United States—History—19th century.
I. Sachsman, David B. II. Rushing, S. Kittrell. III. Morris, Roy.
  E609.W67 2008
  973.7'8—dc22   2008012608

CONTENTS

PREFACE

DAVID SACHSMAN

The Symposium on the 19th Century Press, the Civil War, and Free Expression at the University of Tennessee at Chattanooga since 1993 has hosted hundreds of scholars from across the United States and Canada, and some from as far away as Israel and the United Kingdom. Its purpose is to share current research and to develop a series of monographs on the 19th century press, the Civil War and the press, the Civil War in fiction and history, 19th century concepts of free expression, and images of race and gender in the 19th century press.

Words at War: The Civil War and American Journalism is the second of three books in a series called *The Civil War and the Popular Imagination* being published by Purdue University Press. It follows *Memory and Myth: The Civil War in Fiction and Film from Uncle Tom's Cabin to Cold Mountain*, which was published in 2007, and precedes *Seeking a Voice: Images of Race and Gender in the 19th Century Press*. Every chapter in all three books was first a paper or part of a paper delivered at the annual symposium in Chattanooga.

How does one go from scores of seemingly unrelated conference papers to a three-book series on the Civil War and the popular imagination? The symposium began as a conference on the Civil War and the press, so the concept of a book or books on the Civil War and American journalism was there from the beginning. The conference itself started with a number of questions. What role did Antebellum newspapers and magazines play in setting the agenda for civil war? What influence did northern and southern newspapers have during the war years? And what was the role of the press in the continuing conflict that followed the cessation of arms?

As the symposium evolved, other issues were raised, addressing how the Civil War has been treated both in terms of history and in terms of how it has been constructed—perhaps *mediated* is a better word—through literature and film as well as journalism. The symposium solicited papers that bridge the gap between historical and literary studies, papers that offer a variety of approaches to understanding the Civil War and its meaning in American culture and history. Year after year, the conference organizers sorted the many conference papers into various categories while thinking of two books, *Words at War: The Civil War and American Journalism* and *Memory and Myth: The Civil War in Fiction and Film from Uncle Tom's Cabin to Cold Mountain*.

Finally we reached the point where we were ready to put together the two books—and we had the right team to do it. Kit Rushing and I chose Roy Morris Jr., the former editor of *America's Civil War*, the current editor of *Military Heritage* magazine, and the author of four books on American history, to be the third editor of the books. We also added a highly recommended history honors student, Autumn Dolan, to the team. While Rushing and I had actually heard every paper delivered and already had some ideas as to which papers should be chosen, at this point in the process Morris and Dolan read every paper, and Dolan even developed her own system of stars (four stars = a really great paper). The team met weekly for several months reviewing, ranking, and organizing the conference manuscripts. For every paper chosen for one of the books, three papers were set aside for future consideration.

The idea for the third book, *Seeking a Voice: Images of Race and Gender in the 19th Century Press*, developed out of this sorting process. Through the years the conference had featured many cutting-edge papers on the presentation of race and gender in the newspapers and magazines of the 19th century. The two books so far envisioned could not possibly have included more than a fraction of these papers, and so we began organizing the conference papers in terms of three different books.

The first book published by Purdue University Press, *Memory and Myth: The Civil War in Fiction and Film from Uncle Tom's Cabin to Cold Mountain*, is concerned with artistic responses to the Civil War. From the time of her founding, America has challenged artists to confront both the reality and the myth of their native country. *Memory and Myth* concerns the works of such writers as Harriet Beecher Stowe and Edgar Allan Poe in the years leading up to the Civil War and the works of Civil War and post–Civil War era writers, the men and women who actually lived through the war and then found themselves struggling to make moral and artistic sense of the national calamity. It goes on to look at the wildly disparate ways in which the war has been rendered by succeeding generations of American writers, from Upton Sinclair and F. Scott Fitzgerald to Shelby Foote and Charles Frazier, and it examines the treatment of the Civil War in motion pictures and television, from D.W. Griffith's *The Birth of a Nation* to Ken Burns's *The Civil War*.

The present volume, *Words at War*, begins by examining the fighting words, dueling editors, crusades, murder and mayhem, panic, and hysteria that set the agenda for civil war in America in the four decades leading up to the conflict. Part II examines the roles played by Confederate and Copperhead newspapers during the war years. Part III, "The Union Forever," examines the press in the North from a number of different perspectives, including Abraham Lincoln's relationship with editor–publishers James Gordon Bennett and

Horace Greeley. The fourth and final section looks at the continuing conflict of the postwar years through press coverage of the 15th Amendment, Nathan Bedford Forrest, the Ku Klux Klan, the 1866 riot in Memphis, and lynchings.

Each of the chapters in *Words at War* is considerably shorter than the original papers. It was the editors' goal to produce a thirty-chapter book that was still tight and readable. We wish to thank our authors for the quality and the substance of the final product, and we wish to take full responsibility for leaving so much information and so many details on the cutting room floor.

ACKNOWLEDGMENTS

A project of the complexity of *Words at War* and its companion works requires the dedication, skill, and knowledge of a number of scholars and support staff. An attempt to acknowledge the work of the people involved in the effort with these few words hardly reflects fairly the investment of time, resources, and talents of those named and of the many not named.

Graduate student and administrative assistant Ryan P. Buckholder deserves credit and recognition for his work organizing and managing early versions of the Symposium on the 19th Century Press. Ryan collected and cataloged research papers from the first of the conferences from which originated the chapters of *Words at War*. Kelly Griffin also joined the project in its early years, and her presence continues to provide managerial support through her years of dedicated office management, her bright smiles, and her organizational abilities.

Graduate assistant and office manager Andrea Elkins served the project and the West Chair of Excellence for several years. Honors student and later graduate student Meredith Jagger began the actual organization of the manuscripts. Graduate students Alison Brasher and Victoria Vaughn did much of the preparation work for several of the symposia. Victoria began the process of contacting authors and publishers necessary as a preliminary step in bringing *Words at War* to the public.

It was in 2004 that history honors student Autumn Dolan and author and editor Roy Morris Jr. joined forces with the original editors to prepare the three separate collections that became the current three-book series. Roy with line-by-line dedication edited each paper and each paper collection. Autumn invested hours in computer formatting, pagination, indexing, and manuscript management. Autumn and undergraduate honors student Corrine Vitek devoted hours assisting in the organization and management of the 2005 and 2006 versions of the symposium.

The past and continuing support of university administrators Charles Nelson, Herb Burhenn, John Friedl, Richard Brown, Fred Obear, Bill Stacy, and Roger Brown makes the Symposium on the 19th Century Press, the Civil War, and Free Expression a continuing venue for scholarship. Of importance, too, to the success of the symposium and of the current project has been the financial support and encouragement of Tom Tolar and WRCB-TV3, Tom

Griscom and the *Chattanooga Times Free Press,* Ruth Holmberg, Paul Neely, and the late Frances Alexander.

I must also acknowledge the continued encouragement and support of Fran Bender and Judy Sachsman. Without Fran's and Judy's long-suffering and patient love, the original editors would be seriously handicapped.

Whatever the value of this current project, those named here as well as many unnamed students, faculty, independent scholars, and community supporters must share in the recognition. That support and dedication we acknowledge and cherish.

Kittrell Rushing

INTRODUCTION

— Roy Morris Jr. —

The Civil War did not begin in earnest until the first shots were fired by secessionist forces at Fort Sumter, South Carolina, on the night of April 12–13, 1861.
But the underlying sectional tensions between the North and the South, like
slow-acting cancers, had been developing for decades in the body politic. One
of the agents spreading these tensions was the American press, specifically the
nation's newspapers, which thanks to rapid improvements in transportation
and printing technology were able to reach an ever-larger audience of eager
and contentious readers. Fulfilling their traditional roles of agenda-setting,
information-sharing, and opinion-shaping, American newspapers traced the
steadily worsening relations between the regions in the three decades leading
up to the Civil War.

After the war began, the press continued to play a role in molding the
way in which the war was perceived by participants on both sides of the conflict. These perceptions, in turn, helped shape the course of the war on both
the battlefields and the home fronts. And after the war was over, the nation's
newspapers, particularly in the defeated South, continued to shape public
opinion by influencing the ways in which the war was remembered, the South
was reconstructed, and the nation as a whole was reunited.

Words at War: The Civil War and American Journalism analyzes the
various ways in which the nation's newspaper editors, reporters, and war correspondents covered the biggest story of their lives—the Civil War—and in
doing so both reflected and shaped the responses of their readers. The four
parts of the book trace the evolving role of the press in the antebellum, wartime, and postwar periods. Part I, Fighting Words, begins with a look at the

1

role the press played in setting the agenda for the fiery sectional debate over slavery. It follows that debate through the four contentious decades from the Missouri Compromise of 1820 through the Nullification Crisis of 1832 and John Brown's inflammatory raid at Harpers Ferry.

Part II, Confederates and Copperheads, and Part III, "The Union Forever," concern the coverage of the war in the two regions, with particular emphasis placed on the prosouthern Copperhead movement in the North and the unofficial cooperation between the press and the Lincoln government in Washington. The final part, Continuing Conflict, looks at the lingering aftereffects of the war, the various ways in which newspaper editors sought to influence their readers' responses to the outcome of the war, and the often conflicting ways in which it was remembered by both the victors and the conquered. Taken as a whole, the book presents the picture of a vital and intensely involved press during one of the most momentous times in our nation's history.

FIGHTING WORDS

The Civil War did not fall entirely without warning on the nation in the spring of 1861. Sectional tensions had been growing for decades—indeed, since the very founding of the nation in 1776. Donald Shaw, the dean of agenda-setting studies, and coauthors Randall Patnode and Diana Knott Martinelli take a look at how newspaper editors played a large role in delineating—and in some ways sharpening—those tensions in the four decades immediately preceding the Civil War. By studying selected newspapers in both regions of the country, the authors find the newspapers acting as "a sort of barometer of the underlying political events and public opinion." As the authors note, "No one could have been expected to see war coming, but . . . newspapers did show evidence of a slowly growing social disunion."

Economic differences between the increasingly industrialized North and the agrarian, slave-based South led to bitter disagreements over the proper role of the federal government in raising taxes and regulating trade between the two regions. The so-called Tariff of Abominations, passed in 1828, placed a stiff tariff on manufactured goods imported into the country from abroad. Southern opponents of the tariff, led by Vice President John C. Calhoun, deemed the tariff "unconstitutional, oppressive, and unjust" and maintained that individual states had the right to "nullify," or disobey, any such laws passed by the federal government. It was the first manifestation of the increasingly explosive concept of states' rights, which worried and resentful southerners would insist upon ever more vehemently in the coming decades.

Patricia McNeely's "Dueling Editors: The Nullification Plot of 1832" looks at the corrosive effects of the Nullification debate on one small South

Carolina community. In Greenville, a hotbed of anti-Nullification sentiment, editors of two local newspapers took their political disputes to fatal extremes when they fought a duel over their differences. The death of *Southern Sentinel* editor Turner Bynum clearly showed the dangerous emotionalism developing in the South.

Douglas W. Cupples's "Virginia and Andrew Jackson's Proclamation: The Emergence of an Opposition Party" looks at local reaction to the Nullification Crisis in Virginia, where Governor John Floyd prophetically warned that "these United States will be shaken to pieces in a few years and deluged in blood purely because the Southern States tolerate slavery and the North wishes to destroy this property that they may govern by a majority in Congress and make the entire South subservient to their views."

Bernell E. Tripp looks at the slavery issue from the northern side, focusing on the efforts of New England abolitionist Lewis Tappan to enlist support for the mutinous slaves of the slave ship *Amistad*, which had arrived off Long Island after the slaves murdered the captain and took over the ship in the summer of 1839. Their case was championed by Tappan and other abolitionists, including former president John Quincy Adams, who represented them in court. The slaves eventually were returned to Africa, "a small victory [but] a decisive step forward in the struggle to abolish slavery," writes Tripp.

Another impassioned abolitionist, New York poet and editor William Cullen Bryant, is the subject of Gregg MacDonald's article, "William Cullen Bryant's 30-Year Crusade against Slavery." Although best remembered as the youthful poet of "Thanatopsis" and "To a Waterfowl," Bryant had a long career as editor of the *New York Evening Post*, in which position he worked tirelessly to promote the cause of individual rights by using the newspaper "as both an educational tool and moral force" in the fight against slavery.

The growing discord between the two regions in the wake of the Nullification Crisis, the annexation of Texas, and the Compromise of 1850 is the subject of Mark R. Cheathem's "The Failure of a Moderate Southern Voice: Andrew Jackson Donelson's Tenure as Editor of the *Washington Union*." Donelson, the nephew of Andrew Jackson, was brought to Washington to serve as a moderate voice for the Democratic Party in the South, but as Cheathem writes, he became "a voice of moderation crying in the political wilderness, a voice lost in the cacophony of sectional debate."

Donelson's failure to steer southern opinion away from secessionist impulses reflected the hardening of sentiments on both sides of the Mason-Dixon line in the decade of the 1850s. Katherine A. Pierce's "Murder and Mayhem: Violence, Press Coverage, and the Mobilization of the Republican Party in 1856" looks at the way in which newspaper coverage of two sensational acts of violence in the nation's capital helped pave the way for the development of the antislavery Republican Party. Pierce links the caning of Massachusetts Senator Charles Sumner to the murder of a Washington waiter, both deeds carried out by southern congressmen and both widely reported by an outraged northern press, which helped prepare its readers for a more aggressively antisouthern political party.

In "Tales in Black and White: The Two Faces of 19th Century Abolitionist James Redpath," Bernell E. Tripp goes on to describe the unique journalistic contributions of roving newspaper correspondent Redpath, who wrote pseudonymously as both a white man and a black man. Ironically, the Hamilton brothers clashed with Redpath over the issue of emigration to Africa, but all three strongly championed opposition to slavery in the South. Redpath, in his travels through Bleeding Kansas and the slaveholding South, was one of the first journalists to practice the brand of participatory, firsthand journalism that would become widespread a century later.

One of the many scoops that Redpath authored involved his personal interview with the notorious abolitionist-turned-terrorist John Brown. In "'The Hay Stack Excitement': Moral Panic and Hysterical Press after John Brown's Raid at Harpers Ferry," Brian Gabrial looks at the very different ways in which Brown's raid was reported in northern and southern newspapers, ways that promoted a hysterical response in both pro- and antislavery readers.

CONFEDERATES AND COPPERHEADS

The rise of the Republican Party, the terrifying specter of slave revolts following John Brown's raid, and the growing distrust and anxiety of southerners toward northern abolitionists gave rise to the secession movement in 1860. Newspapers across the South, from New Orleans to North Carolina, reflected the growing unrest in the region, an unrest that was maximized by the election of Republican candidate Abraham Lincoln as president in November 1860. T. Harrell Allen looks at the steady shift of public sentiment away from the Union and toward secession in "North Carolina Newspapers and Secession." The radical change in editorial policies by the pro-Union Greensboro *Patriot* and the Wilmington *Daily Herald* accurately mirrored their readers' drift from unionism to secession after Lincoln's election and the Confederate firing on Fort Sumter.

The onset of the Civil War presented special challenges to southern journalists, challenges that Debra Reddin van Tuyll describes vividly in "Knights of the Quill: A Brief History of the Confederate Press." Van Tuyll finds it fitting that Virginia editor Edmund Ruffin actually fired the first shot at Fort Sumter because Ruffin and his brethren "had been lobbing shells in the rhetoric war for months, if not years, prior to the showdown at Fort Sumter." Once the war was under way, southern newspapers strove mightily to provide their readers with news from the war front, often in the face of physical dangers and material shortages.

Six days after the fall of Fort Sumter, Union soldiers marched into the office of the American Telegraph Company in Washington, D.C., and took possession of the Associated Press, thus depriving southern editors of their main source of telegraphic news. How southern newsmen responded to this challenge is the subject of Ford Risley's "Wartime News over Southern Wires: The Confederate Press Association." Despite a myriad of problems ranging from an uncooperative Richmond press to the loss of key newspapers during the war, the PA, as it was known, managed to serve the basic needs of southern readers for news of the war. As Risley makes clear, this was due in no small part to the aggressive leadership of PA superintendent John S. Thrasher, whose emphasis on succinct, factual writing would become a hallmark of twentieth-century journalism.

Georgia was one of the key Confederate states, and Georgia newsmen struggled mightily to perform their basic duties in the face of endemic shortages of supplies and the slashing invasion of the state by Union troops led by scorched-earth proponent William Tecumseh Sherman. Calvin M. Logue, Eugene Miller, and Christopher J. Schroll detail the various struggles of Peach State journalists in "The Press under Pressure: Georgia Newspapers and the Civil War."

The war brought unique pressures to northern Democrats, many of whom opposed the war and the Lincoln administration's vigorous prosecution of it. These antiwar northerners, labeled Copperheads by their opponents, had to walk a thin line between dissent and treason, a line that increasingly became blurred as the war dragged on with enormous casualties and unremitting partisan bitterness. In "'Another Copperhead Lie': Marcellus Emery and the *Bangor Union* and *Democrat*," Crompton Burton details the cost of such bitterness to one such antiwar northern editor. Accused of standing "heart and soul with the traitors," Emery saw one of his newspapers fold and the other sacked and burned by pro-Union supporters during the course of the war. Nevertheless, he maintained that the right to a free press was the "best guardian" of the people's liberties and defiantly printed a four-page extra edition of the *Democrat* the day after it was destroyed.

The most prominent northern Copperhead is the subject of Giovanna Dell'Orto's "The Arrest and Trial of Clement L. Vallandigham in 1863." Vallandigham's arrest and trial for treason occasioned a spirited debate by the press of the First Amendment's protection of journalistic freedom of expression, in opposition to the government's need for wartime censorship. This debate, centering on the right of individuals to express even widely unpopular ideas, marked a significant evolution in journalists' understanding of freedom of expression under the Constitution, Dell'Orto maintains.

A counterfeit proclamation purportedly coming from President Lincoln himself led to a myriad of troubles for several New York and Washington newspapermen at the height of the war. In "Civil War Spin: The Bogus Proclamation of 1864," Menahem Blondheim analyzes the case of the *New York World*, the *Journal of Commerce*, and the Independent Telegraph Company, all of which were victimized by the fake presidential message calling for another 300,000 men to put down the rebellion. Despite early evidence that the publications had been taken in by a sophisticated financial trickster, the Lincoln administration nevertheless arrested, incarcerated, and harassed the editors of the publications. Blondheim attributes the administration's overreaction to its anger at losing control of the information-dispensing apparatus at a particularly perilous time, both politically and militarily.

"The Union Forever"

In the North, news-hungry readers scanned the headlines and casualty lists of their local newspapers to keep up with the ongoing progress of the war. Northern journalists realized early on that the military conduct of the war could not be divorced from the political sphere. Indeed, like most civil wars, the war between the North and the South was essentially a political contest carried to violent extremes—"politics by other means," as Karl von Clausewitz termed it.

In "Journalism in Civil War Indiana: The Party Press and Free Expression," David W. Bulla examines the special difficulties faced by journalists in Indiana, a border state with a large antiwar contingent of Democrats and Copperheads coexisting uneasily with a fervently patriotic Republican majority. The eventual suppression of Democratic newspapers by Federal authorities inhibited the state's vibrant press and led to a sharp public debate between Union General Milo Hascall and Indiana Congressman Joseph Edgerton on the nature of civil liberties and free expression during wartime.

Civil liberties of a different sort are the subject of Brian Gabrial's "Damning Voices: The Press, the Politicians, and the Mankato Indian Trials of 1862." Gabrial details the massacre of white settlers in Minnesota by Sioux warriors during the Civil War and the subsequent trial and execution of thirty-eight Indians for their part in the massacre. Although some of those executed were probably guilty, Gabrial notes, the trial itself took place in a climate of animosity and fear fanned by incendiary newspaper accounts of the massacre and those accused of the crime.

African Americans naturally watched the progress of the Civil War with great interest. The readers of the *Christian Recorder,* a publication of the African Methodist Episcopal Church, were kept fully apprised of the military course of the war, as well as the moral and political consequences of the war. As Hazel Dicken-Garcia and Linus Abraham note, the religious newspaper was well aware of the conflict between Christian principles and war but found it to be a moral war because it would do away with the infernal institution of slavery while also preserving the federal government under which African Americans could reasonably hope for a future guarantee of full civil rights.

William E. Huntzicker looks at another dilemma facing Civil War journalists—specifically, how much of the truth they should tell if the truth might harm the war effort. In "Independent or Compromised? Civil War Correspondent Sylvanus Cadwallader," Huntzicker details the challenge faced by Cadwallader, a correspondent for the *Chicago Times*, in the summer of 1862, when he accompanied Union General Ulysses S. Grant on a madcap trip up the Mississippi River. Cadwallader observed firsthand Grant's heavy drinking on that trip but avoided writing about it for fear it would cost Grant his position. It was a fateful decision for the North and for the entire course of the war.

Abraham Lincoln, as a brilliant politician, understood the value of well-placed friends in the press corps. As Gene Murray recounts in "Abraham Lincoln's Relationship with James Gordon Bennett and Horace Greeley during the Civil War," the president took pains to consult and in some ways direct the prominent editors, whose influential New York newspapers, the *Tribune* and the *Herald*, were read by thousands in the city and across the North. Both editors grew to respect Lincoln, a respect they passed along to their readers, which in turn translated into crucial political support for the president's policies.

Secretary of War Edwin Stanton also helped mold public opinion through his canny use of the press. In Stanton's case, as Crompton Burton details in "'No Turning Back': The Official Bulletins of Secretary of War Edwin M. Stanton," it was the issuance of official dispatches under the secretary's name that helped control the public consumption of news and further advance the government's wartime agenda.

Journalism of another sort was present in poet Walt Whitman's wartime dispatches, as Roy Morris Jr. notes in "'O the Sad, Sad Sights I See': Walt Whitman's Civil War Journalism." Whitman, who spent the war as a hospital visitor in Washington, D.C., fell back on his prewar experience as a New York newspaper editor to send back poignant accounts of the suffering and heroism he had witnessed among the common soldiers in the hospitals. Whitman's journalism, like his poetry, brought home the awful reality of the war to Americans far removed from the battlefields and hospitals.

Continuing Conflict

The end of the Civil War did not end all the conflicts—social, racial, and economic—that had provoked the war in the first place. As the opinion shapers and reflectors of their communities, postwar journalists still played an important role, particularly in the defeated South. How they used this power—often for disreputable purposes—is a subject of growing scholarly attention.

In "Taking No Right for Granted: The Southern Press and the 15th Amendment," Gregory Borchard examines the reaction of editors at three influential southern newspapers to the passage of the 15th Amendment giving black men the right to vote. The editors of the *Atlanta Constitution*, the *Charleston Daily Courier*, and the *Richmond Dispatch* all opposed the amendment on constitutional grounds, but to varying degrees the editors also exposed readers to a more subtle acceptance of national goals and mores if only because they felt that resistance at that time was futile.

One powerful symbol of southern resistance was Confederate cavalry leader Nathan Bedford Forrest, who had been one of the South's most effective and brutal soldiers during the Civil War. In "What Can We Say of Such a Hero? Nathan Bedford Forrest and the Press," Paul Ashdown and Edward Caudill analyze the press's role in creating and maintaining Forrest's legendary status during and after the war.

Forrest was reputed to be one of the leaders of the Ku Klux Klan, the fearsome secret society created in the South after the Civil War to resist Republican political control (and the expansion of blacks' rights as citizens). In "Partners in Crime: Southern Newspaper Editors and the Ku Klux Klan," G. Michael Bush looks at the role played by southern editors in fostering support for the Klan's excesses by "choosing words intended to alarm black fears and inflame the most racist of white passions."

Marius Carriere also finds the press playing a deleterious role in race relations in "An Irresponsible Press: Memphis Newspapers and the 1866 Riot." It is Carriere's contention that Memphis newspaper editors helped create the conditions for the brutal race riot in the city in early May 1866 that left 48 people dead and 70 more injured. "The articles in the Conservative press before and during the May riots of 1866 were clearly biased at best, and inflammatory at worst," Carriere maintains.

A more positive role was undertaken by the press during the centennial celebrations of 1876. Robert A. Rabe looks at this role in "Race, Reconciliation, and Historical Memory in American Newspapers during the Centennial Year." According to Rabe, the nation's newspapers helped promote sectional reconciliation by stressing the shared history of all Americans—although such an image intentionally underplayed the ongoing racial tensions in the South following the Civil War.

The press's coverage of evangelist Dwight Lyman Moody's famous 1875 revival tour is the subject of Edward J. Blum's "God of Wrath, God of Peace," which discovers a mutually beneficial relationship between the press and the evangelist—each of whom needed the other for financial reasons. Ironically, Blum finds, the massive press coverage inadvertently helped the cause of sectional reconciliation by presenting readers with a religious alternative to "vengeful Reconstruction and social revolution." That alternative, trumpeted by Moody, was northern forgiveness of southern sins, transforming "a God of wrath into a God of peace."

Coverage of lynchings in three Virginia newspapers in the last three decades of the nineteenth century suggests that not all southerners found Reconstruction such a positive transformative process. Indeed, as James E. Hall makes clear in "'Draw Him Up, Boys': A Historical Review of Lynching Coverage in Select Virginia Newspapers," many in Virginia found the threat posed by black emancipation to be pervasive and menacing, which in turn seemed to justify the drastic actions taken by lynch mobs to enforce an extralegal order on the postwar era. They were confirmed in their beliefs by the overwhelmingly supportive coverage of lynchings by leading Virginia newspapers.

From the Nullification crisis of the 1830s, through the steadily growing sectional discord of the 1850s, to the election of Abraham Lincoln, the Civil War, and Reconstruction, newspapers and magazines on both sides of the Mason-Dixon line reported a staggering succession of momentous happenings. Their various accounts—influenced by personal, political, and sectional biases—comprised the true "fighting words" of the nation's most combative years. In bringing the political and military conflict into American parlors and living rooms, they both solidified and expanded the power of the press as it moved into the modern era. For the national news media, as it was for the rest of the strife-torn nation, the Civil War was a watershed event, after which nothing again was ever quite the same.

Part I

—

Fighting Words

Southern vs. Northern News

A Case Study of Historical Agenda-Setting, 1820–1860

— Donald Shaw, Randall Patnode, and Diana Knott Martinelli —

When the Civil War broke out in the spring of 1861, many Americans were surprised. Southerners had threatened secession so often that, by 1860, new threats that the election of Republican Abraham Lincoln would lead to secession were not taken seriously. States in the Upper South—North Carolina, Tennessee, Virginia, and Arkansas—seceded only after the Lower South states left the Union. Before the South fired the first cannon shot of the Civil War at Fort Sumter in Charleston Harbor, southern editors and journalists had, in a sense, been firing verbal shots for decades. Editors and journalists from northern and midwestern states had replied. Then, as now, editors had considerable power to set the agenda of their daily or weekly publications. And although one cannot be sure what influence newspapers had in leading or reflecting public opinion about what turned out to be a terrible war, it is reasonable to assume that newspapers then had at least as much influence as today in terms of social effects.

Agenda-setting research, the study of how the news media set salience agendas for their readers, listeners, and viewers, has documented many conditions under which media do influence audiences.[1] This study assumes that newspapers also reflect public opinion at some level and that cultures leave agenda residues in existing institutions such as newspapers. Agenda-setting may also be used to study historical change. Edward Caudill has argued that the past can be viewed as an arena in which reflections of public opinion can be seen in mass media. He draws upon early sociological work by D.W. Harding and the public opinion research of Lee Benson, historian D.G. Boyce, and agenda-setting scholar Max McCombs, among others, to support this methodology.[2] "In the United States," writes Caudill, "such an approach definitely is plausible for periods since the 1890s, when a true 'mass press' emerged in a few places, and probably since the 1830s, when the 'penny press' expanded the reach of newspapers."[3]

This study sought to see if one could detect traces of the coming war in the content of a sample of newspapers from the 1820–1860 period using the newspapers as a sort of barometer of the underlying political events and public opinion. It found that newspapers reflected regional interests and that editors in the South were very oriented to the issues that affected the South particularly, such as the acquisition of new territories (with the related question of whether slavery would be allowed in them), sectional news presented through the perspectives of states or regions, and finally, news about slavery.

Two 1850s newspaper clippings from the *Rhode Island County Journal* and the *New Orleans Bee*, respectively, provide a glimpse of the growing tension. In an article headlined "The Doom of the Cotton Hand," the *Rhode Island County Journal* reported:

> Iron and steel machinery, and chemical solvents are making of flax fibre a more than rival for the Mississippi fibre, which underlies the southern system of labor, and on which rests the politics of half this Union, and in whose behalf the extreme resort to disruption of the federal tie, and civil war is constantly menaced. [4]

The *New Orleans Bee,* citing "Untenable Views," disagreed:

> Those amiable gentlemen, the Black Republicans, though fully agreeing as to the necessity of waging unrelenting war upon the South, differ somewhat as to the means of carrying their benevolent wishes into effect. Some of them are desirous of securing auxillaries [sic] in the work, while others consider they are quite strong enough to dispense with all extraneous help. The New York Tribune for example is clearly of opinion that however agreeable it might be for Black Republicanism, pure and simple, to elect a President, the object cannot be achieved without the aid of numerous voters.[5]

As Caudill and Boyce note, it is plausible to believe that people turn to newspapers more often in times of crisis than not.[6] Therefore, Caudill says, "It is a reasonable assumption that the press is more useful as a guide to public opinion during times of stress."[7]

The historical agenda also shows that newspapers of the North and South converged in emphasis on the topics of territories, sections, and slavery by 1860, and that when opinion came together, there was nothing left but to fight because the issue could not be continued by political parties any more or resolved by the Congress,[8] suggesting that the time for debate was over. Scholar Fred Siebert has suggested that social systems under pressure become more conservative and tolerate less freedom.[9] News about these three issues— new lands, old sections, and slavery—emerged in distinct patterns in American newspaper agendas, suggesting an evolution of public opinion. News about territories may have led to sectional awareness and then to more news about slavery, as if warning of an earthquake. This pattern occurred in the 1820–1843 period, then repeated itself more strongly in 1844–1860, just before the Civil War. The newspaper agendas suggest that southern and northern newspapers came to almost the same point by 1860, as if there were no room for variance. The outbreak of war shows there wasn't.

Newspaper agendas are reflections of the collective cultural values of the regions in which they are published. Agendas are the result of factors in the selection and presentation of news topics. The content of the mass media is a summary of various social forces because journalists belong to their times. Historians since James Ford Rhodes have recognized the value of newspapers to document events.[10] Newspapers also provide opportunities for historians to make contributions to the broader field of American social history.[11] Political scientist Richard Merritt used a sample of colonial newspapers to ask whether or not one could see the emergence of an American community.[12] Putting a large number of news story samples into a computer database, Merritt discovered that colonial newspapers seemed to refer to each other and to, for example, other states or "governors" more than to "England" or to "kings" in the 1750s. This was, Merritt argues, the emergence of American community, self referents over outside referents.

This study sampled newspapers from all states and territories of the nation in the years between 1820 and 1860 as a source of different types of stories. Newspapers were sampled from historical regions (Lower South, Upper South, Border States, Middle States, New England, and the West)[13] to reflect broad regional patterns. Each year from 1820 through 1860 was represented in each of the six regions by a single newspaper selected randomly from all newspapers for that period. In 1830, for example, the Middle States might have been represented by a newspaper in New Jersey, New York, Pennsylvania, or Washington, D.C., the states and district included in the sample frame for the Middle States.

The universe of available newspapers was constructed using *Newspapers on Microfilm*. The study first identified dailies that were published for more than two years and were located in the capital of each state or territory. If none was available, the study sought dailies of at least two years' life published in other major cities. If dailies were not available (as was often the case in the South and West in the early years of the study), nondailies published in capital cities or other major cities were used. The mixing of daily and nondaily newspapers was found to have little influence on the character of press coverage generally because dailies and nondailies of the period carried highly similar content. In all, 38 dailies and 29 nondailies fell into the study. On average, each newspaper was included in the study's final sample about four times over the 41-year period sampled.[14]

For each sampled newspaper, 12 issue dates were randomly chosen, one for each month of the year being represented. From these particular newspaper issues, individual stories were sampled from news or editorial columns (advertisements were excluded). Coders recorded the first 15 lines of each story selected, or about 150 words. This was judged sufficient to allow coders to determine the subject of the stories. In all, 3,273 stories were sampled. The intercoder reliability was acceptable at .83.[15]

Newspapers shared a great deal in the 1820–1860 years. Table 1 illustrates a breakdown of news in the various publications according to 11 categories. These categories are defined as:

- Politics: This category includes election campaigns and results, political parties and meetings, and foreign relations.
- Governmental: This category includes debates by government agencies, governmental employees and operations, the post office, military news, and political spoils.
- Foreign: This category includes news of Europe, Latin America, and other foreign lands.
- Slavery/Abolition: This category includes abolitionist propaganda and reactions, the Nat Turner Revolt of 1831, fugitive slave news, the slave trade, slave conspiracies, the underground railroad, and Liberia.
- Sectional differences: This category includes the Missouri Compromise of 1820, the Kansas–Nebraska question of 1854, the Dred Scott decision of 1857, the Wilmot Proviso of 1848, the nullification controversies of 1828 and 1832, the Nashville Convention of 1850, and general sectional hostility.
- Territories: This section includes territorial governments, the sale and settlement of public lands, the Oregon question of 1843–1848, the Texas boundary dispute of 1845–1846, the Texas annexation

TABLE 1 Newspaper coverage of topics by region, 1820–1860.

	North %	South %	West %	Total %	$n =$
Politics	7.4	8.7	11.4	8.7	284
Foreign	13.1	12.5	12.2	12.6	413
Governmental	16.8	14.3	20.8	16.1	527
Slavery/Abolition	2.0	2.7	1.2	2.3	74
Sectional Differences	2.1	2.6	2.2	2.4	77
Territories	4.1	4.9	2.8	4.3	142
Economics	10.3	12.9	10.0	11.6	379
Science & Technology	5.1	3.5	4.4	4.2	136
Social Life	24.4	22.5	20.2	22.8	744
Cultural Life	13.1	13.9	12.4	13.4	438
Education	1.6	1.5	2.4	1.7	54
$n =$	1807.0	1680.0	500.0		3267

dispute of 1844–1845, the Mexican War of 1846–1848, the Gadsden Purchase of 1853, news of General William Walker and Nicaragua in 1855–1857, the Cuba question of 1851, and news about Florida and California.

- Economics: This category includes commerce, tariffs, banking, agriculture, government finance programs, land and market speculation, manufacturing and industry, taxation, internal improvements and public construction, and government spending.
- Science and technology: This category includes railroads, the telegraph, steam engines and steam power, canals, and medicine.
- Social life: This category includes spot news, activities of people, celebrations honoring important people, July 4 celebrations, community health, weather, crime and piracy, Indians, obituaries and memorials, disasters, sports, population growth, and attacks on other newspapers.
- Cultural life: This category includes anecdotes, cultural news and reviews, fiction and novels, historical accounts, literary essays, general descriptions of the U.S. and its territories, manners, morals, and religion.
- Education: This category includes general public education, colleges and universities, and private education.

Table 1 shows that the newspapers sampled from all three parts of the nation—North, South, and West—were more often than not in agreement. Table 1 shows all 11 major categories of news, not just news about territories,

TABLE 2   Leading subtopics by region and period.

	North		South	
	1820–1843	1844–1860	1820–1843	1844–1860
Territories	1. Florida 2. Territorial governments 3. Other	1. Mexican War 2. California 3. Other	1. Territorial governments 2. Sale of public lands 3. Florida	1. Mexican War 2. Other 3. Sale of public lands
Sectional	1. Nullification 2. Missouri Compromise	1. Kansas/ Nebraska Act 2. General sectional hostility 3. Other	1. Nullification 2. Missouri Compromise 3. General sectional hostility	1. Other 2. Kansas/ Nebraska Act 3. General sectional hostility
Slavery	1. Slave trade 2. Liberia 3. Other	1. Other 2. Fugitive slaves 3. Slave trade	1. Abolitionist propaganda 2. Liberia 3. Other	1. Abolitionist propaganda 2. Other 3. Fugitive slaves

sections, and slavery—topics that we know, in retrospect, came to represent regional differences with the approach of, it turned out, a major civil war.

Table 2 shows some of the major subtopics represented by these three news categories. Not surprisingly, in the 1844–1860 period, the Mexican War (1846–1848) was heavily emphasized in the news agendas of the sampled newspapers from the North and South. (Hereafter, we are focusing on the agendas of newspapers from the North and South, leaving out newspapers sampled from the West.) In the earlier 1820–1843 years, the sampled newspapers from both North and South focused on news about territorial governments.

Table 2 shows that the northern newspapers put stories about slave trade on the agenda in both periods, whereas southern newspapers did not focus on that issue. By contrast, newspapers of the South emphasized stories about abolitionist literature. Max McCombs has contrasted what he calls Level 1 agenda setting—agreement on the big topics—with agreement on the attributes within any given topic, Level 2 agenda setting. Table 2 shows that the newspapers of North and South might agree that the topic was important but did not necessarily agree on the way they approached the broad topic.

Did northern and southern newspaper agendas suggest a region that was drifting apart? Figure 1 shows the generally declining agreement between the newspapers of the two regions, indicated by declining Spearman's Rho

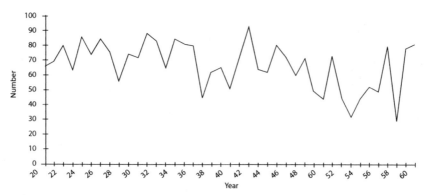

FIGURE 1   Comparison of 11 subject categories, North vs. South (same year) Spearman's Rho correlation.

correlations. All 11 subjects are reflected in the table, including of course news about territories, sections, and slavery, where we have discovered clear regional differences. (Three categories are too few for Spearman's Rho correlations.)

If the newspaper agenda did reflect public opinion in the North and South, this suggests a decline in agreement when all topics are considered. In terms of the coming Civil War, the topics most pertinent—most historians would argue—were those dealing with territories, sections, or slavery. New territories naturally raised questions about whether or not slavery would be allowed in them, often generating lengthy and heated debate. For example, the Missouri Compromise of 1820, which was much discussed in the American press, put a line on the map above which slavery was not to extend. In our analysis we refer to this topic as new lands. Sectional news also focused attention on the local state or nearby states, which presumably represented similar interests because of similar locations. We refer to this topic as old lands in our discussion. Finally, slavery news tended to put the most painful social issue of all on the agenda.

Figures 2 and 3 show that the newspapers of the Upper South emphasized the three issues overall more than did any other region, even the Lower South. Only the Upper South gave slavery very heavy attention in the 1820–1843 years. During this time, the soils of the Upper South became more exhausted from large-scale tobacco and cotton crops, in the production of which large numbers of slaves were employed. By the 1844–1860 years, Upper South newspapers kept focused on the three issues, even as that region "whitened" with the movement of many slaves who were sold down the river, literally, to the Lower South states and Texas. Figure 3 shows that the Lower South states began to reflect the same agenda emphasis on new lands, old sections, and slavery as did the Upper South states.

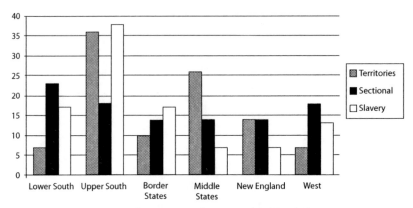

FIGURE 2   Percentage of news types by region, 1820–1843.

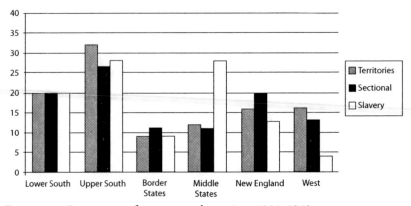

FIGURE 3   Percentage of news types by region, 1844–1860.

Historians can use the newspaper agendas to see if the data suggest any natural periods. Figure 4 shows that news about territories came in most heavily in logical periods, for example, during the periods of the 1820 Missouri Compromise, the approaching war with Mexico over Texas, and the actual war. Texas as a slave state not only provided endless opportunity for expansion of the South's peculiar institution but also would give the South another two senators. Little wonder that the addition of Texas to the Union was a complex issue reflected in the agendas of the sampled newspapers of both North and South.

Figures 5 and 6 show patterns in the coverage of news about sections and slavery. When all three issues are sorted out by the numbers of stories, it is clear that there appear to have been two distinct warning periods, one stronger than the other. The first period was 1820–1843, when the emphasis on these stories in the sampled newspapers showed a large number of stories about territories, then—next in importance—sections, and finally slavery.

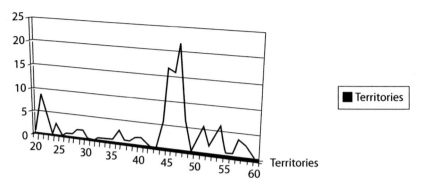

FIGURE 4   Total number of North, South, and West territory stories by year, 1820–1860.

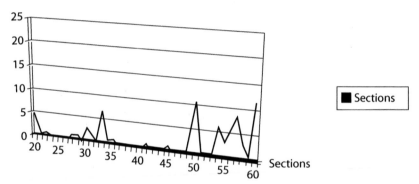

FIGURE 5   Total number of North, South, and West section stories by year, 1820–1860.

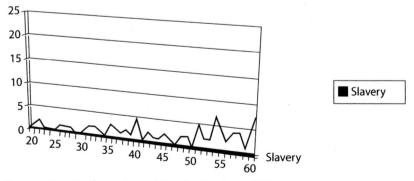

FIGURE 6   Total number of North, South, and West slavery stories by year, 1820–1860.

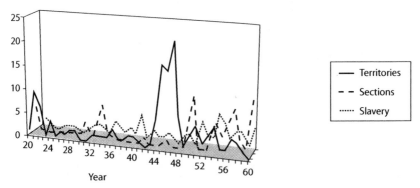

FIGURE 7   Total number of North, South, and West territory, section, and slavery stories by year, 1820–1860.

Like a seismograph's warning of a coming earthquake, the same pattern was repeated in the second period, 1844–1860, but more dramatically—territories, then sections, and finally slavery. Although we have not shown it, this pattern of territories, sections, and slavery, in declining order of emphasis, appeared in the press of all six sampled sections in the study. Figure 7 shows all three patterns combined.

The agendas of the sampled newspapers suggest still more. Figure 8 shows the same three types of news, this time in percentage terms so that the relative emphasis of the North and South is reflected. Newspapers of North and South agreed in general in emphasis on news about territories (with the exception of the 1831–1843 years). The same is true in emphasis on news about sections. Southern newspapers gave dramatically more attention to slavery news than did northern newspapers in the same 1831–1843 years, but otherwise both sections gave about the same quantitative emphasis (although Table 2 shows that the approach within topics differed).

On the eve of the Civil War, 1860, sampled newspapers of North and South not only emphasized all three topics to about the same extent, but there was a clear convergence of emphasis, with about one-third of the emphasis on territories, sections, and slavery in newspapers of North and South. Whatever was felt by individual southerners, certainly southern newspapers did not show much deviation from northern newspapers in focusing on the larger issues. One might not know which issues—territories, sections, or slavery— were most important, but clearly all three topics were part of the key issues that were to set southern against northern brother.

American press news provided hints of coming social disruption, with news about territories first generating additional sectional news and perspectives and finally news about slavery, in that order. These three agenda items

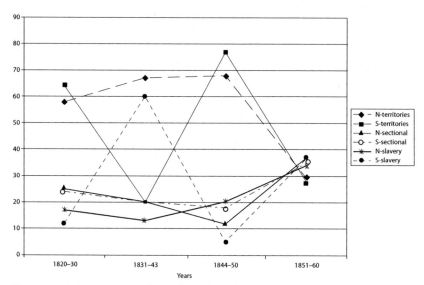

FIGURE 8   Percentages of North and South articles by subject.

were more important in that part of the world than in the newspapers of the other sections. By 1860, there was no getting around the issue, especially in the newspapers that represented the regions of the Upper and Lower South. There is also evidence that the regions came to agree on the key issues, the very ones the political parties and Congress finally could not resolve peacefully.

Caudill suggests that historians consider modern studies to establish the relationships among public opinion and historical events so that we can make better guesses about events in earlier periods in which there are no public opinion data. Obviously our study could not do that. But there is evidence that newspapers of both North and South slipped gradually but distinctly away from consensus on all news topics over the 1820–1860 years and that by 1860 they had converged in terms of space on the topics of territories, sections, and slavery—all topics that framed differences between the two regions. There also is evidence that such events as the 1846–1848 Mexican War influenced news coverage and perhaps made regional differences more evident to the publics of the different American regions. The newspaper agendas suggest that the Civil War began, in a sense, in 1846 with the Mexican War, starting the agenda cycle off in a way that political parties, the Congress, and political leaders ultimately could not resolve.

No one could have been expected to see war coming, but historically one can make a case that newspapers did show evidence of a slowly growing social disunion—the exact opposite, perhaps, of Merritt's consolidation of American community because that study finds stronger evidence that the South as a region kept focus on topics of disruption and that the northern newspapers also began to reflect them. Newspapers of the West and on the border between the South and North never expressed as strong an interest in these issues. But as public and cultural attention came to settle on the same troubling issues, there was not an easy solution. That would require cannons.

NOTES

1.   E.M. Rogers, J.W. Dearing, and S. Chang, "Agenda-Setting Research: Where Has It Been, Where Is It Going?" in *Communication Yearbook*, vol. 11, ed. J. Anderson, 555–593 (Newbury Park, CA: Sage, 1988).

2.   Edward, Caudill, "An Agenda-Setting Perspective on Historical Public Opinion," in *Communication and Democracy*, ed. M. McCombs, D.L. Shaw, and D. Weaver, 169–182 (Mahwah, NJ: Erlbaum Associates, 1997).

3.   Ibid., 181.

4.   *Rhode-Island County Journal,* 6 July 1855.

5.   *New Orleans Bee,* 6 September 1859.

6.   Edward, Caudill, "An Agenda-Setting Perspective on Historical Public Opinion," in *Communication and Democracy*, op. cit., 182.

7.   Ibid., 182.

8.   Roy F. Nichols, *The Disruption of American Democracy* (New York: Collier, 1962).

9.   Fred S. Siebert, *Freedom of the Press in England, 1476–1776: The Rise and Decline of Government Controls* (Urbana: University of Illinois Press, 1952).

10. James Ford Rhodes, *History of the United States from the Compromise of 1850* (New York: Macmillan Company, 1966).

11. For example, see Lucy M. Salmon, *The Newspaper and the Historian* (New York: Oxford University Press, 1923).

12. Richard L. Merritt, *Symbols of American Community, 1735–1775* (New Haven, CT: Yale University Press, 1966).

13. The states (and district) included in each region follow: Lower South—Alabama, Florida, Georgia, Louisiana, Mississippi, South Carolina, and Texas; Upper South—Arkansas, North Carolina, Tennessee, and Virginia; Border States—Delaware, Kentucky, Maryland, Missouri, and (what became) West Virginia; Middle States—New Jersey, New York, Pennsylvania, and Washington, D.C.; New England States—Connecticut, Maine, Massachusetts, New Hampshire, Rhode Island, and Vermont; West—California, Illinois, Indiana, Iowa, Michigan, Minnesota, Ohio, Oregon, and Wisconsin.

14. Donald L. Shaw, "Some Notes on Methodology: Change and Continuity in American Press News, 1820–1860," *Journalism History* 8, no. 2 (Summer 1981): 38–50.

15. For an extensive discussion of the methodology, see Shaw, ibid., 51–53, 76, and Donald L. Shaw, "At the Crossroads: Change and Continuity in American Press News 1820–1860," *Journalism History* 8 (Summer 1981): 38–50.

Dueling Editors

The Nullification Plot of 1832

— Patricia McNeely —

By 1830, after writing for only four years for the *Republican* and the *Greenville Mountaineer* in Greenville, South Carolina, Benjamin F. Perry had already established himself as a major political force in a hotbed of anti-Nullification sentiment. Incumbent legislators felt the growing influence of Perry's passionate editorial voice when they were defeated by the Unionists in Greenville County that year in the fall elections. They blamed their loss on Perry, whose pro-Union editorials had grown so influential that the would-be Nullifiers felt they could not hope to win in Greenville as long as he continued his journalistic crusade. Knowing that the 26-year-old Perry was hot-headed and always willing to fight, the Nullifiers persuaded brilliant and equally hot-headed 25-year-old Turner Bynum of Columbia to become a rival editor in a deadly political battle where Bynum was to be the pawn and Perry the target.

By destroying Perry or his reputation, the Nullifiers hoped to kill or slow the growth of Union sentiment in the upstate region of South Carolina and—not coincidentally—regain their seats in the general assembly. The Perry-Bynum duel was to be played out against a backdrop of national and state politics during the contentious and potentially explosive period following passage of the so-called Tariff of Abominations in 1828. When Congress passed the tariff, the South Carolina legislature declared the new taxes unconstitutional and endorsed a lengthy treatise, written anonymously by United States Senator

John C. Calhoun, affirming the right of an individual state to nullify—that is, refuse to obey—any federal law with which it disagreed. South Carolina's newspapers, which were at the heart of the dispute, quickly chose sides as either pro-Nullification or pro-Union voices. The journalistic war flared.

Of the state's 34 newspapers in 1828, 20 were openly pro-Nullification, whereas 14 favored a strong federal government and no state's right to veto federal laws. The decade that followed the passage of the Tariff of Abominations saw the establishment of 52 new newspapers in South Carolina, all with clear pro- or anti-Nullification alignments. In case there were any doubts, many of the papers announced their affiliation in their mastheads, such as the *Abbeville Whig and Southern Nullifier*, established in 1831; the *State Rights and Free Trade Evening Post*, established in Charleston in 1831; the *Camden Journal and Southern Whig*, established in 1834; and the *Southern Watchman and General Intelligencer*, established in Charleston in 1837. The editors argued eloquently and passionately in their newspapers, and their political disagreements frequently spilled off the printed page into personal arguments, fistfights, and in some cases duels.

Being an editor had never been a safe occupation in South Carolina. Offended by an article in the *South Carolina Gazette* in 1748, a reader sent a message to editor Peter Timothy threatening to cut off his ears. In 1780, Timothy was arrested by the British and shipped to a prisoner-of-war camp. By the early nineteenth century, dueling had become more common in South Carolina than in most southern states,[1] although the deadly practice was also prominent in Georgia, Mississippi, Tennessee, and Kentucky.[2] The most trivial remark could lead to a duel, and almost anything an editor wrote about Nullification or the Union could be construed by the opposition as a personal affront that could only be settled at ten paces. Although illegal in South Carolina, duels had become so common by 1838 that John Lyde Wilson, a habitual duelist who was editor of the *Investigator* and had been governor of South Carolina between 1822 and 1824, published a code of honor that became the standard guide for southern duelists. Until that time duels had been conducted as participants chose, but after the code was published duelers adhered to strict guidelines. Survivors, if tried, were usually acquitted.

Editors were challenged on an almost daily basis. Near the end of his life, Francis W. Dawson, editor of the *News and Courier*, estimated that he had been challenged to hundreds of duels during his life. Dawson never accepted any of the challenges, although he was a second several times. Dueling was outlawed in South Carolina three times—in 1812, 1823, and 1869—but the laws typically were ignored. Soon after a tough death-for-dueling law was passed in 1880, Colonel E.B.C. Cash killed Colonel W.M. Shannon in Camden. Dawson led a litany of newspaper editors across the state in denouncing the practice. With intense newspaper support, a fourth law was passed in 1882 making it illegal to leave the state to issue or receive a challenge or participate in a duel.[3] Dawson's editorial crusade against dueling won him a knighthood from Pope Leo XIII. Ironically, he was killed in 1889 defending the honor of his French governess, although not in a duel.[4]

Other editors also became prime targets for duelists. John C. Calhoun's protégé George McDuffie, who wrote for the *Mercury*, fought two duels with William Cumming of Augusta in 1822. McDuffie's arm was broken in the first duel, and a bullet lodged in his spine during the second duel, crippling him for life. Governor James Hamilton Jr., who also wrote for the *Mercury*, fought and wounded fourteen men who offended him. William R. Taber, an editor with the *Mercury*, died in a much-publicized duel on September 29, 1856. Charleston Judge A.G. Magrath, a candidate for Congress, took offense at an article in the *Mercury* signed "Nullifier" but written by Edmund Rhett Jr. and accompanied by an editorial comment written by Taber. Edward Magrath, the judge's younger brother, challenged Taber and John Heart, also a *Mercury* editor, to a duel. The editors considered Magrath's challenge insulting and instead cross-challenged Magrath, meaning that Magrath would have to fight them both. Taber, who claimed to be defending the liberty of the press, agreed to fight Magrath first and was fatally wounded. The second duel between Heart and Magrath was canceled.

It was during this era that a fiery 20-year-old Greenville law student named Benjamin F. Perry began writing for a new newspaper, the *Republican*, which had been established in 1826. Perry condemned the Tariff of Abominations but opposed Nullification and disunion and began a running editorial battle with the *Yorkville Encyclopedia*, a Nullification newspaper established in 1825 in York County. A year after Perry was admitted to the bar on January 10, 1827, the *Republican* folded, but the owners started a new pro-Union newspaper, the *Mountaineer*, in 1829, with Perry once again on board as editorial writer. He officially became editor in 1830, and at the age of 24 became the leading Unionist editor outside of Charleston and one of the greatest obstacles to the spread of Nullification sentiments in South Carolina.

Perry's primary upstate editorial foe was Dr. Frederick W. Symmes, editor of the *Pendleton Messenger*, which was published near John C. Calhoun's home in the Pendleton District, a staunch Nullification hotbed 30 miles west of Greenville. The *Messenger*, which was established in 1807 as *Miller's Weekly Messenger*, was the oldest newspaper in the upstate, but Symmes, a Nullificationist and one of Calhoun's most loyal supporters, was no editorial match for the passionate and tenacious Perry.

At the beginning of his career, the hot-headed Perry spent almost as much time fighting as writing. He barely avoided a duel with Greenville lawyer and legislator Waddy Thompson and Dr. Henry H. Townes, editor of the *Pendleton Messenger* and a former classmate of Perry's. Challenges were hurled but no duels were fought, although Perry got into a club-and-cane fight with one of Thompson's intermediaries. By 1831, Perry had been in more than a dozen personal fights stemming from his Unionist editorials, and he made it clear that his political beliefs were stronger than any former friendships. "We regret exceedingly those differences in politics which have separated us from some of our warmest and best friends," Perry wrote. "But this separation is a mere feather in the balance, when compared with the honor and glory of our country. Friend has no name, kindred has no ties, when placed in opposition to the Liberty, Independence and Union of the Republic."[5]

With his strong, passionate, and well-written editorials, Perry established an immediate following in Greenville, which had become a hotbed of Union support in South Carolina. In October 1830, incumbent legislators Waddy Thompson, his brother-in-law Dr. William Butler, and fellow lawyer Tandy Walker were hit by the full force of Perry's editorial power when they were defeated by the Unionists in Greenville County. They understandably blamed their loss on Perry, whose *Mountaineer* had expanded its circulation as far south as Charleston to give even wider circulation to Perry's persuasive Union voice.

Against that backdrop, Perry's political enemies decided to establish a Nullification newspaper in Greenville to compete directly with him. To lead the battle, Thompson, who had barely avoided a duel with Perry, persuaded 25-year-old Turner Bynum of Columbia to become editor of the new publication. Perry had already been in numerous fights with both Thompson and William Choice, another legislative candidate, and there was little doubt about the purpose and political direction of the new pro-Nullification newspaper. Thompson and other prominent Nullifiers believed that Bynum could change the political landscape in Greenville and also block the fast-growing pro-Union sentiment upstate. Perry wrote later that Bynum "was the very man my enemies, personal & political, wanted to break down the *Mountaineer* & destroy me, either in character or life! I was aware of their object & determined to act prudently whilst I acted firmly."[6]

The first issue of the *Southern Sentinel* appeared on June 23, 1832, with a challenging motto: "Quick to Discern, and Ready to Defend." Perry tried to calm the gathering storm with a conciliatory editorial:

> The first number of the "Southern Sentinel" edited by Turner Bynum, esq., and published by B. Bynum [Turner's brother] and G.E.W. Nelson was issued in this place on Saturday last. This paper will be devoted

mainly to the great question which now agitates South Carolina. The Editor is a young man of talents and literary attainments and will, no doubt, conduct the Sentinel with great zeal and ability. He says in his address that his course shall be governed by fair, open and manly argument, without descending to the slag, abuse and personalities of a newspaper bully. To such an Editor, conducting his paper on such principles we shall always be happy to extend the right hand of friendship and good feeling. Although we differ on abstract principles, it is no cause for a want of that civility, courtesy and kindness which mark the conduct of friends and honorable men. The question now for the consideration of the people of South Carolina is a great and important one, and both sides should be fairly, honestly and patiently heard. . . . There are in this district sixteen hundred voters and of this number, a very small portion indeed have ever taken the Mountaineer. We do not think that the influence of this paper has been such as some persons have attributed to it. On the contrary, we believe that it has done very little towards the formation of the present sentiments of the district.[7]

Perry knew what the backers of the *Sentinel* intended, but the Nullifiers had painted him into a corner. The week after Bynum's paper appeared, Perry wrote that he wanted to leave the newspaper business, "but circumstances have forced me to continue its Editor. . . . As soon as party spirit subsides, I will lay aside newspapers and devote myself to literature and my profession. If I were to do so sooner, my enemies would attribute it to a want of nerve." No copies of the *Southern Sentinel* have survived from July 1832 to show Bynum's editorials about the Nullification question, but Perry's editorial about the tariff and a surplus of $10 million in the Treasury in the July 28 edition of the *Mountaineer* generated a hailstorm of criticism.

Bynum's editorial "The Late Tariff Act" on August 4 was a bold and angry personal attack on Perry. Bynum wrote directly to and about Perry, calling his newspaper by name in his editorial, referring to him as "Sir Knight of the Mountain," labeling him a "treacherous Delilah," and likening him to the satanic serpent that wooed Eve:

The "Mountaineer" of the last week, with a truckling subserviency to the traitorous dictates of the leading submission presses of the State, has asserted that the tariff has been 'favorably adjusted'; that there is a reduction of $10,000,000; and that the duties, under the late Act, are "infinitely lower," than by the bill of 1816. Such reckless assertions would hardly deserve the notice of a sensible man, were it not that it is necessary to disabuse the public mind, so far as it is influenced by that paper, of wanton and egregious error. . . . It is the SUPPOSITION (!!!) of a "respectable gentleman!"

Be not deceived by the delusion of "compromise"—the lips of the ravisher are full of seductive sweetness. The serpent wooed Eve to commit sin by a tempting lie—and the monopolists with their confederates and apologists here, would lead you to inevitable slavery by offering to bind upon your arms, what they deceitfully call, bracelets of gold—but which, if you heedlessly accept, will be found shackles of iron.[8]

In the face of such a personal attack, Perry had no choice but to challenge Bynum to a duel. Years later, Perry recalled the circumstances:

I once more got into a difficulty. On yesterday morning "The Sentinel" made a most scurrilous and abusive attack on me. I challenged Mr. Bynum the Editor immediately. He accepted the challenge—to fight as soon as he could procure his weapons and send for an acting friend. This is what Bynum and the Sentinel were brought here for. Waddy Thompson, a false-hearted demagogue and a jesuitical slanderer, whose patriotism consists in egotistical declamation, and whose chivalry has been wasted in words, [had] made a tool of Bynum to destroy me. I [was] in his way and in the way of other nullifyers in this place.[9]

Perry chose personal friends Dr. A.B. Crook and Perry Duncan as his seconds, but Bynum's seconds were pointedly political choices. He was accompanied by prominent Nullificationist James H. Hammond, who later would become governor of South Carolina; politician-journalist Colonel Alexander C. Haskell; and Colonel Thomas Pinckney, who had been the Federalist Party's nominee for vice president in 1796. The parties met on an island near Hatton's Ford in the Tugaloo River near the Georgia border on August 16, 1832. Most duels were not fatal, and in fact, most duelists were poor shots who either missed or only slightly wounded their adversaries before declaring themselves satisfied, but Perry had been practicing. Bynum fired first, the shot going over Perry's head. Perry, taking careful aim, fatally wounded Bynum. After Bynum died the next day, his friends took his body on a two-horse wagon to Pendleton to bury him at midnight outside the cemetery wall of the Old Stone Church (church leaders would not permit burial in their cemeteries of anyone who died in a duel).[10] There was no mention of the duel or Bynum's death in the *Mountaineer,* but the *Pendleton Messenger* carried a "melancholy" article about the duel and Bynum's death in its August 22 issue.

Perry wrote later that the duel "has been to me the most painful event of my life. But I could not avoid it without sacrificing character & usefulness in life. Public opinion which sanctions duelling is to blame, and it must continue until there is a change in the opinion of the public. I had no ill will against Bynum & he said he had none against me! Yet we met in fatal combat, & no one attempted to interfere to stop it! I knew full well that sooner or later, I should have to fight for my principles or be disgraced." Perry said Bynum's death "put an end to all the secret slanders & afterwards the Nullifiers treated me with the greatest courtesy. Good results from evil very often. When a man knows that he is to be held accountable for his want of courtesy, he is not so apt to indulge in abuse. In this way duelling produces a greater courtesy in society & a higher refinement."[11]

Left alone by his political enemies, Perry returned to the attack with a vengeance, and the scope of his influence widened. In the fall elections in Greenville, the Unionists won by three-to-one margins. Perry resumed his editorial attack against Nullification, writing bitterly in the December 1, 1832, issue of the *Mountaineer,* "This is the glorious doctrine of Nullification, which has already torn society to pieces, and embittered the nearest and dearest relations of life."[12] Fearing that Thompson and friends would bring in another editor to take up where Bynum left off, Perry wrote in his journal on December 6, 1832, that he would not fight any more duels with editors. Taking advantage of the unwritten code of honor that allowed victors of duels to refuse all subsequent challenges, Perry wrote:

> I have shown that I am not afraid to fight and consequently I am not going to challenge any blackguard of an editor. The next man I fight or challenge shall be a man of some distinction. I am done with lackeys. There is no honor to be acquired in a contest with such men, and I am unwilling to become their executioner. The practice of duelling is a bad one, but a necessary evil, and must some time be adopted in order to avoid a worse one.[13]

With no hope of luring Perry into a duel, the Nullifiers closed their newspaper. The last edition of the six-month-old *Southern Sentinel* was published December 15, 1832, just two weeks after Perry's strident nullification editorial.[14] After the *Southern Sentinel* died, Perry defiantly added a standing head under the American eagle that ran over his editorial column: "The Union Must Be Preserved."[15] Although he was goaded and challenged numerous times in his career, he never fought again.

Thompson had never viewed Bynum and the *Southern Sentinel* as anything other than the political tools they were. Because Bynum had failed to destroy Perry and the Union movement in Greenville, Thompson decided to try another angle. Six months after Bynum's death, he callously converted to Unionism and invited Perry to dinner at his home. Although Perry declined the dinner invitation, he announced that he was "very anxious to be at peace and in friendship with all mankind once more"[16] and promised Thompson that he would not write or say anything about the new Union sympathizer in any future political campaigns. Perry recalled later that "I was unfriendly with General Thompson at that time. I did not, however, hesitate to throw aside personal considerations. This renewed the friendly relations between General

Thompson and myself, and we continued ever afterwards fast friends, enter-
taining the same political views.[17]

After Bynum's death and Thompson's sudden political conversion,
Union sentiment grew ever stronger in Greenville County, and Thompson
flourished in the new political environment. The establishment of the *Southern Sentinel* and the subsequent dispute with the *Mountaineer* was good for
Perry's business, as well. His newspaper went from a circulation of around
250 in July 1832 to almost 400 by December 1832, but a few months later he
stepped down from his position as editor of the *Mountaineer* to practice law.
On March 30, 1833, he wrote what he thought would be his last editorial in
the *Mountaineer*:

> The life of an Editor is, at all time, one of great vexation, great trouble and
> great responsibility, and in time of high political excitement, it is one of
> deep and painful mortification. To me it has been a source of wounded
> pride and lasting regret. It has cost me much of feeling and of trouble.
> Nor has it ever been congenial with my nature to be in constant excite-
> ment and turmoil. The course I have pursued as the conductor of a public
> Journal is before the community, and by it I am willing to be judged. . . .
> In my conduct there may be much of violence but there can be nothing
> of intentional wrong.[18]

Perry turned his attention to the development of railroads, winding up
on committees with his new best friend Thompson and his former classmate
Townes, with whom he had almost dueled. In the spring of 1834, Perry accepted the nomination of the Union Party to run for Congress from the Pendleton and Greenville districts. In one of Perry's few political losses, voters in
neighboring Anderson and Pickens Counties turned against him because of
Bynum's death, and even with a landslide vote in Greenville, he lost by a margin of 70 votes—2,925 to 2,855.

When Congressman Warren Davis died in January 1835, Thompson
announced as a candidate for Congress. Perry kept his word not to write or
say anything derogatory about Thompson in a political campaign. Perry's
old newspaper foe, Dr. Frederick Symmes, baited him in the *Pendleton Messenger*, but Perry refused to fight, and Thompson won by 710 votes. In spite
of the Bynum duel and Thompson's earlier political affiliation, Perry and
Thompson spent hours talking politics.[19] Perry was elected to the General
Assembly in 1836 and served almost continuously through the Civil War.
In another irony, just six years after Bynum's death in 1838, Thompson, secure and happy in his new position in the Union camp, challenged John C.
Calhoun to a duel, a challenge that Calhoun skillfully avoided in a carefully
worded letter.[20]

Perry had been replaced as editor of the *Mountaineer* in 1833 by William Lowndes Yancey, who came to Greenville in 1833 to read law with Perry. Yancey shared Perry's Unionist views. In 1838, Yancey attended a militia muster where congressional candidates Thompson and Joseph N. Whitner of Anderson were speaking. After Yancey made a disparaging remark about Thompson, he was called a liar by Mrs. Thompson's 17-year-old cousin. Yancey slapped the cousin and hit the boy's father with a riding crop. A few days later, Yancey killed the boy's father, who had attacked him with a grain cradle and a knife. Yancey was ably defended by Perry and escaped with a fine of $1,500 and twelve months in jail. Governor Patrick Noble subsequently reduced the fine to $500 and commuted the jail sentence altogether. Yancey returned to Alabama, where he would become a nationally known champion of secession.

By 1840, Nullification was a dead issue, and Calhoun, with his eye on the White House, began unifying the state into a party dedicated to the protection and perpetuation of slavery. In yet another political realignment, Perry joined forces with the Democratic Party and his former nemesis Calhoun, whereas Thompson, his partner and best friend since 1833, joined the opposition Whig Party. By 1847 Perry was seeing eye-to-eye with Calhoun on national issues, whereas Thompson was in the other camp.[21]

President John Tyler appointed Thompson minister to Mexico in 1842, but he returned to Greenville two years later to practice law. By 1850, Thompson owned a plantation with thirty-three slaves, and Perry's former die-hard Union newspaper, the *Mountaineer,* joined forces with his old nemesis the *Pendleton Messenger* to support disunion. The political about-face of the *Mountaineer* drove Perry back into the newspaper business, and in 1850 he started a new Union newspaper in partnership with Thompson. The first issue of the *Southern Patriot,* partially funded by Thompson and edited by Perry, appeared on February 28, 1851, under the somewhat contradictory motto "The Rights of the South and the Union of the States." The 2,000 copies of the first issue sold out, and subscriptions increased at the rate of 100 per week.[22]

Perry's former classmate G.F. Townes was editing the *Mountaineer,* now a secessionist newspaper that became increasingly critical of Perry, who struck back in the *Southern Patriot.* The editorial battle grew so intense that Townes took out a warrant against Perry for libel and had him arrested and held on a $300 bond. The charges were dropped, and Perry edited the *Southern Patriot* until 1855, when he took over the *Mountaineer* again and merged it with the *Southern Patriot* to form the *Patriot and Mountaineer.*[23] Soon after Perry established the *Patriot and Mountaineer,* he was challenged to a duel by William R. Taber, editor of the Charleston *Mercury,* but he refused the challenge. Taber was killed in a duel the next year.

Perry and Thompson had stood with Calhoun in opposition to the Wilmot Proviso of 1846, which excluded slavery from any newly acquired territory. They believed that the exclusion of slavery meant the dissolution of the Union.[24] When South Carolina voted to secede in 1860, Perry wrote in his journal: "That my son should ever fight against the Union is what I never expected. But I may have to do so myself. The dire necessity of self defense [has] fallen on South Carolina & we must defend our independence & Liberty."[25] Perry, who had spent his life fighting to save the Union, volunteered his services to the Confederacy and urged his friends to join the Confederate Army. Perry was appointed district attorney for the Confederacy, which involved confiscating northern property for the state. He was fighting for a cause that he had bitterly opposed for almost thirty years. Ironically, he blamed former *Mountaineer* editor Yancey, whose life Perry had saved in a murder trial, for breaking up the Union by becoming a leading secessionist and inducing southern Democrats to walk out of the presidential nominating convention in 1860, thus ensuring a fatal break in party ranks that led to the election of Abraham Lincoln.

When the Civil War ended, Perry became the first provisional governor of South Carolina. He was elected to the United States Senate in 1865 but was refused a seat by the Republican-controlled body. Although he did not own any newspapers after 1858, he continued to write newspaper articles and books until his death December 3, 1886. His best friend Thompson sold his home and 900-acre plantation in 1867 and moved to Madison, Florida, where he raised cotton until he died in 1868.[26] As for Turner Bynum, Thompson's almost-forgotten political pawn, someone finally put a marker on his grave in the early part of the twentieth century, a modest postscript to a violent era when duels were common and editors sometimes had to defend their editorials—and their honor—at ten paces.

Notes

1. Walter Edgar, *South Carolina: A History* (Columbia: University of South Carolina Press, 1998), 306.
2. David Duncan Wallace, *South Carolina: A Short History* (Chapel Hill: University of North Carolina Press, 1951), 491.
3. Ibid., 612.
4. Herbert Ravenel Sass, *Outspoken: 150 Years of the News & Courier* (Columbia: University of South Carolina Press, 1953), 70–74. Dawson, who was unarmed but carrying a cane, was shot and killed on March 12, 1889, by a married doctor whom he had accused of "paying inappropriate attention" to his French governess. The doctor, who was one of Dawson's neighbors, pleaded self-defense and was acquitted. Sass, 73, 74.
5. *Greenville Mountaineer,* 12 May 1832.

6. Lillian Adele Kibler, *Benjamin F. Perry: South Carolina Unionist* (Durham, N.C.: Duke University Press, 1946), 124.

7. *Greenville Mountaineer*, 30 June 1832.

8. *Southern Sentinel*, 4 August 1832.

9. Benjamin F. Perry, Diary, Roll 2, Southern Historical Collection, University of North Carolina, 5 August 1832.

10. Mildred Woodson Brown of Slater-Marietta, S.C., and Alice Woodson Gantt of Greenville, S.C., are the great-granddaughters of Daniel and Mary Phelps Pike, who lived in a house overlooking the Old Stone Church cemetery in Pendleton, S.C., in 1832. This story has been passed down through generations in their family. The Pikes' granddaughter Edith Cecilia Whitten Woodson of Central told and retold this story many times to her daughters Mildred Woodson Brown of Slater-Marietta, S.C., and Alice Woodson Gantt of Greenville, S.C., when they were children.

    The friends of Turner Bynum stopped to borrow a shovel and a pine knot for a torch at the home of Daniel and Mary Phelps Pike, who lived in the house on the ridge overlooking the cemetery. Bynum's friends, who had fashioned a stretcher from two freshly cut pine trees, buried him by the light of the burning torch. Heavy rains had fallen in the area. Creeks were swollen and overflowing their banks, and the two fresh pine poles, which were stuck at the head and foot of his grave, took root and grew. Years later, residents remembered the Dueling Trees, as they were called, that marked Bynum's grave. After the trees died, Bynum's grave was marked with a gravestone, and when the Old Stone Church cemetery was expanded, the wall was moved, and Bynum's grave was finally inside the cemetery.

11. Kibler, op. cit., 135.

12. *Greenville Mountaineer*, 1 December 1832.

13. Perry, Diary, 6 December 1832.

14. *Greenville Mountaineer*, 15 December 1832.

15. Ibid.

16. Kibler, op. cit., 160.

17. Stephen Meats and Edwin T. Arnold, *The Writings of Benjamin F. Perry*, vol. 3, *Reminiscences of Public Men* (repr., Spartanburg, S.C.: The Reprint Company, 1980), 320.

18. *Greenville Mountaineer*, 30 March 1833.

19. Kibler, 168, 200.

20. Wallace, op. cit., 492.

21. Kibler, op. cit., 219–220.

22. Ibid., 260.

23. Ibid., 310–312, and John Hammond Moore, *South Carolina Newspapers* (Columbia: University of South Carolina Press, 1988), 126, 127.

24. Wallace, op. cit., 503.

25. Kibler, op. cit., 348.

26. Archie Vernon Huff Jr., *Greenville: The History of the City and County in the South Carolina Piedmont* (Columbia: University of South Carolina Press, 1995), 152.

VIRGINIA AND ANDREW JACKSON'S PROCLAMATION

The Emergence of an Opposition Party

— DOUGLAS W. CUPPLES —

The election of Abraham Lincoln as president of the United States in 1860 was the last in a series of events leading to the Civil War. The foundation for sectional discord, however, had existed since the founding of the first permanent English colonies at Jamestown, Virginia, and at Massachusetts Bay in 1607 and 1620. Throughout the republic's early years, the nature and role of federal authority had been a source of contention and debate. The path to secession began accelerating as the Democratic Party's solidarity started unraveling during the Nullification Crisis of 1832–1833.

Andrew Jackson's popularity was ascending at the time of his re-election to the presidency in 1832. His victory that year by a significant margin gave him a 23 percent increase over the number of electoral votes he received in 1828.[1] The combative chief executive and military hero soon became embroiled in a crisis that contributed to party disunity, factionalism, and increased sectionalism.[2] The crisis involved the proposed imposition of a national tariff aimed at protecting American markets from foreign goods. The tariff was strongly opposed by southern states, particularly those with heavy coastal trade. In South Carolina, opposition to the tariff resulted in the passage of an Ordinance of Nullification by the state legislature that declared the tariff null and void. Jackson immediately responded with a strongly worded proclamation warning South Carolinians to comply with the tariff and denouncing the doctrine of nullification as "uncompatible with the existence of the Union."

Although the Nullification Crisis did not lead to armed conflict, the events portended an even greater trial for the nation. Virginia's governor, John Floyd, prophetically confided after the compromise tariff that

> Such is the corrupt state of public morals, produced by the ignorance, vice and bad passions of Jackson and the minions around him that I do believe these United States will be shaken to pieces in a few years and deluged with blood purely because the Southern States tolerate slavery and the North wishes to destroy this property that they may govern by a majority in Congress and make the entire South subservient to their views.[3]

Congress responded to the crisis by passing the Compromise Tariff Act as well as the Force Act, prompting South Carolina to repeal the ordinance nullifying the tariff. By the time of congressional action, the threat of armed conflict had subsided, but a new era had emerged, not only for the nation but also for many states and most definitely for the Democratic Party. South Carolina stood alone during the 1832–1833 crisis, and her actions received little official support from any of the other states. The Nullification Crisis, however, provided a catalyst that fragmented the Democratic Party of Jackson, especially in the southern states, and contributed to the emergence of the Whig Party and other splinter factions.[4]

South Carolina was not the first state to threaten to nullify a federal law. In 1798, the Kentucky and Virginia legislatures passed resolutions to that effect. Written by Thomas Jefferson and James Madison, these resolutions reaffirmed "the state compact theory of the constitution . . . condemned the policy of consolidating the states by degrees into one sovereignty, and declared the alien and sedition laws unconstitutional."[5] The Olmstead case in Pennsylvania occurred in 1809, and Georgia's response to the *Worcester v. Georgia* case in 1825 also advanced the nullification argument.[6] The Olmstead case arose from the appeal of a judgment by the Pennsylvania Court of Admiralty in regard to the distribution of prize money in the case of the sloop *Active* in 1778.[7] The Pennsylvania Legislature successfully denied the jurisdiction of federal authority until 1808. Ruling on the case on February 23, 1809, Chief Justice John Marshall declared that "if the legislatures of the several states may, at will, annul the judgments of the Courts of the United States, and destroy the rights acquired under those judgments, the constitution itself becomes a solemn mockery."[8] When a federal marshal attempted to enforce the writ, the Pennsylvania militia prevented it. The Marshal court eventually succeeded in serving the writ, and several state authorities were tried and convicted for obstructing the process of the United States District Court.[9]

The *Worcester v. Georgia* case was another open defiance of a federal law, this time by the state of Georgia. Chief Justice Marshall had ruled in *Cherokee Nation v. Georgia* that the states lacked jurisdiction over Indian tribes. Georgia ignored Marshall's ruling and defied federal authority again in the Worcester case, which involved a state law that prohibited white men from living among Indians without the approval of state authorities. Upon hearing that Marshall had ruled against the state, Andrew Jackson is supposed to have said, "Well, John Marshall has made his decision. Now, let him enforce it."[10]

Virginia, the home of four of the first five presidents, represented a different challenge to the president during the Nullification Crisis. Governor Floyd, originally a Jackson supporter, was related to the influential Preston family of South Carolina, which numbered some of Vice President John C. Calhoun's most trusted advisers.[11] Floyd had expected that he and Calhoun would play a major role in the Jackson administration; when this failed to develop and Calhoun resigned from office in protest against the tariff, the Virginia governor moved to an antiadministration position.[12]

Elected governor in 1830, Floyd had previously supported the elimination of slavery in the state as a result of Nat Turner's insurrection.[13] Floyd was elected with the support of many Jackson men in the general assembly, and he had not been opposed by the proadministration *Richmond Enquirer*.[14] The governor became disenchanted with Jackson after the president split with the vice president. He then openly supported Calhoun during the Nullification Crisis.[15] On April 16, 1831, Floyd wrote in a letter to the South Carolinian advising him that "Virginia you may be assured, at least we feel assured, will vote for you as president if necessary at the next election."[16]

Despite the increasing distance between Jackson and Floyd, the president remained extremely popular in the Old Dominion, and the pro-Jackson faction dominated the early debate in the state legislature on the nullification issue. Richard Ellis has argued:

> Whatever support existed for nullification was at this time mute and indirect. The main attempt to enlist sympathy for South Carolina came in Governor Floyd's speech to the newly assembled legislature on December 4. . . . Floyd's oblique attempt to lend support to the proceedings in South Carolina did not have any noticeable effect. The President's popularity in Virginia, in early December, was unchallengeable.[17]

Support for nullification in Virginia and throughout the South, although minimal, did exist.[18] Many considered Virginia a border state, and the course of the debate in the general assembly and between the newspapers gave credibility to that belief. The advocates of nullification in South Carolina tried to associate the doctrine with the Virginia Resolutions in order to pull the state to their support.[19] Prior to the president's proclamation, Thomas Ritchie, the influential editor of the *Richmond Enquirer*, asserted on December 4, 1832, that the paper, "the devoted friend of the Rights of the States . . . [was] opposed to the abominable Tariff system" and "equally opposed to the course which South Carolina has taken." The editor continued that the Constitution faced dangers from two sides—the usurping of power by the central government and resistance to federal laws by the individual states. Ritchie would serve as a spokesman for Jackson throughout the crisis.

Anti-Jackson factions existed in Virginia, but they were small and contained within the Democratic Party. In the Virginia legislature, Jacksonians were in the majority, as they were throughout the state, and on December 10 the members elected William Cabell Rives to the United States Senate. Rives characterized himself as "anti-tariff, anti-bank, anti-nullification, and a thorough and decided friend of Jackson's administration." For him, the timing of the election was propitious. After the president's proclamation circulated among the legislators, admiration for the Jackson administration markedly diminished. A political upheaval was in the making.[20]

Jackson's proclamation was the anvil upon which the divisiveness would be hammered. Whereas many Virginians, including former president James Madison, abhorred nullification, they also revered the principles espoused in the Resolutions of 1798 and condemned Jackson's proclamation unequivocally. Jackson's proclamation fell like a thunderbolt on the state Democratic Party.[21] On December 11, General William F. Gordon wrote to Thomas Walker Gilmer that "It [the proclamation] is a very strong document. Its principles you will perceive are at war with all our opinions of state Power and the character of our Confederation."[22] Democratic unity was shattered. Interparty differences became deeply personal and parsimonious. Governor Floyd confided in his diary that "Jackson is the worst man in the Union, a scoundrel in private life, devoid of patriotism and a tyrant withal . . . . I, at this moment, feel assured that we will soon be by that monster and villain, Jackson, involved deeply in a civil war."[23]

The problem was not that Jackson displayed firmness and a resolve to enforce federal law, nor that he opposed nullification. The problem was that he expounded a theory of federal-state relations that struck at the very heart and core of the young republic's formation. More important than the stand against South Carolina's action was his assault on the formation of the original compact between the states, the question of state sovereignty, and the right of secession, which many believed to be a reserved liberty retained by the states.[24] The proclamation declared the concept of a compact between sovereign states and the right of secession to be "fallacious."[25] The president added further damage by asserting that the federal government was one "in which the people of all the States collectively are represented" in opposition to the theory that the people were represented through the sovereign states.[26] Jackson continued by asserting that the government

> operates directly on the people individually, not upon the States; they retained all the power they did not grant. But each State having expressly parted with so many powers as to constitute jointly with the others a single nation cannot from that period possess any right to secede. . . . To say that any State may at pleasure secede from the Union, is to say that the United States are not a nation.[27]

By exhibiting a lack of respect for state rights and advocating greatly enhanced federal power, the president had gone farther than most southerners—who already opposed nullification—could accept.[28] For those Democrats such as Floyd, as well as the pronullification newspapers such as the *Richmond Whig* and the *Petersburg Jeffersonian*, the proclamation provided sufficient cause for an open break with Jackson.[29] The *Whig* referred to the proclamation as being of "unusual eloquence . . . [and] advanced high toned Federal doctrines," even "the highest toned Federal doctrines."[30] A month later the *Whig* editorialized:

> It is most evident that Virginia must choose between two alternatives, vindicate her ancient principles against the proclamation, or consent to see them finally and forever set aside, and incur the damning disgrace of having surrendered to the imperious will of one man—of gen. [sic] Jackson . . . let it not be doubted how she will decide.[31]

The *Alexandria Gazette* attempted to take the lead and extol moderation. On December 19, the editor affirmed under the heading "The Value of the Union" that "the Union must be preserved. Reason dictates, patriotism enjoins it, self interest demands it—the Union must be preserved." The editor warned that force used against South Carolina would ultimately lead to a dissolution of the Union. In summation, the paper laid out a plan for resolving current discord and for an eventual solution to the outstanding question of federal-state relations: "Let the Tariff be so adjusted for the present as gradually to retire within a wholesome and well bounded channel; and let a convention of the States be called as soon as possible and settle the ambiguous article of the Constitution."[32]

In the tension-filled days ahead, the *Gazette* continued to voice moderation and compromise. On December 20, it announced its support of the president's denunciation of South Carolina in advance of the state's deadline to comply with federal authority. It observed in the same comments, however, its disapproval of South Carolina nullification being put down while Georgia nullification had been supported.[33] In the same edition, which appears to have been an effort to press the issue of moderation, a communication from Loudon County asserted that "the course is a plain one—it is the only one, and is founded upon *mutual compromise* and *compassion*." The communication further called for an adjustment of the tariff and a convention of the states along the lines of the *Gazette's* previously ascribed position.[34]

Another letter in the same issue, signed "Grotius," continued the peaceful theme:

> Much diversity of opinion may prevail as to the mode she [South Carolina] has adopted in the assertion of her sovereign rights; but in principle she has not departed from the example which has been set her in various parts of the Union . . . her integrity cannot be suspected, her motives cannot be impeached. Against that separation [of the states] it is our duty to raise our warning voice, and call upon every patriot to solve, if possible. . . . Upon this subject the State of South Carolina has displayed a magnanimity which should win the gratitude of every American.[35]

Grotius continued along this line by endorsing Floyd's remarks that the reserved rights are the "sleeping thunder of the states" and "it is folly and madness to trifle with the reserved power of a most patriotic and united portion of the country."[36]

Virginia was primarily divided along sectional lines that in many ways represented a rift between the older, more settled Eastern portions of the state and the newer Western portions including the Shenandoah Valley. The eastern section primarily supported South Carolina, and the western side lent its backing to the president. The *Lynchburg Virginian* on December 13 called any oppression under the tariff "imaginary" and charged that South Carolina had been "misled." On the 17th, the proclamation was hailed as "a document of eminent ability . . . masterly and well-timed . . . second only in merit to Washington's Farewell Address." Floyd was accused of being in "open opposition to the sentiment of the people whom he represents."[37]

The debate on constitutional theory was conducted in a series of articles by former Senator Littleton Waller Tazewell in the *Norfolk and Portsmouth Herald* that attacked the centralizing authority of the proclamation. The other side was voiced by his replacement in the Senate, William C. Rives, when he took the floor in behalf of the administration's Force Act. Tazewell, writing under the nom de plume "A Virginian," personally opposed nullification. He carefully reconstructed in his essays the origin and formation of civil society.

He pleaded with the president and South Carolina to exhibit forbearance during the crisis. Tazewell reaffirmed the compact theory of a covenant among the states as the basis for the federal Union, and although he denied the legitimacy of nullification, his articles affirmed the right of secession.[38] The essence of the argument was the philosophical foundation of the anti-Jackson faction in the Democratic Party in Virginia. During the writing of his treatise, Tazewell received a letter from John W. Murdaugh, of Richmond, who urged, "The time has now arrived when Congress must be taught by resistance to restrain its action within Constitutional limits, Andrew Jackson must be taught that his will is not the law of the Land."[39]

The Democratic Party was disintegrating.[40] The *Lynchburg Virginian* refused to print Tazewell's essays on the pretext that they were "dull and ethereal."[41] John Tyler, whose foundering political career received new life with the crisis, wrote Tazewell on February 2:

> Were ever men so deceived as we have been—I mean those of the old Democratic school—in Jackson? His Proclamation has swept away all the barriers of the Constitution, and given us, in place of the Federal government, under which we fondly believed we were living, a consolidated military despotism. To this it must inevitably come, if his doctrines be correct.[42]

Tyler's term in the Senate was due to expire in 1832, and he had earlier expressed concerns about "formidable adversaries" posing "hazards" in the next session of the legislature.[43] By the middle of February 1833, Floyd confided in his diary that the Jackson wing in the legislature was attempting to defeat Tyler's reelection.[44] The divisive nature of the crisis was reflected in the fight for the seat held by Tyler. On February 6, Tyler stated in the Senate, during the debate on the Revenue Collection Bill, that Virginia was the "Mediator State."[45] He further contended that the administration had pursued a course that was "too well calculated to chafe the spirit" of South Carolina by sending an army, revenue cutters, and armed ships.[46] Virginia's senior senator described a scene in South Carolina that approached siege warfare. Tyler's speech clearly reflected the changing sentiment in the Virginia legislature. It was an unequivocal indictment of the president, coming a scant ten days before the vote in the legislature, and might have influenced the margin of victory of the pro-Jackson candidate over James McDowell, 81 to 62.[47]

Administration supporters in Virginia contended that a state of tyranny existed in South Carolina.[48] The proclamation was described as a patriotic and able document, whereas nullification was labeled "subtleized treason."[49] Samuel Moore, a member of the house of delegates from Rockbridge, on December 29 argued in the chamber that sovereignty could not be applied to the states except in open rebellion against the federal government.[50] Gatherings and meetings in local communities were held throughout the state. A resolution passed at a meeting in Augusta County on Christmas Eve declared that nullification was "violent and revolutionary."[51] In Powhatan, the right of secession was affirmed, but nullification denounced. Similar resolutions were adopted in Loudon, Kanawaha, Scotland, Washington, Frederick, Botetourt, Page, Fauquier, Rockbridge, Scott, Fluvanna, Montgomery, Jefferson, Amherst, Patrick, Allegheny, Greenbrier, Smyth, and Westmoreland Counties and in western cities such Lynchburg, Staunton, and Wheeling.[52]

Abel Parker Upshur, an influential federal judge in Virginia, denounced Jackson at a meeting in Eastville and argued in a series of articles addressed to Thomas Ritchie at the *Richmond Enquirer* that the Kentucky and Virginia Resolutions of 1798 were compatible with the doctrine of nullification.[53] Meetings issuing statements or resolutions critical of Jackson were held in James City, King William, King and Queen, Richmond Powhatan, Prince Edward, Northampton, Cumberland, Hampshire, Prince George, and Halifax Counties.[54] Although the sectional divisiveness was clear, some counties such as Powhatan split upon the issue of secession or support for Jackson.

The irascible John Randolph of Roanoke, formerly a staunch Jackson supporter and opponent of Calhoun's theories, reacted vehemently against the proclamation.[55] Randolph wrote to the *Norfolk American Beacon* on February 13, 1833, that Virginia was a "free ... Sovereign state," and had never surrendered her sovereignty, even at the time she entered the Union.[56] Randolph, physically ill and prone to periods of mental distress, traveled to various towns and counties where he led citizens in passing numerous resolutions that affirmed Virginia's sovereignty while reprobating nullification.[57]

Floyd's address to the House of Delegates on December 4, 1832, brought the crisis into the legislative chamber.[58] Floyd affirmed in his message that allegiance was owed to the "constitution of the United States" but "none to men, or to a state."[59] He argued that the "oppressive" tariff had been replaced by one "no less injurious."[60] Prudence and wisdom were counseled in the message to the legislators, but it was equally clear that Virginia was charged to lead in the support of South Carolina.

On December 13, the legislature received the Nullification Ordinance and assigned responsibility for action to a committee on federal relations. The committee reported back on December 29, and it was readily apparent that Jackson's proclamation had made a deep impression.[61] The committee did not approve South Carolina's turn to nullification and disapproved and protested against the "principles avowed, and powers assumed by the president of the United States."[62] The committee further reaffirmed the doctrine that the

Union was created by the states, not the people, and secession was declared a solution for a state seeking relief, as a last resort.[63] In support of Virginia's mediating role, it was recommended that two commissioners be sent to South Carolina.

The committee continued to work on the resolutions with amendments in the Committee of the Whole. Thomas Marshall of Fauquier County offered a substitute that requested South Carolina "to rescind the ordinance . . . or at least to suspend its operation until the close of the next session of congress."[64] James McDowell, who had recently been defeated by John Tyler for a seat in the United States Senate, offered a substitute for the pro-Jackson forces that stated that "nullification by a state as a remedy not recognized in the federal constitution—not reserved to the states . . . is dangerous, revolutionary, and practically subversive."[65] John T. Brown of Petersburg submitted the "Preamble and Resolutions," which were adopted and which affirmed nullification was "unconstitutional and dangerous" but reserved for the states as "parties of the constitutional compact, in their sovereign capacity . . . an equal right to judge, each for itself . . . whether the compact be violated."[66]

An attempt by Thomas J. Stuart of Augusta County to pass a resolution approving the president's proclamation was defeated by a vote of 101 to 24.[67] The assembly's adoption of a substitute set of resolutions was bitter for Floyd. He wrote in his diary, "So ends the high character of the State of Virginia and such the end of liberty."[68] By April 1, Floyd was more optimistic and confident, predicting that "States Rights will be restored and our liberty perpetuated."[69] Antiproclamation demonstrations were seen at many subsequent Fourth of July celebrations in eastern Virginia.[70]

Civil war did not occur as a result of the Nullification Crisis. The presidency of Andrew Jackson, however, continued to be clouded by the controversy, which compounded the growing alienation between the state governments in the South and the federal government in Washington. Jackson's proclamation was the Rubicon crossing for those who favored a more centralized authority for the national government. The right of secession had long remained a theoretical and abstract right and a refuge of those who feared too strong a central power. The proclamation forced the debate and closed that haven. Virginia assumed the obligation to provide leadership and resolve the crisis in order to save the Union, yet the Democratic coalition was fragmented in the process.

An opposition party resulted in Virginia and, equally important, the Old Dominion's effort to lead the other states was diminished. The great question of federal-state relations was taken over by the more radical elements of the political spectrum in both North and South. The aftermath of the Nullification Crisis in Virginia reflected the attitude of other southern states. The

Jackson wing of the Democratic Party elected Martin Van Buren to the presidency in 1836 with a 214,012-vote majority.[71] Four years later, however, the Whigs—a synthesis of alienated Democrats who left the party in 1833 and some former Federalists—elected William H. Harrison over Van Buren by a 146,000-vote margin.[72] Jackson's handling of the Nullification Crisis, especially the doctrines advanced in his proclamation, contributed to the emergence of an opposition party. By 1860, his split, compounded by other conflicts in Kansas and at Harpers Ferry, Virginia, resulted in four major candidates for president and the ultimate election of Republican candidate Abraham Lincoln—the very last thing that southern leaders wanted to see happen.[73]

NOTES

1. Charles A. Beard, *Mr. President: The President in American History* (New York: Julian Messner, 1977), 58. *Historical Statistics of the United States: The Colonial Times to 1970*, part 2 (Washington: United States Department of Commerce, 1975), 1076.

2. Some of the most helpful works on Virginia during the Nullification Crisis are Charles Henry Ambler's *Sectionalism in Virginia from 1776–1861* (New York: Russell and Russell, 1910; reprint 1964) and *Thomas Ritchie: A Study in Virginia Politics* (Richmond: Bell Book and Stationery, 1913). Ambler also edited *The Life and Diary of John Floyd* (Richmond: Richmond Press, 1918). The text of official papers is in Herman Vandenburg Ames, *State Documents on Federal Relations: The State and the United States* (Philadelphia: Department of History, University of Pennsylvania, 1906); Massachusetts General Court, *State Papers on Nullification* (New York: Da Capo Press, 1970); and *Abridgement of the Debates of Congress, from 1789 to 1856* (New York: Appleton, 1859). There has been little focus on the response in other states to the nullification issue. Paul Bergeron, "Tennessee's Response to the Nullification Crisis," *Journal of Southern History* 39 (February 1973): 23–44, and Lucie Robertson Bridgeforth, "Mississippi's Response to Nullification, 1833," *Journal of Mississippi History* 45 (February 1983): 1–21, examine two of the southwestern states. The recent work by Richard E. Ellis, *The Union at Risk: Jacksonian Democracy, States Rights, and the Nullification Crisis* (New York: Oxford University Press, 1987) studies the responses of Georgia, New York, and Virginia during the crisis. Excellent studies of nullification and the slavery debate are William W. Freehling, *Prelude to Civil War: The Nullification Controversy in South Carolina, 1816–1836* (New York: Harper and Row, 1965); Allison Goodyear Freehling, *Drift Toward Dissolution: The Virginia Slavery Debate of 1831–1832* (Baton Rouge: Louisiana State University Press, 1982); and Merrill D. Peterson, *Olive Branch and Sword: The Compromise of 1833* (Baton Rouge: Louisiana State University Press, 1982). A number of good books provide an encompassing coverage of Southern history and sectionalism. Among them are Dickson D. Bruce Jr., *The Rhetoric of Conservatism: The Virginia Convention of 1829–1830 and the Conservative Tradition of the South* (San Marino, California: Huntington Library Press, 1982); William J. Cooper Jr., *The South and the Politics of Slavery, 1828–1856* (Baton Rouge: Louisiana State Univer-

sity Press, 1978); and Charles S. Sydnor, *The Development of Southern Sectionalism, 1819–1848* (Baton Rouge: Louisiana State University Press, 1948). Additional readings are Newcomb H. Morse, "The Foundations and Meaning of Secession," *Stetson Law Review* 15 (1986): 419–436; Ulrich B. Phillips, ed., "Original Letters," *William and Mary Quarterly* 21 (July 1912): 1–11; Henry Simms, *The Rise of the Whigs in Virginia, 1824–1840* (Richmond, Va.: William Byrd, 1929). Informative books on Jacksonian America are Charles Sellers, *Andrew Jackson and the State Rights Tradition* (Chicago: Rand McNally, 1963); Edward Pessen, *Jacksonian America: Society, Personality, and Politics*, rev. ed., (Urbana, Ill.: Dorsey Press, 1985); and Robert V. Remini, *The Revolutionary Age of Andrew Jackson* (New York: Harper Collins, 1976). Valuable biographical and primary material sources are Claude Hampton Hall, *Abel Parker Upshur: Conservative Virginian, 1790–1844* (Madison, Wis.: State Historical Society of Wisconsin, 1963); Littleton Waller Tazewell, *A Review of the Proclamation of President Jackson of the 10th of December, 1832* (Norfolk, Va.: J.D. Ghiselin, 1918); Lyon Gardner Tyler, ed., *The Letters and Times of the Tylers*, vol. 1, Richmond (1896; repr., New York: Da Capo Press, 1970); and the State of Virginia, *Journal of the House of Delegates*, 1833; and Norma Lois Peterson, *Littleton Waller Tazewell* (Charlottesville: University of Virginia Press, 1982).

3. Ambler, *Life and Diary of John Floyd*, 16 April 1833, 214–215.
4. In 1860, South Carolina would lead and be joined by ten other Southern states in forming a separate nation.
5. Ambler, *Sectionalism in Virginia*, 68–69.
6. H. Newcomb Morse, "The Foundations and Meaning of Secession," 420; N.S. Shaler, Kentucky 409 (1925); United States v. Peters, 9 U.S. (5 Cranch) 115 (1809); and Worcester v. Georgia 31 U.S. (6 Pet.) 515 (1832).
7. Ames, *State Documents on Federal Relations*, 45.
8. Ibid.
9. Ibid.
10. Remini, *The Revolutionary Age of Andrew Jackson*, 112–113; Pessen, *Jacksonian America*, 298.
11. Calhoun was often accused by the pro-Jackson element of manipulating the nullifiers from behind the scenes. The *Lynchburg Virginian*, 13 December 1832.
12. Ambler, *The Life and Diary of John Floyd*, 97.
13. Nat Turner was a slave who led an insurrection in August 1831 in Southampton County, Virginia. The revolt led to the slaughter of between 50 and 60 whites and the mutilation of their bodies. Most of the victims were women and children. Twenty-one of the 56 Negroes arrested were acquitted, 12 transported out of the state, and 20 were hanged. Sydnor, *The Development of Southern Sectionalism*, 225–226. The Nat Turner insurrection marks a pivotal episode in the history of American Negro slavery. For all practical purposes, emancipation—as a solution to the problem—virtually ceased to be an option in the South. The South's reaction was a tightening of slave laws, even extending to those Negroes who had been granted or had earned their freedom. A small number of southerners, John Floyd among them, continued, for a short time, to argue for emancipation and colonization outside the United States. Both approaches were reacting from a fear of the potential danger that future insurrections might hold. Floyd, perceived

that the growing number of Negroes would eventually be too many to control, and his motive for emancipation was to remove the threat.

14. Ambler, *Life and Diary of John Floyd*, 98–99.

15. "Message of Governor John Floyd to the Virginia House of Delegates," December 4, 1832, State of Virginia, *Journal of the Virginia House of Delegates*.

16. Ambler, *Life and Diary of John Floyd*, 105; Ambler, *Thomas Ritchie* 37; and Merrill Peterson, *Olive Branch and Sword*, 18. Peterson includes the two senators from Virginia, Littleton Tazewell and John Tyler, among Calhoun's presidential supporters.

17. Ellis, *The Union at Risk*, 128.

18. Freehling, *Prelude to Civil War*, 203.

19. Simms, *Rise of the Whigs*, 161.

20. Norma Peterson, *Tazewell*, 221, and Ellis, *The Union at Risk*, 127.

21. *Tyler Papers*, 449.

22. "Original Letters," *William and Mary Quarterly*, 1. Gilmer, A lawyer and future governor of Virginia, was to eventually serve as U.S. secretary of the navy. Gordon, a brigadier general of Virginia militia during the War of 1812, was a representative from Virginia in Congress from 1830 to 1835.

23. Ambler, *Life and Diary of John Floyd*, 204–206.

24. Ibid., 13 December 1832, 203.

25. "Proclamation of the President of the United States," *State Papers on Nullification*, 85.

26. Ibid., 86.

27. Ibid., 86–87.

28. Norma Peterson, *Tazewell*, 220–221.

29. *Tyler Papers*, 449.

30. *Alexandria Gazette*, 17 December 1833.

31. *Niles' Register*, 19 January 1833.

32. Ibid. Also, *Alexandria Gazette*, 19 December 1832. In addition, on January 1, 1833, the *Gazette* editorialized support for the reelection of Tyler to the Senate, further confirmation of the newspaper's compromising efforts.

33. The *Gazette* was referring to the lack of action, and therefore, administration support for the State of Georgia, in contrast to the hard position against South Carolina.

34. *Alexandria Gazette*, 20 December 1832.

35. Ibid.

36. Ibid.

37. *Lynchburg Virginian*, 17 December 1832.

38. Ibid., 222–223.

39. Norma Peterson, *Tazewell*, 222.

40. Ibid. John Hampden Pleasents, editor of the *Richmond Whig*, wrote Tyler on January 1, 1833, "There are three parties, and some shades of other parties on this subject in the General Assembly." *Tyler Papers*, 451–452.

41. *Alexandria Gazette*, 2 February 1833.

42. Sellers, *Andrew Jackson and the States Rights Tradition*, 56.

43. *Tyler Papers*, 444.

44. Ambler, *The Life and Diary of John Floyd*, 11 February 1833, 210.
45. *Debates of Congress*, 67.
46. Ibid.
47. *Norfolk American Beacon*, 13 February 1833; Ellis, *The Union at Risk*, 138. Ambler, *Sectionalism in Virginia*, 217. Three days before Tyler's reelection, South Carolina declared that enforcement of the Nullification Ordinance was suspended until after the Congress adjourned. *Tyler Papers*, 455. Tyler would cast the lone vote against the Force Act on February 20, 1833.
48. *Lynchburg Virginian*, 12 December 1832.
49. Ibid., 20 December 1832 and 3 January 1833.
50. *Journal of the House of Delegates*, 29 December 1832; *Lynchburg Virginian*, 3 January 1833. John R. Wallace, from Fauquier County, argued that South Carolina's complaint was empty because it was the first state to ask for the application of a duty in 1789. *Niles' Register*, 26 January 1833. Wallace argued for Virginia to advise South Carolina to abandon nullification.
51. *Lynchburg Virginian*, 7 January 1833.
52. *Niles' Register*, 12 January 1833; *Lynchburg Virginian*, 24 January 1833; and Ellis, *The Union at Risk*, 133.
53. Hall, *Upshur*, 89–90.
54. Ellis, *The Union at Risk*, 133.
55. Norma Peterson, *Tazewell*, 224.
56. *Norfolk American Beacon*, 13 February 1833.
57. *Alexandria Gazette*, 18–19 February 1833, and *Norfolk American Beacon*, 27 February 1833.
58. For the text of Floyd's message, see the *Journal of the House of Delegates*, 4 December 1832.
59. Ibid.
60. Ibid.
61. For text, see, "Report of the Committee on Federal Relations," Document Number 11, *Journal of the House of Delegates*, 29 December 1832.
62. Ibid.
63. Ibid.
64. Ibid., Document Number 15.
65. Ibid., Document Number 18.
66. Ibid., Document Number 19.
67. *Alexandria Gazette*, 5 January 1833; Ambler, *The Life and Diary of John Floyd*, 5 January 1833, 206–207.
68. Ambler, *The Life and Diary of John Floyd*, 15 January 1833, 208.
69. Ambler, *The Life and Diary of John Floyd*, 1 April 1833, 214.
70. Simms, *The Rise of the Whigs*, 76.
71. Beard, *Mr. President*, 158.
72. Ibid., 160.
73. *Tyler Papers*, 478. The result was the election of a minority president.

Lewis Tappan and the Friends of Amistad

The Crusade to Save the Abolition Movement

— Bernell E. Tripp —

Abolitionist Lewis Tappan sat in the New Haven, Connecticut, law office of Roger Sherman Baldwin. Tappan's task, as defined by the "Friends of the *Amistad*," was to convince Baldwin to serve as chief counsel for the defense of the Mendi captives who had revolted aboard the Spanish schooner *Amistad*. He was not the first visitor to seek out Baldwin, who had established an impressive record in the field of constitutional liberties since his admission to the bar in 1814.[1] He had already received letters from New London abolitionist Dwight P. James, as well as the Rev. Joshua Leavitt, editor of the American Anti-Slavery Society's *Emancipator*, in New York.[2] He had also received visits from prominent New Haven banker Amos Townsend Jr., who arrived at the attorney's office with another Connecticut abolitionist, John F. Norton, and discussed the matter with Baldwin for two hours.[3]

Tappan, a controversial antislavery moralist from New York, implored Baldwin to do everything for the captives that "humanity and Justice require."[4] Uncompromising in his belief that slavery was a moral wrong, Tappan condemned not only those who participated in the enterprise but also those who allowed it to flourish by doing nothing.[5] Baldwin immediately agreed, declining to discuss the financial terms for his services, and departed with Tappan to visit the Africans in jail.[6] The timing of the *Amistad* controversy could not have been better, and abolitionist leaders, particularly Tappan, lost no time in using the case to their advantage. Fearful of losing ground to proslavery supporters after a series of setbacks, including several incidents of antiabolition mob violence in Pennsylvania and Illinois, the abolitionists were eager to find something to unify the movement.[7]

Consequently, what began with the seizure of one "insignificant" African named Sengbe Pieh, a Mendi villager to become known as Cinquez, would result in a battle that wound its way to the top of the judicial ladder— the United States Supreme Court—and made its mark on American society racially, politically, and morally. Although the Africans' case would fail to strike an overwhelming blow against the institution of slavery, it would play a pivotal role in determining the path of the abolitionist movement, serving as a crucial rallying cry to nudge the country ever closer to ending slavery.

The case of the *Amistad* began in West Africa with the capture of several villagers, including Sengbe Pieh. The captives were later herded onto the slave ship *Tecora* to begin the much-dreaded Middle Passage, a two-month trip to Cuba, where they were sold to plantation owner Jose Ruiz and his friend, Pedro Montez, and provided with Spanish names. Thus, Sengbe Pieh became Jose (Joseph) Cinquez.[8] The complex events centering on Cinquez and about three dozen companions and their actions aboard the slave ship *Amistad*, Spanish for *friendship*, began on June 27, 1839. The *Amistad*'s journey was intended to be only a few days. But three nights later, the slaves took over the ship, murdered the captain and the cook, and attempted to force their owners to steer the *Amistad* back to Africa. By steering toward Africa by day and north toward the United States by night, Montez and Ruiz tricked the nonseafaring slaves, arriving off Long Island, New York, on August 26. The ship anchored within half a mile of shore, and the slaves were recaptured by the crew of the USS *Washington*.[9]

Sensational news accounts of the arrival of the mysterious black schooner and the murderous Africans dominated the local newspapers.[10] Many early reports eagerly described the "black pirates" who murdered the crew in cold blood and the brave *Washington* crew who recaptured them.[11] Such news items about the *Amistad* and the captives began to have an effect on the American public, and readers eagerly perused the pages of their daily papers, hoping to find some snippet of information about the mysterious schooner and its occupants. Long before the *Amistad*'s capture, sightings of the "long, low black schooner" cruising haphazardly along the coast had ignited a multitude of speculations and suspicion.[12] Once seized, the schooner presented the answers to innumerable mysteries. The "murderous demons" were described in detail. The *New London Gazette* ran a series of articles intended to excite public opinion against the Africans and for the Spaniards. The Africans were characterized as lustful, stupid, cannibalistic savages, whereas the Spaniards were described as intelligent, gentlemanly, and pious.[13]

Continued coverage of the *Amistad* events would be an essential part of the campaign against slavery, attempting to garner public support for both sides in the conflict. Because of the complex nature of events in the *Amistad* case, there was a judicial hearing and two trials, one criminal and one civil. After the initial hearing on August 29, 1839, District Judge Andrew T. Judson resolved that a grand jury should settle the case.[14] Upon learning of the incident, the abolitionists quickly implemented a plan for assisting the *Amistad* captives. In addition to contacting Baldwin, Dwight James also contacted Joshua Leavitt in New York and charged him with locating someone who spoke the captives' language and with taking that translator to New Haven to hear the Africans' side of the story.

In New York, Tappan called a meeting of the leading abolitionists in the area, including Jocelyn, who had worked with Baldwin in 1831 in confronting an angry mob that resisted efforts to build a black training school near Yale College, and William Jay, son of Vice President John Jay. The New York abolitionists appointed Tappan, Jocelyn, and Leavitt as the Committee for the Defense of the Africans of the *Amistad*, also known as the Friends of the *Amistad*, for the sole purpose of securing defense counsel for the prisoners and ensuring their satisfactory treatment while in jail. The group finally settled on Baldwin in New Haven, along with Seth P. Staples Jr. and Theodore Sedgwick of New York City.[15] The committee drafted a statement of purpose and an appeal for donations to fund their plans, both to appear in the *Emancipator*. Their "Appeal to the Friends of Liberty," signed by the three committee members, appeared in the paper's September 5 issue. It read:

> Thirty-eight fellow-men from Africa, after having been piratically kidnapped from their native land, transported across the seas, and subjected to atrocious cruelties, have been thrown upon our shores, and are now incarcerated in jail to await their trial for crimes alleged by their oppressors to have been committed by them. They are ignorant of our language, of the usages of civilized society, and the obligations of Christianity. Under these circumstances, several friends of human rights have met to consult upon the case of these unfortunate men, and have appointed the undersigned a committee to employ interpreters and able counsel, and take all the necessary means to secure the rights of the accused. It is intended to employ three legal gentlemen of distinguished abilities, and to incur other needful expenses. The poor prisoners being destitute of clothing, and several having scarcely a rag to cover them, immediate steps will be taken to provide what may be necessary. The undersigned therefore make this appeal to the friends of humanity to contribute for the above objects.

Donations may be sent to either of the Committee, who will acknowledge
the same, and make a public report of all their disbursements.

The next day the members of the committee set about fulfilling their assigned tasks. In the office of the *New York Evening Post,* its editor, William Cullen Bryant, proposed that Sedgwick write a series of articles discussing the legal
aspects of the case. Sedgwick, who had already been contacted by Leavitt and
agreed to serve as defense counsel, accepted Bryant's proposal on the condition
that he could sign the articles with the pseudonym "Veto."[16] Meanwhile, Tappan and Baldwin arrived at the New Haven jail with several Africans to act as
interpreters, but only one man, John Ferry, knew enough Mendi to communicate with the prisoners. Most of the prisoners could understand him, although
none of them could speak his dialect. Said Tappan: "You may imagine the joy
manifested by these poor Africans, when they heard one of their own color address them in a friendly manner, and in a language they could comprehend!"[17]

Tappan and the others were also allowed to visit Cinquez, who was
housed in a separate cell. This was the perfect opportunity to begin the cre-
ation of a hero and leader from among the captives. Tappan declared:

> [Cinquez] is with several savage looking fellows, black and white, who
> are in jail on various charges. Visitors are not allowed to enter this strong
> hold of the jail, and the inmates can only be seen and conversed with
> through the aperture of the door. The jailer is fearful that some of them
> would escape if the door was opened in frequently [sic]. Even the other
> African prisoners are not permitted to hold converse with their Chief.
> Before they and he were deprived of this privilege, and when he occasion-
> ally came among them, they gathered around him, all talking at once,
> and shaking hands, as if they rejoiced to see him among them. They ap-
> peared to look up to him, I am told, with great respect.[18]

According to Tappan's account, they found a nearly naked Cinquez lying on the floor with a single blanket partly wrapped around him. Tappan said
Cinquez seemed hesitant at first, unwilling to answer the interpreter's questions, until Ferry convinced him to tell his story for the first time.[19] Similarly,
Tappan provided one of the first detailed descriptions of the Africans and
their behavior among the whites, an account laden with positive comments
regarding the prisoners' physical appearance, behavior, and intelligence. Tappan pointed out:

> The prisoners are in comfortable rooms.—They are well clothed in dark
> striped cotton trowsers, called by some of the manufacturers "hard
> times," and in striped cotton shirts. The girls are in calico frocks, and
> have made the little shawls that were given them into turbans. The pris-
> oners eyed the clothes some time, and laughed a good deal among them-

selves before they put them on. Their food is brought to them in separate tin pans, and they eat it in an orderly manner. In general, they are in good health. . . . They are robust, are full of hilarity, especially the Mandingos. Neither Cinquez nor any of his comrades have been manacled since they have been here. Their demeanor is altogether quiet, kind, and orderly. Cinquez is about 5 feet 8 inches high, of fine proportions, with a noble air. Indeed, the whole company, although thin in flesh, and generally of slight forms, and limbs, especially, are as good looking and intelligent a body of men as we usually meet with. All are young, and several are quite strip-lings. The Mandingos are described in books as being a very gentle race, cheerful in their dispositions, inquisitive, credulous, simple hearted, and much given to trading propensities. The African prisoners are orderly and peaceable among themselves. Some of them sing well, and appear to be in good spirits and grateful for the kindness shown them.[20]

Tappan and Leavitt visited the captives in their cells on at least three occasions, each time returning to write lengthy accounts of the visit designed to arouse sympathy for the Africans. The initial impulse to help the Africans might have come from purely humanitarian concerns, but the abolitionists quickly realized the value in the captives' cause. The human injustice of slavery could be placed against the backdrop of the constitutional processes of liberty. They also reasoned that the *Amistad* case might be God's way of manifest-ing the evils of slavery for all to see. Comparing the *Amistad* uprising to the American rebellion against British control, the *Herald of Freedom* declared:

Cinquez is no pirate, no murderer, no felon. His homicide is justifiable. Had a white man done it it would have been glorious. It would have im-mortalized him. . . . Something important, we feel may grow out of [this] to the anti-slavery cause. God may have cast this chieftain on our shore at this crisis to aid us in the deliverance of his people.[21]

The first criminal trial, beginning on September 19, 1839, in U.S. Circuit Court in Hartford, Connecticut, provided the perfect backdrop for a carnival sideshow atmosphere, courtesy of abolitionists. As many as 4,000 people a day readily paid 12 cents each to catch a glimpse of the Africans, money for the defense and to purchase supplies and clothing for them.[22] Vendors hawked en-gravings of Cinquez, from a portrait completed by Jocelyn's brother Nathan-iel, or of the schooner *Amistad*. An exhibit of a gigantic painting of the mutiny depicting Cinquez murdering the ship's cook traveled from town to town, and engravings of the work were sold to visitors as souvenirs.[23] These same visitors filled theater houses to view *The Black Schooner, or the Pirate Slaver* Amistad, a nautical melodrama based on the Africans' journey. The play included walk-on parts for the slaves and the *Washington* crew, with "Zambra Cinques, Chief of Mutineers" as one of the main characters.[24]

The excitement and attention surrounding the case pleased Tappan and his fellow abolitionists. All the leading New York papers provided correspondents to give the trial extensive coverage. In a courtroom filled to capacity, Tappan sat on a bench next to the little girls from the *Amistad*. The defense team and abolitionists had chosen to focus first on gaining the girls' release for two reasons: first, to focus attention on the girls, who played no role in the mutiny and who could be expected to generate public sympathy for the abolitionist cause and, second, to illustrate that the girls were indeed Africans and had been sold illegally, establishing a precedent for the other Africans.[25]

The scene depicted all the drama the abolitionists had hoped for. Wrapped in white blankets, the girls sobbed loudly and clung to the only people familiar to them, Tappan and their jailer, who tried to cheer them up with apples. They were obviously frightened and probably failed to understand why they were in the courtroom.[26] Newspaper accounts on both sides varied as to the effectiveness of the attorneys' legal maneuvering. In the *New York Commercial Advertiser*, Tappan's characterizations were laced with comments reflecting his abolitionist leanings. According to Tappan, the attorneys for the defense delivered powerful and eloquent arguments, whereas presentations by opposing attorneys were lame and deviously resourceful. Meanwhile, the antiabolitionist *Herald* concluded that the case was primarily a struggle between the government and the abolitionists for possession of the Africans, either to deliver them to the Spanish authorities or "to make saints of them." Despite obvious bias, the *Herald* did concede that the abolitionists' attorneys had made a strong showing, especially Baldwin's closing "with an effective appeal to the sympathies of the court."[27]

The outcome of the trial was not an overwhelming victory for either party. After three days of arguments, Associate Justice Smith Thompson ruled against criminal prosecution but refused to order the Africans' immediate release until the courts decided who held a claim on them as property.[28] In the meantime, the court would adjourn until the third Tuesday in November, and the Africans would receive favorable incarceration in the New Haven jail.[29] The *New York Herald* reveled in the decision, cheerfully reporting that the abolitionists would now have to "send home their darkies and disperse." The writer rejoiced that the abolitionists were "half frantic" at Thompson's refusal to release the Africans, meaning that *Liberator* editor William Lloyd Garrison would not be able to lease a cannibal to the Zoological Institute to pay the paper's debts and Tappan would not realize his hope that intermarriage might someday turn all Americans "copper-colored."[30]

Ironically, the court ruling proved quite advantageous for the abolitionists. They had wanted to keep the Africans and the case before the American public. Not only had they succeeded in gaining the public's attention, but they had also turned the case into one of charitable concern for the prisoners rather than a move against slavery or for racial equality. Even the most prejudiced individuals could not resist feeling paternalistic toward the helpless prisoners, who posed no threat to the white community.

When the court reconvened on January 7, lawyers, interested parties, and curious spectators squeezed into every available seat in the New Haven courtroom. Yale Divinity School and Yale Law School had dismissed classes early so students could attend the trial. Women occupied most of the seats in the small courtroom, while those individuals unable to acquire a seat crowded the doors and jockeyed for standing room among the spectators from throughout the North.[31] Many of the spectators in the crowded courtroom had come to hear the testimony of Cinquez, who had become a hero during the months of his incarceration. Wrapped in a white blanket that exposed only his head, Cinquez had remained silent as he squatted on his haunches among a dozen other Africans. In the afternoon, U.S. District Attorney William S. Holabird challenged Cinquez, the group-appointed leader, almost too rapidly for the interpreter, James Covey, to translate the words into Mendi, Cinquez's native tongue.

As the onslaught of question after question assailed him, Cinquez finally propelled himself to his feet and tossed aside the blanket to reveal the red flannel shirt and white duck pantaloons he had worn while on the *Amistad*. At first, Covey translated Cinquez's words as rapidly as they were spoken. However, Cinquez's passionate account soon became too spirited for Covey to follow. His frenzied story related in Mendi gave way to gestures and movements that mimicked his experiences aboard ship. Finally, his voice crescendoed in Mendi before dissolving into a shriek in English. "Give us free! Give us free!" he implored the crowd before Holabird could demand his removal from the courtroom. The effect of Cinquez's impassioned words on everyone in the room was evident. Tappan bowed his head and sighed in relief as the courtroom erupted in cheers and yells from the spectators in support of his latest hero of the abolitionist movement.[32]

After days of debate, Judson ordered that the Africans be placed under the control of the president and returned to Africa.[33] Although the decision was a small victory, it was a decisive step forward in the struggle to abolish slavery. The case not only increased interest in whether a human being could be declared property; it also permitted the abolitionists to demonstrate that a key argument by supporters of slavery was fatally flawed—that Africans were neither intelligent nor civilized. The case also increased support for the abolitionist cause, especially among northerners who previously had been hesitant about taking a firm stand against slavery. By putting a human face on the enslaved, abolitionists were able to harness a wave of enthusiasm at a time when the abolitionist movement had been weakened by its inability to function as a unit. With the key issues of the antislavery struggle discussed regularly in newspapers throughout the North, national political leaders could no longer evade addressing the situation. Slavery would eventually meet its demise, and Tappan's *Amistad* trials would be seen as key events that provided the momentum to nudge the country toward that painful and protracted end.

NOTES

1. Howard Jones, *Mutiny on the* Amistad (New York: Oxford University Press, 1839), 37.
2. Dwight P. James to Roger Sherman Baldwin, New London, 30 August 1839, reprinted in B. Edward Martin, *All We Want Is Make Us Free: La* Amistad *and the Reform Abolitionists* (Lanham, MD: University Press of America, Inc., 1986), 10.
3. Jones, *Mutiny*, 37. Simeon Jocelyn, pastor of a Congregational church for African Americans in New Haven, had solicited Townsend's help.
4. James to Baldwin, New London, 30 August 1839.
5. Jones, *Mutiny*, 37. See also Lawrence J. Friedman, "Lewis Tappan's Circle," in *The Abolitionists: Means, Ends, and Motivations*, ed. Lawrence B. Goodheart and Hugh Hawkins, 105–115 (Lexington, Mass.: D.C. Heath & Company, 1995).
6. Letter to the *New York Evening Post*, reprinted in the *Emancipator*, 19 September 1839. See also, http://www.law.umkc.edu/faculty/projects/ftrial/amistad/AMI_LTR.HTM. Accessed Dec. 7, 2001.
7. Abolitionist and editor Elijah P. Lovejoy was murdered in Alton, Ill., in 1837, and Philadelphia's Pennsylvania Hall, where abolitionist meetings were held, was destroyed. The Philadelphia mob continued its rampage throughout the city, terrorizing African American neighborhoods.
8. John W. Barber, *A History of the* Amistad *Captives* (New Haven, CT: E.L. & J.W. Barber, 1840), 6–8; Mary Cable, *Black Odyssey: The Case of the Slave Ship* Amistad (New York: Penguin Books, 1977), 3–16; Howard Jones, *Mutiny on the* Amistad (New York: Oxford University Press, 1839), 14–30. *Charleston Courier*, 5 September 1839; *New York Journal of Commerce*, 28 August 1839; *New York Morning Herald*, 2 September 1839, 9 September 1839.
9. Ibid.
10. *New York Journal of Commerce*, 10 January 1840, 11 January 1840; Barber, *History*, 19–21; "Testimony of Cinque, January 8, 1840, U.S. Dist. Ct. Records for Connecticut," reprinted at http://amistad.mysticseaport.org/library/court/district/1840.1.8.cinquetest.html. Accessed December 14, 2001.
11. *Morning Courier & New York Enquirer*, 30 August 1839; *New York Morning Herald*, 28 August 1839; *New York Evening Star*, 4 September 1839; *New Haven Daily Herald*, reprinted in Cable, *Black Odyssey*, 9.
12. See *Norfolk Beacon*, 24 August 1839, reprinted in the *New York American*, 27 August 1839; *New York Advertiser and Express*, 28 August 1839; and *New York Commercial Advertiser*, 26 and 27 August 1839.

13. See, e.g., *New London Gazette*, 26 August 1839.

14. Transcript of the trial. Reprinted at http://amistad.mysticseaport.org. Accessed Dec. 7, 2001.

15. James to Baldwin, 30 August 1839; Lewis Tappan, *History of the American Missionary Association: Its Constitution and Principles* (New York: AMA, 1855), 4.

16. Tappan cleverly draws attention to the work of his colleague "Veto" through the letters publicizing his visits to the Africans. In a September 9, 1839, letter, he wrote: "I have read an ingenious and well written article in the *Evening Post* signed Veto, in which the learned writer presents a pretty full examination of the case of the schooner *Amistad*. . . . If *Veto* will turn to *Niles' Register* for 1823, he will find an elegantly written and very able opinion of Chief Justice Tilghman, of Pa., on this subject, in which that eminent jurist, in giving his own judgment against the claim of a foreign government in the case of a fugitive charged with treason or murder, where there exists no treaty stipulation, as there does not at present between the United States and Spain, refers also to the corroborative opinions of all the preceding Presidents of the United States, (with the exception of the elder Adams, who had not given an opinion) very clearly and satisfactorily shows that the government of this country ought not to surrender persons situated as are Joseph Shinquau and his unfortunate countrymen, who are, by the act of God, thrown upon these shores to find, I trust, that protection and relief of which they had been, probably, forever deprived had it not been for this remarkable and providential interposition." Letter to the *New York Evening Post*, reprinted in the *Emancipator*, 19 September 1839.

17. Letter to the *New York Evening Post*, reprinted in the *Emancipator*, 19 September 1839. See also, http://www.law.umkc.edu/faculty/projects/ftrial/amistad/AMI_LTR.HTM. Accessed Dec. 7, 2001.

18. Ibid.

19. Ibid.

20. Ibid.

21. *Herald of Freedom*, reprinted in the *New York Colored American*, 28 September 1839.

22. Jones, *Mutiny*, 65.

23. Cable, *Black Odyssey*, 38.

24. Cable, *Black Odyssey*, 38. The drama played to packed houses throughout the North, taking in $1,650 in the first week.

25. Barber, *History*, 16–18; Jones, *Mutiny*, 64–74; Owens, *Black Mutiny*, 175–188.

26. Ibid.

27. *New York Morning Herald*, 23 September 1839.

28. *New York Morning Herald*, 25 September 1839; *New York Colored American*, 28 September 1839; *Richmond Enquirer*, 25 September 1839.

29. Jones, *Mutiny*, 78. The prisoners received favorable treatment in the jail. They were permitted almost unrestricted visitation privileges, religious instruction from Yale University faculty members, and exercise periods on the green.

30. *New York Morning Herald*, 1 October 1839.

31. *New York Journal of Commerce*, 10 January 1840; Barber, *History*, 19–21.

32. *New York Journal of Commerce*, 10 January 1840, 11 January 1840; Barber, *History*, 19–21; "Testimony of Cinque, January 8, 1840, U.S. Dist. Ct. Records for Connecti-

cut," reprinted at http://amistad.mysticseaport.org/library/court/district/1840
.1.8.cinquetest.html. Accessed December 14, 2001.

33. *New York Journal of Commerce*, 13 January 1840, 15 January 1840; Barber, *History*, 23–25. Appeals before the U.S. Circuit Court and finally the U.S. Supreme Court, including a nine-hour argument from John Quincy Adams, prolonged the Africans' incarceration until 1841. Following the Supreme Court's decision affirming the Africans' freedom, Cinquez and his comrades concluded that it was time to go home. After several more months of waiting while the *Amistad* committee raised funds to send them home, the 35 Mendi survivors left New York aboard the *Gentleman* in November 1841. They were accompanied by members of the Mendi Mission Committee, abolitionists traveling to Africa to establish a mission for ministering to the religious needs of the country's inhabitants.

William Cullen Bryant's 30-Year Crusade against Slavery

— Gregg MacDonald —

William Cullen Bryant's poetic merits have been well documented. He was the first native-born American poet to gain worldwide fame, and his best-known poems, including "Thanatopsis" and "To a Waterfowl," have become part of the nation's acknowledged literary heritage. But Bryant's talents and interests far exceeded the Romantic poetry upon which the bulk of his fame rests. He was also an inveterate traveler and an accomplished attorney, and as editor of the *New York Evening Post* from 1829 to 1878, he was New York's foremost crusader for individual rights. Bryant used his paper as a moral force to educate and to "advocate views of political and social subjects which he believed to be correct."[1]

A descendant of a long line of New England ministers, Bryant publicly opposed slavery long before abolitionist movements gained popular momentum in New York in the 1840s. Indeed, his masterful condemnation of the slave trade in the pages of the *Evening Post* has been called "one of the genuine journalistic landmarks of the nineteenth century."[2] Bryant, for his part, regarded the newspaper as both an educational tool and a moral force with which to diffuse to the common man practical information and encourage prudence, which he defined as "wisdom applied to the ordinary affairs of life."

Bryant believed strongly that a journalist should mold opinion and influence events. In the *Evening Post* of July 30, 1830, he voiced his philosophy.

"In combating error in all shapes and disguises," he wrote, satisfaction came to an editor in the ability "to perceive that you are understood by the intelligent, and appreciated by the candid, and that truth and correct principles are gradually extending their sway through your efforts."[3] It was a task he undertook with unflagging zeal for nearly half a century.

Bryant arrived in New York in 1825, two years before the city's final emancipation of slaves. In 1799, the New York legislature provided that the children of slaves born after July 4, 1799, would eventually acquire complete freedom (females at the age of twenty-five, males at twenty-eight).[4] Another act in 1817 declared that all blacks born after that date would become free after July 4, 1827.[5] In 1826, Bryant began working at the *Evening Post* as an editorial assistant. By 1829 he had become editor-in-chief and acquired a financial interest in the paper. Prior to Bryant's editorship, the newspaper had not changed much from its origins in 1801 as a Federalist Party organ, except that it had switched allegiances to the Democratic Party. Bryant's original share as editor was one-eighth of the net profits. The next year it rose to one-fourth, and by 1833 it was one-third.[6]

Bryant's steady opposition to protective tariffs, monopolies, and the extension of slavery often found him at odds with his own party.[7] In 1835, the *Post* was formally disowned by President Martin Van Buren's administration organ, the *Washington Globe*.[8] In a subsequent letter to a friend, Bryant wrote, "Let me counsel you against excessive sensitivity to what people say of you. . . . I know very well that I am much railed at and that I pass with a very large class of well-meaning persons as a man of no moral principles. I hear frequent intimations of the injustice that is done me."[9]

Bryant espoused the doctrines of free trade and free expression. It therefore was not surprising that he vehemently opposed slavery. Whenever he had the chance to speak of slavery, he condemned the practice as a violation of the fundamental principle of individual rights. As a boy, he had been taught by his father, a surgeon who served in the Massachusetts legislature, to question conventional ideas and speak his mind unwaveringly when he was convinced that the convention was not right. So it was with slavery.[10]

Bryant's management of the *Evening Post* greatly enhanced profits and brought the paper "into a position of influence for its honesty, ability, and high clean methods."[11] By 1834, the paper boasted that it "had never been in a more prosperous condition."[12] As newspaper historian Allan Nevins has noted:

> For the half year alone ending May 16, 1833—the figures for the full year are lost—the profits [of the paper] were $6,000.35, making Bryant's income for six months exactly $2,000. . . . In those days an [annual] income

of $4,000 or above was handsome, and Bryant was able to sail in the summer of 1834 with a full purse.[13]

Bryant's adept management enabled him to finance his favorite avocation, traveling. On June 24, 1834, he took his family on a two-year tour of Europe. It was during this tour that he was able to see firsthand how the United States was perceived abroad. In a letter to the *Evening Post* staff from Heidelberg, Germany, on December 9, 1835, Bryant lamented, "It is a source of constant vexation to Americans residing in Europe to see in the publick [sic] prints, and hear reported in conversation, exaggerated stories of riots, Lynch trials, and violence of various kind committed in the United States."[14] Bryant was alluding to an incident in New York City on July 7, 1834, when a white mob tried to prevent a group of blacks from using a chapel on Chatham Street for a belated Fourth of July celebration. Similar riots occurred in other eastern American cities while Bryant was abroad. He was shocked and abashed to discover that these atrocities were so well publicized in Europe and that, for the most part, they were factually correct. "The injury to the American character abroad, and to the cause of freedom in general, is great," he noted. "The misfortune is, that a part of what is laid to our charge is true, and that disorders have been perpetuated in America, which can neither be denied nor excused."[15]

Returning to his work on the *Evening Post* in March 1836, Bryant immediately began investigating the slavery issue. On April 21, he wrote an editorial titled "How Abolitionists Are Made." In it he chided South Carolina Senator John C. Calhoun and New York Senator Nathaniel P. Tallmadge for trying to have a petition to abolish slavery in the District of Columbia summarily dismissed. His European experience is evident in his language:

> [Mr. Tallmadge] should have condemned those acts of violence and tumult which made the friends of despotism abroad to exult, and which covered with shame the faces of those who were looking to our country as a glorious example of the certainty which with good order and respect for personal rights are the fruits of free political institutions.[16]

On May 18 of that same year, a gag rule was proposed to the House of Representatives by a committee headed by South Carolina Representative Henry Pinckney. It called for all antislavery petitions to be tabled without discussion, and it characterized such petitions as "foul slander on nearly one-half of the states of the union."[17] In his May 20 editorial, Bryant retorted:

> That they wished to gag the mouths of those who desired the abolition of slavery in that district we well knew; but we had no idea, 'til now, that

they denied even to the resolute enemies of abolitionism the right of being less violent and fanatical than themselves.[18]

To Bryant, this was a deliberate effort to break down the fundamental liberties of the constitution. He added: "We feel it the more of our duty to notice these indications of intolerance . . . because they form part of a plan for breaking down the liberty of speech and of the press by a most odious, tyrannical and intolerable censorship."[19]

Bryant eventually associated slavery with these types of government restrictions and with dangerous social and political pressures within the North. He saw slavery as posing a "double-barreled threat aimed at the heart of free society."[20] The New York state constitution of 1821 required free blacks to have a much higher property qualification for the right to vote than whites. On February 7, 1837, Bryant commented on the rejection of a petition that would allow blacks the same voting rights as whites. The rejection was based on the assertion that it was an abolitionist issue and therefore would upset the South:

> [I]t is very unwise to connect this question with that of the principal object of the abolitionists, which is to do away with slavery. . . . The great objection . . . hitherto, has been that they were inter-meddling with a matter with which they had no concerns. . . . The moment we allow ourselves to be restrained in legislating on this subject, by a regard to what is or may be said at the South, or anywhere else, we submit to external interference. . . . The law, as it now stands, is pregnant with absurdities.[21]

Bryant believed that individual freedom, free speech, and freedom of the press were universal rights. On August 10, 1836, he faced a situation in which these fundamental beliefs seemingly conflicted with one another. The *Evening Post* and Bryant were lambasted by the abolitionist newspaper the *Emancipator* for printing an advertisement that offered a reward for the return of an escaped slave. The *Emancipator* went on to ask whether "The *Post* was going to turn slave-catchers."[22] Bryant replied that although the practice of slavery was "contrary to natural rights and pernicious in its consequences,"[23] the right to advertise was a universal one that did not transgress the law.

On August 4, 1837, the self-proclaimed Republic of Texas petitioned the United States government for annexation to the Union. This action was seen by Bryant as a major strike against the abolition of slavery. He knew that slaveholding states were allowed proportional representation in the House of Representatives based in part on their slave populations. If annexed, Texas would be a gigantic slaveholding state. He railed against the move in his editorial that same day:

The project is to annex to the Union a territory in which slavery is an established political institution—a territory so ample that half a dozen states as large as Kentucky might be carved out of it. . . . The slaveholding states, by the Constitution of the Union, are disproportionately represented in Congress . . . allowed an additional number of representatives for a certain species of their property.[24]

Bryant used the issue to voice his feelings about the institution of slavery as a whole. "Holding, as we do, its existence among us to be a great evil," he said, "a great misfortune, and a monstrous anomaly in our institutions, we cannot but regard with the strongest alarm the project of adding to the nation a vast territory which holds that evil within its bosom."[25] The petition was denied three weeks later by President Van Buren.

By 1838, Bryant's outspoken and unpopular stance against slavery and his advocacy of the right of abolitionists to publish and petition Congress had caused him to be ostracized by the Democratic Party. According to William Cullen Bryant II, he was cast aside by "most of the New York Press, as well as the Tammany Hall leadership of his own party."[26]

The next year was an eventful one for Bryant. A new edition of his poems was released; his assistant editor, fellow poet, and friend, William Legget, died; and the controversial *Amistad* affair occurred. *Amistad* was a schooner sailing from one location in Cuba to another with a number of African slaves on board. The slaves revolted, took control of the ship, and attempted to sail it back to Africa. Instead, they landed in Long Island Sound, New York, where they were seized as criminals. A court sentenced them to slave labor.[27] The importation of slaves from Africa had been outlawed in America since 1808.[28] Bryant asked his friend Theodore Sedgwick Jr., an attorney, to investigate the law. Sedgwick came to the conclusion, which he expounded at length in the *Evening Post*, that the blacks could not be held.[29] Ultimately, they were released when the court upheld Sedgwick's view.[30]

In March 1843, Bryant traveled to the South for the first time. After firsthand contact with southern slaves, he surprisingly seemed almost complacent. In a letter to the *Evening Post* from South Carolina dated March 29, Bryant noted that "the blacks of this region are a cheerful, careless, dirty race, not hard worked, and in many respects indulgently treated." To Bryant, the practice of slavery seemed to have achieved "a compromise in which each party yields something, and a good-natured though imperfect and slovenly obedience on one side is purchased by good treatment on the other." As for white southerners, he found them "extremely agreeable. Whatever may be the comparison in other respects, the South certainly has the advantage over us in point of manners."[31]

Returning to New York, Bryant reentered the political battles of the day. The most pressing issue was still the unsettled question of Texas annexation. Hearing rumors that southern Democrats in cooperation with President John Tyler were planning to revive the Texas annexation scheme, Bryant warned on March 22, 1844, against the admission of Texas. He said it would increase dissension between the North and the South and expose the nation to "a war more formidable than any to which we are exposed from Great Britain or any other power."[32]

In early April, Bryant published six articles written by his friend, attorney Theodore Sedgwick. Sedgwick asked, "Should Texas, equal to one-sixth of the present U.S., be added as a slave-holding territory from which five or six states could be formed?"[33] Bryant also led a committee of antiannexationists. Later that month they met at the Broadway Tabernacle. The meeting degenerated into a riot, and Bryant denounced the outrages committed by the rioters in attempting to break up the gathering. Three days later, on April 27, he devoted the entire front page and five columns on page four of the newspaper to the draft of a proposed treaty with Texas and the government's confidential correspondence, none of which had been made public. The publication led to the appointment of a Senate committee to investigate how the newspaper had obtained its information. Bryant, subpoenaed to testify, explained that he had merely found a copy of the treaty on his desk. He never revealed his source for the information.

Bryant's opposition to the annexation of Texas soon wavered, however. In a July editorial, he announced, "As soon as the just claims of Mexico can be disposed of—as soon as the question of slavery can be got out of the way, we abandon our opposition to the annexation of Texas."[34] His somewhat conciliatory tone may have resulted from the nomination of dark horse candidate James K. Polk, a Tennessee slave owner, to run for president on the Democratic ticket. Although disagreeing with Polk on the Texas issue, Bryant supported the party nominee against Whig candidate Henry Clay, whose views on reestablishing the national bank Bryant fundamentally opposed. Bryant's support was crucial in holding New York state for the Democrats, whose 32 electoral votes ultimately decided the race in Polk's favor.

Bryant hoped to use his influence with the new president to work out a compromise on the Texas issue, but it was not to be. For all his determination and vigor however, the opposition triumphed. In November 1845, Texas was annexed to the United States. The next May, the country declared war on Mexico. Three months later, Pennsylvania Congressman David Wilmot proposed the so-called Wilmot Proviso, which prohibited slavery in any new acquisition of territory resulting from the war. The Wilmot Proviso became the rallying point for opponents of slavery. Bryant gave his wholehearted support to the cause, even going so far as printing the names of five free-state senators who had voted against the proviso and anathematizing New York Senator Daniel S. Dickinson for ignoring the instructions of the New York Assembly to vote in favor of Wilmot's measure. Said Bryant:

> A man who does not approve of slavery in the abstract may tolerate it where it exists, from want of constitutional authority to extinguish it, or from regard to the actual conditions of society, and the difficulties of change; but how can he justify himself in instituting it in new communities, unless he believes with Mr. Calhoun that it is in itself a 'great good'? . . . The federal government represents the free as well as the slave states; and while it does not attempt to abolish slavery in the states where it exists, it must not authorize slavery where it does not exist.[35]

In 1848, at war's end, Bryant switched political parties. He had said of the Democrats just before the transfer: "Talk of an acquisition of territory, and you are met with a demand that it shall be open to the introduction of slavery. Propose a scheme of finance, and you will find it opposed because it is feared that it may affect the interests of slavery."[36] Bryant joined the fledgling Free-Soiler Party, whose slogan was: "Free soil, free speech, free labor and free men."[37] The Free Soilers tried to resolve the slavery issue by committing the party to the Wilmot Proviso. Again, however, Bryant's altruism was not enough to win his cause. The Wilmot Proviso was defeated by the United States Senate.

On March 4, 1850, Senator Calhoun proposed to the Senate that the South be given an equal share of the territory acquired from Mexico as a result of the war.[38] On March 7, Massachusetts senator and famous orator Daniel Webster urged passage of a compromise allowing the organization of territory ceded by Mexico without restriction on slavery except in California. In his editorial of March 9, Bryant castigated the "folly" of Webster's alliance with Calhoun:

> Mr. Calhoun sees clearly what Mr. Webster does not see . . . that the slave states should never be left in a minority in Congress, and who will consent to no policy on the part of the federal government which does not look to the maintenance of their political power.[39]

Bryant insinuated that Webster had caused great harm in supporting the whims of the wily Calhoun, declaring, "Mr. Calhoun, therefore, very properly realizes the plan of Mr. Webster as meeting the wishes of those who desire the extension of slavery, and as removing the principal barrier to its introduction into our new possessions."[40]

That summer, Congress enacted a compromise that was accepted by moderates of the North and South. The Compromise of 1850 called for the

organization of New Mexico and Utah into territories without reference to
the slave issue; the admittance of California as a free state; the payment of
$10,000,000 to Texas for separating New Mexico from its bounds; the aboli-
tion of slavery in the District of Columbia; and the strengthening of the existing Fugitive Slave Act. Bryant did not care for the compromise and opposed
the abandonment of any principle. He called the compromise "a blanket poul-
tice, to heal five wounds at once, when the common sense method was to dress
every sore separately."[41]

Bryant wrote that the question of slavery must be settled by "principles
alone and not through compromise."[42] The *Evening Post* urged its readers to
petition Congress against the compromise. Bryant stridently opposed the Fugitive Slave Act. In his editorial of October 4, 1851, he blasted the unnatural-
ness of one man's being made to "shackle" a member of his community:

> Its operation is revolting. The people feel it to be an impeachment of their
> manhood, to be asked to assist in manacling for the purpose of reducing
> to slavery, one who has lived among them the life of an industrious and
> honest citizen.[43]

In 1854, Congress passed the Kansas-Nebraska Act. This bill repealed
the Missouri Compromise, which had prohibited slavery north of the parallel
36°30' in the old Louisiana Purchase territory. The *Evening Post* helped launch
a public crusade against the bill's northern supporters, most of whom were
Democrats. The newspaper never again supported Democratic candidates so
long as Bryant remained at the helm.

In July 1855, Bryant committed himself to the burgeoning Republican
Party, which had a main platform plank urging the abolition of slavery. The
Republicans held their first national convention in 1856. The Dred Scott decision, which denied citizenship to blacks descended from slaves, was handed
down by Chief Justice Roger Taney in 1857. From that moment, the *Evening
Post* treated slavery as a serpent upon which the nation must set its heel. With
Bryant's wholehearted support, the Republicans organized for the presidential
election of 1860. For Bryant, the old party differences over the basic political
and economic issues were to be suspended until the influence of slavery had
been contained within its old limits.[44]

Bryant hailed the nomination of Abraham Lincoln at the Republican
convention in Chicago. In his first editorial after Lincoln's nomination, Bryant declared:

> There are many points in his character fitted to call forth the enthusiasm
> of his party and to unite upon him the support of that numerous class
> who floated loosely between the two parties, and are found sometimes on

one side and sometimes on the other, as popular qualities of one candidate or another attract their suffrages.[45]

Two days later, the editor hailed Lincoln as the ultimate representative American, noting, "Whatever is peculiar in the history and development of America, whatever is foremost in its civilization, whatever is granted in its social and political structure finds its best expression in the career of such men as Abraham Lincoln."[46]

The Republican Party went on to elect Lincoln in the most divisive election in American history, and the war that many had been predicting between the North and the South began five months later. Bryant, through his unwavering opposition to slavery and his support for emancipation, had been an important catalyst for that war. In the words of historian Edward K. Spann, "Little did [Bryant] and other Republicans realize that they had set in motion forces which, far from restoring the old order, were to radically change the nature of American society.[47]

NOTES

1. Andrew James Symington, *William Cullen Bryant: A Biographical Sketch* (New York: Harper & Brothers, 1880), 115.
2. Curtiss S. Johnson, *Politics and a Bellyfull* (New York: Vantage Press, 1950), 91.
3. *New York Evening Post* (hereafter *Post*), 30 July 1830.
4. David Maldwyn Ellis, *New York: State and City* (New York: Cornell University Press, 1979), 116.
5. Ibid.
6. Allan Nevins, *The Evening Post: A Century of Journalism* (New York: Boni and Liveright Publishers, 1922), 136.
7. William Cullen Bryant II, "No Irish Need Apply: William Cullen Bryant Fights Nativism, 1836–1845," *New York History* 74, no. 1 (January, 1993): 30.
8. Ibid.
9. William C. Bryant, *The Letters of William Cullen Bryant* (hereafter *Letters*), ed. William Cullen Bryant II and Thomas G. Voss, vol. 2 (New York: Fordham University Press, 1975), 99.
10. Symington, 30.
11. Richard Burton, *Literary Leaders of America* (Norwood, Mass.: Norwood Press, 1903), 172.
12. Nevins, 135.
13. Ibid., 136.
14. William Cullen Bryant, *Letters*, vol. 1, 475–477.
15. Ibid.
16. "How Abolitionists Are Made," *Post*, 21 April 1836.
17. "Petitions Against Slavery," *Post*, 20 May 1836.
18. Ibid.
19. Ibid.

20. Edward K. Spann, *Ideals and Politics: New York Intellectuals and Liberal Democracy, 1820–1880* (New York: SUNY Press, 1972), 158.
21. "Negro Suffrage, New York State," *Post*, 7 February 1837.
22. "Slave Catching," *Post*, 10 August 1836.
23. Ibid.
24. "The Proposed Annexation of Texas," *Post*, 4 August 1837.
25. Ibid.
26. "No Irish Need Apply," *New York History*, 38.
27. Nevins, 172.
28. Ellis, 116.
29. Nevins, 172.
30. Ibid.
31. *Letters*, vol. 2, 201.
32. Charles H. Brown, *William Cullen Bryant* (New York: Charles Scribner's Sons, 1971), 290.
33. Ibid.
34. "Texas," *Post*, 25 July 1844.
35. Ibid.
36. Spann, 166.
37. Johnson, 98.
38. William Cullen Bryant, *Power for Sanity: Selected Editorials of William Cullen Bryant, 1829–1861*, ed. William Cullen Bryant II (New York: Fordham University Press, 1994), 261.
39. "A Recipe for the Extension of Slavery," *Post*, 9 March 1850.
40. Ibid.
41. Nevins, 245.
42. Johnson, 101.
43. "Fugitive Slave Riots," *Post*, 4 October 1851.
44. Spann, 179–180.
45. Brown, 417.
46. Ibid., 417–418.
47. Ibid.

THE FAILURE OF A MODERATE SOUTHERN VOICE

Andrew Jackson Donelson's Tenure as Editor of the *Washington Union*

— MARK CHEATHEM —

Andrew Jackson Donelson served as editor of the *Washington Union*, a Democratic newspaper in the nation's capital, from April 1851 to May 1852. During his thirteen-month tenure, he attempted, through his avowed platform based on devotion to the Constitution and the Union, to steer the Democratic Party toward moderation and away from the secessionist impulse that was becoming more prevalent within the party. However, Donelson's moderate editorial tone alienated him from many Democratic leaders, ultimately causing him to abandon the party of his now-deceased uncle, Andrew Jackson.

Donelson had served the Democrats in a variety of capacities before taking over the *Union* in 1851. He had been a member of the notorious Kitchen Cabinet during his uncle's presidency, his work with that body leading Martin Van Buren to consider him for a cabinet post when he won the 1836 presidential election. After returning to Tennessee in 1837, Donelson spent the next several years helping Jackson solidify the party's standing in their home state. His loyalty to the Hero of New Orleans led to his appointment as chargé d'affaires to Texas, where he played an instrumental role in securing the United States' annexation of the Lone Star Republic. President and fellow Tennessean James K. Polk, who also had contemplated making Donelson a cabinet member, appointed him minister to Berlin, then Frankfort, from 1846 to 1849.

Upon returning to Tennessee in early 1850, Donelson was immersed in $40,000 of debt, a not uncommon predicament for southern planters. He found time that year to serve as a moderate candidate at the Nashville Convention, which debated southern reaction to what some of the region's leaders considered attacks on the institution of slavery. This political activity was not paying the bills, however, so Donelson began casting about for some position that would help him turn a profit. Cognizant of Donelson's precarious financial situation, Democratic leaders approached him in early 1851 with the prospect of taking over the party's mouthpiece in the nation's capital.[1]

The *Washington Union* had replaced Francis P. Blair's *Globe* in 1845 as the official organ of the Polk administration and now served as the Democratic Party's major newspaper. During the 1850 Compromise negotiations, *Union* editor Thomas Ritchie had espoused Henry Clay's peaceable settlement, infuriating the states' rights wing of the Democratic Party. Using the excuse that Ritchie was too old and opinionated to serve as party editor and that accusations of corruption were hindering his credibility, a number of nationally known Democrats, including Lewis Cass and Stephen A. Douglas, forced his resignation and immediately chose Donelson as his replacement. Having written extensively for a Democratic newspaper in Nashville, Donelson had been many party leaders' original choice to head the *Globe* in 1845, a position that he had turned down. Now they assured him that his talents were needed to unite the party as the next presidential election year loomed.[2]

To convince Donelson to take the post, party leaders made two promises. They agreed to find someone else to provide the necessary capital to purchase the newspaper from Ritchie, relieving Donelson of the necessity of going further into debt. They also assured him that Congress would pass legislation giving the *Washington Union* a printing contract for the 1850 census returns, an agreement that would garner the newspaper's editor and proprietor between $100,000 and $200,000. With these lucrative financial inducements before him, Donelson put aside any compunction and agreed to accept the position in March 1851.[3]

Initial reaction to Donelson's appointment as editor was mixed. Some politicians, such as Pennsylvanian James Buchanan, were favorable. "With Donelson," Buchanan declared, "I am both personally & politically satisfied." By his very name, he noted, Donelson possessed the emotional influence and political prestige of Andrew Jackson's memory. In addition, he was "a shrewd man & able writer."[4] Others were not as confident about Donelson's chances of uniting the Democratic Party and the South. Fellow Tennessean Cave Johnson questioned "whether Donelson . . . will conciliate the fire-eaters." Robert M.T. Hunter, a Virginia Democrat and avid supporter of southern rights, possessed little faith in Donelson, whereas Democratic newspapermen Francis Blair and John Rives were suspicious of the influence that potential Democratic presidential contender Lewis Cass had over him. Blair also questioned Donelson's motives. The Tennessean's financial woes were common knowledge in Washington, and it seemed to Blair that Donelson was looking for financial gain more than he was hoping to defend the party's principles.[5]

With such discussion swirling around him, Donelson began preparing the platform by which he hoped to govern the newspaper. He consulted several prominent Democratic leaders and asked for their counsel on what direction he should take. Buchanan offered the only substantive advice. After congratulating Donelson on his new position as party spokesman and expressing his hopes that "it may prove a source of profit to yourself as well as a means of restoring harmony and strength" to the party, Buchanan made three important recommendations. First, the *Union* should "adopt the Virginia Resolutions," a set of declarations made by the Virginia legislature promoting the 1850 Compromise as a final settlement of the slavery question and calling for South Carolinians and other southerners to cease agitating for secession. Winning the next presidential election, Buchanan emphatically declared, depended upon reconciling the states' rights and Union wings of the Democratic Party. Secondly, Donelson had to come out strong for the faithful execution of the fugitive slave law. Above all, Buchanan counseled, the new editor "had better pursue [his] own independent course" at the *Union*.[6]

Bearing that advice in mind, Donelson took over the *Union*'s columns on April 16, 1851, and announced his prospectus one week later. His first editorial, while strongly Democratic in principle, clearly stated his determination to exercise political independence when it came to his ideological principles. "This paper, whilst under my control," Donelson declared, "will never become the organ of any combination of aspiring individuals, banded together to promote their own selfish or ambitious purposes." It would also not become the mouthpiece of any one individual and would only sustain the Democratic Party when it pursued "truly national measures by constitutional and just means." Just as Buchanan suggested, he called for Americans to support the 1850 Compromise and be moderate on slavery, while also demanding the enforcement of the fugitive slave law.[7]

Donelson's opening editorial and prospectus emphasized the principles he held dear. He noted that the North and the South now faced a situation similar to the one confronting the American colonies before the Revolution. In the 1760s and 1770s, the colonies and Great Britain had grown farther apart because of Parliament's repressive acts. That rift had led to war. Donelson compared that time to the current political atmosphere. Just as the Americans and British had enjoyed a close relationship and then split acrimoniously, the United States faced the same outcome unless northerners and southerners worked to reconcile their differences over slavery. The most important way to defuse the situation, Donelson advised, was to remove slavery as a divisive issue. To do so, the South had to abide by the 1850 Compromise, whereas the North had to enforce the stronger fugitive slave law provision. Otherwise, "the preservation of the Union will become an impossibility," he concluded.[8]

Donelson made it clear that he considered himself the party's spokesman for moderation. "The Constitution as administered and expounded by Washington, and the authority of those great minds which afterwards effected the civil revolution of 1800, shall be my guide," he stressed, "on the one hand in insisting on the love of the Union, and the avoidance of whatever can tend to the alienation of one portion of the people from another; and, on the other, in guarding against the dangers of consolidation." Donelson urged both northern and southern Democrats to pursue compromise. Extremists were attacking "the cause of popular self-government," he warned, and Democrats in both sections needed to "pause, and unite once more with their true friends to strengthen the party which has never failed heretofore, with constitutional means, to foil all serious assaults upon the rights of the people and the States." Donelson also made it clear that he had little patience for southern arguments in support of secession, northern advocacy of abolition, or any other radical solutions that threatened to divide the nation. He intended to rely only on tried-and-true republican principles and institutions, values the new editor believed were sufficient to resolve any dilemma the nation or one of its regions might face.[9]

Realizing that southerners would question his commitment to slavery and states' rights, Donelson endeavored to clarify his stance on those issues in his second editorial, titled "Our Position as a Citizen of the South." "[Having] been familiar from our infancy . . . [w]ith the institution of slavery," Donelson declared himself a southerner "for weal or for wo[e]." "Not that we would characterize the institution of slavery as a blessing," he admitted, "but such is the mysterious connexion [sic] with which Providence binds man to the institutions under which he is born." Slavery, he argued, "postpones the corruptions that are incident to the states of civilization in which human beings sink nearly to the level of the machines with which they earn a scanty subsistence." It had played an important role in the nation's founding, encouraging "the diversification of our interests" and causing southerners to limit the power of the federal government. "It is better to improve and expand our blessings by strengthening the basis of existing relations," Donelson remarked, "than by changes which can never be incorporated into our system without alienating its parts. Let us, then, all resolve . . . that the constitution is our unchangeable hope and guide," he concluded, and slavery a permanent southern institution.[10]

As Donelson's first editorials appeared, Democrats remained divided over his benefit to the party. Archibald Campbell Jr., one of New Yorker William L. Marcy's strongest supporters, liked Donelson's editorials. "It is truly refreshing to read his good manly sense after being deluged so long with the twaddle of the amiable but *shallow* old man Ritchie," he proclaimed. Other leading Democrats, including Buchanan, Cass, and Franklin Pierce of New Hampshire, added their approbation of his editorial voice. Some Democrats expressed reservations, however. Robert Tyler, son of the former Virginia president, criticized Donelson's perceived opposition to Buchanan's presidential candidacy. Francis P. Blair was also lukewarm toward Donelson's editorials.[11]

Donelson was not oblivious to such criticism. He informed his wife, Elizabeth, that "*false friends*" constantly approached him, "men that calculated to use me, and are not a little mortified to find that I can think for myself." Donelson, however, remained undeterred. By the end of his first week at his new post, he informed his son, Jackson, that the newspaper was already making a profit, enough to enable his family to move to Washington. Within the month, however, Donelson noted to his wife that he was barely able to pay the $500 in weekly expenses the newspaper regularly accrued. "My patronage is better in the West and in the middle states than in the South," he told her. "The democratic [sic] party is scattered and broken down in many places. It can be rallied and will elect the next President. . . . To be instrumental in that is my work here."[12]

Donelson churned out editorials for the *Union*'s readers six times a week, usually writing them late at night. He described the daily grind of writing editorials as "more laborious than chopping with an axe." His task was made easier by the assistance of a number of correspondents scattered throughout the United States and in Europe. During these first months, Donelson's only editorial assistance came from Robert Armstrong, his financial backer; Charles Eames, former editor of the *Nashville Union*, who joined the *Union*'s staff in August 1851; and a man named Overton, a Virginian who drank too much and had helped Ritchie before his retirement.[13]

Many topics, both foreign and domestic, filled the columns of the *Union* during Donelson's first few months as editor. He carried on numerous running disputes with the *Washington Republic*, the official organ of President Millard Fillmore's administration, and the *Southern Press*, a Washington newspaper established by southern fire-eaters. Slavery also received thorough treatment because Donelson attempted to present himself as a supporter of the institution while denying the need for its sectional divisiveness. In all his editorials, Donelson emphasized the necessity of moderation to maintain the nation's republican ideology and institutions.

Donelson's most forceful statement in support of the Union and political moderation came in July 1851. The Fourth of July holiday inspired him to publish a lesson on the importance of the United States in the eyes of the world. "The stately fabric of a free government, and the cheering spectacle of a prosperous and powerful people," he began, "vindicate before the world the eminent supremacy of republican institutions." As Americans celebrated their independence, "dangerous and designing men have shut their eyes on the past, and forgotten the lessons taught by the revolution. . . . Factionists have kindled the fires of sectional strife, reckless of the consequences which may follow. . . . Misguided men, dead to every patriotic impulse, and mindful only of personal aggrandizement, have attempted to depart from the safe example of our fathers, and to turn the government from its legitimate course," he warned. Americans had forgotten from where their freedom came, Donelson admonished: "[c]ustom has made us callous." If sectionalists persisted in pressing their "insane" claims, he predicted that civil war would come. "It would be an announcement of the triumph of tyranny in the Old World—the beginning of a saturnalia in the New World. . . . Standing armies and ruinous military establishments will consume the substance of the people." Donelson believed, however, that Providence would intervene and that the American people would remain "firmly united by the remembrance of a common ancestry, and bound together by the thrilling memories of a glorious past."[14]

This grandiose statement did not improve Donelson's standing within the Democratic Party. Appeasing all of its factions was a difficult task for someone who had to make frequent public pronouncements on the state of the nation and its political parties. Warning of dire consequences if the sections continued their course was not popular. Moderation was becoming less and less of an option for southern politicians, as many would discover in coming years. To mute some of the criticism directed at him, Donelson increased his attacks on the Whigs and their putative association with corrupt officials and fanatical abolitionists.

Still, his editorials kept coming back to a persistent theme: the Union was paramount. The continued agitation for secession by states' righters galled him. Donelson acknowledged the right of secession only as a last resort against "oppression and tyranny" when all other avenues for redress had failed. In that instance, secession was more rightfully labeled revolution, he argued. Seceding "to destroy at pleasure" the federal compact that the Constitution had established, Donelson claimed, was an absurdity at odds with the republican system. From his vantage point, fire-eaters' charges that the 1850 compromise constituted "intolerable oppression" blasphemed the intentions of Jefferson and other supporters of the idea of states' rights and secession. By denying the primacy of the Constitution and the laws of the land, Donelson believed southern secessionists were just as guilty as northern abolitionists of placing the nation in danger of dissolution over slavery.[15]

Despite his attempts to unify Democrats, in early 1852 Donelson discovered that members of his own party were working to force him out as *Union* editor. One justification they used was Donelson's supposed favoritism of various presidential candidates. From the first rumor that he was replacing Ritchie at the helm of the *Union*, many Democrats believed that the new editor, despite his claims of neutrality, had already committed himself to a nominee for the 1852 election. The names of William L. Marcy, Lewis Cass, James Buchanan, Stephen Douglas, and Sam Houston all appeared in the *Union's* columns as possible candidates for the party's nomination, leading supporters and opponents of each to count the number and length of articles on other potential nominees and speculate on their meaning. Donelson, in fact, publicly supported no single candidate. He clung fiercely to the slogan "principles and not men," and if he privately favored a particular nominee, neither his correspondence nor the *Union's* columns revealed his preference. The criticism that some Democrats directed against him was unwarranted.[16]

The argument about favoritism was merely a smokescreen, however. Donelson knew that his editorials were alienating him from fellow southerners, and his refusal to support the South unquestionably was the primary reason for his eventual removal from the *Union*. He advised his wife in October 1851 that "the influence of the *seceding* gentlemen is every where [sic] against me, not openly, but more effectively in the dark. Men that you would not suspect are at the bottom of it." Donelson was right; southern fire-eaters were prominent in the movement to replace him, but moderates also found his editorials objectionable. Georgia Democrats Robert Toombs and Alexander H. Stephens, both Unionists, criticized Donelson's moderation as "expedient" and dangerous to the South. Edward W. Hubard, one of Robert M.T. Hunter's associates, especially criticized Donelson's efforts. "The [*Washington Union*] was clearly for Cass from the start," he observed. "He [Cass] would establish the inquisition if the Union [sic] would suggest it, or the alien and sedition laws. Should he be elected[,] the country might look out for the most high handed measures, all proved by the editor of the Union [sic] to be in accordance with the doctrines of Jefferson, Madison, and Jackson. May the Lord deliver our party from the hands of the quacks of Tennessee and Michigan." Even Houston, a moderate southerner and old friend, had no faith in Donelson.[17]

As a southern moderate intent on accepting the 1850 Compromise as the final settlement of the slavery question, Donelson found it difficult to please either staunch southern Unionists or states' rightists. Fire-eaters hated him for lambasting their advocacy of secession, whereas Unionists criticized him for trying to preserve the Democratic Party with all of its disparate elements. With northern Democrats critical of Donelson's alleged favoritism of southern candidates, and southern Democrats upset at his attempt to mediate the various factions' differences, party leaders in Congress launched two lines of attack to force Donelson's retirement.[18]

Donelson had accepted the *Union*'s editorship with the promise that the newspaper would receive a congressional contract for the 1850 census printing. Whatever his stated ideological commitment to maintaining the Democratic Party and its republican principles, Donelson took the job to make money that he desperately needed. Democratic leaders knew his situation, of course, and used his precarious financial position to oust him. On December 9, 1851, Senator Jesse Bright of Indiana introduced a resolution authorizing Congress to negotiate a census printing contract with Donelson and Armstrong. The Joint Committee on Printing reported the resolution back to the Senate for debate on January 6, 1852. The resolution immediately bogged down in mundane discussion over the question of who in Congress should negotiate the contract with the *Union*'s proprietors and whether the contract should go to Donelson and Armstrong or to the lowest bidder. There were also intimations that the entire bidding process was corrupt and smacked of political favoritism. When debate resumed on January 12, opponents of the resolution attacked the necessity of a speedy passage. "Surely the worthy and highly-respectable gentlemen, who are the proprietors of the *Union*, are not in a state of starvation," one senator facetiously said. Why not allow printers to bid for the job, as was customary, the resolution's opponents inquired, instead of risking the possibility that Donelson and Armstrong would try to bilk the government out of a substantial amount of money? When it came time for the House to vote on the resolution, its members tabled the measure indefinitely by a vote of 134 to 51, and the Senate did likewise, 28 to 16. This move effectively ended any hope that Donelson had of making a substantial profit at the *Union*, but in the short term he persevered, even without the financial inducement.[19]

As if denying the *Union* the promised congressional printing contract were not enough, Democrats further accused Donelson and Armstrong of trying to obtain steamship mail subsidies, government money used to support private entrepreneurs who promised to deliver mail to California and across the Atlantic. Democrats who advocated only limited government support of private enterprise attacked Armstrong because his son-in-law, Arnold

Harris, was a steamship subsidies lobbyist to Congress, and castigated Donelson because he portrayed himself as a strict constructionist Democrat so long as it did not affect his own pocketbook. There is no evidence that Donelson was connected to Harris's lobbying, but his cautious approval of the idea in a March 1852 editorial provided his opponents with enough ammunition to label him corrupt.[20]

In the census debate and the steamship subsidies controversy, opponents of the *Union* expressed concern about corruption, but everyone involved knew what the real issue was. Donelson had offended numerous factions within the Democratic Party, and they were determined to force his ouster by any means possible. Donelson's attempts to defend himself in the *Union*'s columns failed to relieve the pressure. He finally gave in May 12, 1852, when he informed the newspaper's subscribers that he was resigning. The newspaper's failure to receive the census printing had made it "more than my pecuniary means could bear to remain here with no prospect of remuneration for my services," Donelson informed his son, Jackson. In his valedictory editorial, Donelson assured his readers that he had "endeavored faithfully to maintain the old and settled principles of the democratic [sic] party." In truth, however, his expectation of establishing the *Washington Union* as a "rallying point" for the party had failed.[21]

Donelson was bitter. He had been the victim of the "baneful influence of the presidential schemers," he told Howell Cobb. "Free-soil and secession are allowed to play what [pranks] they please, because leading men standing on our platform are unwilling to provoke their wrath." To his son he confided that "[a]t a proper time[,] the public will be informed more particularly than would be now useful, of the character of the opposition which has been made to my political views."[22]

Donelson hoped that whoever won the Democratic presidential nomination would recognize his contributions to the party and, should that candidate win the presidency, reward him in some fashion, perhaps even restoring him to the *Union*'s editorship. Franklin Pierce's nomination in early June gave him reason to be optimistic. To Donelson, Pierce represented the victory of his efforts at the *Washington Union*. At the convention, he had urged Democrats to cease fighting over the 1850 Compromise and accept its tenets, whatever qualms they possessed. Donelson had also been satisfied in his one past encounter with Pierce in May 1851, when the New Hampshire Democrat had applauded his editorial tenure at the *Union*. "There is a great battle before us," Pierce had written Donelson, "a battle for the Union—a battle for the ascendancy of the principles, the maintenance of which so nobly signalized the administration of Gen. Jackson. The tone, vigor, and statesmanlike grasp which you have brought to the columns of the *Union* are not merely important, they are absolutely indispensible [sic] at this crisis." Just in case Pierce had forgotten his compliments, Donelson sent him a reminder in July 1852 and lauded his support for the 1850 Compromise. Pierce was a true Constitution man, Donelson believed, one who could "be reproached with no sectionalism." "I trust the impulse which has been given to sound, patriotic, and national views by your nomination," he told Pierce, "will force all extremists to their proper level, and leave you, as Genl. Jackson was, free to pursue the dictates of a policy which looks alone to our progress as one people, and which guards alike the interests of the states and the powers of the Federal Government."[23]

Donelson's assumption that Pierce would reward his loyalty should he win the presidency led the Tennessean to write and speak in support of the Democratic candidate. He told Tennesseans at political rallies that some disgruntled Democrats had orchestrated his dismissal from the *Union*, but the Baltimore convention's moderate candidate and platform demonstrated that the party as a whole "endorse[d] the course of the [*Washington*] *Union*" under his direction. When Pierce won the election that November, however, he ignored Donelson in making his cabinet and other government appointments. It was a slight that Donelson never forgave.[24]

In Donelson's mind, as a reward for his many sacrifices at the head of the *Union*, the Democratic Party had repaid him by chasing him out of Washington without the financial incentives promised to him. When Donelson turned his political acumen to winning the election for the Democratic nominee, Pierce, the victorious candidate, a man who had once congratulated him for his ideological stance, failed to acknowledge his efforts with a compensatory appointment. At the end of 1852, Donelson considered himself politically and financially bankrupt, and he blamed Pierce and the Democratic Party for his quandary. After a brief political retirement, he returned to the fray but not as a Democrat. In late 1854, he became a member of the Know-Nothing Party, a move that earned him both political and personal exile from middle Tennessee. No doubt, he saw little difference from his earlier exile in Washington.

NOTES

This chapter is reprinted by permission of Louisiana State University Press from Mark Cheathem's book, *Old Hickory's Nephew: The Political and Private Struggles of Andrew Jackson Donelson*. Copyright © 2007 by Louisiana State University Press.

1.   Robert B. Satterfield, "Andrew Jackson Donelson: A Moderate Nationalist Jacksonian" (PhD diss., The Johns Hopkins University, 1961), 428.

2.   Roy Franklin Nichols, *The Democratic Machine, 1850–1854* (New York: Longman, Green, 1923), 32–34; Charles H. Ambler, *Thomas Ritchie: A Study in Virginia Politics* (Richmond, Va.: Bell Book & Stationery, 1913), 278–288; and William Ernest

Smith, *The Francis Preston Blair Family in Politics*, 2 vols. (New York: Macmillan, 1933), 1:269–270.

3.   Andrew J. Donelson to Elizabeth R. Donelson, 24 February 1851 and 7 March 1851, Andrew J. Donelson Papers, Library of Congress, Washington, D.C.; Smith, *Blair Family*, 270; and Nichols, *Democratic Machine*, 33–34.

4.   James Buchanan to Cave Johnson, 22 March 1851, James Buchanan Papers, Historical Society of Pennsylvania, Philadelphia, Pennsylvania; Francis P. Blair to Martin Van Buren, 15 March 1851, Martin Van Buren Papers, Library of Congress, Washington, D.C.; *National Intelligencer* (Washington, D.C.), 17 April 1851, in *Republican Banner and Nashville Whig*, 24 April 1851; and Boston *Post*, 7 June 1851, in *Washington Daily Union*, 10 June 1851.

5.   Cave Johnson to James Buchanan, 30 March 1851, Buchanan Papers; Robert M.T. Hunter to George N. Sanders, 27 March 1851, in Charles H. Ambler, ed., *Correspondence of Robert M.T. Hunter, 1826–1876*, in *Annual Report of the American Historical Association for the Year 1916*, 2 vols. (Washington, D.C.: GPO, 1918), 2:126; and Francis P. Blair to Martin Van Buren, 10 March 1851 and 15 March 1851, Francis P. Blair to John Van Buren, 24 March 1851, Van Buren Papers.

6.   James Buchanan to Andrew J. Donelson, 27 February 1851, Donelson Papers; Andrew J. Donelson to William L. Marcy, 15 March 1851, William L. Marcy Papers, Library of Congress, Washington, D.C.; James Buchanan to Andrew J. Donelson, 20 March 1851, in St. George L. Sioussat, ed., "Selected Letters, 1846–1856. From the Donelson Papers," *Tennessee Historical Magazine* 3 (1917): 268–269; and Arthur C. Cole, *The Whig Party in the South* (Washington, D.C.: American Historical Association, 1914), 191–192.

7.   *Washington Daily Union*, 16 April 1851 and 23 April 1851; and Andrew J. Donelson to James Buchanan, 15 April 1851, Buchanan Papers.

8.   *Washington Daily Union*, 16 April 1851.

9.   Ibid.

10. *Washington Daily Union*, 17 April 1851.

11. A[rchibald] Campbell to William L. Marcy, 26 April 1851, Marcy Papers; Ivor Debenham Spencer, *The Victor and the Spoils: A Life of William L. Marcy* (Providence, R.I.: Brown University Press, 1959), 195; William L. Marcy to Andrew J. Donelson, 7 May 1851, James B. Bowlin to Andrew J. Donelson, 5 May 1851, Richard K. Meade to Andrew J. Donelson, 7 May 1851, Lewis Cass to Andrew J. Donelson, 16 May 1851, James Buchanan to Andrew J. Donelson, 16 June 1851, Robert Tyler to Andrew J. Donelson, 4 May 1851, in Sioussat, ed., "Selected Donelson Letters, 1846–1856," 274–276, 271–274, 276–278, 278–279, 279–280, 270–271; Francis P. Blair to Martin Van Buren, 30 April 1851 and 14 May 1851, Van Buren Papers; and Benjamin C. Howard to Andrew J. Donelson, 19 May 1851, Franklin Pierce to Andrew J. Donelson, 30 May 1851, Andrew J. Donelson to Elizabeth R. Donelson, 16 May 1851, Donelson Papers.

12. Andrew J. Donelson to [Jackson Donelson], 20 April 1851, Andrew J. Donelson to Elizabeth R. Donelson, 11 May 1851 and 16 May 1851, Donelson Papers.

13. Andrew J. Donelson to Elizabeth R. Donelson, 11 May 1851 and 16 May 1851, Theodore Fay to Andrew J. Donelson, 24 May 1851 [fragment], Benjamin C.

Howard to Andrew J. Donelson, 19 May 1851, Donelson Papers; Francis P. Blair to Martin Van Buren, 30 April 1851, Van Buren Papers; and *Washington Daily Union*, 6 July 1851, 20 August 1851, and 26 August 1851.

14. *Washington Daily Union*, 4 July 1851.

15. *Washington Daily Union*, 22–23 August 1851, 25 August 1851, 27 August 1851, 29 August 1851, 2 September 1851, 4–7 September 1851, 9–10 September 1851, 14 September 1851, 16–19 September 1851, 21 September 1851, 24–25 September 1851, 3 October 1851, 5 October 1851, 9 October 1851, 16 October 1851, 21 October 1851, 18 December 1851, 21 December 1851, 4 January 1852, 6 January 1852, 23 January 1852, 13 February 1852, and 20 February 1852.

16. Nichols, *Democratic Machine*, 35; Smith, *Blair Family*, 1:270; Larry Gara, *The Presidency of Franklin Pierce* (Lawrence: University Press of Kansas, 1991), 23; M.R. Werner, *Tammany Hall* (Garden City, N.Y.: Doubleday, Doran, 1928), 70; Spencer, *Victor and the Spoils*, 194.

17. Andrew J. Donelson to Elizabeth R. Donelson, 6 October 1851, Donelson Papers; Andrew J. Donelson to Howell Cobb, 22 October 1851 and 26 October 1851, Alexander H. Stephens to Howell Cobb, 26 November 1851, Robert Toombs to Howell Cobb, 2 January 1851 [1852], in Ulrich B. Phillips, ed., *Correspondence of Robert Toombs, Alexander H. Stephens, and Howell Cobb*, in *Annual Report of the American Historical Association for the Year 1911*, 2 vols. (Washington, D.C.: GPO, 1913), 2:262–263, 264, 265–267, 218–220; Edward W. Hubard to Robert M.T. Hunter, 8 May 1852, in Ambler, ed., *Correspondence of Robert M.T. Hunter*, 141–142; and Llerena Friend, *Sam Houston: The Great Designer* (Austin: University of Texas Press, 1954), 283.

18. Allan Nevins, *Ordeal of the Union: Fruits of Manifest Destiny, 1847–1852* (New York: Scribner's, 1947), 357–358, 375–376; Philip Clayton to Howell Cobb, 25 August 1852 [1851], in Phillips, ed., *Correspondence of Toombs, Stephens, and Cobb*, 2:317; and *Washington Daily Union*, 20 January 1852, 21 January 1852, 23 January 1852, 27 January 1852, 3 February 1852, 22 February 1852, 28 February 1852, and 5 March 1852.

19. *Journal of the Senate*, 32nd Congress, 1st Session, 41; *Congressional Globe*, 32d Congress, 1st Session, 203–207, 245–251, 259–266; Mark W. Summers, *The Plundering Generation: Corruption and the Crisis of the Union, 1849–1861* (New York: Oxford University Press, 1987), 44–45; and Nichols, *Democratic Machine*, 35–36.

20. Summers, *Plundering Generation*, 44, 103–106; Nichols, *Democratic Machine*, 35; Francis P. Blair to Martin Van Buren, 15 March 1851, Van Buren Papers; James Buchanan to Cave Johnson, 22 March 1851, Buchanan Papers; and *Washington Daily Union*, 26 March 1852.

21. Albert G. Brown to Jefferson Davis, 1 May 1852, in Lynda Lasswell Crist, Mary Seaton Dix, and Richard E. Beringer, eds., *The Papers of Jefferson Davis*, vol. 4, *1849–1852* (Baton Rouge and London: Louisiana State University Press, 1983), 255–258; *Washington Daily Union*, 28 January 1852, 1 February 1852, 15 April 1852, 16 April 1852, 17 April 1852, 18 April 1852, 20 April 1852, 22 April 1852, 24 April 1852, 25 April 1852, and 12 May 1852; and Andrew J. Donelson to Jackson Donelson, 12 May 1852, Andrew J. Donelson to Elizabeth R. Donelson, 6 October 1851, Donelson Papers.

22. Andrew J. Donelson to Howell Cobb, 10 [12] May 1852, in Phillips, ed., *Correspondence of Toombs, Stephens, and Cobb*, 2:294–295.

23. Gara, *Presidency of Franklin Pierce*, 29–36; Franklin Pierce to Andrew J. Donelson, 30 May 1851, Donelson Papers; and Andrew J. Donelson to Franklin Pierce, 26 July 1852, Franklin Pierce Papers, Library of Congress.

24. Speech by Andrew J. Donelson [at Nashville, Tennessee], n.d. [September 1852], Andrew Ewing to Andrew J. Donelson, 3 September 1852, speech by Andrew J. Donelson [at McNairy County, Tennessee], n.d. [29 September 1852], and Democratic corresponding committee of McNairy County to Andrew J. Donelson, 14 September 1852, Donelson Papers; and Gara, *Presidency of Franklin Pierce*, 36–37.

MURDER AND MAYHEM

Violence, Press Coverage, and the Mobilization of the Republican Party in 1856

— KATHERINE A. PIERCE —

By 1856, two new political parties, the nativist American Party, or Know-Nothings, and the exclusively northern Republicans, jockeyed for position to succeed the rapidly declining Whigs as the major electoral opponent of the Democrats.[1] At the start of the year, many observers believed the Know-Nothings would prevail, but by summer's end the Republicans had emerged victorious. Republican hopes for success in the upcoming presidential campaign, however, depended on forging a workable coalition of northern Know-Nothings, former Whigs, and dissatisfied Democrats behind the candidacy of former military officer and explorer John C. Frémont.[2]

The northern press, particularly those newspapers associated with the Republican Party, proved central in attracting undecided voters. Contemporary historians have focused on the caning of Massachusetts Senator Charles Sumner by South Carolina Congressman Preston Brooks in May 1856 as a singularly vivid act of southern aggression that, taken in combination with the sacking of Lawrence, Kansas, by proslavery guerrillas earlier that same month, outraged the northern public and aided Republicans in their recruitment efforts.[3] Few historians, however, have emphasized the role that Republican newspapers played in preparing northern opinion for an explosive reaction to the Sumner episode by sensationalizing a seemingly unrelated

85

murder that occurred precisely two weeks earlier at Willard's Hotel in the capital city.

On May 8, California Congressman Philemon T. Herbert, a boarder at Willard's Hotel, arrived too late for breakfast but still demanded service. A brawl ensued with the kitchen staff, and Herbert shot and killed the Irish head-waiter, Thomas Keating. The *New York Daily Tribune* account on May 9 stated that after Herbert and a friend William Gardiner, a fellow Californian, had been directed to request service from the main office, Herbert verbally abused the staff. After the congressman and Keating exchanged words, Herbert struck him in the face. A wild melee erupted with "chairs and crockery broken pro-fusely" as Keating, his brother Patrick, and the two Californians tossed plates, turned over chairs, and beat each other with fists and trays. The fighting ex-panded as friends of Herbert and kitchen staff rushed into the dining room. When the combatants finally drew apart, Thomas Keating lay dead.

Horace Greeley, editor of the *New York Daily Tribune*, condemned the use of violence and called on the House of Representatives to "decide whether a Member may shoot down a fellow-man during its sittings . . . [and] walk into the Hall and take his seat with the blood of a human being red upon his hands." The *Tribune*'s story was a parable of class inequity and the "unmanly" use of a concealed weapon. Although the *Tribune* clearly disparaged Herbert's arrogance and his fatal response to Keating's perceived insolence, there were no sectional references. Herbert's friends testified that he fired in self-defense only after six or seven waiters assaulted him with murderous intent.[4] The *Philadelphia Ledger* characterized Herbert as a "quiet, inoffensive man" and portrayed the killing as a "difficulty" resulting from insolent waiters banding together to assault Herbert as he ate breakfast.[5]

The next day, the *Tribune* shifted its focus from abuse of congressio-nal privilege to a biting commentary on sectional attitudes. Earlier identified as a Democratic congressman from California, Herbert was revealed to be southern born, a native of Alabama. From this point, the "affray" became a "murder," and although occasional elements of class rhetoric remained, Gree-ley increasingly adopted a tone of sectional indictment. Herbert became the aggressor, "a man easily excited and prompt to take offense" and "given to agi-tations of passion." Keating assumed the role of sacrificial victim. "No apology can be made for the shooting of an unarmed, defenseless man . . . with the intent to kill simply because he is resisting assault," Greeley thundered.[6]

Greeley's changed language transformed a contested case of manslaugh-ter into an example of southern aristocrats' assault on northerners' rights. Herbert, representing the so-called Slave Power, stood in opposition to honor, justice, free labor, and northern values. References to his youth and passionate nature served to belittle him in contrast to middle-class values of self-discipline, control, and virtue.[7] The morality tale of class disparity evolved into one of sectional censure. In a solitary line item under a bold summary headline, the paper noted, "The killing of a menial is not reckoned a grave offense south of Mason and Dixon's Line."[8]

Local magistrates sent the matter to the District of Columbia's criminal court to decide if Herbert should be released on bail. Greeley commented, "Does any man believe, if a waiter in Willard's Hotel had first insulted, then struck and finally shot dead, Mr. Herbert or any other Member of Congress" that such a "wavering, hair-splitting decision" would result? He focused on the threat to "our Republican institutions" of such unequal justice.[9] Greeley highlighted the testimony from the hotel staff. Ten of twelve witnesses called before the magistrate reported that Herbert was abusive and aggressive and that he and Gardiner had attacked the staff with canes and chairs prior to the shooting. Herbert's four friends testified that he had been besieged by a "gang of waiters" and fired only in self-defense. Stymied by the conflicting evidence amassed in seven hours of testimony, Judge Thomas Crawford noted that the evidence was "not only contradictory, but utterly irreconcilable." He announced that it was either manslaughter or justifiable homicide and released Herbert on $10,000 bail.[10]

Rejecting Crawford's release of Herbert as a denial of "even-handed justice," Greeley focused on the magistrate's class bias rather than his political affiliation.[11] The next day, his characterization of the judge changed as he marked Judge Crawford as "a slavedriver at heart" because of his past prosecution of resisters of the Fugitive Slave Act. Greeley tied Crawford and slaveholders to the Democratic Party and derided northern laborers who supported it for making "slaves of themselves."[12] The *Tribune* attributed the lack of justice to the Slave Power's ability to flout the law with impunity. Greeley directed his editorials to the common people, noting that "the laboring people of the United States—those called upon to fill what are usually regarded as humbler occupations—will do well to take it into serious consideration" that the judge's decision "may be characterized as slaveholder's doctrine and slavedriver's law," which answered any disobedience with violence. Crawford would have the hotels of Washington subject to this law "whether the attendants of those hotels are black or white, bond or free." Henry McCloskey, editor of the *Brooklyn Eagle*, doubted that Herbert would be punished, making "our whole system of criminal jurisprudence a delusion and a mockery" as "no man identified with a political party" need fear the law.[13]

Not one to let political opportunity pass, Greeley quoted from the *Richmond Enquirer* to remind readers of the autocratic vision that southern leaders applied to all men, white or black. "Conservative men everywhere," wrote one of the South's leading Democratic editors, "are about to adopt the principle that men should be governed, not let alone, and that each should be governed according to his wants and moral and intellectual capacity." Greeley also tied southern philosophies to Kansas. If slavery extension was not opposed, he warned, then the North must accept "not merely murders in Kansas, but shootings at Washington—pistols at the breakfast table." In that same issue, James S. Pike, the *Tribune's* most vitriolic Washington correspondent, charged:

> South of Mason and Dixon's line, society is divided into two classes, the gentlemen and the menials. The slaying of a colored servant, or an Irish servant by one of the upper class, is regarded as an unfortunate affair, but an excusable offense. However culpable the individual, the tragedy at Willard's is rather chargeable to the state of society created by Slavery than to him. The paternity of the crime, as well as the character of the man who committed it, belongs to Slave society. Blame the institution that engenders such offenses rather than the individual. . . . The responsibility rests on a society that teaches the gratification instead of the control of the passions. A society that defends and sustains Slavery will not allow one of the ruling class to suffer for the killing of an underling.[14]

Out on bail, Herbert returned to the House of Representatives on the 16th; there the *Tribune* noted he was "countenanced by gentlemen of the South . . . but the tone of Northern sentiment is of a directly opposite character. Nothing discloses more clearly the radical difference of character between North and South than the view which is taken of this transaction by the two sections."[15] The day before, Representative Ebenezer Knowlton of Maine introduced a recommendation that the House Judiciary Committee consider expelling Herbert. In debate on the House floor, southerners opposed the resolution and moved to table it.[16] Maine Republican Israel Washburn, objecting that tabling was the same as suppressing the investigation, challenged the decision and called for a vote. The *Tribune* printed the 79–70 vote that tabled the resolution and gave the names and votes of all members voting, noting that another 83 had either abstained or were absent.

In the same issue, the *Tribune* highlighted the sectional disparity in response to the "slaughter" at Willard's:

> This truth is, that though we are but one nation we are two peoples. We are a people of equality, and a people of inequality. We are a people of Freedom and a people of Slavery. The instincts, the principles, the sentiments, the feelings, and the education of the two sections are totally different from one another. On the one side are moderation, and justice, and equality, and humanity. On the other, a haughty precipitancy, a lofty disdain of the humbler classes, an urgent denial of human equality, and an

equally urgent claim for the immunities of caste. These two peoples are united by a bond of political union, but whenever a collision comes which brings out the peculiar characteristics of the two, they are seen to be as unlike as almost any two civilized nations on the face of the globe.[17]

On May 20, the *Chicago Daily Tribune* printed a full column account of the Herbert shooting titled in bold type, "A Congressman Killing an Irishman." Charles Ray, one of the paper's editors, depicted the suppression of the House attempt to investigate "the murder" as a united effort of pro-Nebraska Democrats and Know-Nothings.[18] All Illinois representatives' votes were tallied and the epithet *doughface* stuck on supporters of Herbert. Denying any interest in swaying Celtic voters, Ray wrote:

> The Republican members believe in equal rights, justice, and humanity to all men. But the sham democracy representing a party made up of Slavery, Cast [sic], and special privileges voted against it. And why? Because the murdered man was only a laborer, a servant, an Irishman. . . . The murderer belongs to the upper crust democracy; he goes for Slavery Extension—for oligarchy. [19]

As the press continued its focus on Kansas, abusive behavior by southern congressmen, and the need to save the Constitution and the Union from the "domination of the desperate and despotic slave power," Charles Sumner began his two-day oration, "The Crime against Kansas," on the Senate floor. Sumner had promised abolitionist Theodore Parker a radical speech on slavery in early May to strike at the Slave Power and undermine antislavery support for Massachusetts Know-Nothings, who intended to replace Sumner with a candidate of their own in the 1857 election. [20] On May 21, *Tribune* correspondent James Shepherd Pike highlighted the boorish behavior of Democratic senators during Sumner's speech and speculated on the desires of an unidentified southern senator who "declared that if he could have his way, he would hang Sumner on the spot." He lamented the fate of Kansas and warned the free states to "prepare for that further debasement which will be at once their due and their doom."[21] These comments primed a fuse that the next day's events would light around the North.

House member Preston Brooks and fellow South Carolina Congressman Lawrence Keitt sought out Sumner in the Senate chamber shortly after noon on May 22. Brooks, waiting until the Senate had adjourned, found Sumner seated at his desk franking copies of his speech. Declaring that Sumner's speech had slandered his cousin, Senator Andrew P. Butler, and the entire state of South Carolina, Brooks struck the older man repeatedly about the head with a one-inch gutta-percha cane that shattered under the force of the blows. [22] Seriously injured, Sumner did not return to his Senate seat for three years. In a letter to his brother, Brooks boasted that supporters were seeking fragments of his cane as "sacred relics."[23]

The next day, in the *New York Daily Tribune*, Greeley explicitly connected incidents of southern violence across the nation, creating a sketch of malevolent southern designs to enslave white men:

> The South has taken the oligarchic ground that Slavery ought to exist, irrespective of color—that there must be a governing class and a class governed—that Democracy is a delusion and a lie. Northern men will be assaulted, wounded or killed . . . as long as the North will bear it. The acts of violence during this session—including one murder—are simply overtures to the drama of which the persecutions, murders, robberies and war upon the Free-State men in Kansas constitute the first act. We are to have Liberty or Slavery.

Repeatedly, the *Tribune* used binary opposition to make its readers' choices appear raw and stark: "We are to have Liberty or Slavery," aristocrats or menials, free speech, soil, and labor opposed to repression, plantation slavery, and curtailed opportunity for social and economic mobility.[24] Using racially charged and gendered language, the newspaper inveighed against the Senate's refusal to support Sumner. Calling on northern manhood, Greeley declared, "If indeed, we go on quietly to submit to such outrages, we deserve to have our noses flattened, our skins blacked, and to be placed at work under task-masters, for we have lost the noblest attribute of freemen; and are virtually slaves." Other newspapers picked up the theme. The *Pittsburgh Gazette* announced that "neither religion nor manhood requires submission to such outrages . . . and if our representatives will not fight, when attacked, let us find those who will." In a half-column article, it reprinted from the *Cleveland Leader* a nine-point mockery of a Democratic Creed—with the final item as "pro-slavery members of Congress may shoot Irish waiters with impunity."[25]

In an extensive commentary shortly after the attack, the *Tribune* explicitly linked Willard's murder and the assault on Sumner to escalating northern resentment of southern arrogance:

> The youth trained to knock down his human chattels for "insolence"— that is for any sort of resistance to his good pleasure—will thereafter knock down and beat other human beings who thwart his wishes—no matter whether they be Irish waiters or New England Senators.[26]

Reviewing the actions of the previous six months, the *Tribune* enumerated the Slave Power's threat to northern liberties and the overall sentiment of approval of such threats in southern newspapers:

In the main, the press of the South applaud the conduct of Mr. Brooks, without condition or limitation. Our approbation at least is entire and unreserved. We consider the act good in conception, better in execution, and the best of all in consequence. These vulgar abolitionists in the Senate are getting above themselves. They have been humored until they have forgot their position. They have grown saucy, and dare to be impudent to gentlemen. THEY MUST BE LASHED INTO SUBMISSION. . . . Southern gentlemen must protect their own honor and feelings. [27]

Keating's death and Sumner's battered head remained linked in the press and the public's mind as vindication of Republicans' clamor over Kansas. Although the "facts" reported from Kansas over the summer tended toward the sensational, their veracity was decreasingly questioned in the aftermath of the violence in Washington.[28] Incidents of southern violence validated for many northerners, regardless of party affiliation, images of violence in Kansas. The *National Anti-Slavery Standard* reprinted the text of a sermon delivered in Philadelphia on May 25 that condemned President Franklin Pierce's complicity in the violence in Kansas and concluded:

But, contradictory as accounts from Kansas may have been, what the real state of things there is, and on which side the truth lies, no man now needs doubt. When acts of ruffianism are committed at the center, and by men standing high in office, by members of Congress, who kill inoffensive waiters and brutally assault Senators, when such things take place in the center, what else is to be expected on the borders but just what we hear? The Slave Power is the same in Missouri that it is in Washington.[29]

Regional papers such as the *New Hampshire Statesman* also highlighted the conspiratorial nature of the events' timing, characterizing the assault on Sumner as "one link in the chain of flagitious outrages upon the North by which we are debased forever; one further evidence that the South intends to 'drive us to the wall and nail us there'; new proof that the South desires to treat us as it does its bondsmen at home."[30]

Delayed repeatedly by Sumner's poor health, Brooks's trial began on July 8, with District Attorney Philip Barton Key representing the government and Judge Crawford again presiding. (Herbert's trial also dragged into July, slowed by difficulties in juror selection, and a second trial resulted in a hopelessly deadlocked jury.) Brooks's testimony, delivered over a month after his caning of Sumner, was widely interpreted as the shared opinion of his fellow southerners on the right to employ violence against personal insults:

In extenuation of my offense permit me to say that no extraordinary power of invention is required to imagine a variety of personal grievances which the good of society and even public morality require to be redressed, and yet no adequate legal remedy may be had . . . wholesome public opinion, embodied in an intelligent and virtuous jury, always had and always will control the law, and popular sentiment will applaud what the book may condemn.[31]

Fortunately for Brooks, Judge Crawford agreed, assessing him a fine of $300 dollars without comment on his actions.[32] The *Chicago Daily Tribune* ridiculed the decision with the comment, "position, party and the perverting spirit of slavery are the influences by which the verdict of 'not guilty' was rendered in this case, in violation of the truth, justice and common sense."[33]

Two weeks later, Herbert was acquitted of all charges, and Greeley seized on the verdict to decry yet another incident among many of the past year that he said "shows what the free white people of this country . . . the free white laboring people . . . [can] expect from the triumph of the Slave Power." He added:

Perhaps they [the Irish] coincide in the opinion of the slaveholders that all industrious employments, and especially domestic service, are degrading, and that all who thus stand on a social level with slaves ought to be content to be treated like slaves. Next to the privilege of flogging his own niggers at home, nothing can be more essential to the comfort . . . of 'gentlemen' of the Brooks and Herbert school than the privilege of shooting Irish waiters at Washington and elsewhere.[34]

The *Pittsburgh Gazette* ran its account of Herbert's release under the bold headline, "The Party of Murder and Violence," describing Washington as a city where senators were beaten insensible and servants shot down by congressmen who were released with the aid of a "democratic judge, aided by a jury selected by a democratic marshal." Comparing the violence in Washington and Kansas, the *Gazette*'s editor speculated, "It is a question for peaceable and Christian men to ask whether a party which thus hugs murder, violence, and oppression to its breast, is fit to rule the country."[35] The next day's issue of the *New York Tribune* tied the acquittal to Kansas and the actions of "Border Ruffians" in Washington and the territories. "All must allow that killing Irish waiters is dog cheap at Washington, since that may be done for nothing. Even this is surpassed in Kansas where murder, robbery, arson . . . and even rape are not only unpunished, but paid for by the Federal government."[36]

On August 8, New York Know-Nothing Congressman Russell Sage contrasted the *Alabama Mail*'s warning to northern white laborers—"We hope that this Herbert affair will teach them prudence"—with his own past. "Born and bred to toil . . . I look upon labor as honorable," said Sage. "I am a Northern laborer!"[37] He listed various incidents of congressional violence and sectional bias since January: the murder of Keating by Herbert, the assault on

Sumner, the solid opposition of the slave state members to sending an investigating committee to Kansas or expelling Brooks or his associate Keitt, and the rejection by the House of Congressman Knowlton's resolution to investigate Herbert by all but two Democrats. "Is Slavery not sectional and aggressive?" he wondered. "Or is the murder of a poor Irish waiter not worth investigating?" Sage denounced slavery in the territories as "not an unimportant question of the day, but [one that] concerns the stability of the Union, the preservation of the Constitution—that instrument of universal Freedom, contemplated as such by its framers, and interpreted as such by all men, South and North, until a few years past." Echoing the earlier public defection of long-time Democrat Hannibal Hamlin of Maine, Sage switched to the Republicans and asked that his colleagues do the same.[38]

While references to both Washington attacks and Kansas continued throughout August and September, the *Chicago Daily Tribune* recapitulated nine separate confrontations and violent episodes involving congressmen during the current session: two separate attacks on newspaper editors, one attack and four aborted challenges, a fistfight on a public omnibus, and the assaults by Preston Brooks and Philemon Herbert.[39] The *Tribune* identified Brooks and Herbert as two of Buchanan's top supporters, along with David Atchison, "leader of the Southern Border Ruffians" supporting the proslavery government in Kansas.[40]

The *New York Daily Tribune* office rushed to distribute a speech given on October 8 in rural New York by one "John Jay, esq." prior to the presidential vote in November. The rhetoric deliberately recalled the revolutionary heritage of militant northern farmers who were needed to resist "a sectional and aristocratic oligarchy . . . [that] aspires to rule American people." To ensure "the mighty future of this continent, possibly to the end of time," free men must oppose destruction of freedom in the territories and reject those "scenes recently enacted in the Capital."[41] Demonstrating again the influence the Party's press network and a keen instinct for the inflammatory, Jay quoted an offensive paragraph from a small paper in Alabama, the *Muscogee Herald*, identical in length and content to the text printed in a Young Men's Frémont and Dayton Union pamphlet circulated in New York City, *The New "Democratic" Doctrine: Slavery Not to be Confined to the Negro Race*; the September 18 edition of the *Chicago Daily Tribune*; and a Republican pamphlet printed in Providence, Rhode Island, for use by party speakers:

> Free society, we sicken at the name. What is it, but a conglomeration of greasy mechanics, filthy operatives, small-fisted framers, and moonstruck theorists? All the Northern, and especially the New-England States, are devoid of society fitted for well-bred gentlemen. The prevailing

class one meets with is that of mechanics struggling to be genteel, and small farmers who do their own drudgery, and yet who are hardly fit for association with a Southern gentlemen's body servant.[42]

He contrasted the Republican support of freedom and free labor with James Buchanan, "the candidate not only of Pierce and Douglas, but of Herbert who shot the Irishman, of Brooks who assaulted Sumner, of Keitt, who proposes, if Fremont is elected to march to Washington and rob the Treasury." Jay castigated the Democrats for their broken oaths, truckling to the Slave Power and their "tolerance, if not encouragement, of fraud, outrage, robbery, and murder."[43] In a final rhetorical flourish he harangued the crowd:

Shall our constitutional liberties be preserved? Shall the mission of the country be accomplished? Shall peace and freedom shower their blessings over our Western territories? Or shall club-law rule at Washington? Shall honorable murderers stalk unpunished in the capital? Shall military despotism trample the life-blood from our territories, and an arrogant oligarchy of slave masters rule as with the plantation whip, twenty millions of American citizens?[44]

Throughout the fall, Herbert and Brooks still commanded a symbolic stature along with Kansas as exemplars of Southern violence, Democratic corruption, and the threat to white Northern freedom. Conspiracy metaphors infused political pamphlets. William G. Brownlow, Tennessee parson, editor, and Know-Nothing supporter, condemned the Democrats for five episodes of violence involving congressmen—including the Keating shooting and the attack on Sumner—which he said disgraced the capital and signaled the need to reject the Democracy.[45] In a direct appeal to northern Democrats, Samuel Ingham, Andrew Jackson's first treasury secretary, implored fellow Democrats in the North to support Frémont and asked whether their children would be the "free sons of noble sires who fought the battles of liberty for their country and conquered, or will you doom them to be the harassed, dragooned, impressed victims of slavery domination, if they have the manliness to speak or act for freedom?"[46]

The murder of Keating, the caning of Sumner, and the vividly contrasting sectional accounts reinforced the specter of the Slave-Power threat to northern liberties and validated Republican party and media claims regarding the depredations of southern-backed "border ruffians" terrorizing antislavery settlers in Kansas. The success of Republican editors and publicists in mobilizing northern voters exceeded their expectations.[47] The separate but serial events planted distrust of the moral fitness of southern leaders to control federal power and stimulated undecided voters to shift their allegiance to the Republicans. At the same time, the Democratic Party lost credibility with northern voters as each attempt to prosecute these cases seemed to expose the corruption of the executive branch, legislature, and courts. Violence in the political system triggered outrage in most Americans. The 1850s were marked by fears of slavery's expansion, corruption, reactions against immigrants, and worries about the future of the Republic. Although narrowly defeated in 1856, the Republicans and their allies in the media wove together an enduring tapestry of antisouthern narratives that endured until 1865.[48] Once this interpretive frame was in place, additional events like the Dred Scott decision, further violence in Kansas, and the southern response to John Brown were simply added to the hostile perception many northerners now held of the South. Republican success in creating the sense that northerners must protect their own sectional interests by rejecting candidates deemed overly sympathetic to the South set the stage for the sectional electoral sweep that elevated Abraham Lincoln to the White House in 1860. Celebrating the election of a Republican governor in Illinois and Frémont's narrow defeat, one of the evening's final toasts at a state party dinner promised "there is a good time coming boys!"[49]

NOTES

1. Nativism attracted disaffected voters with its hostility to Catholics and immigrants and its stress on the Union and an end to party corruption. Know-Nothings perceived Catholics and foreigners as a greater danger to the republic than slave owners. By late 1854, their estimated membership surged to between 800,000 and 1,500,000 nationwide while the Whig, Republican, and Democratic Parties struggled to retain adherents. Michael Holt, *The Political Crisis of the 1850s* (New York: John Wiley and Sons, 1978), 150.

2. Works representative of the historiography of the rise of the Republican Party and the political realignment of the 1850s in the last thirty years include: Eric Foner, *Free Soil, Free Labor, Free Men: The Ideology of the Republican Party before the Civil War* (New York: Oxford University Press, 1970); William E. Gienapp, *Origins of the Republican Party, 1852–1856* (New York: Oxford University Press, 1987); Michael Holt, *The Political Crisis of the 1850s* (New York: John Wiley and Sons, 1978); Michael A. Morrison, *Slavery and the American West* (Chapel Hill: University of North Carolina Press, 1997); Richard H. Sewell, *Ballots for Freedom: Antislavery Politics in the United States, 1837–1860* (New York: Oxford University Press, 1976); Joel Silbey, "The Surge in Republican Power: Partisan Antipathy, American Social Conflict, and the Coming of the Civil War," in *Essays on American Antebellum Politics, 1840–1860*, ed. Stephen E. Maizlish and John J. Kushkia, 199–229 (College Station: Texas A&M University Press, 1982).

3. William E. Gienapp, "The Crime against Sumner: The Caning of Charles Sumner and the Rise of the Republican Party," *Civil War History* 25, no. 3 (1979); Gienapp, *Origins*, 299–302; Holt, *Political Crisis*, 194–196.

4. *New York Daily Tribune*, 9 May 1856.

5. *Philadelphia Ledger*, 9 May 1856.

6. *New York Daily Tribune*, 10 May 1856.

7. For additional detailed description of the critical relationship among religion, reform, and personal morality as it contributed to sectional stereotypes see: Richard J. Carwardine, *Evangelicals and Politics in Antebellum America* (New Haven, Ct.: Yale University Press, 1993); Daniel Walker Howe, "The Evangelical Movement and Political Culture during the Second Party System," *Journal of American History* 77, no. 4 (March 1991): 1231–1239; and Bertram Wyatt-Brown, *Yankee Saints and Southern Sinners* (Baton Rouge: Louisiana State University Press, 1985).

8. *New York Daily Tribune*, 10 May 1856.

9. *New York Daily Tribune*, 13 May 1856.

10. *New York Daily Tribune*, 12 May 1856. *Daily National Intelligencer*, 12 May 1856; *Philadelphia Ledger*, 12 May 1856. The *Chicago Daily Tribune* first printed the story four days after the shooting as a confused report of multiple woundings and killings.

11. *New York Daily Tribune*, 13 May 1856. Although he was a Pennsylvania Democrat, Crawford's past decisions consistently supported the rights of slaveholders regarding recovery of fugitive slaves in the District of Columbia. He was a close friend of South Carolina Senator Andrew P. Butler, chairman of the judiciary committee, who exercised oversight of the D.C. judiciary and was appointed to the bench by President Polk. James A. Garaty and Mark E. Carnes, eds., *American National Biography*, vol. 4 (New York: Oxford University Press, 1999), 87–89. Crawford had served in Congress with Butler, and there are hints that while Crawford was investigating Creek land claims in Alabama in the 1830s he was involved with Butler family members in Alabama.

12. *New York Daily Tribune*, 14 May 1856.

13. *New York Daily Tribune*, 14 May 1856. *Brooklyn Eagle*, 14 May 1856.

14. *New York Daily Tribune*, 14 May 1856.

15. *New York Daily Tribune*, 16 May 1856.

16. Thomas Clingman (NC), Howell Cobb (GA), and Alexander Stephens (GA).

17. *New York Daily Tribune*, 17 May 1856. The *Chicago Daily Tribune* commented that same day on the need for vigilance in response to the state Democratic platforms of Georgia and South Carolina, calling on free white men to unite to save the Constitution and the Union from the "desperate and despotic slave power." *Chicago Daily Tribune*, 17 May 1856.

18. Ray himself was tied to the Know-Nothings, but his hostility to slavery's expansion into the territories was stronger than his nativism. His comments were a harbinger of the split later that summer that shattered the Know-Nothing Party when its members divided over the relative importance of slavery versus nativism.

19. *Chicago Daily Tribune*, 20 May 1856.

20. Michael Pierson, "'All Southern Society is Assailed by the Foulest Charges': Charles Sumner's 'The Crime Against Kansas' and the Escalation of Republican Anti-Slavery Rhetoric," *New England Quarterly* 68, no. 4 (1995), 541–543.

21. *New York Daily Tribune*, 21 May 1856.

22. *New York Daily Tribune*, 22 May 1856.

23. Gienapp, "Crime against Sumner," 220.

24. *New York Daily Tribune*, 23 May 1856.

25. *Pittsburgh Gazette*, 24 May 1856. Quote beginning "If indeed, we go on quietly . . . " reprinted in *Pittsburgh Gazette* on May 24 from the May 23 *New York Daily Tribune*.

26. *New York Daily Tribune*, 24 May 1856. The private citizen referred to is Greeley himself, who was beaten by Rep. Albert Rust of Arkansas for comments made during the vote for speaker of the house in January. There was minimal interest in or public response to the attack when it occurred.

27. *Richmond Enquirer*, quoted from the Michigan Republican State Committee, *Important Facts drawn from Authentic Sources, Proving beyond a Doubt the Approaching Presidential Election Is to Decide the Question between Freedom and Slavery* ([Detroit]: H. Barns, 1856), 19–20. The same quotation was reprinted in *The Republican Scrap Book*, a party pamphlet containing the platforms of all parties, key quotations from candidates, speeches, and historical references justifying Republican resistance to the Democrats and emphasizing the southern threat to the republic. *The Republican Scrap Book* (Boston: John P. Jewett & Co, 1856), 75. The *Richmond Enquirer* commented with approval that University of Virginia students endorsed Brooks's actions and bought him a cane "with a heavy gold head . . . which will bear upon it a device of the human head, badly cracked and broken." Quoted from Charles Sumner, *Charles Sumner: His Complete Works*, vols. 5 and 6 (New York: Lee and Shepherd, 1900; repr., New York: Negro Universities Press, 1961), 277.

28. The most widely disseminated reports came from correspondents such as James Redpath, under contract to both the *Chicago Daily Tribune* and the *New York Daily Tribune*, who fed copy to both a regional and national market. To keep Kansas and Sumner in the public mind, beginning in early June the *Pittsburgh Gazette* ran daily ads offering free copies of Sumner's speech, "The Crime against Kansas," paired with the address of the Kansas Aid Society for those stimulated to contribute.

29. *National Anti-Slavery Standard*, 31 May 1856.

30. *New Hampshire Statesman*, 31 May 1856, quoted in Randall R. Butler II, "New England Journalism and the Question of Slavery, the South, and Abolitionism, 1820–1861" (PhD diss., Brigham Young University, 1980), 113.

31. *Daily National Intelligencer*, 9 July 1856.

32. *Daily National Intelligencer*, 9 July 1856.

33. *Chicago Daily Tribune*, 15 July 1856.

34. *New York Daily Tribune*, 29 July 1856. During closing arguments, Senator Butler, chairman of the Judiciary Committee with oversight over Crawford and Key, entered the courtroom and sat at the defense table with Herbert. *Daily National Intelligencer*, 24 July 1856.

35. *Pittsburgh Gazette*, 29 July 1856.

36. *New York Daily Tribune*, 30 July 1856.

37. Russell Sage, *Speech of Hon. Russell Sage, of New York, On the Professions and Acts of the President of the United States; the Repeal of the Missouri Compromise; the Outrages in Kansas; and the Sectional Influence and Aggressions of the Slave Power* (Washington, D.C.: Buell & Blanchard, Printers, 1856), 11. Although Sage

invoked a shared heritage "of hard labor" in his appeal to New York farmers, his wealth rested on investments in the state's railroads.

38. Sage, 12–14. The complete fourteen-page speech was also published in *The Republican Scrapbook* (Boston: John P. Jewett, 1856). Angered by Sage's comments, a drunken Preston Brooks sought Sage at Willard's Hotel on August 23, but the two were kept apart, and Brooks later "regretted" giving offense. *Chicago Daily Tribune*, 25 August 1856.

39. *Chicago Daily Tribune*, 22 August 1856. A similar summation linking violence in Washington and Kansas was contained in a 480-page party textbook published in August that is suffused with republican imagery and historical references that trace the party's history back to Washington. Benjamin Hall, *The Republican Party and Its Candidates* (New York: Miller, Orton & Mulligan, Publishers, 1856), 443–444.

40. *Chicago Daily Tribune*, 12 September 1856.

41. John Jay, *America Free—Or America Slave. An Address on the State of the Country. Delivered by John Jay, esq., at Bedford, Westchester County, New York, October 8th, 1856* (New York: Office of the *New York Tribune*, 1856), 2.

42. Jay, 11. Young Men's Frémont and Dayton Union, New York, *The New 'Democratic' Doctrine: Slavery Not to be Confined to the Negro Race, but Made the Universal Condition of the Laboring Classes of Society* (New York: J.W. Oliver, 1856), 2. *Facts and Figures for Fremont and Freedom* (Providence: Office of the *Daily Tribune*, 1856), 20. The only variation was an additional final sentence in the *Chicago Daily Tribune* that stated, "This is your free society which the Northern hordes are endeavoring to extend into Kansas." *Chicago Daily Tribune*, 18 September 1856.

43. Jay, 13. This pairing of Herbert and Brooks appeared frequently in party materials—five times in three of the four pages of the pamphlet in *The Murder of Thomas Keating, by Herbert: To the Voters and Working Men of the First Congressional District* (N.p.: n.p., 1856), 1–3; Michigan State Committee, *Important Facts*, 27; Charles Billinghurst, *A Review of the President's Message. Speech of Hon. Charles Billinghurst, of Wisconsin in the House of Representatives, August 9, 1856* (Washington, D.C.: Buell & Blanchard, 1856), 8.

44. Jay, 19.

45. William G. Brownlow, *American Contrasted with Foreignism, Romanism, and Bogus Democracy, in the Light of Reason, History, and Scripture* (Nashville: n.p., 1856), 170.

    See also Josiah Quincy's fury at the pattern of southern violence and perfidy against the North represented by the Fugitive Slave law, the Kansas-Nebraska Act, events in Kansas, and the attack on Sumner. *Republican Scrapbook*, 76.

46. Samuel D. Ingham, *Another Old-Line Democrat for Fremont: Letter from Hon. S.D. Ingham; Former Secretary of the Treasury under General Jackson* (Trenton, NJ: n.p., 22 September 1856), 8. For an example of rhetoric linking Kansas to eastern outrages in a conspiracy see: *The Election and the Candidates: Governor Reeder in Favor of Frémont* (N.p.: n.p., 1856), 7, in which Reeder is quoted: "This plot progressed step by step and always successfully, how each and every outrage

perpetuated upon our people tends directly and inevitably to its accomplish-ment . . . the man who regards them as isolated occurrences, due to surrounding circumstances, labors under a delusion." See also *The Murder of Thomas Keating*, 1–3. For ethnic composition of the First District see: Kenneth C. Martis, *Histori-cal Atlas of Political Parties in the United States Congress, 1789–1989* (New York: Mcmillan, 1989).

47. After a poor showing in Connecticut in the spring of 1856, when Republicans re-ceived only 11 percent of votes cast, the correspondence of state party leaders and various editors revealed a leadership lacking confidence in its chance to carry the North and convinced its best hope was to lay a foundation for the campaign of 1860. Gienapp, "Caning of Sumner," 219.

48. John C. Frémont polled 1.3 million votes to James Buchanan's 1.8 million with-out appearing on the ballot in a single southern state. These impressive tallies for a new party were collected and made available for voters in the 1860 campaign. Horace Greeley, *Political Textbook for 1860: Comprising a Brief View of Presi-dential Nominations and Elections, Including all the National Platforms ever yet Adopted* (repr., New York: Negro Universities Press, 1969), 239.

49. *Knox (Illinois) Republican*, 17 December 1856.

TALES IN BLACK AND WHITE

The Two Faces of 19th-Century Abolitionist James Redpath

— BERNELL E. TRIPP —

By 1856, abolitionist John Brown and members of his family were well known—indeed, notorious—in both the North and the South. His violent brand of protest had finally found an outlet through murderous confrontations with slavery supporters. Having gone back to Kansas to stage his own personal war against slavery, Brown helped generate a reign of terror throughout the state that would earn it the unwanted nickname of "Bloody Kansas."

One night in 1856, a young reporter working as a correspondent for several eastern newspapers wandered through the forests of the Kansas countryside searching for the self-proclaimed savior of southern slaves. Originally from Scotland, James Redpath was a former *New York Tribune* reporter who had made three previous trips to the South and West to see slavery with his own eyes and converse with the bondsmen about their condition. He had heard much of "Old Captain Brown," and his sympathies were firmly on Brown's side.

Stumbling upon Brown's son Frederick, who immediately recognized the stranger as a supporter he had seen in Lawrence, Redpath was soon ushered into the confines of the secret camp. After only an hour in the camp, Redpath was convinced that Brown and his men were "earnestness incarnate." He later wrote:

I left this sacred spot with a far higher respect for the Great Struggle than ever I had felt before and with a renewed and increased faith in noble and disinterested champions of the right; of whose existence—since I had seen so much of paltry jealousy, selfishness, and unprincipled ambition among the Free State politicians—I was beginning to doubt, and to regard as a pleasant illusion of my youth. I went away, thoughtful, and hopeful for the cause; for I had seen for the first time, the spirit of the Ironsides armed and encamped. And I said, also, and thought, that I had seen the predestined leader of the second and the holier American Revolution.[1]

The meeting with Brown served to reaffirm Redpath's convictions that slavery was a moral and legal wrong and that blacks deserved to be free. Newspapers were filled with the rhetoric of abolitionists of both races, as well as the counter-arguments of slavery supporters, but no one had bothered to talk to the slaves themselves. The history of the black and abolitionist presses of the nineteenth century was intricately intertwined with the history of black enfranchisement in a white-dominated society. Redpath established his goal as one of aiding the slaves, no matter what. He declared:

If I found that slavery had so far degraded them, that they were comparatively contented with their debased condition, I resolved, before I started, to spend my time in the South, in disseminating discontentment. But if, on the other hand, I found them ripe for a rebellion, my resolution was to prepare the way for it, as far as my ability and opportunities permitted.[2]

Redpath would become one of the first journalists to practice participatory journalism. His plan was to make several forays into slaveholding states to talk to the slaves and to provide an eyewitness perspective on their condition. However, the correspondence he would send to the abolitionist and mainstream newspapers would be representative of white, as well as black, perspectives. To *Liberator* and *National Anti-Slavery Standard* readers he would be John Ball Jr., a young, free-born black man from Iowa. To readers of the *Boston Daily Traveller*, the *New York Tribune*, and numerous other mainstream newspapers, he would be Jacobius, James Redpath, or one of several other pen names.

Born in 1833 in Scotland, Redpath immigrated to the United States in 1849. Before long, he landed a job as a reporter with Horace Greeley's *New York Tribune*. One assignment, to compile a regular column, "Facts of Slavery," based on information clipped from southern newspapers in 1854, soon piqued his interest. His resulting curiosity about the nature of slavery encouraged him to look for answers firsthand. In the book that chronicled his travels, he explained, "My object in travelling was, in part, to recruit my health, but chiefly to see slavery with my own eyes, and personally to learn what the bondmen said and thought of their own condition."[3]

On his first trip, beginning in March 1854, Redpath traveled by foot, railroad, and boat to Virginia, North Carolina, South Carolina, and Georgia. After returning to New York in the summer, he began his second tour in September 1854, visiting slaves in Virginia, North Carolina, South Carolina, Georgia, Alabama, and Louisiana. By mid-1855, Redpath departed for Missouri and Kansas, later returning to the East to traverse Virginia again in 1857. To the slaves he interviewed during his travels, Redpath immediately identified himself as "a northern abolitionist, travelling in the South for the purpose of ascertaining the real sentiments of the African population on the subject of involuntary bondage."[4] To Garrison's black readers, however, he was a young black Iowan who felt it his duty to reveal what he had seen and heard of slavery in the South.[5]

Masquerading as John Ball Jr., Redpath strolled down the streets of Richmond, Virginia, noting the shuttered windows and closed doors of stores still closed in the early-morning silence. This was his first extended trip outside of Iowa, a trip taken for his health, and he was eager to explore his new surroundings. As a light rain began to fall, he sought shelter in the doorway of a house. Invited in, he waited out the rain by reading a newspaper and gazing toward the cemetery at the end of the street, the next stop on his walking tour of the city. At first touched by the sentiment expressed with the elegant marble tombstones and the custom of remembering loved ones, he was soon saddened by another tradition that reminded him of the current state of American society. No headstones bore the names of deceased people of color. When he inquired where the slaves were buried in the cemetery, he was told, "Why, in the nigger bury-ing ground. You don't suppose we allow slaves to be buried here?" Redpath later observed in his journal and in a letter to the *Liberator*, "Slaves, and even freemen of color, are not buried in the white man's cemetery. I wonder if heaven and hell will be partitioned off, as our own planet is, to suit the prejudices of our Southern brethren!"[6]

Thus was John Ball Jr. ushered into the columns of Garrison's *Liberator* and introduced to its black and abolitionist readers. The correspondence was the first of many that Garrison's readers would encounter from the young correspondent, but they would never know that the "black" man who wrote diligently to his relatives and friends back home in Iowa about the atrocities he saw on his travels was really a white abolitionist. The letters that appeared in the *Liberator* and later in the *Anti-Slavery Standard* were filled with anecdotes and transcripts of interviews with blacks, as well as with Redpath's interactions with southern whites. He wrote:

The Wandering Gentile has at length reached his southern home, and thereby ended his journeying—for the present year! Since I copied the last extracts that I sent you from my diary, I have travelled several hundred of miles, and have spoken with several hundreds of bondsmen on the subject of slavery. . . . I have partaken of their bread and slept in their cabins; have trusted them and been trusted by them. I have spoken, also with the slavers, as well as with the slaves.

Brothers! Rejoice—*and work*! Wherever I have gone, I have found the bondsmen discontented, and the slaveholders secretly dismayed at our recent victories in the Northern States. Little did any of them think, as they confessed to each other in my presence, that "'the fanatics' would force them to abolish slavery before many years are over—little did they think that they were basking in the company of an Abolition Spy! of one who solemnly swore, when a child, to devote his life to avenging the oppressed; and who glories in betraying tyrants.[7]

Redpath's writings documented not only instances of cruelty and mistreatment, but also the daily discrimination blacks endured. In the following missive, he explained a Richmond custom:

He [an older black man] told me that it was an offence in Richmond, punishable with imprisonment and stripes on the bare back, for a coloured person, whether bond or free, male or female, to take the inside of the sidewalk in passing a white man. Negroes are required to "give the wall," and, if necessary, to get off the sidewalk into the street. Rowdies take great pleasure, whenever they see a well-dressed coloured person with his wife approaching, to walk as near the edge of the pavement as possible, in order to compel them to go into the street—or to incur the extreme penalty of the law. Gentlemen, of course, never enforce this brutal law. But, alas! the majority of the male sex, in Richmond as elsewhere, are neither men nor gentlemen.[8]

The alleged identity of Redpath's black counterpart was revealed again and again throughout his correspondence from the South, often reiterating his dangerous undertaking. He implored Garrison and his readers:

You know that I am a radical Abolitionist. Born a member of a disfranchised class, I have always opposed oppression, in every form in which I have encountered it. . . .

Had I acted as C.K.W. seems to advise, what would have been the result? Probably, I would have been shot or hanged, or tarred and feathered, or ridden on a rail; certainly, I would speedily have been compelled to leave the slave States, and been 'passed round' by the pro-slavery press.[9]

Redpath made clear several times in his letters to abolitionist editors why he chose the persona of John Ball Jr.—to protect his life. Abolitionist words were extremely unwelcome in the South. Laws forbade the circulation of antislavery literature in the South, and an avowed abolitionist ran the risk of death should he be caught interviewing slaves to record their opinions of slavery. Because he would also be providing reports to white-owned newspapers in the North as well as to abolitionist papers, Redpath took great pains to ensure his secrecy. He possessed the constant fear that someone would note the similarities of writing styles between those of James Redpath and John Ball Jr. To avoid suspicion, a letter containing fictitious biographical information was dispatched to Garrison at the start of the series.[10] When writing for the *National Anti-Slavery Standard*, he devised an elaborate plan that not only required multiple-stop mailing routes but also demanded that the *Standard* stop exchanges with newspapers in cities where he would be residing. Also, the editors were never to mention his true identity to anyone.[11]

His fear of being discovered was probably warranted. Serving as the correspondent for the *Tribune*, as well as several smaller papers in different states, Redpath took great pains to describe everything he saw and experienced. Often, those descriptions paralleled those produced by John Ball Jr. In describing the procedures for a slave auction in Virginia he remarked:

> Dickinson, Hill & Company, body-sellers and body-buyers, 'subject only to the Constitution,' carry on their nefarious business in Wall street—I believe its name is—within pistol shot of the capital of Virginia and its executive mansion. Near their auction-room, on the opposite side of the street, is the office of another person engaged in the same in human traffic, who has painted, in bold Roman letters, on a sign-board over the door:
>
> > E.A.G. Clopton,
> > AGENT
> > For Hiring Out Negroes,
> > AND
> > Renting Out Houses.
>
> Both negroes and houses, by the laws of Virginia, are "held, adjudged and reputed" to be property! This is Southern Democracy![12]

To express his outrage, Redpath/Ball concluded with a poem by an author unknown to him, who condemned:

> Curses on you, foul Virginia,
> Stony-hearted whore!
> May the plagues that swept o'er Egypt—
> Seven—and seventy more,
> Desolate your home and hearths.[13]

As a white man, Redpath easily gained access to situations and events that his alter ego could never have entered. His eyewitness accounts were

enlightening and enlivening. While traveling through Missouri and getting
the impulse to visit the site of a former abolitionist newspaper whose editor
had been run out of town, Redpath made his way to Parkville, where he happened upon the tarring and feathering of a 25-year-old white male who had
tried to leave the town with a young girl and a couple who were slaves. He
detailed:

> A ruffian named Bird, and the wretch who [had earlier] proposed to burn
> the prisoner—*birds of a feather*—then cut two paddles, about a yard long
> (broad at one end), and proceeded slowly, amid the laughter and jests of
> the crowd, which [the abolitionist] Atkinson seemed neither to see nor
> care for, to lay the tar on, at least half an inch deep, from the crown of his
> head to his waist; over his arms, hands, cheeks, brow, hair, armpits, ears,
> back, breast, and neck. As he was besmearing Mr. Atkinson's cheeks,
> one of the operators bedaubing his lips, jocularly observed, that he was
> 'touching up his whiskers,' a scintillation of genius which produced, as
> such humorous sparks are wont to do, an explosive shout of laughter in
> the crowd. All this while the only outward sign of mental agitation that
> the prisoner exhibited, was an increased and extraordinary activity in
> chewing and expectorating.[14]

Atkinson was then seated on two crossed poles and paraded through
the streets, accompanied by the jeers of his tormentors and the cheers of by-
standers. Redpath later learned that the man was "put over the river" that
night and the slaves were whipped and punished.[15]

As Jacobius, Redpath frequently added examples of his distaste for many
areas of the South and his disgust with some of the practices of its inhabitants—both blacks and whites. He remarked on a trip through Alexandria,
Virginia:

> The first characteristic that attracts the attention of a Boston traveller in
> entering a southern town, next to the number, and the dull, expressionless
> appearance of the faces of the negroes—is the loitering attitudes, and the
> take-your-time-Miss-Lucy style of walking of the white population. The
> number of professional loafers, or apparent loafers, is extraordinary.[16]

The greatest intensity of his wrath was reserved for the southern politicians who dared to criticize Greeley and the *Tribune* during a "Commercial
Convention" in Charleston, South Carolina. Said Redpath:

> Everybody, North and South, has heard of the great Commercial Con-
> ventions, which regularly assemble, now here, now there, but always in
> the Slave States, to discuss the interests, and "resolve" on the prosper-
> ity—immediate, unparalleled, and unconditional—of slaveholding trade,
> territory, education, Legree-lash-literature, and "direct commerces" with
> Europe. These assemblies are generally regarded, in the Slave States, as

the safety-valves of the Southern Juggernaut-institution, without which, for want of ventilation, that political organization could speedily explode, and scatter death and destruction to the ends of the earth.[17]

After the end of the last trip into the South, Redpath wrote in the book of his travels:

The reader must have noticed that I took particular pains to ascertain the secret sentiments of the Southern slaves. He must have seen, also, that I never stepped aside to collate or investigate any cases of unusual cruelty, or to portray the neglect of masters in the different States, to provide their bondmen with the comforts of a home or the decencies of life. That I had material enough, my summary will show.

I did not go South to collect the materials for a distant war of words against it. Far more earnest was my aim. . . . Whatever falls, let slavery perish. Whoever suffers, let slavery end. If the Union is to be the price of a crime, let us repent of the iniquity and destroy the bond.[18]

Although Redpath's motives to keep his identity a secret during his travels are understandable, his adoption of the persona of John Ball Jr. raises the question of why someone would risk his well-being for as little as $2.50 per letter, his pay for writing for the *Standard*. Although Redpath's abolitionist interests ignited long before meeting Brown, his connection with Brown might provide an explanation for his willingness to venture into "enemy" territory not just once, but three times.

Upon Brown's death, Redpath was asked to complete a book on his life. In the preface, Redpath declared his unwavering support for Brown and his cause: "When the news of the arrest of John Brown reached Boston, I could neither rest nor sleep; for I loved and reverenced the noble old man, and had perfect confidence in his plan of emancipation."[19] He later dedicated another book, *The Roving Editor, Or Talks with Slaves in the Southern States*, to Brown, noting:

To you, old Hero, I dedicate this record of my Talks with the Slaves in the Southern States. . . . You are willing to receive the negro as a brother, however inferior in intellectual endowments; as having rights which to take away, or withhold, is a crime that should be punished without mercy—surely—promptly—by the law, if we can do it; over it, if more speedily by such action; peacefully if we can, but forcibly and by bloodshed if we must! So am I.[20]

Even as Ball, Redpath made his rebellious, antislavery position clear—that the slaves should be freed by whatever means necessary. His words were strongly reminiscent of his friend and mentor, John Brown. He prophesied:

All fanatics are prophets to the extent of their vision—for fanaticism is the ardent worship of a truth; and by its light we can—nay, must—see the sequences of acts performed in accordance or in violation of it. And I am a fanatic.

Slavery will be speedily abolished. That I see. I think, by violence; nay, I know by bloodshed, if the present spirit long pervades the South. Unless it repents it shall utterly perish.[21]

The 19th century was a time of change for all Americans, and many felt it their duty to play an active part in that transformation. Ultimately, this would mean the sacrifice of money, property, philosophy, and lives. For Redpath, it would also require his identity for a short time. Redpath's belief in Brown's cause and his need to view the problem with his own eyes forced him to risk his life on a daily basis. By masquerading as a black man, he believed he could step into the world of the slave and find out firsthand what bondage was really like. As a white man, he thought that he would be able to more readily observe daily discrimination and its far-reaching effects on both the North and the South. Ironically, he learned that both views were one and the same.

Notes

1.   James Redpath, *The Public Life of Capt. John Brown, with an Auto-Biography of His Childhood and Youth* (Boston: Thayer and Eldridge, 1860), 114.
2.   Ibid., 248.
3.   Ibid., 20.
4.   *Liberator*, 11 August 1854.
5.   *Liberator*, 4 August 1854.
6.   Ibid.
7.   *National Anti-Slavery Standard*, 2 December 1854.
8.   *National Anti-Slavery Standard*, 21 October 1854.
9.   *Liberator*, 8 December 1854.
10. *Liberator*, 4 August 1854.
11. Redpath to Gay, letters of 6 and 17 November 1854 and 23 January 1855, Gay Papers; Redpath to Garrison, July 26, 1854, Garrison Papers. All reprinted in James Redpath, *The Roving Editor, Or Talks with Slaves in the Southern States*, ed. John R. McKivigan (University Park, PA: Pennsylvania State University Press, 1996), xvi–xvii.
12. *Boston Atlas and Bee*, 30 October 1859. Reprinted in McKivigan, 220.
13. Ibid.
14. *St. Louis Daily Missouri Democrat*, 24 October 1855.
15. Ibid.
16. *Boston Daily Evening Traveller*, 23 May 1857.
17. *New York Tribune*, 19 April 1854.
18. James Redpath, *The Roving Editor, Or Talks with Slaves in the Southern States* (New York: A.B. Burdick, 1859), 248–249.
19. Redpath, *Capt. John Brown*, 7.
20. Redpath, *Roving Editor*, 4.
21. Redpath, *Roving Editor*, 249.

"THE HAY STACK EXCITEMENT"

Moral Panic and Hysterical Press after John Brown's Raid at Harpers Ferry

— BRIAN GABRIAL —

"The excitement in Virginia is at a boiling point," the *New York Herald* reported the day before John Brown's hanging on December 2, 1859. Without a doubt, Brown's raid at Harpers Ferry a month and half earlier had ignited a flashpoint of sectional animosity between northern and southern states and revealed, as historian David M. Potter observed, "a division between North and South so much deeper than generally suspected."[1] According to Potter, John Brown's execution "aroused immense emotional sympathy" in the North while causing "a deep sense of alienation" in the southern states, which thought Brown a "fiend" who wanted "to plunge the South into a blood bath" of slave insurrection.[2]

From mid-October through December, events at Harpers Ferry and nearby Charlestown, where Brown's trial and execution took place, dominated daily news coverage, as did reports of rumored rescues of "Old Brown." If radical abolitionists could commit such an outrageous act once, southerners reasoned, they certainly would do it again. Newspaper accounts reflected those fears. The writer of a special dispatch to the *Baltimore Sun*, for example, warned he "would not be surprised . . . there will be an attempt made by the Abolitionists of the North to release Brown and his associates from the Charlestown Jail."[3]

Brown's invasion of a southern state combined with nearly constant rescue rumors to create a "moral panic" that sociologists Erich Goode and Nachman Ben-Yehuda have defined as a fear that "evil doings are afoot" and that "certain enemies of society are trying to harm some or all of the rest of us."[4] To southern slave owners, Brown and the abolitionists defined that category of "certain enemies of society." As rumors of possible abolitionist invasions spread southward, the Georgia legislature considered a resolution pledging support for Virginia and urging the "utmost vigilance in guarding against a recurrence of a similar conspiracy, in our own borders, or elsewhere at the South."[5] Tensions mounted to such a degree that a November 20 *New York Herald* editorial cautioned, "Ridiculous rumors are spread from mouth to mouth, and eagerly swallowed and believed in, of there being another abolitionists incursion on foot." It observed, "The consequence is that the citizens are arming and enrolling themselves in volunteer companies, and are, in fact, preparing for civil war."

The hysteria that gripped Charlestown, Harpers Ferry, and indeed, all of Virginia and the South in the weeks preceding Brown's execution was reflected in a "hysterical style of the press" that media scholar Roger Fowler describes as "constantly alarming and hyperbolic" and focused on an indistinctly defined "evil" whose power is blown out of proportion.[6] According to Fowler, "Hysteria is not simply behavior which is in excess of the events which provoke it, it is also behavior which attains autonomy, which sustains itself as expressive performance, independent of its causes."[7] Sociologist Robert Bartholomew calls such imagined threats "collective delusions" that involve the "rapid spread of false, but plausible, beliefs that gain credibility within a particular social and cultural context."[8]

Often, social elites, including governmental, political, religious, educational, or economic groups, as well as the mass media, may demand repressive actions that are seen as perfectly normal responses, according to Levin, to "defend the American way of life against serious danger."[9] Just as elites can and do commit repressive acts, the masses can and do act in passive agreement to preserve order.[10] One result may be ad hoc vigilante groups, heightened conspiracy fears, even repressive legislation. After Harpers Ferry, for example, Charleston, South Carolina, witnessed renewed calls for a local "Fire Guard" to be on guard.[11] The November 8 issue of the *Charleston Courier* published the letter from a "Citizen" who reasoned that if Harpers Ferry had had such a guard, "the ringing of the fire bell would have summoned a sufficient number of armed citizens to have at once put a [sic] end to 'Old Brown's' murderous plans."

To northern and southern conservative political leaders and newspaper editors, Brown's abortive raid represented a worst-case scenario—a "social

catastrophe"—because it involved a white man "invading" a slave state to arm
and free slaves. Slavery, to them, represented an aspect of "Americanism," and
they considered abolitionism a moral evil, un-American, and a threat to their
way of life. Brown and his supporters, along with their deeds and words created, in historian Stephen Oates's words, a "'Great Fear' in the South."[12] Thus,
southern and sympathetic northern conservative elites found sympathetic
voices to the abolitionist cause, including antislavery Republican politicians,
newspaper editors, even moderate Democrats, contemptible.

By 1859, slavery's advocates viewed abolitionists as true threats. In November 1859, a "SLAVE OWNER" wrote the *Charleston Mercury* urging fellow South Carolinians to "cultivate a spirit of embittered hatred, and active
and implacable hostility" toward abolitionists, whom he called a "mischievous
rabble of conspirators."[13] To slave owners, John Brown represented abolition's
most dangerous and radicalized faction. In the North, abolitionists and Republicans had gained increasing support arguing that a "slave power" conspiracy threatened to turn the entire United States into slave-holding country.[14]
Although they believed Brown's methods wrong, they considered many of his
ideas right. As for "Old Osawatomie" Brown, he had already earned infamy
leading antislavery raids into "Bloody Kansas" and Missouri in the mid-1850s.
By the time of the Harpers Ferry raid, he had lost one son in the Kansas fighting and stood accused of killing six proslavery men.

Despite Brown's reputation, several powerful and wealthy northern abolitionists continued to fund his activities, which enabled him to carry out his
Harpers Ferry raid. During the summer of 1859, he and his 21 men, including five blacks, lived on a nearby Maryland farm. They began their move on
Sunday, October 16. For more than 24 hours, the small band controlled the
town and the federal arsenal. But as news reached surrounding communities, organized militia joined other armed men at Harpers Ferry who teamed
with federal troops to force Brown's surrender. A seriously wounded Brown
was removed to nearby Charlestown, where prosecutors quickly tried him for
treason. The state of Virginia hanged Old Brown on December 2.[15]

During this period, as Brown biographers Oswald Garrison Villard
and Stephen B. Oates have noted, Charlestown was in a state of perpetual
excitement—by December, 4,000 troops guarded the town and protected
the prisoners.[16] According to Villard, "The whole countryside behaved as if
in a state of siege."[17] In late October, a *Tribune* editorial criticized the Virginia courts for refusing to "allow any one to see or converse with Brown,
fearing that he would say that which might, by being published, inflame the
slaves against their masters."[18] The *New York Times* warned of "The Panic at
the South," which "thanks to the encouragement of rumor, is rapidly rising

to a most intemperate temperature."[19] Three days before Brown's execution, the *Richmond Enquirer* reported on precautions taken at Charlestown "should any rescuers make their appearance from getting unobserved to Charlestown in the confusion of a large crowd." Although no rescue attempts were made, newspaper reports reflected a state of alarm that, according to Oates, was partially exacerbated by Virginia Governor Henry Wise's nearly constant mobilization of troops in the area.[20]

A "hysterical style of the press" was evident in newspaper headlines after Brown's raid and trial. Northern and southern newspaper headlines contained words like *rumors, excitements, frights*, or *panics* as they drew reader attention to stories discussing possible "new" invasions.[21] As Brown's execution date neared, southern newspapers and the *New York Herald* contained headlines that indicated new and "Alarming Intelligence" or the "Rumored Rescue of John Brown."[22] The newspapers warned of "Troubles on the Border"[23] or "Another Rumor of Rescue"[24] or "Another Alarm!"[25] November 20 *New York Herald* headlines told of "Excitement and Alarm in Virginia" or of the "Dread of Another Abolitionist Insurrection."[26] Other northern newspaper headlines referred to "The Virginians in Distress,"[27] "The Virginia Fright,"[28] or "The Great Virginia Panic."[29] The *Charlotte (North Carolina) Bulletin* reported rumors that Governor Wise's sons at Yale "would be executed" if Virginia executed Brown. The *Bulletin* item urged extremely reactionary behavior: "[If] violence be done to a Southern man, as a retaliatory measure, for the execution of Brown, [then] every suspicious Northern man, not a resident, caught in the South, [should] be immediately executed—put to death."[30]

In contrast, most northern newspaper reports and editorials tended to criticize Virginia for its excessive concern and repressive measures. A *New York Times* editorial expressed this about Virginia's panics: "These insane exhibitions of terror will only encourage more fanatics at the North."[31] The *Boston Evening Transcript* reprinted the *Baltimore Exchange*'s comments after one of Brown's dramatic courtroom speeches:

> Brown's speech created the greatest excitement. The citizens look upon it
> as a trick. The guard has been increased. *Three men selling patent medi-*
> *cines had been ordered out of town.* The people are arming everywhere,
> and are ready for any emergency."[32]

The Boston newspaper also contained this observation from the *Providence Journal*: "The good people of Charlestown are right. There is more danger in three quack doctors than in the whole army of abolition."[33] A *Times* editorial headlined "The South and the Insurrection" observed this about Southern repression and fears:

We reproach and denounce them [Southerners] for their hostility to free discussion [of slavery], for excluding anti-slavery publications, for their suspicion of tourists and travelers from the Northern States, and for the violent and lawless vengeance with which they resent any attempt to interfere with their slaves at home. They live in the midst of the most fearful perils which can haunt the social life of any community. They are in the power of the slaves who surround them.[34]

Any sudden event, no matter how slight, could set off a panic. Even "a sentinel firing his gun" could, as the *Herald* reported, "cause a very great panic among women and children, and some men, whose nervous systems have become much disordered by late events."[35] The *Tribune* noted, "It was ascertained that the sentinel had mistaken a cow for a man—that he challenged her—she wouldn't halt and he fired." The November 18 *Evening Post* reported "The Anti-Pedler [sic] Panic in Virginia": "The troops have been called out against an imaginary expedition to rescue the famous captain of Harper's Ferry."[36] A *Richmond Whig* item, headlined "A Fulmination from Virginia" in the *Times*, declared, "The truth is we have no longer any use for the vagabond tourists or itinerant peddlars [sic], of unknown character, who have heretofore found free counsel among us."[37] The *Times*'s editor labeled it an "amiable exhortation."

The newspapers reported unsubstantiated rumors of an abolitionist rescue of Brown or reprisals. The November 18 *Richmond Enquirer* reported "Alarming Intelligence" that Wise had received "anonymous communications" about the abolitionists' "intended raids" along the Virginia and Kentucky borders that included kidnapping "prominent citizens." Wise had also been informed that a "guerilla war" had begun and property had been destroyed.[38] The November 20 *Herald* reported from its Richmond correspondent that "anonymous communications received by the Executive in the last two days" have warned of the intended border raids in Virginia and Kentucky that would result in the kidnapping of "prominent citizens or members of their families" to keep "as hostages for the pardon of the culprits."[39]

Wire reports in the *Herald*, headlined "Excitement and Alarm in Virginia" and "Dread of Another Abolitionist Insurrection," said that Andrew Hunter, Brown's prosecutor, "professes to be convinced that an attempt will be made to rescue the prisoners."[40] The *Richmond Enquirer* printed letters from "reliable persons, with names attached" warning of rescue plots. A Pennsylvania writer, for example, claimed a "lawless band of fanatical abolitionists and Black Republicans" called "The Noble Sons of liberty" had 500 supporters and planned to enter Charlestown and "demand the release of that old villain John Brown." Another letter postmarked Ohio contained a warning that, in "a desperate effort . . . to save the notorious Brown from being executed," there would be a "sudden and tremendous rush on the guard."[41] Reports in the *Enquirer* and *New Orleans Daily Picayune* said that Ohio Governor Salmon P. Chase had sent a dispatch to Governor Wise that a hundred to a thousand men were heading to Charlestown.[42] The November 21 *Tribune* reported these rumors, but its Charlestown correspondent remarked, "[T]hese stories produced a terror the more intense and pervading from its intangibility."[43]

Northern and southern newspapers reported that the people of Charlestown viewed all strangers with great suspicion. A week after Brown's conviction, the *Tribune*'s Charlestown correspondent said that "martial law holds sway," adding:

> The examination of strangers is never relaxed. The surveillance is uninterrupted from the time they arrive until they leave. If they stay too long, it is popularly decided that they mean no good, and if they stay but a very short time, every one is satisfied that they mean very ill.[44]

When mysterious "incendiary fires" occurred, Charlestown's mayor issued a proclamation that "there should not be longer permitted to remain in our town or county, any stranger who cannot give a satisfactory account of himself."[45] Another proclamation rationalized the action: "This measure of precaution is taken to prevent serious consequences to life, should any rescuers make their appearance from getting unobserved to Charlestown in the confusion of a large crowd."[46]

The words of "A True Virginian" appeared in the *Richmond Enquirer* and called on "Southerners [to] rid yourselves of everything antagonistic to your peculiar institutions." The letter urged:

> Drive it out! Purge the land of the kankering [sic] pest. Look around you. Abolitionism partakes of your hospitality and sits at your fireside! Get rid of it! Drive it out! Peddlars, preachers, merchants, travelers, school-teachers! Off with them, every one, old and young, male and female.[47]

The *Enquirer* reported, "Should any suspicious-looking characters be found lurking around us, require them to give a satisfactory account of themselves, or compel to make their *exit* in *double-quick time*."[48] The December 1 *New York Herald* reported that three Cincinnati merchants had been arrested on a Baltimore and Ohio train for expressing sympathetic remarks about John Brown. The *Tribune* reported that Northern reporters were told to leave and go to Baltimore, and "Passengers now riding on the railroads are required to procure passports from Governor Wise."[49] On Brown's execution day, the *Boston Evening Transcript* reported that "several persons, editors of the abolition newspapers . . . were ejected from the cars for Harper's Ferry."

Anyone perceived as abolition sympathizers, including members of the northern press, came under strict scrutiny. The October 25 *New York Herald* reported that those reporters "who are attached to abolition and black republican newspapers . . . have been getting scared lest the people of the Ferry . . . molest and ill use them." And in some cases their fears were justified. A "traveling daguerreotype operator" seeking a likeness of John Brown for his employer, a Boston sculptor, was chased out of Charlestown.[50] A *Boston Evening Transcript* item headlined "The Terrors of a Camera" reported that the sculptor "has been told that he is 'marked man.'"[51] According to published accounts, "This was rather too much. Two strange men with a camera inside of a jail was a prospect not to be calmly contemplated."[52] The people of Charlestown chased out of town an artist for *Frank Leslie's Illustrated Newspaper* for being a suspected "correspondent for the *New York Tribune*."[53] The November 15 *New York Times* quoted Mr. W.S.L. Jewett, the frightened illustrator, about his escape:

> We were never left alone for so much as five minutes at a time; and we should have been happy to enjoy this pleasing state of society much longer, but for a sudden conviction that hanging by a mob might injure the graceful proportion of our necks; that riding on a rail might jolt our systems seriously out of order, and that a coat of tar and feathers would be infinitely unbecoming to our complexions.[54]

George Hoyt, a lawyer for Brown, also fled and remarked what he "feared most was an attack on the jail."[55] According to the *Tribune*'s Charlestown correspondent, Jewett's and Hoyt's "last moments were, alas, not tranquil." The correspondent added, "The painful event was witnessed by the entire population of Charlestown."[56] The *Richmond Enquirer* also reported Jewett's unfair treatment but included a line noting the *Tribune* had "recently published some letters from Charlestown of an irritating character."[57] One incident receiving news coverage was the mysterious mid-November burning of a wheat stack near Charlestown, which caused the "wildest terrors . . . among the people."[58] The event prompted Northern editorial reaction ridiculing Virginians. A November 19 *New York Evening Post* editorial headlined "The Hay Stack Excitement in Virginia" said that "The Virginians are evidently going daft; old John Brown has addled them. . . . Their terror exaggerates the slightest occurrences. If that poor old prisoner only coughs in his solitary cell, they think it is a pistol shot and fly to arms." A *Tribune* editorial scoffed at the panic over the "burning wheat stack," joking, "He [John Brown] seems to have infected the good people of Virginia with a delusion as great as his own. It seems to be impossible for them to get over the terror which his bold seizure of Harper's Ferry inspired."[59]

A *Times* editorial remarked, the "whole State seems to be in a condition of a frightened frenzy," and continued, "The wildest rumors from the North—the appearance of a stranger—the burning of a hay stack; inspire the liveliest and most fearful apprehensions."[60] The *Boston Evening Transcript* editor compared Virginia to Don Quixote because "Old Virginia seem[s] anxious to wage [contests] with shadows."[61] A letter from "A Colored Gentlemen in Self-Defence" observed that Virginians' "heroic imaginations now convert every harmless pillow into an infernal machine," every abolitionist into John Brown, and "every colored man" into "the dusky ghost of Gen. Nat. Turner, the hero of Southampton."[62] Even the *Herald*'s editor regretted "to see evidences of such a panic on the part of the people of Virginia" and the "accidental burning of a corn stack is magnified into visions of armed hosts carrying fire and sword into the Old Dominion." Said the *Herald*:

> Let the people of Virginia, strong in their own consciousness of strength, pay no heed to the imaginary fears of a few thoroughly scared militia men, but rely on their own ability to repel all lawless invasions, and at the same time feel double security in the power of the federal government and in the patriotism and good sense of the people of the North.[63]

The newspaper blamed numerous fires and rumors for causing panics,[64] and an editorial, "The Panic in Virginia," observed that the "people of Virginia appear to be easy victims of practical jokers in their midsts" and expressed regret "that their excitement and alarm should have carried them so far as to subject them to ridicule."[65] The *Tribune* also blamed persistent rescue rumors as the cause of the "tremendous excitement."[66]

Evidence that southern elites used moral panics to maintain or broaden control is suggested. One *Enquirer* editorial on November 25 defended troop buildup in Charlestown as a way to keep an eye on strangers and to keep "an outraged people from seeking vengeance upon the authors of their wrongs."[67] A November 29 *Charleston Mercury* editorial said that Governor Wise "possesses information warranting the assembling of this extraordinary force," and the *Charleston Courier* warned of possible "multitudes" from free states at Brown's execution, noting that soldiers would be present to make sure "they can do no harm."[68] Similarly, a *Picayune* editorial argued that, while Virginia authorities "are beset with news-mongers and alarmists," Wise must ensure "ample preparations" to prevent a "gang of desperadoes, who might fearlessly and successfully sweep in, when unexpected, and hurry their recovered saint away from his bondage."[69] The item "Safety of the South" appeared in the December 5 *Mercury* and called for increased protection from "Northern Abolition emissaries."

Some northern newspaper editorials indicated that Southern elites perpetuated fears of slave uprisings, abolitionist invasions, and other panics for political leverage. The *New York Evening Post* editor, for example, called the panics "A Cry for Help" and claimed, "By exciting the fears and inflaming the passions of the South, and through the South operating upon the timidity of the North, they hope to continue their ascendancy, yet for a while."[70] A November 21 *Boston Evening Transcript* item said that Wise made more out of the various alarms and panics because he had presidential aspirations: "One cause for the groundless alarms proceeds from the efforts of Virginia politicians to make themselves conspicuous."[71] A November 21 *Times* editorial expressed concern that "The excitement in Virginia, thanks to the encouragement of rumor[,] is rapidly rising to a most intemperate temperature." An editorial two days later expressed this concern: "There is no actual war between the North and South, yet the panic is no less intense."[72]

A *Charleston Mercury* editorial held abolitionists responsible for increased tensions but concluded:

> This is a sad state of things. In our indignation at the aggressions of the North, we are in danger of dealing with men as if they were guilty, without proof. . . . The very worst effect of Northern Abolitionism must be that it divides us amongst ourselves.[73]

Two southern newspapers even suggested misuse of the telegraph as causing moral panics. Both the *Enquirer* and the *Mercury* accused northern telegraph operators of wiring misleading reports about Virginia panics. A November 25 *Richmond Enquirer* item warned that "reliable Virginians in New York city [sic]" believed that most telegraph operators, agents and reporters were "of Black Republican and abolition tendencies, [who] contribute to give a false coloring to everything" happening in Virginia. The *Mercury* reported that "those in possession of the telegraph were in league to ridicule the South and make us a laughing stock to ourselves and before the world."[74] The Charleston editor noted that "every intelligent man in the South has been completely disgusted at the broad and pathetic farce that has been played off before the public about the hanging of that hoary villain, 'Old Brown.'"

In general, both northern and southern newspapers examined for this study reported frequent instances of imagined "frights" or panics at Charlestown and nearby Harpers Ferry. Despite the suspicions that abolitionist invasion tended to be magnified for political purposes, examples of the "hysterical style of the press" found in southern newspapers created a moral panic indicating beliefs that abolitionists and their supporters planned to rescue Brown and destroy the southern way of life. In general, southern newspaper editorial reaction supported military action to ensure public safety. As for northern editorial response, it tended to focus on southern overreaction to the "evil" and to criticize southerners for their irrational fears. The research indicates that northern editorials also thought some southern political elites might be causing a moral panic to maintain power.

NOTES

1. David M. Potter, *The Impending Crisis, 1848–1861* (New York: Harper and Row, 1976), 384.
2. Potter, 378–383. See also James A. Rawley, *Secession: The Disruption of the American Republic, 1844–1861* (Malabar, FL: R.E. Kreiger Publishing Co., 1990), 103.
3. *New York Tribune*, 29 October 1859.
4. Erich Goode and Nachman Ben-Yehuda, *Moral Panics: The Social Construction of Deviance* (Oxford: Blackwell, 1994), 11.
5. *Charleston Courier*, 9 November 1859.
6. Roger Fowler, "Hysterical Style in the Press," in *Media Texts: Authors and Readers*, ed. David Graddol and Oliver Boyd-Barret, 90–99 (Philadelphia: Open U Multilingual Matters, 1994), 91. Fowler observes, "We are bound to be concerned about it, but its outlines are indistinct, like some huge threatening shape on the horizon in a bad horror movie."
7. Ibid., 91.
8. Robert Bartholomew, "Collective Delusions: A Skeptic's Guide," *Skeptical Inquirer* 29, no. 3 (May–June, 1997). http://findarticles.com/p/articles/mi_m2843/is_n3_v21/ai_19524417. Accessed June 17, 2008.
9. Murray B. Levin, *Political Hysteria in America: The Democratic Capacity for Repression* (New York: Basic Books, 1971), 220.
10. Ibid., 146.
11. *Charleston Mercury*, 10 November 1859.
12. Stephen B. Oates, *To Purge this Land with Blood: A Biography of John Brown* (New York: Harper and Row, 1970), 322–323.
13. *Charleston Mercury*, 23 November 1859.
14. Leonard L. Richards, *The Slave Power: The Free North and Southern Domination, 1780–1860* (Baton Rouge: Louisiana State University Press, 2000), 1–4.
15. Any number of John Brown histories provide sufficient context. This research relied on several John Brown biographies. See Richard J. Hinton, *John Brown and His Men* (New York: Funk and Wagnalls Company, 1894); Stephen B. Oates, *To Purge this Land with Blood* (Amherst: The University of Massachusetts, 1984); Oswald Garrison Villard, *John Brown, 1800–1859: A Biography Fifty Years After* (New York: Alfred A. Knopf, 1943). See also *The John Brown Invasion, an Authentic History of the Harper's Ferry Tragedy* (Boston: James Campbell, 1860); *Report of the Select Committee of the Senate Appointed to Inquire in to the Late Invasion and Seizure of the Public Property at Harper's Ferry* (Washington, D.C.: U.S. Government Printing Office, 1860).
16. Oates, 322. See also, Villard, 524.

17. Villard, 525.
18. *New York Tribune*, 26 October 1859.
19. *New York Times*, 21 November 1859.
20. Oates, 322.
21. For example, a *New York Tribune* headline, "Reported Attempt to Rescue the Harper's Ferry Insurrectionists," appeared on October 27. The headline "News, Rumors, and Gossip from Harper's Ferry" appeared in the *Richmond Enquirer* on November 4. The article reported that many slaveholders feared John Brown's men had "tampered" with their slaves.
22. *Richmond Enquirer*, 18 November 1859.
23. *Richmond Enquirer*, 22 November 1859.
24. *Charleston Courier*, 22 November 1859.
25. *Charleston Courier*, 23 November 1859.
26. Another *New York Herald* headline that day warned, "Virginia Arming for Civil War." Other *Herald* headlines referred to the "Panic in Virginia" on November 22 or "The Panic in Charlestown" on November 27.
27. *New York Tribune*, 18 November 1859. The *Tribune* headline "Another Fright at Charlestown" also appeared that day.
28. *Boston Evening Transcript*, 18 and 19 November 1859.
29. *New York Evening Post*, 20 November 1859.
30. *Charleston Courier*, 3 December 1859.
31. *New York Times*, 22 October 1859.
32. *Boston Evening Transcript*, 1 November 1859.
33. *Boston Evening Transcript*, 1 November 1859.
34. *New York Times*, 22 November 1859. The state of things had deteriorated so that on November 28, a *Times* headline read, "New Yorkers Warned away from South Carolina." The *New York Evening Post* on November 16 reported the arrest of a man in Memphis caught holding a letter addressed to John Brown.
35. *New York Herald*, 24 November 1859; *New York Times*, 25 November 1859. See also *New York Tribune*, 24 November 1859; *Richmond Enquirer*, 25 November 1859. The newspapers also reported that men "under the influence of whiskey" caused another alarm.
36. The *New York Times* of November 28 reported on "Another Pernicious Peddler" and noted that "the Virginians have caught another of those pestilent peddlers, who fret the lives out of the chivalry."
37. *New York Times*, 17 November 1859. Another *Times* article on October 21 said, "Every stranger that comes here [Charlestown] is looked upon with suspicion." A *New York Tribune* article made a similar statement on November 5: "All strangers are regarded with particular suspicion."
38. A separate article that day headlined "Rumored Rescue of John Brown" indicated that "No one in Richmond believes any such rumor." Similar reports from the *Richmond Whig* appeared in the *Charleston Courier* on November 21 and 23, 1859.
39. *New York Herald*, 20 November 1859.
40. *New York Herald*, 20 November 1859. The *Herald* called the rumors "doubtless all humbug" and blamed the people of Alexandria as "trying to get up another

excitement." The newspaper also reported from a Baltimore dispatch dated November 19 about "Rumors in circulation that armed men are crossing or have crossed the river from Ohio, at or near Wheeling."

41. A Tennessee letter from a "Northern man" with "no sympathy with these scoundrels, who would murder innocent women and children," said the writer received a letter from a friend "in the North" telling of a rescue plot. *Richmond Enquirer,* 22 November and 2 December 1859. The *Charleston Courier* also reported on rumors to rescue Brown on November 19, 22, and 23, 1859.

42. *Richmond Enquirer,* 22 November 1859, and *New Orleans Daily Picayune,* 22 November 1859. Wise said that, if this were true, "he would enter proceedings against [Chase] on the charge of treason."

43. Later the *Tribune* noted that Governor Wise had sent spies into Pennsylvania and Ohio to learn of large bodies of men "arming and moving toward Virginia." See *New York Tribune,* 29 November 1859. Similar reports about the "most plausible plan yet devised for the release of 'old Brown'" appeared in the November 21, 1859, *New York Times,* which credits the *Richmond Examiner* as its source.

44. *New York Tribune,* 9 November 1859.

45. *Richmond Enquirer,* 18 November 1859.

46. *Richmond Enquirer,* 29 November 1859.

47. *Richmond Enquirer,* 22 November 1859.

48. *Richmond Enquirer,* 25 November 1859. The newspaper also noted the arrest of "a very suspicious looking fellow" in Monroe County who was "evidently a Yankee from his peculiar accent" and seemed capable of "anything desperate or disreputable."

49. *New York Tribune,* 30 November 1859.

50. *New York Tribune,* 7 November 1859; *New York Times,* 11 November 1859.

51. *Boston Evening Transcript,* 10 November 1859.

52. *New York Tribune,* 7 November 1859; *New York Times,* 11 November 1859.

53. *Boston Evening Transcript,* 14 November 1859; *New York Tribune,* 14 November 1859; *New York Evening Post,* 14 November 1859.

54. The *Boston Evening Transcript* contained the same article on November 16, 1859.

55. *New York Tribune,* 17 November 1859. In the letter, George Hoyt added, "Deeming it no valor but sheer foolhardiness to brave the populace, Mr. Jewett and I packed our bags and quitted the municipality of Charlestown."

56. *New York Tribune,* 16 November 1859.

57. Under the headline "Excitement at Charlestown, VA," the *Richmond Enquirer* informed readers of Jewett's and Hoyt's expulsions on November 18.

58. *Daily National Intelligencer,* 19 November 1859, and *New York Times,* 19 November 1859. On November 21 the *Charleston Courier* published a single sentence regarding this panic, "There was not the slightest cause for the ridiculous panic. The fire seen was simply a stack of wheat burning."

59. *New York Tribune,* 19 November 1859. The newspaper also alluded to New York City's sad chapter more than a hundred years earlier that resulted in the deaths of innocent slaves: "The present panic which prevails in Virginia calls to mind the bloody delusion with which this City of New-York was visited a hundred years

and more ago, and at the bottom of which, then as now, lay the terror of negro insurrections."

Two days later, on November 21, the *Tribune*'s Charlestown correspondent noted such stories produced new slave insurrection fears: "Taken in connection with the recent wheat-stack and stable conflagrations—which, beyond a doubt, were caused by the negroes, who, however, ignorant of the fact their owners may be, have a pretty effective and secret Free Masonry among them—" Historian John Stauffer has suggested that slaves in and around Charlestown and Harper's Ferry "responded to Brown's capture by burning and destroying property." See John Stauffer, *The Black Hearts of Men: Radical Abolitionists and the Transformation of Race* (Cambridge: Harvard University Press, 2002), 257.

60. *New York Times*, 21 November 1859. A *Times* editorial of November 24 assailed Virginians for irrational behavior and for giving themselves up to "vaguest panic terrors."
61. *Boston Evening Transcript*, 21 November 1859.
62. *New York Times*, 22 November 1859. The letter from C.H. Langston originally appeared in the *Cleveland Plain Dealer*.
63. *New York Herald*, 20 November 1859.
64. *New York Herald*, 21 and 22 November 1859.
65. *New York Herald*, 22 November 1859.
66. *New York Tribune*, 18 November 1859.
67. On November 25 and 29, 1859, the *Enquirer* reported on troops amassing in Charlestown to keep order at Brown's execution. One article said that "Wise exhibits no sort of fear of a rescue being attempted" and dispelled rumors that "a party of outlaws" may attempt a rescue. It also reported the town as being under martial law. See *Richmond Enquirer*, 25 November 1859.
68. *Charleston Courier*, 28 November 1859.
69. *New Orleans Daily Picayune*, 30 November 1859.
70. *New York Evening Post*, 26 November 1859.
71. Two days later, a *Boston Evening Transcript* editorial asserted, "We regret that Virginia has not the cool head and firm hand of its Governor elect, Letcher, to guide it in this crisis."
72. *New York Times*, 23 November 1859.
73. *Charleston Mercury*, 30 November 1859.
74. *Charleston Mercury*, 29 November 1859.

Part II

Confederates and Copperheads

NORTH CAROLINA NEWSPAPERS AND SECESSION

⎯ T. HARRELL ALLEN ⎯

The months preceding North Carolina's decision to secede from the Union revealed the powerful and competing forces that were working to mold public opinion and ultimately take the state down the road to secession. These influences were often expressed in the state's newspapers. Some papers reflected a strong desire to stay in the Union, others expressed a forceful desire to secede. Both groups accurately reflected the mood of the people of North Carolina at the time. Certainly in the fall of 1860 most North Carolinians were committed to staying in the Union. Eventually this would change, and North Carolina would become one of the last southern states to secede.

In attempting to understand how public opinion shifted from pro-Union to prosecession during this tumultuous time, it is useful to examine two newspapers that in the beginning were strongly pro-Union but that eventually would call for North Carolina to secede. Such an examination also provides an opportunity to apply a late twentieth-century mass media theory, agenda-setting, to nineteenth-century newspapers to gain a greater understanding of the relationship between newspapers and their readers in the antebellum period.[1] Donald Reynolds, in his book *Editors Make War,* argues that southern newspapers played a significant role in fashioning public opinion toward secession.[2] He accords southern journalism "a share of the blame for the most fatal step that the South ever took."[3]

One way to test Reynolds's assumptions is to examine two newspapers that in the fall of 1860 were decidedly pro-Union and to compare their editorial positions with their readers' attitudes and voting behaviors on the crucial issues that would come before them over the next six months. The newspapers selected, the *Greensboro Patriot* and the *Wilmington Daily Herald*, were chosen because of the significant shift in their stance on secession between the fall of 1860 and the late winter and early spring of 1861. One extremely prosecession newspaper, the *Wilmington Journal*, was also examined as a contextual measure for comparing its prosecession views to the pro-Union views expressed in the *Patriot* and the *Daily Herald*.

As the presidential election neared in the fall of 1860, the *Patriot*, published in Greensboro by M.S. Sherwood and James A. Long, endorsed John Bell of Tennessee for president and Edward Everett of Massachusetts for vice president. The *Patriot* made it clear that by voting for Bell and Everett, voters would "proclaim to the world that they are determined to stand by the country and the Constitution." The *Daily Herald,* edited by A.M. Waddell, likewise urged people to stay in the Union and endorsed Bell and Everett, asking: "Are you in favor of disunion and all its train of horrors? If so vote for Breckinridge and Lane. If you are not vote for Bell and Everett." John C. Breckinridge, the candidate of southern Democrats, eventually carried North Carolina by only 848 votes. Breckinridge received over 60 percent of the vote in New Hanover County, where slavery was prevalent and where the *Daily Herald* was published. In Guilford County, where the *Patriot* was published and an area of strong pro-Union sentiment, Bell, the Constitutional Union candidate, received over 60 percent of the vote.

Despite the vote for Breckinridge, public opinion indicated that North Carolina was overwhelmingly in favor of maintaining the Union.[4] The election of Republican candidate Abraham Lincoln caused concern but did not cause a public outcry for leaving the Union. The *Patriot* said about the election: "That Lincoln is elected we have no doubt. We regret the result deeply. We know that in North Carolina there are but few, very few, who regard the election of Lincoln, of itself, a sufficient cause of disunion."[5] The paper went on to advise its readers to let Lincoln assume office, adding, "We say to our people not to be carried away, but to wait and be still." The *Daily Herald* admonished those who would secede because of Lincoln's election:

> Peaceable secession is an impossibility. The State that secedes must pass through a baptism of blood. Self defence, which is nature's first law, can alone justify such a course on the part of any state, and the necessity for self defence does not exist. The ostensible reason for secession, and indeed, the only reason given, is the election of Lincoln, and it is admitted that he is powerless to do harm to the South, if he is desired, inasmuch as he has neither judicial nor legislative power to aid him.[6]

Reflecting the apprehensive mood and anxiety of the people, the *Patriot*, warned:

> We, ourselves, feel that imminent danger threatens the Republic. We do not believe in, nor do we concede to any State the right of secession. There is a heavy responsibility resting upon the democracy of North Carolina. The time has come when everybody must take sides, and he that is afraid to utter his sentiments, may be set down as a good subject out of which to make a traitor.[7]

Similar sentiments were expressed by the *Daily Herald* in a column headed, "Are We Getting Scared?" The paper offered the view:

> It makes no difference what a man's views are . . . we wish to see and hear a perfectly free, and independent expression of them in all public meetings. We have been pained to see some of our friends, whose opinions coincide with our own . . . to see them apparently averse to talking about the Union. Can we not manfully claim our right in the Union before we resolve to go out of it?[8]

The impulse for secession took the form of a call for a state convention to discuss the current crisis. Governor John W. Ellis, leaning toward secession, called for a state convention to discuss what action North Carolina should take. The *Patriot* reacted strongly to Ellis's stance for leaving the Union:

> We presume the people of North Carolina will think and act for themselves in this matter; they will not be led by Governor Ellis. If on calm and sober reflection, they should think it best to go out of the Union, they will go, but if they should come to the conclusion to remain, they will do so, and if Gov. Ellis is not satisfied to remain with them, why he can take his departure.[9]

The division of opinion soon engulfed the state legislature, with secessionists on one side and Unionists on the other. The former wanted to take immediate steps to withdraw from the Union, whereas the latter saw no reason to take any action that might lead to withdrawal. In late November, the *Patriot* brought the convention issue to its pages in a story headlined, "Shall We Have a Convention?" The paper acknowledged that the people seemed split on this issue but said, "In this conflict of opinions, we feel at liberty to express our own sentiments, and we say most unhesitatingly, let us have a Convention."[10] The paper said that such a convention would allow the people to "define their position as regards their staying in or going out of the union and also to make a State Constitution. We are not afraid to trust the people."

In Wilmington, home city of the *Daily Herald,* the secession mood was growing, as reflected in a large November 19 public meeting where a resolution was passed that called for a convention of the people for the stated purpose of withdrawing from the union. However, during this uneasy time, the *Daily Herald* was oddly silent on the state convention question and did not express a position on the call for the convention. The paper had repeatedly urged calmness and a wait-and-see stance on those who favored secession: "We ought to suppress, as much as possible, our feelings, and exhaust every resource of calm reflection, before we determine now to take the final step which will separate us forever from our Northern countrymen."[11]

For reasons that are unclear, the *Patriot* shifted from its earlier position of calling for a state convention to one of opposition. On December 13 it ran a long article, "Our Position," in which it said it was opposed to calling a state convention, noting: "We are most decidedly opposed to any convention of the people being called, at this time, to take into consideration the question of severing the ties which have so long held us together as a united, prosperous and happy people."[12] Perhaps the editors, in shifting from their earlier position, thought the result of the convention would be a majority vote for secession, for the article conjectured, "It is said that the Convention is to be called, that North Carolina, acting in her sovereign capacity, may go out of the union, [but] we answer that at least nine-tenths of her people vastly prefer, under present circumstances, to remain in the Union." The paper also worried that such a convention would create a "false and unjustifiable inference South Carolina and the other Cotton States would draw from such an act," and "would have the effect of hastening, or precipitating our Sister states of the South into revolution."[13]

The *Patriot* went on to advocate the increased circulation of the newspaper as a vehicle for spreading information and thus disarming the disunionists:

> The disunionists of North Carolina, though few in number, have succeeded by noise and bluster, to make the impression that they are a strong party. . . . The way to head them then, is to give the people information. Let every man see that his neighbors take the *Patriot,* for so long as our people are properly informed, there is no danger that they will be led away into treasonable purposes. . . . Secession is not only wrong in principle, but it is unwise, impolite, cowardly, wicked and devilish.[14]

During this volatile time, an event of major significance and lasting impact occurred: South Carolina on December 20, 1860, seceded from the Union. In Wilmington, 100 guns were fired in honor of the choice. The *Herald,* following South Carolina's action, asked its readers whether North Carolina should follow its sister state to the south: "People of North Carolina, shall this programme be carried out? Are you submissionists to the dictation of South Carolina? Are you to be called cowards because you do not follow the crazy lead of that crazy state?"[15]

Despite the radicals' attempt to use this event as a means of getting North Carolinians agitated, the majority still supported the Union. The *Daily Herald* in an editorial, "The Fearful Leap Taken," wrote, "we have not yet abandoned all hope, we shall still cling fondly, even if desperately, to the union, we will not give up the ship, the noble ship which has borne us so bravely through all the storms of our history, until the last plank is swept from under our feet."[16]A short time after South Carolina's secession, the *Patriot* wrote in an editorial, "A Leap in the Dark," that the state seemed to have no plan for a new government, "Before South Carolina seceded, her people thought they needed nothing but secession; they may soon feel that they need everything else but secession."[17]

Despite efforts on the part of Unionists to make sure the radical mood in South Carolina did not take root in North Carolina, the majority of the Unionists now took a conditional position; they would prefer to stay in the Union, but if efforts at finding a suitable compromise with the North failed, then they would join South Carolina and other southern states in secession. This stance signaled a shift in their earlier position. The thrust of the efforts to leave or remain in the Union focused on the question of whether to call a state convention to vote on the issue. Both sides began to develop and advance arguments, often expressed vividly and with increased emotion in the pages of the newspapers. The *Patriot,* perhaps beginning to soften a bit on its pro-Union stance, wrote:

> But suppose . . . the best interests of North Carolina were to secede, even
> then we should say, that to secede before the end of two years from this
> date would be unwise, impolite, would show a great want of prudence. . . .
> And why do we say so? In the first place, we are now totally unprepared to
> secede; we have neither arms nor money with which to buy them.[18]

The *Patriot* went on to argue that North Carolina should not join the cotton states because its interests would be sacrificed in favor of "King Cotton."

As the debate grew, the secessionists took actions that were designed to influence public opinion and persuade people to join their side. One such event occurred in Wilmington on January 10, when a group of radicals seized Fort Caswell, situated on the Cape Fear River. The more radical secessionists had asked the governor to allow them to take the fort so that it could not be used to garrison federal troops. Governor Ellis refused, saying he did not believe the federal government intended to put troops there, but a group of citizens from Wilmington and Smithville marched on the fort and took it.

The *Daily Herald*, while condemning the taking of Fort Caswell, appeared to reflect the growing unrest and fading hopes of compromise that would hold off secession, and public opinion began to reflect this attitude.

An early indication of the editors' weakening resolve and a sense of hopelessness appeared in the *Daily Herald* in late December:

> If war results from secession, it will not surprise us, for we have always contended that peaceable secession was an impossibility. We have contended against it to the last, but, if war is to come, *all* Southern men, we trust and believe, will be found shoulder to shoulder in the fight. We have denounced the disunionists, because we thought it to be our duty to do so, but after powder has been burned in this contest, the men of the South are brothers.[19]

For the first time, the pro-Union paper moved from its earlier unconditional stance to a new and radical one. A few days later, the *Daily Herald* again struck a more strident position on staying in the Union:

> We are no nearer being a secessionist now, than at any time heretofore . . . but if, regardless of our protestations and arguments, and those of other conservative men, disunion comes, and with it the necessary consequence *civil war*, the time for argument will have passed and all men of all parties *must* take sides. We hope there has never been any doubt that the Union men of the South will be laggards in defence of their homes and firesides.[20]

Increasingly the people began to earnestly debate whether to call a state convention to settle the issue of secession. Public meetings held in December and January seemed to reflect the majority opinion that such a convention should be called. A majority of the state's newspapers wanted a convention.[21] The *Patriot*, differing somewhat from its earlier view, now took the position that a national convention should be called but that it should be done by the people and not by the legislature. The paper called for the state legislature to pass a bill that would allow the people to vote on calling a national convention.[22] On January 29 a bill passed calling for an election on February 28, at which time the people would vote for or against a state convention.

The mood of the *Daily Herald* was gloomy as the new year began. In an unusually bleak editorial, "Peace or War," it observed:

> We are in a dreadful condition, from which there seems to be no escape except along the bloody path of revolution. All efforts at conciliation and compromise have failed miserably. All hope of the Union seems to be abandoned. The people of the South will be acting on the defensive at any rate, and in that event will have both right and might on their side.

We confess that our heart has been made sick by hope long deferred and finally dashed to the earth.[23]

Again reflecting the anxious and uncertain public mood, the *Patriot* noted:

> We are truly grateful to be able to say that we are satisfied beyond a doubt, that an overwhelming majority of the people of North Carolina have no sympathy with the mad schemes of those who, for their selfish, wicked and ambitious purposes would precipitate us into revolution. It is a fixed fact, that North Carolina is devotedly attached to the Union.[24]

As the convention vote neared, the *Daily Herald* reflected the public mood as it reported on public meetings in Wilmington. It reported a Union meeting in which various pro-Union citizens spoke, "There was a large assemblage of citizens at the Theatre last evening, to witness the proceedings of the Union meeting." However, the paper realistically gauged the public mood and wrote, "We hope the gentlemen who participated in the meeting and who are certainly greatly in the minority here, will yet be heart and hand with those who, seeing no hope for our rights in the union, are making preparations to abandon it."[25] In a terse editorial announcing its support for two secessionist convention delegates, the paper noted: "We vote for them because they are disunionists. We shall support them because we believe that immediate secession is the best thing for North Carolina."[26]

As the people discussed and debated the need for a convention, the *Daily Herald* seemed to move even more toward a secessionist stance, noting:

> The issue now presented to the people of North Carolina to decide, is not whether they will preserve the union . . . but the issue is very different from this. It is whether North Carolina will go with the South or with the North. The conviction that we are two peoples in feeling and interests, and that we ought to separate is growing stronger in the South every day. There is, therefore a simple choice left to North Carolina, between a Northern and a Southern Republic. Can any true North Carolinian hesitate in making the choice? We have no doubt whatever as to the result of their [the delegates] deliberations. Union delegates may be in the majority, but North Carolina will sooner or later certainly unite her destinies with those of her Southern sisters.[27]

The ensuing election resulted in a victory for the Unionists. The convention was voted down by the people, 47,323 to 46,672, and 78 of the 120 delegates chosen were Unionists.[28] The statewide vote reflected the divided public opinion of the people and the delegate vote more accurately reflected the geographic or sectional divisions in the state. Across the state, 52 counties elected Unionist delegates, but only 30 chose secessionist delegates. An event that likely played a major role in the outcome was a peace conference in Washington, D.C. Wire reports from Washington that a compromise had been reached at the conference were published in pro-Union papers and influenced some people to vote against the state convention, believing a compromise would be reached between the North and South. That the reports were false was only learned after the North Carolina vote. The Unionists believed the convention vote signaled a death blow to secession. The *Patriot* concluded, "The result of the late election has not only been the defeat, the overwhelming defeat of the disunionists in this state. It has shown the people of North Carolina to be Union loving people."[29]

The secessionists, on the other hand, still called for secession. The *Daily Herald* admitted that the convention had failed but warned, "We think it is not improbable that such a revulsion of feeling as was never witnessed will take place in less than sixty days and then some people had better get out of the way."[30] Within two weeks following the convention's defeat, the paper called for another convention on the basis of Lincoln's inaugural address, in which he firmly denied the right of a state to secede.[31] In an unusual editorial, the *Daily Herald* felt compelled to defend its change from pro-Union to secessionist:

> Some of our Union friends have complained exceedingly of our inconsistency in advocating secession after having fought so faithfully for the Union. We lost some subscribers by it. We were honest in our efforts to secure our constitutional rights in the Union, and when we saw that could not be done, we were equally honest in our advocacy of immediate secession.[32]

Public opinion was now rapidly moving toward secession. Lincoln's remarks seemed to signal war against South Carolina, and many of the Unionists now seemed ready to give up the struggle. Secessionist editors used their papers to attack Lincoln and persuade conservatives to join them in revolution. Despite the efforts of the Unionists to stem the tide of public opinion now running against their position, they were soon overtaken by events. In early April, Lincoln announced that he was sending provisions to Fort Sumter. Reacting in a belligerent editorial on April 6, the *Daily Herald* advocated, "Let us take Fort Caswell. We will doubtless be called a revolutionist for these remarks. Be it so." Two months earlier, when Fort Caswell had been taken by local militia, the *Daily Herald* had condemned the action and called it illegal. Now it urged the same action and justified it by stating, "Lincoln has showed his hand at length . . . he intends to go into a war with the Confederate States. We think war is inevitable." On April 10 the *Herald* again beat the war drums, asking: "Is there a man in North Carolina that would say he was indifferent to the issue of such a conflict? Abe Lincoln's authority will never be exercised in North Carolina, except at the point of a bayonet."[33]

On April 12 came the extraordinary news that Fort Sumter had been attacked by Confederate troops and surrendered the next evening. The Unionist newspapers were dazed by this news. The *Patriot* wrote in an editorial, "It is with deep regret that we announce to our readers that the war has commenced. We intend to wait as calmly and quietly as possibly until the facts are fully disclosed and before we will presume to advise others."[34] But time for cautious and calm reasoning had come and gone. On April 15 Lincoln issued a proclamation calling for 75,000 troops to combat the rebellion in the South. In addition, Secretary of War Simon Cameron demanded that North Carolina furnish two regiments. Governor Ellis immediately replied, "You can get no troops from North Carolina."[35] Lincoln's call for troops realistically destroyed all Union sentiment in North Carolina. Even the staunchly pro-Union *Patriot* now joined the ranks of the secessionists:

> Our devotion to this union has been strong and sincere. North Carolina is in a revolution; all the Southern states are in a revolution; we are for the South and against the North. Let no dissentions divide us. We all have a common destiny, let us then make a common fight—for in doing so we will discharge our duty to our country.[36]

The Unionists were now in a hopeless situation. Although they loved the Union, they would not support coercion at the point of armed troops on their soil. The normally calm statements of the *Patriot* gave way to shrill rhetoric and passion:

> We regard Lincoln and his advisers and abettors, as tyrants and oppressors, and in their unholy, unrighteous object of subjugation of the South, should be resisted to the bitter end. We regard Lincoln's call upon North Carolina for troops to aid in subduing their brethren as an insult and should cause her sons to rush to arms to drive back any invasion of her soil.[37]

The entire pro-Union press now strongly supported the South. The crisis swept everything in front of it toward secession and civil war. A second state convention was called, and the delegates assembled in Raleigh on May 20. There was little disagreement among the people; about the only discussion was how to get out of the Union—by secession or revolution. Everyone understood that the purpose of the convention was to separate North Carolina from the Union. By an almost two-to-one vote, the convention approved the ordinance of secession. The next day North Carolina became a member of the Confederacy. Although a fierce proponent of the Union, the Old North State now had joined ranks to fight against it.

NOTES

1. S. Kittrell Rushing, "Agenda-Setting in Antebellum East Tennessee," in *The Civil War and the Press*, ed. David B. Sachsman, S. Kittrell Rushing, and Debra Reddin van Tuyll, 147–159 (New Brunswick: Transactions, 2000).
2. Donald E. Reynolds, *Editors Make War: Southern Newspapers in the Secession Crisis* (Nashville: Vanderbilt University Press, 1970).
3. Reynolds, 5.
4. Joseph C. Sitterson, *The Secession Movement in North Carolina* (Chapel Hill: University of North Carolina Press, 1939), 175.
5. *Greensboro Patriot*, 8 November 1860.
6. *Wilmington Daily Herald*, 9 November 1860.
7. *Greensboro Patriot*, 9 November 1860.
8. *Wilmington Daily Herald*, 11 December 1860.
9. *Greensboro Patriot*, 22 November 1860.
10. Ibid.
11. *Wilmington Daily Herald*, 19 November 1860.
12. *Greensboro Patriot*, 13 December 1860.
13. *Greensboro Patriot*, 20 December 1860.
14. Ibid.
15. *Wilmington Daily Herald*, 5 December 1860.
16. *Wilmington Daily Herald*, 21 December 1860.
17. *Greensboro Patriot*, 3 January 1861.
18. *Greensboro Patriot*, 10 January 1861.
19. *Wilmington Daily Herald*, 28 December 1860.
20. *Wilmington Daily Herald*, 21 December 1860.
21. Sitterson, 206.
22. *Greensboro Patriot*, 10 January 1861.
23. *Wilmington Daily Herald*, 1 January 1861.
24. *Greensboro Patriot*, 24 January 1861.
25. *Wilmington Daily Herald*, 2 February 1861.
26. *Wilmington Daily Herald*, 23 February 1861.
27. *Wilmington Daily Herald*, 19 February 1861.
28. Ralph A. Wooster, *The Secession Conventions of the South* (Princeton, N.J.: Princeton University Press, 1962), 193.
29. *Greensboro Patriot*, 23 February 1861.
30. *Wilmington Daily Herald*, 4 March 1861.
31. Dwight Lowell Dumond, *The Secession Movement* (New York: Octagon Books, 1963), 259.
32. *Wilmington Daily Herald*, 19 March 1861.
33. *Wilmington Daily Herald*, 10 April 1861.
34. *Greensboro Patriot*, 13 April 1861.
35. Governor John W. Ellis, Governor's Letter Book, 394.
36. *Greensboro Patriot*, 25 April 1861.
37. Ibid.

KNIGHTS OF THE QUILL

A Brief History of the Confederate Press

— DEBRA REDDIN VAN TUYLL —

At 4:27 a.m. on April 12, 1861, irascible Virginia newspaper editor Edmund Ruffin happily accepted the burden another Virginia journalist had declined. He took the lanyard offered by Confederate General Pierre G.T. Beauregard and fired the first cannon shot at Fort Sumter. Standing beside Ruffin was Roger Pryor, the journalist and former Virginia congressman who had balked at being the man to actually begin the war. Both Ruffin and Pryor were ardent secessionists who had abandoned Virginia for Charleston when their home state declined to secede following Abraham Lincoln's election as president in November 1860. Neither man was at Charleston Battery as a journalist; they had come to join the troops and fight for the fledgling Confederate States of America.

Although Ruffin has been credited with firing the actual first shot of the war and Pryor was one of the three men sent on April 11 to persuade Major Robert H. Anderson to surrender Fort Sumter, they were not the only journalists culpable in starting the war. Their brethren who stayed home to run the South's newspapers also helped foment the Civil War, for they had been lobbing shells in the rhetoric war for months—if not years—prior to the showdown at Fort Sumter. Between their editorial debates over tariffs, the westward expansion of slavery, abolition, and states' rights, the South's 800 or so newspapers had, as a whole, done much to help bring the country to the brink of war.

Following the 1860 presidential election, the most emotional editorial debates were over the question of secession. Some newspapers, the *New Orleans Picayune*, for one, were cautious and tried to warn their readers of the inherent dangers of secession:

> It may be doubted whether, even at the South, the public are aware of the fact that the Union is entirely and hopelessly destroyed and the Government on the eve of dissolution. Many have gone into the secession movement without intending that it should lead to a perpetual and total separation of the North from the South, and perhaps to several distant and separate and sovereign confederacies.[1]

Other newspapers, like the *Troy (Alabama) Southern Advertiser,* were certain that secession of the entire South was the right action. That paper's editors had no doubts and no regrets about South Carolina's precipitous secession or about the responsibility of the other southern states to support her action:

> If war must come, let it come. We hail it as the harbinger of independence and security. The Southern States are bound by honor and patriotism to stand to South Carolina. To remain silent and see her butchered, would be yielding up our right bower to our enemies through craven fear.[2]

Still others rode the fence rails somewhere between the unionist and secessionist positions. These "cooperationist" newspapers were not antisecession, but they did not want to see the Union broken up over the relatively innocuous matter of the election of a Republican president. Cooperationists maintained that the election of Lincoln, in itself, was insufficient justification for breaking up the Union. The cooperationists' position was that Lincoln could do relatively little as president to set the Republican party's antislavery agenda in motion. Without a Republican Congress to pass abolitionist legislation, slavery would be safe. Further, the Supreme Court had demonstrated in its 1857 Dred Scott decision that it was no friend to abolitionists. Cooperationists, including their newspapers, preferred to wait to act until Lincoln took some overt action that was contrary to southern interests.

The South's newspapers led the debates over secession in 1860, but editorial content was to play only a supporting role in Civil War–era newspapers. Once the firing started at Fort Sumter, southerners wanted to read about what was happening with the war. The expansion of their news function was a big change for many southern newspapers, especially those in the smaller towns and villages. Southerners had lived and died by politics and political debates for most of the nineteenth century, and so political commentary had been a particularly important component of that region's press for a long time. With the coming war, though, the interest in political debate diminished. Readers wanted information, and that meant they wanted news. "Everybody wants to hear the news," according to the *Atlanta Southern Confederacy*. The *Southern Confederacy* was right on target in its observation, as demonstrated by a bidding war that broke out in Montgomery with the arrival of the first copy of the *Charleston Mercury* that reported on the shelling of Fort Sumter.[3]

Even before the April 1861 showdown in Charleston Harbor, the southern press had already had to cover nearly a dozen major news stories, including the election of Lincoln, South Carolina's secession the previous December, and the subsequent secession of five more states through the first few weeks of 1861. Then, in early February, reporters from both the South and the North flocked to Montgomery for the convention of the southern states that turned into a constitutional convention for the Confederate States of America and the first meeting of its Provisional Congress. The two big issues facing the newly seceded states, according to the *New Orleans Picayune*'s unnamed correspondent, were forming a government and seeking recognition by foreign powers. Depending on how the United States received the idea of secession, the correspondent wrote, a new government would either have to organize a common defense for the South, or if the North was reasonable and let the states go peacefully, then a new government would have to oversee the separation negotiations. In an overly optimistic letter to his editors, the correspondent predicted virtually automatic international recognition:

> We do not doubt the readiness of all the principal governments in the world to recognize a Southern Confederacy, provisional or otherwise, as soon as formed and set in motion. It is consistent with the uniform practice of modern times, and has grown into the force of public law, that governments *de facto* are acknowledged for all purposes of trade immediately, in spite of all paper proclamations of the intention to reclaim them, thrown out by the authorities they repudiate. To a regular formed Southern Confederacy, with even eight or nine States, England and France will concede at once the fact of independence.[4]

Perhaps the biggest story of the Montgomery convention was the inauguration of Jefferson Davis and Alexander H. Stephens as president and vice president of the Confederacy. The *New Orleans Picayune* correspondent proclaimed the inaugural proceedings to be "the grandest pageant ever witnessed in the South." The chief justice of the Alabama Supreme Court administered the oaths of office to Davis and Stephens while members of the Provisional Congress, military leaders, and high civil authorities watched. "The city was alive, from early morning, with delegations from the various States and people from the adjoining country," the correspondent wrote, "and long before the hour for the inauguration arrived, the Capitol Hill was filled with the beauty and chivalry of the South. A large number of military companies from this State, Mississippi and Georgia were also present, and gave eclat to the occasion."[5]

Scarcely had the Confederacy gotten the workings of its national government set up when the crisis over Fort Sumter erupted. Correspondents in Washington kept the telegraph wires humming with speculation over whether Lincoln would resupply or reinforce the garrison at Fort Sumter and the refusal of U.S. Secretary of State William H. Seward to negotiate with—or even recognize—Confederate peace commissioners. "It is now placed beyond all possible doubt that the attempt will be made by the United States Government to throw a full supply of provisions into Forts Sumter and Pickens," reported the *Charleston Mercury*'s Washington correspondent. "The great military and naval preparations now going on mean COERCION. All disguise is now thrown off." The correspondent, whose letter was dated April 8, correctly predicted, "There will be a collision in less than a week."[6] The *Mercury*, along with other fire-eating newspapers, took the opportunity to goad the South Carolina and Confederate governments about the armed buildup of Confederate troops and to put pressure on them to defend southern honor by ousting Major Anderson and his garrison:

> We have partially submitted to the insolent military domination of a handful of men in our bay for over three months after the declaration of our independence of the United States. The object of that self-humiliation has been to avoid the effusion of blood, while such preparation was made as to render it causeless and useless. It seems we have been unable, by discretion, forbearance and preparation, to effect the desired object; and that now the issue of battle is to be forced upon us. The gage is thrown down, and we accept the challenge. We will meet the invader, and the God of Battles must decide the issue between the hostile hirelings of Abolition hate and Northern tyranny, and the people of South Carolina defending their freedom and their homes. We hope such a blow will be struck in behalf of the South, that Sumter and Charleston harbor will be remembered at the North as long as they exist as a people.[7]

After Sumter, there was no stopping the march toward war. Federals and Confederates alike, even the former Unionist southerners, were ready for a fight. So many men volunteered for military service in the South that many had to be turned away; there was no way the Confederacy could arm everyone who wanted to serve. Editors and printers likewise stepped up to volunteer through the winter, spring, and summer of 1861. The two Montgomery, Alabama, newspapers, the *Advertiser* and the *Mail*, had each lost one-third of their editorial staffs—one junior editor each—by the middle of January 1861, and others soon followed. In fact, more Confederate newspapers closed in 1861 than in any other year of the war, and the loss of labor to the military was one of the major factors in many of the closures.

Reader demand for news was demonstrated by the stunning increases in new subscriptions in the early part of the war. The *Augusta Chronicle and Sentinel*, already with one of the larger circulations in the South, was receiving as many as 75 new subscribers each week in the spring of 1861. Large numbers of men and women crowded around to read the latest telegraphic news from newspaper bulletin boards or availed themselves of newspaper reading rooms where they could read the back issues of exchange newspapers from throughout the Confederacy—and, more commonly than one might expect, even from the North. Some newspapers, such as the *Southern Confederacy* of Atlanta, even made maps of the theaters of war available in their reading rooms.[8] People crowded into post offices on mail day in eager anticipation of the latest news from "dingy half sheets."[9] Later in the war, men would pay telegraph operators to divert the Confederate Press Association's dispatches to them. In response, the CPA sought and attained congressional action that allowed its dispatches to be copyrighted.[10]

While reader demand for news and newspapers soared, the resources to produce them were not always available to members of the southern press. With the exception of the large New Orleans dailies that fell under Union domination in April 1862, the Confederate press was made up primarily of small to mid-sized dailies and country weeklies. At 17,000 subscribers, the *Augusta Evening Dispatch* had one of the largest circulations in the Confederacy. Its closest in-state rival was another Augusta paper, the *Chronicle and Sentinel*, whose combined daily and weekly circulation was 13,000. Few newspapers had more than a few thousand subscribers.[11] As a result, most southern newspapers did not have the kind of resources that allowed the large metropolitan newspapers of the North to field dozens of correspondents at a cost of hundreds of thousands of dollars. Most southern newspapers could, however, recruit local residents serving in the Confederate Army to write regular accounts about their experiences. Even weeklies made arrangements to have soldier-correspondents send letters home. An Alabama newspaper, the *Cahaba Gazette*, solicited writers from a local unit in an editor's note that headed a recent letter from a soldier: "We would be much obliged to our friends of the [Cahaba] Rifles if some of them would write every week, if not oftener. Every little particular connected with them would be read with interest by their friends."[12]

Newspapers often had what appear to have been more formal arrangements with correspondents who would file stories as regularly as their military duties would allow. Often, though, newspapers would also receive letters from volunteer correspondents, military men who were writing in, frequently with an axe to grind. This led to interesting copy because generally such writers were responding—often quite vehemently—to what they considered erroneous first reports of battles. These correspondents often framed their reasons for writing as being to correct the record, and they would sign their letters with noms de guerre like *Truth*. Truth was an officer, perhaps a colonel, who was serving with Confederate troops in southern Kentucky in the winter of 1862. He wrote a scathing response to the initial reports of the Battle of Fishing Creek for their criticisms of the commanding officer there, Brigadier General George Crittenden. The battle had been a disaster for the Confederates, who were forced to retreat into Nashville. The rout opened an invasion route into the heavily unionist areas of eastern Tennessee and even led some Atlanta journalists to fear for the safety of their city.[13] Truth summarized his account of the battle, which squared more with reports filed with the Confederate war department, but then in his final paragraph, he wrote:

> The reports against the loyalty and courage of Gen. Crittenden are basely false. A more loyal and brave man does not hold office in the Southern Confederacy. This much, Messrs. Editors, I have felt inclined to say, in order to remove from the public mind the erroneous impressions made by the fabricated falsehoods of those miserable cowards who fled from the field in disgraceful fear, and promulgated these reports in order to shield themselves from the burning curses of an indignant people.[14]

The South was not without its professional journalist war correspondents, however, though they were considerably fewer in number than their northern counterparts. Among the top Confederate war correspondents was a former *New York Herald* reporter, Felix G. de Fontaine, who had come to Charleston to cover the dispute over Fort Sumter. De Fontaine's sympathies apparently lay with the South. By May he had joined the staff of the *Charleston Courier* as a war correspondent and marched off to Virginia as a major with the First South Carolina Regiment. The rank was assigned to de Fontaine in his role as a war correspondent. The former *Herald* reporter, who wrote for the *Courier* under the nom de guerre *Personne*, was probably the best writer of any of the South's war correspondents. His letters were always lively and detailed. De Fontaine was a writer of strong emotion, and he never failed to let his readers know exactly what he thought about the events he covered. Writing from Richmond, he began an article about the skirmishing that would culminate in the First Battle of Manassas with this diatribe:

> A thousand rumors are flying through the city in relation to the recent encounters in the Northwest, and from the tangled web of facts and fancies, fears and doubts, causes and results, it is almost impossible to weave

a fabric upon which any sort of reliance can be placed. It is beyond question, however, that we have suffered a disaster.[15]

De Fontaine did not stay in the field throughout the war, however, and for that reason, he must be considered the South's number-two war correspondent. In 1864, he purchased the daily newspaper in Columbia, South Carolina, the *South Carolinian*, and settled down there until forced to flee Sherman's invasion in early 1865. De Fontaine's main competitor for the title of best Confederate war correspondent was Peter W. Alexander, a lawyer and former editor of the *Savannah Republican*. De Fontaine beat Alexander into the field by several weeks. When Fort Sumter was bombarded, Alexander was still practicing law in Thomaston, Georgia, but he headed to Virginia shortly after Fort Sumter. There he covered the war not only for the *Republican* but also for the *Memphis Appeal*, the *Mobile Advertiser and Register*, and several other newspapers.[16]

Alexander was far more serious than De Fontaine. He virtually never cracked a joke in any of his dispatches. Alexander's correspondence was most noted for its advocacy on behalf of the Confederate soldiers in Virginia. In the fall of 1861, Alexander took on the Confederate Medical, Quartermaster, and Commissary Departments. He criticized those departments for allowing baggage to rot in the field rather than getting it delivered to troops who needed it. After Alexander's dispatches began to arrive, the *Savannah Republican*'s editors began looking into the matter and found that supplies shipped to Richmond at the beginning of September had still not reached the army a month later, noting, "Winter clothing and supplies of every kind, intended for our brave volunteers, have thus been allowed to lie neglected by the way side, and, as a consequence, our troops to suffer for the absolute comforts and necessaries of life."[17]

Alexander followed up his advocacy on behalf of the troops the next fall with a compelling dispatch about the lack of necessary supplies for Southern forces. His reporting provoked an overwhelming response by southerners. Alexander wrote:

> It is now (midnight) raining and has been for several hours. The army has not had a mouthful of bread for four days, and no food of any kind except a little green corn picked up on the roadside, for thirty-six hours. The provision trains are coming up, but many of the troops will have to go another day without anything to eat. Many of them are also barefooted. I have seen scores of them to-day marching over the flinty turnpike with torn and blistered feet. They bear all the hardships without murmuring; since every step they take brings them that much nearer in bleeding Maryland. As for tents, they have not known what it was to sleep under one since last spring.[18]

Throughout the Confederacy, citizens made donations of shoes and other supplies to supply the army for the coming winter. "Everyone who has read the able correspondence of 'P.W.A.' for the *Republican*, has been delighted and instructed," wrote the editor of the *Natchez Courier*. "His glorious appeal in behalf of the suffering volunteers in our army was a masterpiece of the pen, glowing with noble sentiments and calculated to produce—as it did produce—the results intended." One result of Alexander's story was the proposal by a *Republican* reader to raise $1,000 to buy a service of silver plate for Alexander to thank him for his advocacy on behalf of the troops. The reporter wrote in a later dispatch that he would prefer the money to be donated to the fund to buy shoes for Confederate soldiers.[19]

Alexander's advocacy was sufficient to earn him the honor of being the South's greatest Civil War correspondent, but he deserves that position for other reasons as well. Not only did Alexander remain in the field for virtually the whole war; his writing set him apart from other Confederate war correspondents, including De Fontaine. Alexander's style was very much a product of the Victorian romanticism of his day. Rather than writing in the straightforward prose of De Fontaine, Alexander was more likely to conjure images through metaphors and extravagant language. His report of the Second Battle of Manassas began this way:

> Another great battle has been fought on the bloody plains of Manassas, and once more has heaven crowned our banners with the laurel of victory. The conflict opened Friday afternoon, and last night not a Federal soldier remained on the south side of Bull Run, except the prisoners we had taken and those who sleep the sleep that shall know no waking until the great day of judgment. Never since Adam was planted in the garden of Eden did a holier cause engage the hearts and arms of any nation, and never did any people establish more clearly their right to be freemen.[20]

Alexander and De Fontaine were the two best correspondents, and they were not the only professional journalists who covered the war for southern newspapers. Some of the better-known correspondents included John H. Linebaugh of the *Memphis Daily Appeal*, who died on his way to Tennessee to report on General John Bell Hood's campaign in the fall of 1864; Dr. George W. Bagby, the *Charleston Mercury*'s faithful Richmond correspondent whose weekly dispatches from the Confederate capital appeared like clockwork; Henry Timrod, who would become the Confederacy's poet laureate and who reported on the Corinth, Mississippi, campaign for the *Mercury*; Henry Watterson, who would become one of the South's most famous postwar editors, and who may have been the *Daily Appeal*'s mysterious correspondent, "Shadow"; Samuel Chester Reid Jr., perhaps the Confederacy's most energetic correspondent, who wrote for no fewer than seven different newspapers but who was primarily connected with several Alabama newspapers, including the *Montgomery Daily Advertiser*; and Robert Ette of the *Memphis Daily Appeal*. In addition to these men, there were a number of other southern correspondents, many of whose real names are unknown, but many others about whom we know nothing more than their pseudonyms and their reportage. In this latter class are the three women known to have served as Confederate war correspondents, including "Joan," of the *Charleston Courier*; "Virginia," of the *Mobile Daily Advertiser and Register*, and "E. L. McE," of the *Knoxville Register*.[21]

Southern war correspondents worked long hours under unbelievably difficult circumstances for very little pay and with few of the resources or luxuries of the wealthy New York papers. Timrod, a soldier-correspondent who would become the unofficial poet laureate of the Confederacy and editorial writer for the *Columbia South Carolinian*, received $6 a day plus traveling expenses for the reporting he did from the Army of the West for the *Charleston Mercury*. This fee would have been in addition to his military pay but still was quite meager. The Southern Associated Press, a predecessor of the Confederate Press Association, as well as the Richmond newspapers, were paying their correspondents in Fredericksburg, Virginia, $100 a month in 1863.[22] When the army was in the field near the Rappahannock River in Virginia in the summer of 1862, correspondents were foraging with the troops and sleeping on the ground. "We live on what we can get—now and then an ear of corn, fried green apples, or a bit of ham broiled on a stick," reported De Fontaine. "But quite as frequently do without either from morning until night. We sleep on the ground without any other covering than a blanket, and consider ourselves fortunate if we are not frozen stiff before morning."[23]

Illness and fatigue often plagued the correspondents who, because they were essentially living with the troops, were victim to the same camp diseases; nor were injuries on the battlefield unknown among the correspondent corps. Following the first Battle of Bull Run in late July 1861, Alexander fell ill from exposure and fatigue. He had eaten little on the day of the battle and was then forced to walk 20 miles in hot sunlight after the battle. When he returned to the battlefield several days later, he was overcome by the stench of rotting horseflesh. The horses had been killed in the battle and left unburied afterward. Alexander fell ill a second time during the retreat after the Battle of Sharpsburg. "My condition is such as to render it impossible for me to rejoin the army for the present," he wrote to the *Mobile Daily Advertiser and Register*, another paper for which he wrote regularly. "I was not prepared for the hardships, experiences and fastings the army has encountered since it left the Rappahannock, and like many a seasoned campaigner, have had to 'fall out by the way.'"[24] The *Sandersville Central Georgian* had a stalwart soldier-correspondent whose will to serve his country and his readers was apparently greater than his constitution. The *Central Georgian* reported in early 1862 that its "popular correspondent" Ivy W. Duggan had taken ill for the third time and had been forced to return to the hospital. The paper's editor commented, "Mr. Duggan's patriotism is greater than his strength."[25]

Newspaper work was arduous and risky, even before the Civil War started. According to the *Carolina Spartan* of Spartanburg, South Carolina, a successful editor needed "the constitution of a horse, obstinacy of a mule, impudence of a beggar and entire resignation to the most confounded of all earthly treadmills; he must be a moving target for everybody to shout at, and is expected to know everything, and to assist busybodies, to pry into the business of his neighbors."[26] Once the war began and war-related shortages and other problems kicked in, that list would need to be expanded to include patience, courage, negotiating skills, and nerves of steel.

Problems related to the actual manufacture of newspapers began early in the war, but they did not become a crisis immediately, and a circulation boom kept profits up even though advertising dollars declined as northern clients pulled their advertisements from southern newspapers and southern businesses closed when their owners and employees went off to fight. That circulation boom, though, had both good effects and bad effects. Getting subscribers to pay up was a perennial problem for antebellum newspaper editors. The problem became more pressing during the war, when more people wanted subscriptions but fewer seemed able to pay for them. By the end of 1861, the *Charleston Mercury*'s subscribers owed the newspaper $17,000, and its advertisers were some $20,000 in arrears. Most newspapers pretty quickly went to a cash system, which required subscribers to pay for their subscriptions in cash, in advance. When the scarcity of cash and the ravages of inflation truly hit crisis levels, some editors instituted a bartering system. They would accept just about anything of value in payment for subscriptions. The *Hillsborough (North Carolina) Recorder* announced a subscription price increase in January 1864 but added that the editor would be willing to barter subscriptions for $1 plus "wood, corn, wheat or flour, or butter, eggs, or potatoes, or any article of the kind used in a family." The *Sandersville Central Georgian* had been accepting produce for subscriptions since 1862.[27]

Lack of cash was not the editors' only problem. Prices for paper and other raw materials soared, and labor shortages became a tremendous burden, given the increased demand for newspapers. Nearly three-quarters of the South's printers served in the Confederate military. This rate of service by printers was not uncommon among white Southern men. In South Carolina, for example,

44,000 men out of a voting population of 68,000 volunteered for the army in the first 18 months of the war. Nearly half the printers who served died on the battlefield and thus did not return when their enlistments were up. Many of those who did make it home were disabled by injury or disease. Given that it took about three printers to support the work of one editor, even the loss of a single printer could have a profound effect on the production capacity of a newspaper. The decline in printers did not have as severe an effect as it might have had due to the difficulty of obtaining an adequate supply of newsprint and ink. In 1860, the South had fewer than one-tenth of the country's paper mills, and several of those that were located in the Confederacy were shut down for long periods during the Civil War. The paper mill at Bath, South Carolina, burned in April 1863 and was out of business until the fall of 1864. Other paper mills were plagued by strikes and destruction by enemy armies.[28]

Newspapers coped with the paper shortages in different ways. Some printed only enough copies for subscribers and gave up on newsstand or street sales. Others reduced the number of pages they printed each day or even reduced their page size. In September 1861, the *Charleston Courier*, for example, reduced its page size from eight to seven columns, or from 30 × 44 inches to 18 × 36 inches. The paper's size would shrink even more as the war continued. Other newspapers went to smaller type faces for body copy or even printed on other kinds of paper. A number of newspapers farther to the west found a truly unique solution to the shortage of newsprint. They printed their news on the back side of wallpaper or on other kinds of paper. The Vicksburg papers are well known for printing on wallpaper. On January 18, 1862, the *Augusta Chronicle and Sentinel* noted that it was receiving other newspapers in a multitude of colors. The *New Orleans Delta*, for example, recently had come in a shade of bright orange, and a Mississippi newspaper had arrived in a brilliant vermillion.

The quality of the news produced on those presses has been a subject of disagreement among critics and historians, many of whom believe that neither the southern nor the northern press did a particularly good job covering the war. A common criticism is that Civil War journals focused on writing about the battles and not on the important ancillary military matters such as corruption in the quartermaster corps or problems enforcing the conscription laws. Modern Mississippi newsman Hodding Carter, however, believed the Civil War produced some good journalism and more firsthand reporting than had been possible in most later American wars. J. Cutler Andrews, author of the only history of how Confederate newspapers covered the war, would side with Carter. In Andrews's opinion, the best southern correspondents in the Civil War were easily as good as the best northern correspondents. Even competing papers recognized the quality of the reporting by Alexander and de Fontaine. The *Charleston Mercury* referred to Alexander as "The War Correspondent of the Savannah *Republican* who has hitherto earned the reputation of being one of the most discriminating and best informed of the letter writers with the Army of the Potomac."[29]

When the Civil War began, war coverage was in its infancy, and American newspapers were only beginning to adopt many of the practices that are today assumed to be the way journalism ought to be done. The South's journalists were not nearly so doctrinaire in their thinking. These were practical men who had to figure out as they went along how to make enough profit to stay in business and how to meet the public's demand for a new sort of content with dwindling resources. The differences between the ways the northern metropolitan press was able to cover the Civil War and the ways in which the southern press covered it are legion, but they are the product of social, economic, political, and even military differences between the two regions. It is possible to quibble with the political ideologies that animated a good number of southern journalists. But it impossible to dismiss their contributions and dedication to their readers and even to their cause, unjust as it may seem to some from the retrospective vantage point of later times.

NOTES

1. *New Orleans Picayune*, 1 February 1861.
2. *Southern Advertiser*, 4 January 1861.
3. *Charleston Mercury*, 18 April 1861; *Southern Confederacy*, 14 August 1861.
4. *New Orleans Picayune*, 5 February 1861.
5. Ibid.
6. *Charleston Mercury*, 9 April 1861.
7. Ibid.
8. *Augusta Chronicle and Sentinel*, 27 April 1861; *Albany Patriot*, 11 April 1861; *Gate-City Guardian/Southern Confederacy*, 16 February 1861, 15 August 1861; *Southern Confederacy*, 14 August 1861; *Charleston Mercury* 16 April 1861.
9. Cornelia Phillips Spencer, *The Last Ninety Days of the War in North Carolina* (New York: Watchman Publishing Co., 1866; repr., Wilmington, N.C.: Broadfoot Publishing Co., 1993), 244.
10. *First Annual Meeting of the Press Association* (Montgomery: Memphis Appeal Job Printing Establishment, 1864); *Minutes of the Board of Directors of the Press Association, Oct. 14, 1863 and Jan. 14, 1864* (Atlanta: Franklin Steam Publishing House, 1864.)
11. These circulation figures are for daily and weekly issues combined. Daily circulation was minuscule compared with weekly. For the *Evening Dispatch*, daily circulation was 2,000, whereas weekly circulation was 15,000. The *Chronicle and Sentinel*'s daily circulation was 1,000, and its weekly was 13,000. The circulation figures are from the 1860 U.S. Census, results reported in Kenneth W. Rawlings,

"Statistics and Cross-Sections of the Georgia Press to 1870," *Georgia Historical Quarterly* 23 (March 1939): 177–179.

12. *Cahaba Gazette*, 24 May 1861.

13. J. Cutler Andrews, *The South Reports the Civil War* (Princeton: Princeton University Press, 1970), 127–128.

14. *Memphis Appeal*, 9 February 1862.

15. *Charleston Courier*, 21 July 1861.

16. Andrews, 52.

17. *Savannah Republican*, 24 September 1861, 11 October 1861; Andrews, 112, 113.

18. *Mobile Daily Advertiser and Register*, 10 September 1862.

19. Ibid.; *Natchez Courier*, n.d., quoted in the *Savannah Republican*, 12 December 1862.

20. *Mobile Advertiser and Register*, 10 September 1862.

21. *Montgomery Daily Mail*, 16 November 1864; Andrews, 94–95; *First Annual Meeting of the Press Association; Minutes of the Board of Directors of the Press Association, Oct. 14, 1863 and Jan. 14, 1864.*

22. Andrews, 48.

23. *Charleston Courier*, 30 August 1862.

24. Andrews, 93; *Mobile Daily Advertiser and Register*, 4 October 1862.

25. *Sandersville Central Georgian*, 8 January 1862.

26. Quoted in John Calhoun Ellen Jr., "Political Newspapers in the Piedmont Carolinas in the 1850s" (PhD dissertation, University of South Carolina, 1958), 119.

27. Robert A. Rutland, *The Newsmongers: Journalism in the Life of the Nation, 1690–1972* (New York: The Dial Press, 1973), 196; Andrews, 47; Catherine Patricia Oliver, "Problems of South Carolina Editors Who Reported the Civil War," (master's thesis, University of South Carolina, 1970), 54, 64; John Nerone, *The Culture of the Press in the Early Republic: Cincinnati, 1793–1848* (New York: Garland Publishing Inc., 1989), 47; *Sandersville Central Georgian*, 8 January 1862.

28. *Augusta Constitutionalist*, 9 November 1864; *Columbus Enquirer*, 15 November 1864.

29. *Charleston Mercury*, 15 October 1861.

Wartime News over Southern Wires

The Confederate Press Association

— Ford Risley —

Six days after the surrender of Fort Sumter, a detachment of United States Army soldiers marched into the headquarters of the American Telegraph Company in Washington, D.C., and quietly took possession of the office. Although most southern editors still were dizzy with excitement over the victory at Charleston, it did not take them long to recognize the immediate impact of the company's seizure: the South's main source of vital telegraphic news—the Associated Press—had been lost.[1]

Confederate editors realized that a reliable southern replacement for the AP would be needed if papers were going to receive timely and complete news of the fighting. Even so, they struggled for nearly two years to come up with an effective mutual arrangement for gathering and distributing telegraphic news. The organization that the editors finally settled on, the Press Association of the Confederate States of America, was beset with problems, including an uncooperative Richmond press and the loss of key newspapers over the course of the war. Still, thanks to an aggressive superintendent and a core group of dedicated members, the PA, as it was often known, managed to serve the basic needs of the South's readers for news of the Civil War. That was no small matter considering the wide-ranging fighting that took place during the war and the fact that, unlike those of the North, few Confederate newspapers could afford to send full-time reporters into the field.

The persistence of southern editors in finding a mutual arrangement for sending and receiving telegraphic news from the war was a clear signal that the journalism practiced in the region was changing from the old partisan practices that had dominated newspapers for so long. News was beginning to replace opinion as the main emphasis of the South's newspapers, just as it had done decades earlier in the North. Moreover, the organization and practices that guided the work of the Confederate Press Association for two years foretold the shape of cooperative news reporting in the new nation that was to emerge from the Civil War.[2]

Cooperative news-gathering in the United States began in the 1820s when three New York City dailies banded together to cover harbor and shipping news. The development of the telegraph in 1844 prompted groups of local and regional newspapers to form cooperatives to more efficiently cover and distribute news to members. Commonly known as associated presses, or AP, the cooperatives became gradually more formalized, settling on established rates and guaranteed daily transmission of news. Permanent cooperatives were established, first along the growing telegraphic lines linking the major East Coast cities, and later along the trunk lines, including the one linking Washington, D.C., to cities in the South.[3]

Cooperative news-gathering in the South dated back to 1847, when a group of editors banded together to pay the cost of receiving telegraphic news. On the eve of the Civil War, two telegraphic lines served the South. The American Telegraph Company's trunk line extended from New York through Washington and down to Richmond, Raleigh, Columbia, Macon, Montgomery, and Mobile. The Southwestern Telegraphic Company's line extended from Louisville through Tennessee, Alabama, and Mississippi to New Orleans. The principal telegraphic news agency in the South was operated by William H. Pritchard. The editor of the *Augusta Constitutionalist*, Pritchard also had served as the AP's agent in Georgia, South Carolina, and Alabama since 1856, coordinating the distribution of news to members in those states.[4]

Soon after the American Telegraph Company's line to the South was severed, the southern section of the line was reorganized as the Southern Telegraph Company under the direction of William S. Morris, a major stockholder in the old American Telegraph Company who lived in the South. Around the same time, the lines of the Southwestern Telegraph Company, which extended from Louisville south through Kentucky, Tennessee, Alabama, Mississippi, and Louisiana, were severed. A separate Confederate headquarters was set up in Nashville with George L. Douglass, the treasurer of Southwestern, as president. Recognizing that vital news would be emanating from the new Confederate government, Pritchard, the former AP agent, had set up an office in

Montgomery. When the government was relocated to Richmond, he moved his office there as well. However, Pritchard contracted diphtheria and died in Richmond on March 24, 1862. His son, William H. Pritchard Jr., took over the operation that had become known as the Southern Associated Press.[5]

Even before the elder Pritchard's death, there had been growing dissatisfaction with the high cost and poor quality of the news dispatches sent by the Confederacy's news-gathering agency. The *Memphis Appeal* said there was "universal complaint" with the "present unorganized and imbecile arrangement." The telegraphic news reports were "vague and unsatisfactory, unmeaning, unreliable, and, in many instances, flagitiously false," the newspaper claimed. "They come to us in a roundabout way, after two or three repetitions by as many agents, thus securing exaggeration as well as additional expense."[6]

The *Augusta Chronicle & Sentinel* agreed, declaring:

> The present "associated press" as a vehicle of news, has become nearly useless. If, by chance, any thing of importance is transmitted, we, in many cases, find that it has been anticipated by mail. We often receive news from Richmond by the papers within an hour or two after we have received the same by telegraph, and dispatches from the West, via Nashville are generally utterly useless.[7]

Meanwhile, the *Mobile Register and Advertiser* made clear its own concern with the veracity of some of the reports provided by the AP. From time to time, the newspaper ran the headline "News by Telegraph—Hopeful if True" over its columns of telegraphic news.[8]

The *Charleston Mercury* joined a handful of other Confederate newspapers in calling for a meeting of editors to discuss setting up an alternative service. "It is high time for the journals of the South to be making arrangement for a permanent, extended, better organized, and, at the same time, more economic agency,"[9] the *Mercury* reported. In January 1862, the editors of six daily newspapers met in Atlanta to discuss setting up a new mutual association. The editors agreed that a more systematic arrangement was needed to secure reliable service, and they agreed to meet again in March to iron out details. While that meeting duly took place, the editors apparently made little progress toward securing suitable arrangements.[10]

In the meantime, problems continued with the telegraphic reports, and Confederate editors became increasingly impatient and angry. Wild rumors regularly found their way into news reports. Moreover, when a press association story from the battlefield was sent to members, more often than not it was days late. The first reliable report of the Confederate victory at Second Manassas on August 29–30, 1862, for example, was not published in the *Richmond*

Daily Dispatch until September 5. And more than a week after the Confederacy was defeated at the Battle of Antietam on September 17, press association reports did not know the whereabouts of the Army of Northern Virginia.

The telegraphic reporting provided from the Battle of Seven Pines so outraged James R. Sneed, editor of the *Savannah Republican,* that he expressed his anger in the columns of his newspaper. "Whilst private individuals are telegraphing important information from Richmond concerning the late battles," he wrote, "we would be glad to know what the individual is doing who has set himself up at the capital as the agent of the Press and regularly comes forward with a bill for his services."[11]

Apparently frustrated at the lack of progress toward a cooperative arrangement, the editors of four Richmond newspapers—the *Dispatch, Enquirer, Examiner,* and *Whig*—established their own mutual news agency in November 1862. Known as the Richmond Associated Press, the agency had its headquarters in the Confederate capital and was headed by John Graeme, editor of the *Dispatch.* A notice in the newspaper said that all the resources of the association would be used to appoint news correspondents "at every important point in the Confederacy." Moreover, special arrangements would be made to obtain news from the Confederate army as well as the North. The notice also claimed that a large majority of the daily journals in the Confederacy had united to form the new Associated Press.[12]

Despite the claims of the *Dispatch,* there seemed to be little agreement that the Richmond arrangement was going to serve the needs of the Confederate press any better. Moreover, the news reports distributed by the Richmond Associated Press differed little from those provided by the old system. For example, the telegraphic stories from Fredericksburg provided by the Richmond Associated Press were timelier than those from many other major battles fought during the year but still were generally incomplete. There also was little in the way of follow-up reporting from the battlefield because later accounts of Fredericksburg depended almost entirely on northern papers.[13] Recognizing the problems, the editor of the *Atlanta Southern Confederacy* lamented that "the persons employed by the press and well paid to send us news, have proven themselves incompetent to the task."[14]

Apparently resolved to finally set up an effective news-gathering arrangement, a group of southern editors met again on January 5, 1863, this time in Macon, Georgia. The group sent out a notice to every daily newspaper in the Confederacy asking editors to meet the following month in Augusta. Editors of 12 papers came to the meeting on February 4 and 5; three more were represented by proxy. The editors approved a constitution, elected officers, agreed to hire a superintendent, and settled on a name: the Press Association of the Confederate States of America.[15] The editors elected R.W. Gibbes of the *Columbia South Carolinian* as president and Nathan S. Morse of the *Augusta Chronicle & Sentinel* as secretary and treasurer. The board of directors was comprised of James Gardner of the *Augusta Constitutionalist*, W.G. Clark of the *Mobile Advertiser & Register*, George W. Adair of the *Atlanta Southern Confederacy*, Joseph Clisby of the *Macon Telegraph*, and James R. Sneed of the *Savannah Republican*.

Noticeably absent from the meeting were representatives of the Richmond or Charleston press. Recognizing the importance of those newspapers, members agreed that if the newspapers of either city joined the association, they would be represented on the board.[16] According to its constitution, the Press Association's purpose was "to arrange, put in operation, and keep up an efficient system of reporting news by telegraph . . . under the exclusive control and employed for the exclusive benefit of the members." Any daily newspaper published in the Confederacy could become a member upon paying an initiation fee of 50 dollars. Each member newspaper had one vote in the election of president, secretary-treasurer, and board of directors. The board would establish the policy of the association as well as hire a superintendent and correspondents. The board also would assess members "fairly and equitably" for the cost of operating the association.[17]

The board hired John S. Thrasher as superintendent, and he took over the post on March 9. The 46-year-old Thrasher was born in Portland, Maine, but had moved to Cuba with his parents as a youth. After working as a clerk, he joined a group of revolutionary agitators and helped edit an anti-Spanish newspaper. He was court-martialed for his activity and briefly imprisoned off the coast of Africa. After his release, he moved to New Orleans and worked for Cuban annexation by the United States. He later was hired by the *New York Herald* as a correspondent, traveling in Mexico and South America before the war began.[18]

Thrasher plunged into his new job with great enthusiasm and worked diligently to set up the association. During a six-week period, he traveled to many of the Confederacy's key news centers, including Charleston, Atlanta, Montgomery, Mobile, Jackson, and Vicksburg. He hired correspondents to report from Richmond and Charleston, as well as from some of the Confederacy's largest armies, including those of Robert E. Lee and Braxton Bragg. To secure reporters, who were paid 25 dollars a week, Thrasher ran notices such as one that appeared in the *Atlanta Southern Confederacy*: "Desiring to extend the connections of the Press association, gentlemen having experience as reporters or correspondents for newspapers, may contribute by sending me by mail information of their previous experience, present residence, customary terms for business and whether short hand writers or not."[19] Apparently concerned about the lack of correspondents in the west, Thrasher also asked his reporter in Mississippi to look for soldiers in the area who would be willing to telegraph occasional reports of no more than 50 words. It is not clear how successful the Association was in finding these soldier correspondents. Nonetheless, by summer of 1863 the PA had about 20 correspondents scattered from Virginia to Mississippi, men whom the *Savannah Republican* described as being "for the most part men of intelligence, judgment, and well acquainted with the wants of the press."[20]

Thrasher admonished his reporters in the importance of "securing early, full, and reliable" telegraphic news. Correspondents were instructed to write clearly and concisely, using short sentences and avoiding ambiguous words. The superintendent also ordered that reports should be free of opinion and comment. He urged correspondents "to sift reports" and "to not send unfounded rumors as news." Finally, he warned correspondents to "see that you are not beaten" by reporters from other journals. Thrasher took great pride in his orders, calling them a "complete revolution" in the work practices of the southern journalists. "It has been left to our young Confederation, to exhibit to the world the first instance of the entire Press of a people combining in one body to prosecute the labors of its high mission; giving an adequate and worthy form to itself, and presenting to all a tangible representation of 'the fourth Estate,'" he wrote.[21]

Thrasher instructed correspondents that they represented the "whole daily press" of the Confederacy and that they should request "early intelligence of events." Correspondents were instructed to transmit all news that in their judgment was publishable without harming the military effort of the Confederate Army. He warned that the "greatest caution" should be exercised in reporting troop movements, and in all cases, commanding generals should be consulted about information that was appropriate for transmission. In the event censors refused to approve the transmission of a story, Thrasher told reporters to send him a copy of the story, along with the name and rank of the person prohibiting the transmission and the reason given. When news of "absorbing public interest" was occurring, correspondents were told to transmit "four or five reports" during the course of a day. Finally, to maintain good relations with their sources, correspondents were expected to visit them "twice daily" and "freely exchange news" in order that the reporters might get information in return. Correspondents also were asked to supply governors of the states where they were working with any information of interest to them that was being transmitted to association members.[22]

An important aspect of the association was the insistence of organizers that it be a truly cooperative news organization. Although the superintendent hired correspondents to be stationed at "points of interest," association members were expected to send "all news of interest occurring in their vicinity" at times when no correspondent was available. And although terms of the association did not prohibit "individual enterprise," if a member wanted to make arrangements with another paper to receive special news dispatches, members could not exclude other member papers from joint participation on equal terms.[23]

In March, telegraphic service began to 31 daily newspapers in the Confederacy, the majority of which had subscribed to the old Richmond Associated Press. By May, the number of member papers had grown to 44, including four dailies in Richmond and two in Charleston. In a report to the PA's board, Thrasher also moved his office to Atlanta, a city that he said, combined "the advantages of a central geographic position" and also allowed "communication by telegraph and rail with all parts of the country.[24]

Thrasher and the association were immediately confronted with major challenges to the South's telegraphic news coverage during the spring and summer of 1863. It soon became clear that in spite of the superintendent's organizational efforts, telegraphic reporting in the Confederacy still had plenty of hurdles to overcome. The PA's stories on the Battle of Chancellorsville drew heavily from the news columns of the Richmond newspapers, which in turn, had taken much of their information from the northern press. The editor of the *Augusta Constitutionalist* expressed his outrage at the "ridiculously and pitifully false accounts" of the battle that he received from the Press Association and refused to print them in his newspaper.[25]

To its credit, the PA provided almost daily reports during the long siege of Vicksburg, Mississippi. Still, there were numerous problems with the stories. Most of the telegraphic dispatches never gave an accurate picture of the seriousness of the Union threat to the so-called Gibraltar of the South. By the spring of 1863, civilians and troops in the city were suffering tremendously from the Federal stranglehold. Yet reports repeatedly told how there were plenty of provisions for everyone. Stories of the fighting around Vicksburg variously reported the wholly unfounded tales that 10,000 Union troops had been killed and that 40,000 more had been captured.[26] A major reason for the problems was that most of the reports on Vicksburg came from the Press Association reporter in Jackson, who was cut off from regular communication with the city and had to depend on the accounts of people who had left. Nonetheless, the *Richmond Examiner's* editor referred to the PA reports from Jackson as "an unintelligible compound of gas, braggadocio, blunder, absurdity, and impossibility." He also accused the PA correspondent of wild exaggeration in reporting enemy losses.[27]

Despite the problems with many reports, Press Association correspondents seemed to heed Thrasher's warning about sifting truth from fact. On the whole, they did not write the kind of atrocity stories about the Union Army often found in Confederate newspapers during the war. As they were instructed, PA reporters avoided using the first-person in their telegraphic accounts. They also were generally successful at following Thrasher's instructions to keep their opinions out of stories and stick to facts.[28]

But although some of Thrasher's ideas for the Press Association were successful, others did not work as well. The superintendent was concerned about the cost of transmitting stories over the telegraph and sought various means to save money. He became convinced that "several classes of words" could be deleted from stories without unduly changing their meanings. Articles, pronouns, prepositions, conjunctions, and auxiliary verbs constituted about two-fifths of the words used by good writers, he claimed, and more than one-half of the words used by bad and careless writers. Thrasher instructed correspondents to

> read every message over after writing it out, and purge it of every word not required to convey your meaning; and see where you can use one word to express what you have put in two or three. Omit articles, pronouns, prepositions, conjuctions, and auxiliary verbs, when by so doing the plain sense of your meaning will not be lost. [29]

In response to the complaints of some members regarding the new policy, Thrasher sent a circular defending the practice. He argued that it was not "the object of the Press Association to reduce all its members to one procrustean level" in editing stories. Nor, he wrote, was it the duty of the superintendent "to supply the want of a knowledge of geography, of the history of current events, of the antecedents of men who came into public notice." Nonetheless, criticism from members forced Thrasher to soon abandon his idea.[30]

Southern editors made great use of the daily telegraphic news items they received from the Press Association. Many days it was not unusual for subscribing papers to have 12 or more telegraphic dispatches in a single issue. Because of layout considerations, several items might be nothing more than updated dispatches from the same locale. The old, outdated stories were never removed. In fact, some issues would have a series of dispatches with headlines like "News from the Front," "Good News from the Front," and "Latest News from the Front." The vast majority of dispatches provided by the PA concerned news of the war, but mixed in occasionally was news from Richmond such as congressional action or a speech by the president. News items not related to the war were rare, but occasionally member papers would provide news of a

calamity in their locale, such as a fire. Some of the most complete PA reporting was done during the series of naval battles in Charleston Harbor in the
summer and fall of 1863. The association provided daily accounts of the Federal shelling of Fort Sumter, Battery Wagner, and Charleston itself. In some
cases, as many as three telegraphic reports were filed in a single day.[31]

With the battles of Chickamauga and Chattanooga, Thrasher was confronted with a new obstacle for the PA: an uncooperative Confederate command. General Braxton Bragg had a long-running feud with the press that
culminated in September when he refused to allow the PA correspondent
to report from his army in North Georgia.[32] Without a reporter at the front,
Thrasher, who was back in Atlanta, had to compile stories about the Confederate victory at Chickamauga based on information gleaned from wounded
soldiers and others who had returned from the fighting.[33]

The Confederate victory at Chickamauga did not ease Bragg's feud with
the press. The Confederate commander still refused to admit a Press Association reporter, and so Thrasher was forced to continue compiling incomplete
telegraphic reports from Atlanta. Among the mistakes that occurred as a result of such an arrangement was the erroneous report that General John Bell
Hood had been killed in fighting at Chickamauga. The PA later correctly reported that Hood's wounded leg had been amputated. Right up to the battle of
Missionary Ridge, telegraphic reports originated either from Atlanta or were
based on the accounts of member newspapers that had managed to get a reporter to the front.

Despite the problems in reporting, as 1864 opened Thrasher was buoyed
by the success of the Press Association, claiming that it was "the first known
instance of an union of the whole press of a country for the purpose of collecting and diffusing intelligence of general interest to the people." In fact, that
was not true because the Confederacy's weekly newspapers were not permitted to join the PA, despite a great deal of interest. Nonetheless, Thrasher contended in this report that the organization of the association had done much
to ensure the "preservation of journalism" in the Confederate states.[34]

Yet 1864 was to prove a difficult year for the Press Association. At the
group's first annual meeting, held on April 6 in Augusta, the turning tide of
the war clearly was on everyone's minds. President Gibbes welcomed members
by noting that the press could greatly help the South's cause by maintaining
unanimity in support of the Confederate government and reminding readers
of the sacrifices required.[35] Perhaps the most significant action taken at the
meeting was the decision to permit weekly and semiweekly newspapers in the
Confederacy to join the association. The nondaily papers would be permitted
to print all telegraphic reports provided by the PA at a rate of one-fifth that

assessed to the daily press. Thrasher reported that eleven weekly and semi-weekly newspapers had applied for membership.[36] Also significant was the absence of the Richmond press from the annual meeting. Thrasher reported that the publishers of the city's newspapers had announced their intention to leave the association and set up a separate cooperative news arrangement. The cost of membership in the association and the overall quality of telegraphic news supplied were cited as the chief reasons for dissatisfaction with the PA.[37]

By the spring of 1864, it had become clear that Georgia was going to be the war's next major battleground. It was also clear that the PA was going to have more problems reporting the fighting. General Joseph E. Johnston had succeeded Bragg as commander of the Army of Tennessee, but he too imposed strict censorship on all news from the army. Military authorities ordered that control of censorship be taken away from the provost marshal and given to the inspector general, who was far stricter in what he allowed through.[38] In May, Thrasher traveled to the army's headquarters in an attempt to get daily press service restored. But the trip apparently accomplished little because most of the PA's dispatches over the next several weeks originated from Atlanta. Many of the stories used information from secondhand sources. The superintendent also apparently was having difficulty with his correspondents because in late May he sent two "competent" men to Allatoona to report from the army there.[39]

Despite Thrasher's admonition that correspondents stick to the facts, a clear sense of morale building was evident in many of the Press Association accounts as the fighting got closer to Atlanta. Even while reporting the bad news, many dispatches sought to portray the situation in the best terms possible. A July 12 story that described the Union Army crossing the Chattahoochee River just north of the city nonetheless ended by noting: "Everything is working right. The highest confidence prevails."[40] Three weeks later, after the Confederacy had suffered a series of defeats around the city, the PA dispatch went so far as to proclaim, "Atlanta is safe. All is hopeful and in the best of spirits."[41] Probably due to telegraph difficulties, news of the fall of Atlanta did not appear over the PA wires until September 4 and then only with a brief, incomplete story. A slightly longer story the following day told how the Confederate Army had exploded its extra ammunition and burned supplies in the city that were not needed by troops. Despite the gloomy news, the Press Association story ended by saying, "While the fall of Atlanta is regretted, the army and people are not at all discouraged."[42]

More problems appeared the following month when the PA transmitted a widely published story claiming that Allatoona had been recaptured by Confederate forces. The story stated that Sherman's supply line had been destroyed and the general was cut off from the main portion of his army. It was a startling story that was completely false. In fact, Hood had been checked at Allatoona, the Confederate Army's first setback since evacuating Atlanta.[43] By mid-October, the Press Association was depending almost entirely on northern papers for news from the fighting in Georgia. Among favorite newspapers quoted in the PA's dispatches to members were the *New York Herald, Washington Chronicle,* and *Baltimore American.* The little news that came from association reporters or members generally was about the fighting around Petersburg and Mobile. The first clue of Sherman's plans after capturing Atlanta appeared in the *Augusta Chronicle & Sentinel* on November 19. The PA account was taken from the *Chicago Times* and said the 75,000-man army would sweep through Georgia and South Carolina. The story also gave an indication of how Sherman planned to conduct his march, noting that the army would live off the land before destroying anything of value.[44]

Meanwhile in August, four of Richmond's five daily newspapers—the *Dispatch, Enquirer, Examiner,* and *Sentinel*—carried out their threat to leave the Confederate Press Association. A month later, they announced the formation of the Mutual Press Association with James W. Lewellen of the *Dispatch* as president. Organizers apparently wanted to reduce news-gathering costs by having member papers report news on a reciprocal basis. Member newspapers would agree to pay five dollars a month in advance and to provide to the association's Richmond agent all the important news from their vicinity.[45] The impact of the Richmond newspapers' leaving the Press Association is difficult to determine. The PA still had a correspondent in the capital to report on the Congress and administration. Moreover, members of the Confederate press had repeatedly complained about the unwillingness of the Richmond press to cooperate with the PA.[46] The *Macon Telegraph & Confederate*'s editor dismissed the plan of the Richmond papers and noted that the four had never provided much news from the capital to the Press Association anyway. If the newspapers were successful in forming their own mutual association, he wrote, "the public will have to thank" those papers if the Confederate press contained "only the meager and semi-occasional dispatches which are to be found in the Enquirer, Examiner, Dispatch, and Sentinel."[47]

While Thrasher was contending with a rebellious Richmond press, the superintendent also was on the move. Threatened by Sherman's army in July, he and the rest of Atlanta's press fled south to the safety of Macon. With travel and communications to the North blocked from Atlanta, Thrasher decided in September to visit the Trans-Mississippi area. He did not return until January 1865 after most of the Union Army had left the state. In his absence, Graeme, the PA's Richmond agent, was put in charge of business affairs. By the time of Thrasher's return, a significant portion of the Confederate press had been silenced, making the work of the Press Association all the more difficult. Adding to the problems was the fact that the Union Army had destroyed many miles of telegraphic lines in the South.[48]

Most of the news the PA managed to send over the telegraph centered on the work of the Confederate Congress. The news that a Confederate delegation had discussed peace negotiations was reported in several brief and incomplete stories, as was the case with the news that the negotiations had failed.[49] The Press Association reports largely depended on northern newspapers like the *New York Times*.[50] Inaccuracy also still plagued some of the reporting by the PA. For example, a dispatch published in March erroneously reported that 6,000 Union troops had been killed during fighting in North Carolina. In the same story, it was alleged that during fighting in Tennessee, captured Confederate soldiers were given the choice of either joining the Union Army or being shot.[51]

The news that Richmond was evacuated on Sunday, April 2, was not transmitted for two days from Danville, Virginia, where a temporary government was established.[52] For the next week, Danville became the main source of news from the fighting in Virginia. But there were still problems in learning the results of the fighting and transmitting dispatches. On Sunday, April 9, the day Lee surrendered to Grant, the Press Association sent a story saying there had been heavy fighting in the area on Saturday.[53] On April 16, the *Augusta Constitutionalist* reported that superintendent Thrasher had made a "flying visit" to the city. By that point, the *Chronicle & Sentinel* still did not have news of Lee's surrender, and in fact, five more days went by before telegraph news of the surrender was published in the newspaper.[54]

With the war over, the Confederate Press Association came to an abrupt end. For various reasons, including the destruction of so many telegraph lines in the South, Associated Press service was not resumed immediately to most old Confederate journals. That did not pose a major problem because even before the war ended, many southern newspapers had suspended publishing either because of damaged equipment or Federal occupation. The Associated Press restored service to most newspapers in the South by autumn and, in a few cases, by the end of the year.[55]

The Confederate press clearly had struggled to find a suitable mutual arrangement for gathering and transmitting telegraphic news. The most ambitious and longest lasting system, the Confederate Press Association, dealt with a host of problems in reporting news of the war. Although the quality of news reports provided by the PA often came under repeated criticism from editors, the organizational efforts put forth to create a mutual newsgathering association drew strong praise and, in fact, served as a model for the Associated Press after the war. Moreover, there is little question that without the Press Association reports, most Confederate newspapers would have had virtually no timely news of the war and would have been forced to rely mainly on northern accounts. In his insistence on conciseness and objectivity in PA reports, Thrasher was portending the emphasis on succinct, factual writing that was to become one of the hallmarks of twentieth-century journalism. Finally, the persistence of editors in establishing a Confederate version of the Associated Press was a clear signal that the focus of the newspapers was finally changing in the region. Due largely to the tremendous demand for news from the battlefield, a more modern, news-oriented press had begun to emerge in the South.

NOTES

This manuscript was the basis for a later article, "The Confederate Press Association: Cooperative News Reporting of the War," that was published in *Civil War History* 47, no. 3 (September 2001).

1. J. Cutler Andrews, "The Southern Telegraph Company, 1861–1865: A Chapter in the History of Wartime Communication," *Journal of Southern History* 30 (1964), 320–321.

2. Mutual news-gathering in the South, particularly the Confederate Press Association, has been the subject of two earlier but generally incomplete studies: Quintus C. Wilson, "Confederate Press Association: A Pioneer News Agency," *Journalism Quarterly* 26 (June 1949), 160–166; and Ruby F. Tucker, "The Press Association of the Confederate States of America in Georgia" (master's thesis, University of Georgia, 1950). As their titles indicate, both studies examined only the PA. The Wilson study focused exclusively on the organizational structure of the PA, whereas the Tucker study examined the PA from the perspective of Georgia newspapers exclusively.

3. Richard A. Schwarzlose, *The Nation's Newsbrokers* (Evanston, Ill.: Northwestern University Press, 1998), 1–121. Victor Rosewater, *History of Cooperative News-Gathering in the United States* (New York: D. Appleton, 1936), 4–73.

4. Robert L. Thompson, *Wiring a Continent: The History of the Telegraph Industry in the United States, 1832–1856* (Princeton: Princeton University Press, 1947), 373–376. J. Cutler Andrews, *The South Reports the Civil War* (Princeton: Princeton University Press, 1970), 55–56.

5. Thompson, 373–376; Andrews, "Southern Telegraph Company," 319–344. *Augusta Chronicle & Sentinel*, 25 March 1862. Andrews, *The South Reports*, 55–56.

6. As quoted in the *Boston Advertiser*, 20 January 1862.

7. *Augusta Chronicle & Sentinel*, 21 January 1862.

8. *Mobile Register and Advertiser*, 16 April 1862.

9. Quoted in Rabun Lee Brantley, *Georgia Journalism of the Civil War Period* (Nashville, Tenn.: George Peabody College), 91.

10. The newspapers represented were the *Memphis Appeal, Atlanta Southern Confederacy, Savannah Republican, Augusta Constitutionalist, Nashville Republican Banner,* and *Charleston Mercury.*

11. *Savannah Republican*, 5 June 1862.

12. *Richmond Dispatch*, 5 November 1862. A story in the *Richmond Enquirer* praised the new organization and said it was a welcome improvement over Pritchard's system. That press association only employed "five or six" correspondents, the *Enquirer* contended, and was "more profitable" to Pritchard than "advantageous to the press." *Richmond Enquirer*, 26 November 1862.

13. *Charleston Courier,* 17 December 1862.

14. *Atlanta Southern Confederacy,* 17 December 1862.

15. *The Press Association of the Confederate States of America* (Griffin, Ga.: Hill & Swayze's Printing House, 1863), 6.

16. Ibid., 6–7.

17. Ibid., 8–10.

18. "John Sydney Thrasher," *Dictionary of American Biography*, vol. 18 (New York: Charles Scribner's, 1936), 509–510. What prompted Thrasher to move to the Confederacy or how he came to the attention of the association's board is not clear.

19. "Report of the Superintendent," *The Press Association of the Confederate States of America* (Griffin, Ga.: Hill & Swayze's Printing House, 1863), 44. Thrasher made an initial favorable impression on at least one newspaper. The *Atlanta Southern Confederacy* commented that he "comprehends the duties of the business which he assumed and has taken hold with a will. He has untiring energy and the most extensive experience in journalism—thoroughly comprehending the wants of the Press in the telegraphic line." *Atlanta Southern Confederacy*, 26 March 1863; "Press Reporters and Correspondents," *Atlanta Southern Confederacy*, 6 May 1863.

20. *Savannah Republican*, 6 May 1863.

21. "Report of the Superintendent," *The Press Association of the Confederate States of America* (Griffin, Ga.: Hill & Swayze's Printing House, 1863), 29, 41.

22. Ibid., 54.

23. Ibid., 9–10. Schwarzlose concludes that requiring members to transmit news in their locale had never been tried by the Associated Press, yet it would become "widely adopted" by the AP after the war. Schwarzlose, *The Nation's Newsbrokers*, 269.

24. Ibid., 39. The number of member newspapers gradually decreased as the Union Army occupied more of the Confederacy and as other newspapers ceased publishing for economic reasons. The original members of the Association were: *Mobile (Alabama) Advertiser & Register, Montgomery (Alabama) Advertiser, Jackson (Mississippi) Appeal, Charlotte (North Carolina) Bulletin, Winchester (Tennessee) Bulletin, Augusta (Georgia) Chronicle & Sentinel, Vicksburg (Mississippi) Citizen, Atlanta (Georgia) Commonwealth, Macon (Georgia) Confederate, Augusta (Georgia) Constitutionalist, Charleston (South Carolina) Courier, Natchez (Mississippi) Courier, Richmond (Virginia) Dispatch, Columbus (Georgia) Enquirer, Richmond (Virginia) Examiner, Petersburg (Virginia) Examiner, Petersburg (Virginia) Express, Columbia (South Carolina) Guardian, Wilmington (North Carolina) Journal, Montgomery (Alabama) Mail, Charleston (South Carolina) Mercury, Jackson (Mississippi) Mississippian, Port Hudson (Louisiana) News, Raleigh (North Carolina) Progress, Chattanooga (Tennessee) Rebel, Knoxville (Tennessee) Register, Selma (Alabama) Reporter, Lynchburg (Virginia) Republican, Savannah (Georgia)*

*Republican, Richmond (Virginia) Sentinel, Selma (Alabama) Sentinel, Colum-
bia (South Carolina) South Carolinian, Atlanta (Georgia) Southern Confederacy,
Raleigh State (North Carolina) Journal, Columbus (Georgia) Sun, Macon (Geor-
gia) Telegraph, Columbus (Georgia) Times, Mobile (Alabama) Tribune, Lynchburg
(Virginia) Virginian, Richmond (Virginia) Whig,* and *Vicksburg (Virginia) Whig.*
Ibid., 37.

25. *Augusta Constitutionalist,* 14 May 1863. The editor of the *Savannah Republican*
    complained that during a period of three weeks after the battle, "We have not seen
    the casualties of a single Georgia Regiment in a Virginia paper." *Savannah Repub-
    lican,* 25 May 1863. For a summary of the problems that the Confederate press in
    general faced in reporting the war, see Andrews, *The South Reports,* 506–542.

26. *Augusta Chronicle & Sentinel,* 24 May 1863 and 26 May 1863.

27. *Richmond Daily Examiner,* 6 June 1863 and 25 June 1863. The editor of the *Sa-
    vannah Republican* complained bitterly about the tendency of the press to accept
    reports at face value, noting, "there is a heavy weight of responsibility resting on
    somebody's shoulders for the regular and systematic lying that has been put upon
    the public regarding the ability of this place to hold out. The western Press in the
    vicinity of the unfortunate city have been quite badly imposed on as anybody
    else." *Savannah Republican,* 10 July 1863.

28. On the use of atrocity stories in newspapers during the war, see James W. Silver,
    "Propaganda in the Confederacy," *Journal of Southern History* 11 (1945), 499–501.

29. *The Press Association of the Confederate States of America,* 45–46.

30. Ibid., 45–46. The *Savannah Morning News* published an example of one Press
    Association dispatch from Jackson: "Eight boats passed Vicksburg last night;
    one burnt two disabled five succeeded. Rumor canal Milliken's Bend reach Mis-
    sissippi near New Carthage believed construction Batteries opposite Vicksburg
    Jew paid burn bridge Big Black Vicksburg attached within ten 10 days all offic-
    ers absent ordered report opposite Vicksburg sixty-four steamers left Memphis
    for Vicksburg soldiers niggers no papers allowed below Cairo Yankees fortifying
    Rolla RR north Memphis Bulletin argues suppressed editors arrested."

31. See, for example, *Augusta Chronicle & Sentinel,* 24 November 1863.

32. *Minutes of the Board of Directors of the Press Association, Embracing the Quar-
    terly Reports of the Superintendent* (Atlanta: Franklin Steam Publishing House
    1864), 10, 23–24. The reason given for refusing to grant press access to the army
    was "the indiscretion of special correspondents in regards to army matters."

33. See for example, *Augusta Chronicle & Sentinel,* 23 September 1863.

34. *Minutes of the Board of Directors of the Press Association, Embracing the Quar-
    terly Reports of the Superintendent* (Atlanta: Franklin Steam Publishing House,
    1864), 41–42, 51–52.

35. Ibid., 8. In making his remarks about the need for unanimity and sacrifice, Gibbes
    no doubt was referring to the association's secretary-treasurer, Nathan S. Morse,
    editor of the *Augusta Chronicle & Sentinel.* Morse had become an outspoken
    critic of the Davis administration and a supporter of the peace movement. See
    Ford Risley, "Nathan S. Morse: Georgia's Controversial Civil War Editor," *Geor-
    gia Historical Quarterly* 83 (1999), 221–241.

36. *Minutes of the Board of Directors of the Press Association, Embracing the Quarterly Reports of the Superintendent* (Atlanta: Franklin Steam Publishing House, 1864), 24.

37. *First Annual Meeting of the Press Association* (Montgomery: Memphis Appeal Job Printing, 1864), 30–31.

38. Andrews, *The South Reports*, 439.

39. *Charleston Courier*, 27 May 1864; *Atlanta Southern Confederacy*, reprinted in *Augusta Chronicle & Sentinel*, 28 May 1864.

40. *Augusta Chronicle & Sentinel*, 12 July 1864.

41. Ibid., 10 August 1864.

42. Ibid., 6 September 1864.

43. *Augusta Chronicle & Sentinel*, 12 October 1864.

44. Frequently, PA stories taken from Northern papers carried headlines such as "News from Yankee Land" and "Yankee Idea of Things"; *Augusta Chronicle & Sentinel*, 19 November 1864.

45. *Richmond Dispatch*, 20 October 1864.

46. Writing to Vice President Alexander Stephens early in 1864, Atlanta editor J. Henley Smith noted, "I am astonished at the Richmond Press. They regard themselves as metropolitan, and ignore anything from any other quarter of the Confederacy. They have all the while been an impediment in the proper working [of] the Press Association." Alexander H. Stephens Papers, Library of Congress.

47. *Macon Telegraph & Confederate*, 27 October 1864.

48. So little telegraphic news was getting through to the press, in fact, that a Virginia newspaper published a rhyme copied by other Confederate papers: "The wires that once through Dixie's land / The 'notes' of 'press' men spread / Now on their posts as mutely stand / As if the Press was dead." *Atlanta Southern Confederacy*, 7 February 1865.

49. See, for example, *Augusta Chronicle & Sentinel*, 29 January 1865.

50. Ibid., 21 March 1865.

51. Ibid.

52. For unknown reasons, the account of Richmond's evacuation was not published in the *Augusta Chronicle & Sentinel* until April 6.

53. *Augusta Chronicle & Sentinel*, 11 April 1865.

54. Ibid., 21 April 1865. There is no record of the Press Association's annual meeting, scheduled for April in Augusta, ever taking place. Likewise, there is also no record of the superintendent's quarterly report for 1865 being compiled.

55. The *Richmond Whig*, for example, suspended publishing from April 1 to December 9. When it resumed operations, the paper was again subscribing to the Associated Press. During the postwar fragmentation that plagued the Associated Press, the Southern Associated Press was reorganized in 1866 as a branch of the New York AP. Growing conflicts among regional APs led the Southern Associated Press to incorporate in 1892. Richard A. Schwarzlose, *The Nation's Newsbrokers,* vol. 2 (Evanston, Ill.: Northwestern University Press, 1990), 36.

THE PRESS UNDER PRESSURE

Georgia Newspapers and the Civil War

— CALVIN M. LOGUE, EUGENE MILLER,
AND CHRISTOPHER J. SCHROLL —

The press contributed vitally to the South's Civil War effort by mobilizing support for the war and by informing citizens and soldiers about its progress. It performed both tasks diligently, even when facts were hard to obtain and difficult to reconcile with editorial assurances of ultimate victory. Many southern newspapers were driven out of business by the hardships of war, but others were highly resourceful in devising ways to keep their news-gathering operations alive. The press in Georgia faced particularly daunting problems in the latter years of the war. By 1864, Georgia had become the scene of heavy fighting that was crucial to the war's outcome. In that year, Union Major General William Tecumseh Sherman marched on General Joseph E. Johnston's Army of Tennessee in northern Georgia, bent on destroying the regional resources needed to sustain the South's war effort and demoralizing the enemy.[1] As Sherman advanced, Georgia's press made every effort to promote civil and military resistance to the northern troops. Outnumbered approximately 107,000 to 71,000, Johnston employed a defensive strategy,[2] delaying Sherman's capture of Atlanta until September and enabling the state's newspapers to mount an attack upon Yankee depredations and exaggerate Confederate successes.[3]

    Bad weather, sickness, and broken machinery could interfere with newspapers' business operations at any time, and southern editors often experienced financial problems prior to 1861.[4] Nevertheless, the war greatly intensified long-standing difficulties and brought new problems of its own, including dislocations caused by advancing armies,[5] disruptions of communication and transportation facilities, shortages of necessary supplies, and soaring costs. Deliveries of all kinds were disrupted by the war. The destruction of bridges and railroad tracks interrupted the delivery of mail. When mail did arrive, it accumulated at depots, straining the ability of the post offices to handle it.[6]

As fighting shifted from one setting to another, even the locale of publication, ownership, and personnel of newspapers could change with little public warning. When Sherman threatened Atlanta, editors moved their offices southward to safer ground. By early July 1864, journalists from several Atlanta papers were preparing to evacuate the city. The *Atlanta Intelligencer* set up its operations in a boxcar that could be quickly relocated.[7] Finally, only the *Atlanta Appeal* submitted reports on the course of the battle for Atlanta. For a time, it was difficult to know whether northern sympathizers or loyal southerners published the *Macon Daily Telegraph and Confederate*.[8] Editors sometimes tried to capitalize on these hardships in courting new subscribers. For example, Jared Irwin Whitaker, proprietor of the *Atlanta Daily Intelligencer*, although "driven from Atlanta by the advance of Sherman's hosts," persisted in "contend[ing] for the 'Lost Cause' at a pecuniary sacrifice. . . . Send up your subscriptions."[9]

Although the fighting increased southerners' demand for news, owners had great difficulty publishing newspapers profitably.[10] The war caused severe shortages of materials and personnel required to maintain operations.[11] Even when supplies were available, they were of poor quality. Editors complained in particular of the poor quality of paper.[12] The *Augusta Chronicle* had to use unreliable printing ink.[13] Owners constantly sought to purchase necessary products, such as ink, type, and cordwood, and struggled to keep worn-out presses and typographical machines running.[14]

Keeping reliable workers at an affordable wage was also a problem, and newspaper owners continually advertised for personnel replacements. Most able bodied men were in the army.[15] Within the first two years of the fighting, 18 printers from the *Macon Daily Telegraph* "had enlisted" in the military.[16] By 1864, at least 75 percent of printers working in the South in 1863 had been or were in the army. Help-wanted ads called not only for pressmen, printers, and compositors, but also for blacks, who were excluded by law from typesetting, to work as porters and delivery men.[17] Belying what were likely the paper's own racial stereotypes, the editor and proprietor of the *Atlanta Southern Confederacy* advertised for "an intelligent, smart, reliable . . . negro" man to work "till next Christmas." To guard against any alien philosophy corrupting the paper's Confederate bias, the ad required that even this temporary employee had to be "Georgia-raised."[18]

As the war progressed, hiring and retaining reliable delivery persons became difficult. To assure anxious subscribers of reliable distribution, publishers advertised their extra efforts to deliver newspapers or to make them available at press offices. The owner of the *Atlanta Southern Confederacy* described for city subscribers and military personnel the improved arrangements for distribution he had negotiated. Any buyer from "residence, office, shop or camp" not receiving an "early morning" paper should "call at our office and leave written directions for finding their residences."[19] Within one month, however, the *Southern Confederacy*'s carrier arrangements apparently had been transferred to two black residents of Atlanta. Readers were assured that delivery of the newspaper was "now so perfected by 'Uncle Jesse' and 'John Wesley' that every residence, office, and shop in the city can get the *Confederacy* in good time every morning."[20]

Although the Confederate government granted special postage rates to newspapers and permitted copies to be mailed to soldiers free of charge, the cost of producing a newspaper increased dramatically during the war years as a result of severe shortages and rapid price inflation. For example, the owner of Macon's *Georgia Journal and Messenger* explained to his readers that whereas subscription rates had doubled, the price of paper had increased fifteenfold: "We cannot afford a larger sheet when we have only increased our rates from two dollars and fifty cents to five, while the quantity of paper for which we paid three fifty, we now pay fifty five dollars."[21] When workmen in the typographical association increased their rates by 50 percent, the owner of the *Georgia Journal and Messenger* agreed to suspend publication till other arrangements could be made.

Printers and pressmen, however, had a strong incentive to continue working, even at lagging wages, because editors and other newspaper employees, along with ministers and government employees, were exempt from military service, an exemption that no longer applied to striking workmen in the typographical association.[22] Reporting that the strikers had been enrolled by the conscript officers, the *Georgia Journal and Messenger* warned that "they will probably find some difference between the [military] pay of eleven dollars per month, and the exorbitant prices they had been receiving, as well as in the comforts and commissariat [food supplies] of their new vocation."[23]

In order to remain solvent, newspaper owners were required to supplement their incomes, cut publishing costs, and increase the price of subscriptions. In addition to selling advertisements, owners typically offered a variety of printing services and products. Moreover, they used every possible means to reduce the cost of printing their papers, including reductions in length and content.[24] As shortages and rising costs forced them to cut the length of their newspapers, often to a single sheet, editors faced the dilemma of whether to reduce advertising or news coverage. In explaining this choice to his readers, the owner of the *Georgia Journal and Messenger* pledged that he and other owners were willing to sacrifice advertising income rather than reduce their coverage of the war: "We shall endeavor to give the same amount of reading matter as heretofore, by dropping most of our advertisements and using a smaller type."[25]

Despite the tremendous increases in their own costs, newspaper owners were hard-pressed to justify even modest increases in subscription prices because their readers complained that newspapers were a necessity for obtaining information about loved ones fighting for the Confederacy and about the war effort generally. Thus newspaper owners frequently chided suppliers for raising their prices and pleaded with readers to understand why the cost of subscriptions would also have to rise. To justify the decision by "the weekly papers" of Georgia to "demand $4 per year" after June 1, 1863, the editor of the *Athens Southern Watchman* reprimanded producers generally for "selling *their* products at such extravagant prices." To defend the increase in subscription costs, this editor gave his readers an elementary lesson in price inflation and relative monetary values, drawing his comparisons from their own work experiences: "When we published our paper at $2, we could buy four bushels of corn for that amount. Our paper was therefore worth four bushels of corn. Four bushels of corn is now worth $12 in this market; and further up the country $20. Our paper is therefore worth $12 by the corn standard." "To bring newspapers to a level with everything else," he concluded, would fix their price at from $12 to $20 per year.[26]

Angered by "many farmers complain[ing] of the high prices of newspapers," the publisher of Macon's *Georgia Journal and Messenger* insisted that "the press certainly could claim to have acted with greater liberality, in regard to its charges, than any other class of the community."[27] A year later, at the war's end, this same publisher was still trying to justify increased subscription prices.[28] In another editorial, after noting that he too had shared in the sacrifices that the war had imposed upon his readers, the editor voiced exasperation with the "large number" who "have paid us in what is not, just now palatable—promises. It is very easy for them to send us flour, meat, butter, eggs, or any thing eatable. If those who are receiving our paper, and whose time is out, do not, within a few days we shall be compelled to discontinue their papers.[29] The next month, his patience finally exhausted, the publisher berated subscribers for their indolence: "We shall *most positively*, on and after next Saturday, stop sending our paper to all those who are, at that time, *in arrears with us*. Our expenses are, necessarily, cash, and we must exact cash from them."[30]

As fighting throughout the South disrupted established channels of communication, editors struggled to satisfy their readers' insatiable appetite for timely information about results of particular battles and the well-being of their loved ones or neighbors. To assuage readers eager for any scrap of news about the fighting, editors routinely explained that they lacked reliable details from the front. "For several days we have had no information of any particular movements, either in advance or otherwise," a Macon editor noted.[31] He admitted that his "information" from north Georgia "is not very definite or reliable, but from what we learn probably Atlanta is now being evacuated by Sherman's army—leaving it the tattered fragments and remains of what Atlanta has been."[32] Upon publishing news of coastal fighting, the Macon editor learned early in the war that information received from persons who appeared to be reliable, and in a position to observe what they reported firsthand, was not always dependable: "The favorable reports which reached us yesterday morning from those who watched the contest between the enemy's batteries and our garrison in Fort Pulaski, had not prepared us for the startling intelligence of the surrender of the Fort, which reached us [by courier] about ten o'clock last night."[33]

Although reliable news was in short supply, rumor, conjecture, and opinion were plentiful. Rumors flew in southern communities as fast as bullets. One could not easily differentiate fact from fiction because, as an editor explained, although stories forged in the heat of battle could be false, their general notoriety became a source of belief. For example, after a unit of Sherman's army tested Macon's fortifications, a thousand stories were told of what they stole and burned and how they might have been better repelled. Keenly aware that, for many lay readers, claims were synonymous with truth and legend with reality, a journalist advised readers not to rely upon word of mouth because "a verbal account" could not "cross the street and return in the shape in which it started."[34] One war correspondent noted a reason for the conflicting accounts sent home from the battlefront. A "greasy private" or an officer in battle, he said, saw only what happened in his immediate front. For a fuller picture, one must read newspaper reports, but even these were "sometimes inaccurate."[35]

Georgia editors sought information from diverse sources. Editors avidly read each other's newspapers, and when they could not obtain them by traditional means, they sought copies through private channels. Faced with an extraordinary burden of weighing—and deciding whether and how to pass on information given to them by a wide range of sources—editors processed information about whose reliability they were uncertain in three main ways. First, they might simply refuse to print it. One editor, in attempting to decipher what actually had occurred at "Missionary Ridge and Knoxville" from "sensational reports" brought by train, decided: "We hear so many conflicting reports from [Lieutenant General James] Longstreet that we dare not publish any, as we desire to make these 'front' articles as correct as possible."[36]

A second way of dealing with uncertain information was to print what was received without any speculation or disclaimers as to its possible unreliability.[37] Editors were particularly uncritical of reports that were linked, however tenuously, to authoritative witnesses. Readers of the following account in the Atlanta Confederacy likely assumed that General Johnston's troops would soon run Sherman's invaders back into Tennessee:

> We have before us a letter from one of the highest official sources in the Army of Tennessee, from which we extract the following: "We are in superb spirits. The Yankees have got to fight for Atlanta, and when they do fight, we are certain to whip them [as] decisively as the sun is certain to rise on that day."[38]

Sometimes editors would conjecture confidently about the latest news from the front, even while warning against conjecture: "To speculate editorially is wholly useless, and may tend to deceive our readers. We can, however, say this, most unmistakably—that the enemy are evidently foiled and severely disappointed."[39] An impatient Augusta editor went so far as to defend the publication of news items that might turn out to be false. Even "lies are better than nothing," he suggested; "we at least know, that men are alive when they lie vigorously."[40]

A third and more common way that editors dealt with uncertainty was to print the information at hand but to warn readers that it might be unreliable or even try to help them sort out facts from improbable reports and martial hyperbole. In an article headlined "Raids and Rumors," an editor endeavored to pin down the facts amid the conflicting claims given to him: "For the last few days we had more rumors than any one man or woman could believe and most of them 'reliable' and 'unquestionable.'"[41] Another editor reported how refugees from towns overrun by Federals claimed that the enemy had lost 2,000 killed and wounded but cautioned readers not to consider that hearsay a fact.[42] The Macon editor advised readers to be judicious when interpreting daily reports, only, in the end, to ignore his own counsel:

> With regard to the many telegraphic dispatches we cannot vouch for the correctness of all. The reader must have patience and await results before

coming to decided conclusions, on the awful struggle now going on. Our hopes have not diminished of a final and over-whelming success, and that we shall be able to chronicle it in the next issue.[43]

Editors pointed with pride to steps that permitted them to receive reports directly from war correspondents in the field.[44] The owner of Atlanta's *Southern Confederacy* boasted that "arrangements have been completed which will enable us to receive the latest and most reliable intelligence from every point of interest."[45] When possible, these reporters traveled with the troops and became familiar with the rigors of military life. Aware of the unreliability of the ordinary mails, some particularly conscientious correspondents forwarded letters by courier or carried their own reports to a major city for distribution.[46]

To add an air of authenticity and intrigue as well as to protect the reporter, the war correspondents' reports were often published under pseudonyms, aliases, or code names.[47] Thus one editor boasted of how an "Army Correspondence" had been received "By Private Express from the battlefield," providing the "latest telegraphic news from our special correspondent '290' [Samuel Chester Reid Jr.] from the front, in advance of all other press reports."[48] In some instances, correspondents painted for the reader an astonishingly vivid and detailed word-picture that engages all the senses and evokes a sense of horror at the war's destructiveness. From reports such as the following by "PERSONNE" (Felix Gregory de Fontaine)[49] after the Battle of Shiloh, one can see why officials would be concerned about the impact of battlefront reporting on civilian and military morale:

> The wounded still continue to come in, and the houses in Corinth [Tennessee] are rapidly filling up. The hotel has been turned into a hospital, and five hundred men are already here covering the floors. While I write I am sitting on the floor of one of the corridors, with the bodies of the living and the dead ranged on either side and opposite as far as the eye can reach. Groans fill the air, surgeons are busy at work by candle-light, a few women are ministering to the wants of the suffering, the atmosphere is fetid with the stench of wounds, and the rain is pouring down upon thousands who yet lie out upon the bloody ground of Shiloh.[50]

To cope more effectively with wartime difficulties, newspaper owners and editors united professionally.[51] After a March 1862 meeting in Atlanta to discuss mounting costs, disruption in the flow of telegraphic news, and military restrictions, newspaper representatives from Georgia and elsewhere in the South met the following February in Augusta and formed a new Press Association.[52]

J.S. Thrasher, the association's superintendent, emphasized that the southern press had voluntarily subjected itself to rules and regulations for the common good. As the 1864 convention of the Press Association approached, some editors increasingly viewed the association's primary role as one of asserting leadership in shaping policy and in forming public opinion around some plan for peace. This "reunion of talent would be equal to a convocation of Generals," predicted the *Atlanta Southern Confederacy*: "we are of those who believe that the pen has not lost its magic because of the prominence of the sword, and rely upon it as one of the chief influences which will bring us peace."[53]

Wartime impediments to the gathering and reporting of news arose not only from economic constraints and the physical disruption of communication channels but also from censorship. One editor reported that a Confederate official had walked unannounced into the office of the *Augusta Register* and recorded the military status of the persons working there.[54] Correspondents on whom editors depended for news often found military officers uncooperative or hostile.[55] Because correspondents at the front lines depended upon the army for support, short of banning reporters from following the troops and entering encampments, military officials could stifle the press simply by withholding food, horses, and other supplies from them.[56]

Elected officials and military officers in the Confederacy pressured editors not to publish details about the war effort that might endanger soldiers. No doubt they would have disapproved of reports such as the one in the *Macon Daily Telegraph and Confederate* describing how the "enemy's shells coming over our lines of battle fall far in the rear close to the colored cooking squadrons."[57] Leaders also discouraged press criticism that could lower military and civilian morale. Examples here might be complaints in the *Augusta Constitutionalist* and the *Savannah Republican* about the "vice of intemperance which now prevails largely in portions of our army"[58] or the *Macon Journal and Messenger*'s criticism of the government's "conscription and impressment" practices.[59]

Editors could be maligned, boycotted, and even subjected to physical harm by their readers for publishing items that were perceived to be unpatriotic. One victim of such retribution was J.C. Swayze, editor of the *Bugle Horn of Liberty*, a pictorial monthly published in Griffin. In the autumn of 1863, editor Swayze published a satire that, he later explained, was meant as "a burlesque on slender efforts of other journals to present tasteful illustrations of passing events." Unfortunately for him, Swayze chose as the object of his satire not a Yankee general but the heroic Confederate cavalry officer John Hunt Morgan. Incensed by this satire, as well as by an article relating to the impressment of private houses in Griffin for medical uses, a group of about 100 convalescing soldiers who were mostly from Morgan's home territory of Kentucky and Tennessee chased Swayze down, mounted him on a sharp-edged rail, and transported him through the streets of Griffin, followed by "a procession of at least a thousand" who were "laughing and expressing their merriment and perfect approbation in various ways." Although rescued from a coat of tar and feathers by military surgeons, Swayze was compelled "to give repeated 'three cheers for John Morgan and the Surgeons in Griffin' waving his hat over his head as he did."[60]

As if tracking a deadly tornado winding through Georgia, journalists followed Sherman's army as it moved relentlessly from the Tennessee border to Atlanta and beyond, leaving devastation in its wake. They reported the "enemy . . . concentrating heavily at Ringgold" and "gradually advancing."[61] There was general alarm at Acworth. The enemy was now fording the river near Roswell and approaching Marietta.[62] "The ground is caving in."[63] Atlanta residents are "removing their goods."[64] Near Macon, "everything has been swept as with a storm of fire. . . . The whole country around is one wide waste of destruction."[65] To improve their newspapers' credibility in the face of swirling rumors, inaccurate accounts, and fantasies about what Yankees and Rebels were achieving on the battlefield, editors probed for reliable information, formed a press association, hired correspondents in hopes of receiving more trustworthy firsthand reports, and attempted to establish reliable lines of communication. At times, faced with a deadline and agitated readers, they carried dubious stories without comment or knowingly printed materials whose accuracy could not be corroborated or corrected for several days. More customarily, however, editors printed the most reliable information they could find, accompanied by cautions, qualifications, and admonitions that readers purchase tomorrow's paper for further details. Behind their reporting even of defeats and failures was an unswerving allegiance to the Confederate cause.

NOTES

This article was previously published as "The Press under Pressure: How Georgia's Newspapers Responded to Civil War Constraints," *American Journalism* 15 (Winter 1998): 13–34.

1. James M. McPherson, *Battle Cry of Freedom: The Civil War Era* (New York: Oxford University Press, 1988), 721–722.

2. Ibid., 743–744.

3. See Cal M. Logue, "The Rhetorical Complicity Indigenous to Winning the North Georgia Campaign," *Communication Studies* 43 (1992), 124–131; Logue, "Coping with Defeat Rhetorically: Sherman's March through Georgia," *Southern Communication Journal* 58 (1992), 55–66.

4. Hodding Carter, *Their Words Were Bullets: The Southern Press in War, Reconstruction, and Peace* (Athens: University of Georgia Press, 1969), 9; Carl R. Osthaus, *Partisans of the Southern Press: Editorial Spokesmen of the Nineteenth Century* (Lexington: University Press of Kentucky, 1994), 10, 13.

5. The *Columbus Daily-Sun* reported that northern troops made a special effort to destroy daily newspapers because of their greater potential to bolster civilian and military morale, 21 March 1865, 14 April 1865.

6. On January 18, 1863, A.G. Ware, agent for the Macon & Western Railroad in Atlanta, gave this "fair notice": "I am authorized by the . . . Superintendent of this Road . . . to notify Consignees . . . that after the expiration of five days . . . NO FREIGHT of any kind, will be received . . . for SHIPMENT TO ATLANTA, until . . . cars here have been emptied"; *Atlanta Confederacy,* 20 January 1863; see also Louis Turner Griffith and John Erwin Talmadge, *Georgia Journalism: 1763–1950* (Athens: University of Georgia Press, 1951), 72; Rabun Lee Brantley, *Georgia Journalism of the Civil War Period* (Nashville: George Peabody School for Teachers, 1929), 87–92; Cedric Okell Reynolds, "The Postal System of the Southern Confederacy," *West Virginia History* 12 (1951): 200–279.

7. Brantley, 28. The record for changing locations by rail no doubt belonged to the *Memphis Appeal,* whose press and type were removed from the city on a flatcar shortly before Memphis was captured in June 1862. Its editor and staff evaded capture for almost three years until April 1865, by which time "the *Appeal* had been published in ten towns and four states," including more than a year in Atlanta. Its nickname was "the moving *Appeal.*"

8. When Macon was threatened a second time, early reports indicated that Union officials were now publishing this newspaper under a new title, the *Daily News.* Later, the paper's original personnel insisted that they had not lost control. *Augusta Chronicle,* quoted in the Macon *Daily Evening News,* 4 May 1865.

9. *Atlanta Daily Intelligencer,* 23 July 1864.

10. Discouraged by a lack of supplies and services, editors of many smaller papers in Georgia ceased publishing. Griffith and Talmadge, 67. Brantley calculates that of 111 newspapers and periodicals published in Georgia during the period 1860–1865, 59 "were forced to suspend finally during the Civil War," Brantley, 128.

11. In short supply were newsprint, ink, and labor. Osthaus, 41–42, 103–104.

12. *South Carolinian,* quoted in *Macon Telegraph and Confederate,* 13 August 1864, 19 October 1864.

13. Earl L. Bell and Kenneth C. Crabbe, *The Augusta Chronicle: Indomitable Voice of Dixie, 1875–1960* (Athens: University of Georgia Press, 1960), 60.

14. At the beginning of the war, there were 15 paper mills in the seceding states, which supplied only half the amount of newsprint required to satisfy the South's newspaper consumption. With the destruction of the largest paper mills in Augusta in 1863 and Bath, South Carolina, Georgia newspapers were forced to depend upon blockade-run paper hauled in wagons over the mountains. Ruby Florence Tucker, "The Press Association of the Confederate States of America in Georgia" (master's thesis, University of Georgia, 1950), 58, 82.

15. The Confederacy approved the exemption from conscription of one editor of each newspaper now being published, and such employees as the editor or proprietor might certify, upon oath, to be indispensable for conducting the publication. Steven A. Smith, "Freedom of Expression in the Confederate States of America," in *Free Speech Yearbook,* ed. Gregg Phifer, 17–37 (Falls Church, Virginia: Speech Communication Association, 1978), 20.

16. Griffith and Talmadge, 72.

17. A Georgia law enacted in 1829 had stated that "no slave or free person of colour shall be employed in the setting of types." An editor found guilty "shall forfeit the sum of ten dollars for every slave or free person of colour who may be so employed on any day or part of a day." State of Georgia, *Acts of the General Assembly of the State of Georgia* (Milledgeville: Camak and Ragland Printers, 1830), 175.

18. *Atlanta Confederacy*, 10 January 1863.

19. Ibid., 9 January 1863.

20. Ibid., 5 February 1863.

21. *Georgia Journal and Messenger*, 4 February 1864.

22. When Atlanta printers went on strike in the spring of 1864, publishers threatened to have them drafted; however, military authorities pointed out that if there were no printers, there could be no papers, and the publishers and editors were equally liable for conscription. Henry T. Malone, "Atlanta Journalism during the Confederacy," *Georgia Historical Quarterly* 37 (1953): 217–218.

23. *Georgia Journal and Messenger*, 13 April 1864.

24. Before the war, most daily newspapers ran to four pages; in 1862 they published on half (single) sheets. J. Cutler Andrews, *The South Reports the Civil War* (Princeton: Princeton University Press, 1970), 25–26, 42.

25. *Georgia Journal and Messenger*, 24 February 1864.

26. *Athens Southern Watchman*, quoted in *Georgia Journal and Messenger*, 17 June 1863.

27. *Georgia Journal and Messenger*, 25 May 1864.

28. Ibid., 4 April 1865.

29. Ibid., 31 May 1865.

30. Ibid., 30 June 1865.

31. Ibid., 16 July 1862.

32. Ibid., 16 November 1864.

33. Ibid., 16 April 1862. Eliza Frances Andrews writes in her journal of inviting Jim Chiles to dinner because he had as "much news to tell . . . as the county paper," and it was "more reliable"; *The War-Time Journal of a Georgia Girl* (Macon: Ardivan Press, 1960), 84.

34. *Macon Telegraph*, 17 May 1864.

35. Ibid., 10 June 1864, 24 June 1864.

36. Ibid., 25 November 1863.

37. Inaccurate accounts were sometimes followed by corrections, as in this case: "In our notice of the shooting of Henry Pagnoncelli . . . by Joseph Ryan . . . several errors occurred. We gave the information then as we received it, supposing it to be correct. We learn from Mr. Ryan himself that he is not absent from his command without leave, as was reported to us. . . . Every body . . . whom we have heard . . . approves of Mr. Ryan's conduct in this case. He has not been arrested . . . as previously reported." *Atlanta Confederacy*, 15 January 1863.

38. Ibid., 29 June 1864.

39. *Georgia Journal* and *Messenger*, 1 June 1864.

40. *Augusta Chronicle and Sentinel*, quoted in *Georgia Journal* and *Messenger*, 4 June 1862. Editors might assist the military by printing false information in journals

that were permitted to fall into Union hands. Quintus Charles Wilson, "A Study and Evaluation of the Military Censorship in the Civil War" (master's thesis, University of Minnesota, 1945), 261; see also Robert Freeman Smith, "John R. Eakin: Confederate Propagandist," *Arkansas Historical Quarterly* 12 (1953): 16–26.

41. *Georgia Journal and Messenger*, 27 July 1864.

42. *Macon Telegraph*, 28 May 1864.

43. Ibid., 17 June 1863.

44. Griffith and Talmadge, 67.

45. *Atlanta Confederacy*, 14 December 1864.

46. *Macon Telegraph*, 31 May 1864; Andrews, 435.

47. Through assiduous research, Andrews established the identity of many volunteer soldier correspondents, editorial correspondents in the field who published under pseudonyms, including that of "290" (Samuel Chester Reid Jr.). Andrews, 548–551. We use Andrews's identifying references in our essay.

48. "In another column," the editor continued, "we publish a most interesting general description of the great battle of Chickamauga, from the graphic pen of our talented correspondent '290'"; see also Andrews, 550.

49. Andrews, 50–51, 548–549.

50. *Charleston Courier*, quoted in *Georgia Journal and Messenger*, 23 April 1862.

51. Representatives from Charleston, Memphis, Knoxville, and New Orleans, as well as from the Georgia cities of Savannah, Columbus, Augusta, Macon, and Atlanta, convened in Atlanta. *Journal* and *Messenger*, 19 March 1862. See Tucker, "Press Association," 3–56; E. Merton Coulter, *The Confederate States of America, 1861–1865*, A History of the South Series, vol. 7 (Athens: University of Georgia Press, 1950), 497; Brantley, *Georgia Journalism*, 91–93; Griffith and Talmadge, *Georgia Journalism*, 72–75; F.N. Boney, "War and Defeat," in Kenneth Coleman, ed., *A History of Georgia* (Athens: University of Georgia Press, 1977), 196; Quintus C. Wilson, "Confederate Press Association," *Journalism Quarterly* 26 (June, 1949): 160–166.

52. *Atlanta Confederacy*, 10 February 1863; for notices of the meeting see ibid., 3 January 1863, 5 February 1863.

53. Ibid., 2 March 1864.

54. *Augusta Constitutionalist*, quoted in *Macon Telegraph*, 6 October 1864.

55. Some military officers placed their encampments off-limits to reporters, refused interviews, and found other ways to discourage newspaper coverage; see Andrews, 81, 60–61, 103, 360–361, 429, 433, 436; Tucker, 64; Carter, 298; and Griffith and Talmadge, 75.

56. A Richmond editor explained how "the collection of news in a great army is very laborious, for the lines are often ten or fifteen miles long. A horse, therefore, is indispensable. But food for horse and rider is notoriously impossible of attainment near a great army, except from its stores. As the request of the Press Agents is so narrow in its application, and as a public wish otherwise unattainable is thereby to be facilitated and promoted, we sincerely hope Congress will not refuse its consent." *Richmond Sentinel*, quoted in *Atlanta Confederacy*, 16 June 1864.

57. *Macon Telegraph and Confederate*, 23 November 1864.

58. *Macon Journal and Messenger*, 29 January 1862.

59. Ibid., 15 February 1865.

60. *Atlanta Intelligencer*, 15 October 1863; see also William F. Thompson, *The Image of War: Pictorial Reporting of the American Civil War* (Baton Rouge: Louisiana State University Press, 1994); Osthaus, 108–109.

61. *Atlanta Reveille*, 29 April 1964.

62. *Macon Telegraph*, 23 May 1864, 25 May 1864.

63. Ibid., 29 June 1864.

64. *Macon Republican*, quoted in *Macon Telegraph*, 13 July 1864.

65. *Columbus Daily Times*, 30 November 1864, quoted in T. Conn Bryan, *Confederate Georgia* (Athens: University of Georgia Press, 1953), 169.

"ANOTHER COPPERHEAD LIE"

Marcellus Emery and the *Bangor Union* and *Democrat*

— CROMPTON BURTON —

Mount Hope Cemetery in Bangor, Maine, is a serene resting place for men who left their mark on the state's Civil War experience. Hannibal Hamlin, vice president during Abraham Lincoln's first term, is buried there. So is Colonel Charles Roberts, hero of the Second Maine Regiment. Not far away rests Marcellus Emery. A newspaper editor in Bangor during the conflict, Emery enjoys far less recognition or reputation than his distinguished neighbors. Although he may repose for eternity in the proximity of the state's great men, his place in history is considerably more obscure. Historical narratives have relegated him to a mere footnote, his personal ordeal in pursuit of free speech during the war largely—and unfairly—unremembered.

Born in Frankfort, Maine, in 1830, Emery prepared for college at Yarmouth Academy and entered Bowdoin College in 1849. Although somewhat reserved in his demeanor, he was an energetic student, and upon graduation he accepted a position as a teacher at Hallowell High School. Before the year was out, Emery resigned and accepted a post as a private tutor in Mississippi, later going on to work in a law office in Evansville, Indiana. Returning to Maine in 1857, Emery passed the bar exam and entered into a law partnership. Later that same year, he joined with other leading Democrats in Penobscot County to purchase the *Bangor Daily Journal* and *Bangor Weekly Democrat*. Appointed editor of both journals, Emery changed the name of the daily to the *Union* and managed the two newspapers until the summer of 1861.[1]

By the time Fort Sumter was fired upon in April 1861, Emery had already been editing his weekly and daily newspapers for almost four years, and his support of southern interests and sensibilities was widely known and disdained by his competition and their readers. Samples of these portrayals survive from the spring of 1861 in the columns of the *Daily Whig and Courier*. According to one issue:

> It [the *Union*] whines about the stupendous danger to "our liberties" which will arise from the exercise of power now displayed by the Executive, and would have the people believe that great outrages have been committed upon our "constitutional liberties" in the vigorous measures which have been taken to crush the vipers who are endeavoring to sting the life out of the Republic.[2]

Emery's passionate rhetoric prompted the files of the *Union* to be pitched from the Mercantile Association reading room that same month. The association, founded in 1844 to establish a library, hold lectures, and foster an atmosphere of inquiry for its member firms and individuals, was strong in its condemnation of the *Union*'s political tilt, which it said had "justly brought upon itself and its supporter the contempt and detestation of all honorable men by its bold and unblushing advocacy of the causes of secession and rebellion and its violent denunciation of the Government." The pro-Union *Jeffersonian* joined the fray, querying, "Is there any punishment too severe for Northern traitors?" Another newspaper maligned Emery as standing "heart and soul with the traitors," while still another advocated abandoning such laws as would protect such "disloyal" newspapers as the *Union* and the *Democrat*.[3]

Under siege from his competition, Emery finally admitted defeat and suspended publication of the *Union* on June 1 for want of advertising and business support. William Wheeler and the *Whig* were quick to place a proadministration perspective on the folding of the journal:

> The business men of the city have simply done their duty in refusing to aid in sustaining a traitorous organ in our city, and have taken precisely the right course to suppress it. If the Union had acted a loyal and manly part, and stood by the country, instead of taking part with the traitors, it would have received its share of support.[4]

Later, in that same edition of the *Whig*, it is possible to sample in detail the true nature and impact of Emery's copy. Prefacing a glimpse of the surviving *Democrat*'s content, Wheeler chided:

Not many of our readers ever see the Democrat, and we will, therefore, give an extract, showing its present tone: "But it is now plain to the people that Lincoln and Seward have been plotting a scheme from the very beginning to raise a large standing army wherewith to subjugate the South, and then to change our Government into some kind of a despotism."[5]

Quick to make certain that his presentation of copy from the *Democrat* would not be mistaken for an endorsement, Wheeler further admonished his readers:

No man who wishes to be regarded as a loyal citizen, ought to allow his name to continue in the advertising columns of the Democrat, or suffer the paper to be seen on his premises. The determined disloyalty of that sheet, and the utter recklessness of its course, justifies us in recommending all proper and peaceable measures for its suppression.[6]

Emery did enjoy some support for his views, albeit far from Bangor. The practice of borrowing or clipping articles from other newspapers to fill out sparse columns was as old as the first journal in the American colonies. The custom had evolved into an extensive system of exchanges by the time of the Civil War, accounting for wider exposure of Emery's editorials. The *Arkansas Weekly Courier* presented a Confederate view of his struggle:

We clip a few noble extracts from several Northern papers, to show how fearlessly some of our gallant contemporaries brave the felon's halter, to speak out their condemnation, in unmeasured bitterness against the damnable usurpations of Abe Lincoln and his cowardly abettors, in their attempt to manacle the proud limbs of Southern freemen. Far up in frigid Maine the editor of the Bangor Democrat thus fearlessly talks to the infuriated brutes around him.[7]

On July 21, 1861, Confederate forces routed the Union army of Brigadier General Irvin McDowell, sending Federal troops reeling back to Washington from nearby Bull Run Creek. Whereas the war's opening campaign ignited southern confidence, the immediate aftermath of the battle produced nothing short of panic in northern supporters. Horace Greeley, influential publisher of the *New York Tribune*, dropped the paper's bellicose banner, "Forward to Richmond!" from the masthead and penned a despairing letter to President Abraham Lincoln. "On every brow sits sullen, scorching, black despair," Greeley wrote. "If it is best that we make peace with the rebels at once and on their own terms, do not shrink even from that."[8]

Against this backdrop of shock and uncertainty, Emery issued the opposition viewpoint in a strong and relentless measure. The July 30 issue of the *Democrat* was emblazoned with such headlines as "Total defeat and route [sic] of the Federal Army," and "President Davis's account of the great battle." The journal's articles were neither shy nor timid in their southern sympathy, asking, "But alas! What was their errand? Could the God of our Fathers smile on their mission of subjugation and death?" Emery continued:

> Onward the shouting myriads will pour, until again met by the un-equalled and invincible genius of Davis, Beauregard, Johnston and Lee, and the iron nerves of these noble men, who are defending their fire-sides and their homes, from the ruthless assaults of fanaticism and fury. Victory may again perch upon their banners for a short time, but long ere they will have reached Richmond, disaster will again have overtaken them, and, defeated and routed they will once more fly back to the Po-tomac in wild confusion, leaving the battle-field, and the wayside stained with the blood of thousands.[9]

Contemporary accounts of unfolding events in Bangor over the next two weeks survive with a decidedly Unionist slant. James B. Vickery describes Emery's growing anxiety in his *Illustrated History of the City of Bangor, Maine* and portrays Mayor Charles Stetson as a man powerless to protect the *Democrat*'s editor in the face of growing public outcry: "the embattled Mayor made no promises. How could he assign men to guard a man so universally hated as Emery? The answer was he could not—and he did not."[10] Stetson was unwilling to remind local Unionists that Emery, like Wheeler, was permitted his forum, even for dissent, under provisions of the Maine Constitution providing "that every citizen may freely speak, write and publish his sentiments on any subject, being responsible for the abuse of this liberty. No laws shall be passed regulating or restraining the freedom of the Press."[11]

Joseph Griffin's *History of the Press in Maine* adds to the weight of pro-administration interpretation of those unsettled days in Bangor, absolving Stetson of any responsibility for what was soon to take place, observing:

> No vigilance of his could provide against the cool determination of a community that felt itself outraged by what they conceived to be attacks upon the principles which they had been educated to believe sacred, and stabs at the heart of the country.[12]

Apparently, freedom of speech failed to sufficiently qualify as a sacred principle held close to the heart in Bangor during July and August 1861. For local historians like Vickery and Griffin, it appeared more important that future readers appreciate the disloyalty of Emery rather than the abandon-ment of fundamental freedom of the press in times of national crisis. As David Lowenthal notes, "Unlike memory or relics, history usually depends upon someone else's eyes and voice: we see it through an interpreter who stands between past events and our apprehension of them."[13] In such a context, it is not unreasonable to believe that to the victor go more than the spoils. In fact, the conquerors have always enjoyed the right to chronicle the very conflict in which they have prevailed, and the weight of Unionist perspective colors Emery's memory and the judgment of his journalism.

In light of such a pro-Union perspective, there is agreement between the *Daily Whig and Courier*, the *Daily Evening Times* and the *Jeffersonian* on the sequence of events that took place in Bangor at approximately a quarter of one o'clock on the afternoon of August 12, 1861. With the bell of the First Parish Church ringing a fire alarm, a small crowd gathered in front of the *Democrat* office, and several men entered Emery's rooms, destroying the large cylinder press and pitching stands, cases, and other equipment into the street, where the materials ultimately were set aflame. Returning from dinner, the embattled editor was able to escape personal injury, but his newspaper enterprise was shattered. It would be eighteen months before Emery could print another issue of the *Bangor Democrat*.[14]

The *Daily Evening Times* went to press first on August 12 and offered a rare departure from pro-Union sentiment in its summation of the afternoon's confusion. "The work of illegal violence was witnessed by citizens with varying emotions," the paper noted. "Many were rejoiced, a few indignant, but we believe the sentiment of the cooler and wiser, while holding in abhorrence the course of the Democrat, was one of regret."[15]

Still, the *Times*'s conscience was tempered by its disclaimer in the same issue, "Of the treasonable and mischievous character of the obnoxious paper, there is no dissenting voice, except among the faction for which it spoke."[16] No such qualifications came from the *Daily Whig and Courier* the next day. Wheeler's description of the sacking of the *Democrat* gave way to the sheet's self-vindication. "It has been found impossible to prevent an outbreak of public sentiment—deplore it as we may," the newspaper noted somewhat disingenuously.[17] Consistent with contemporary Unionist sentiment in the city, R.H. Stanley and George O. Hall, in their postwar account, *Eastern Maine and the Rebellion, Being an Account of the Principal Local Events in Eastern Maine during the War and Brief Histories of Eastern Maine Regiments*, wondered aloud:

> The younger portion of our people can hardly realize that there was printed in our midst a paper whose whole sympathy was with the rebels, and which with no uncertain sound denounced the Northern patriots in their efforts to subdue the South. . . . Small wonder then that the loyal citizens of Eastern Maine, holding that it was an evil that could not be reached by law, and that it was due to our brave soldiers in the field, that they be not subjected to a "fire in the rear," decided that "the Democrat" should not be tolerated at home.[18]

It should come as no surprise that the common recollection of the events in Bangor in August 1861 includes no expression of regret from the *Times* but rather the approbation of the *Whig* and the *Jeffersonian*. It is a fact of history that subsequent accounts in New England newspapers embraced a proadministration memory of Emery's misfortune. In 1909, the *Boston Globe* revisited the incident with the headline, "How the Indignant Citizens of Bangor put an End to Discouraging Utterances Against the Army of the North During the Civil War."[19] Thirty years later, the *Bangor Daily News* used subheads such as "Smashed a 'Copperhead'" and "Loyal Anger" to preserve history's take on Emery's trials that summer of 1861.[20]

Far from the forefront of history's treatment of Bangor's suppression of its Copperhead press is a four-page extra of the *Democrat* printed in secrecy by local resident Samuel Smith on behalf of Emery. So fearful of reprisal was Smith that he entered into a written agreement with Emery that it would be reported that the extra was printed in Portland. Stanley and Hall termed the extra "an exceedingly interesting number." So it is, for in its columns Marcellus Emery takes his leave not with a whimper but rather with a display of final defiance. Emery's account of the destruction of the *Democrat* is followed by his unwavering commitment to the right to print an opposing viewpoint. "Thus hath the freedom of the Press been stricken down here in Maine, not from any patriotic impulse, but through the wicked instigation of a band of abolitionist politicians who would willingly subvert all law and all order for the maintenance of a mere party dogma," Emery stated, adding, "I still believe that there is yet virtue and intelligence enough in the people to maintain their liberties, and protect the free Press, which is their best guardian."[21]

It is illuminating to contrast Emery's experience with that of fellow newspaper editor Samuel Medary, whose Columbus, Ohio, *Crisis* was sacked by members of the Second Ohio Cavalry in March 1863 for printing articles critical of the Northern war effort. Medary was subsequently arrested for "conspiracy against the Union" in May 1864. As Reed W. Smith points out, Medary's experience was by no means unique in the Civil War. In fact, Smith notes that "no other war in U.S. history has seen more instances of prosecution of the press by military authorities or private citizens." Editors with southern sympathies were often the targets of persecution, and Smith provides needed perspective when he states, "During the war rabid Unionists damaged or destroyed nearly one hundred opposition newspapers. Unionists instigated many of these acts in retaliation for the dissenting opinions of the Democratic press." Smith paraphrases John Stevens in assigning Medary the status of a crusader. "There are always individuals who believe in their cause so passionately 'that they seek out controversy, challenge community values. . . . Courting martyrdom, daring society to crush them.'"[22] The question for historians remains: What makes Marcellus Emery any less deserving of such praise than Medary?

Part of the answer may lie in the scarcity of Emery's published record. No wartime issues of the *Bangor Union* appear to have survived, and the Bangor Public Library counts only three editions of the *Bangor Democrat* among its holdings. Most of what is known of Emery's rhetoric and his ideological stand is to be found in the columns of his hometown competition, the *Jeffersonian Daily Evening News*, the *Daily Evening Times*, and the *Daily Whig and Courier*. All battled for circulation, and their editorial content, often colored by their political leanings, was not particularly favorable to their Copperhead contemporary. By contrast, Smith's research into Medary's ordeal as editor of the *Columbus Crisis* benefits from the fact that a complete collection of the *Crisis* and Medary's personal papers is preserved at the Ohio Historical Center.

Still, Emery's story is every bit as compelling as Medary's, especially when given the challenges faced by the Maine editor in publishing his contrary views. Medary was in close ideological and geographical proximity to the hotbed of the Copperhead movement in the Midwest, rallied by Ohio Congressman Clement Vallandigham, who provided Medary with moral, if not practical, support. Emery, on the other hand, labored far from the seat of the Peace Democrat movement, yet persevered in spite of that handicap.

Another reason for Emery's obscurity lies in what historian Howard Zinn terms "that inevitable taking of sides which comes from selection and emphasis in history."[23] Histories of the Civil War era chronicling Copperhead politics typically emphasize the minority's controversial convictions that "the Republicans had provoked the South into secession; that the Republicans were waging the war in order to establish their own domination, suppress civil and states rights and impose 'racial equality'; and that military means had failed and would never restore the Union."[24] Thus, Unionists' perspectives dominate the available literature and largely discredit Emery and his political colleagues as defeatists who threatened the noble northern war effort with "fire in the rear." Frank L. Klement writes in *The Copperheads in the Middle West*: "Radical Republicans like 'Thad' Stevens had their names written in gold ink. The Copperheads, Democratic critics of the Lincoln administration, were depicted as irrational men who flirted with treason and who expressed pro-Southern sympathies. The war was described as glorious, noble and inevitable." Although much of the war's military and political histories has been rewritten, Klement notes that the Copperhead story has been immune to revision. "Only the Copperhead story remains the same—those critics of the Lincoln administration are still viewed as men whose hearts were black, whose blood was yellow, and whose minds were blank."[25]

Those willing to search beyond the convenient and acceptable record, however, are rewarded with a worthy equal of Samuel Medary. Upon Emery's death from cancer in 1879 at the age of forty-eight, the *Whig* remembered him for unfulfilled potential saying, "but it has seemed to us that a dire political mistake at a period of unprecedented excitement may have warped a growth that otherwise might have lifted golden fruit into the sunlight of a successful life."[26] By the standard of Smith and other scholars, Emery frustrates attempts to consign him to failure. His stand, although ultimately unpopular and untenable, endures as significantly more important than the actions of the mob. Says Smith, "There have always been and continue to be Americans who persist in defining freedom of the press in their own terms, testing its power—proving its integrity."[27] Marcellus Emery was one such individual, and his place in history emerges as the equal of Hamlin and Roberts for courage and conviction. He lies at Mount Hope not in their shadow but as their rightful companion in helping to define the Civil War experience.

NOTES

1. *Bangor Daily Whig and Courier*, 24 February 1879.
2. *Bangor Daily Whig and Courier*, 30 May 1861.
3. John E. Dimeglio, "Civil War Bangor" (master's thesis, University of Maine, 1967), 21. See also the Bangor Public Library, *Seven Books in a Footlocker: A Commemorative History of the Bangor Public Library* (Dexter, Michigan: Thomson-Shore Inc., 1998), 6.
4. *Bangor Daily Whig and Courier*, 3 June 1861.
5. Ibid.
6. Ibid.
7. As postmaster of Boston, John Campbell issued what is generally regarded to be the first newspaper in Colonial America on April 24, 1704. In the *Boston News-Letter*, Campbell included "extracts from the *London Flying Post* and the *London Gazette* of the previous December." Indeed, as early as 1747 an editor of a New York newspaper was lamenting the irregular arrival of material saying, "Local news being held in such low estimation as it was, editors had to rely upon the arrival of papers or letters by ship or postrider to fill their news columns." See George Henry Payne, *History of Journalism in the United States* (New York: Appleton-Century Company, 1941), 26, and Frank Luther Mott, *American Journalism: A History of Newspapers in the United States through 260 Years, 1690 to 1960* (New York: Macmillan Publishing, 1962), 62. See also the *Bangor Daily Whig and Courier*, 6 July 1861.
8. Shelby Foote, *The Civil War: A Narrative; Fort Sumter to Perryville* (New York: Random House, 1974), 85.

9. Reprinted in R.H. Stanley and George O. Hall, *Eastern Maine and the Rebellion, Being an Account of the Principal Local Events in Eastern Maine during the War and Brief Histories of Eastern Maine Regiments* (Bangor: R.H. Stanley & Co., 1887), 82.

10. James B. Vickery, *An Illustrated History of the City of Bangor, Maine, formerly the Plantation of Conduskeag or Kenduskeag in ye Country of Arcadia on the River named Penobscot* (Bangor: Bangor Bicentennial Committee, 1976), 42.

11. Frederic Hudson, *Journalism in the United States* (New York: Harper & Brothers, 1873), 754.

12. Joseph Griffin, ed., *History of the Press in Maine* (Brunswick, ME: Press of J. Griffin, 1872), 137.

13. David Lowenthal, "How We Know the Past: History," in *The Past Is a Foreign Country* (New York: Cambridge University Press, 1985), 216.

14. Stanley and Hall, *Eastern Maine and the Rebellion*, 83–90.

15. Ibid., 85.

16. Ibid., 87.

17. *Bangor Daily Whig and Courier*, 13 August 1861.

18. Stanley and Hall, 82–86.

19. *Boston Globe*, 10 October 1909.

20. *Bangor Daily News*, 12 February 1939.

21. Stanley and Hall, 93, 97.

22. Reed W. Smith, *Samuel Medary and the Crisis: Testing the Limits of Press Freedom* (Columbus: Ohio State University Press, 1995), 12.

23. Howard Zinn, "Columbus, the Indians, and Human Progress," in *A People's History of the United States, 1492–Present* (New York: Harper, 1995), 10.

24. Patricia Faust, ed., *Historical Times Illustrated Encyclopedia of the Civil War* (New York: Harper & Row, 1986), 564.

25. Frank L. Klement, *The Copperheads in the Middle West* (Chicago: University of Chicago Press, 1960), vii.

26. *Bangor Daily Whig and Courier*, 24 February 1879.

27. Smith, vii.

The Arrest and Trial of Clement L. Vallandigham in 1863

— Giovanna Dell'Orto —

No single man outside the Confederate armies represented a greater threat to the Union than Clement L. Vallandigham, a slightly built Ohio congressman who came to epitomize Copperheadism, the prosouthern faction of northern sentiment that the Lincoln administration considered an explosive "fire in the rear." After a May 1863 speech attacking the war as unnecessary and unconstitutional, Vallandigham was arrested, tried, and found guilty of treason by a military commission under Major General Ambrose Burnside's April 1863 order that those "declaring sympathies for the enemy would be so tried." He was sentenced to imprisonment in Boston's Fort Warren for the duration of the war, but Abraham Lincoln commuted the sentence and ordered Vallandigham exiled to the Confederacy instead. The Democratic press railed against Lincoln's "despotism," while Republican editors faced the dilemma of defending the right of free expression for someone espousing ideas that they loathed.

The Vallandigham case represented a major test of First Amendment protection of press freedom, as the Northern government tried to prevent the circulation of "hated ideas"—political opinions opposing majority views and government objectives. Editorial support for the limiting of traditional press freedom illustrates historian John Lofton's assertion that "this tendency merely to endorse the government's posture hardly indicates a readiness by editors to take a bold independent position in behalf of freedom of the press."[1] Northern editors' suppressive tendencies appear all the more rigid when one considers that these same editors railed against attempts to censor their own newspapers and limit their efforts to gather news. Journalism historian Donna Lee Dickerson has said that "[w]ith few exceptions, editors wailed as loudly against the censorship of their telegraphic dispatches as they railed against government's refusal to suppress opposition journals."[2]

The Vallandigham case spurred a chain reaction that captured national attention. The day after the arrest, riots erupted in Dayton, and a mob burned down the office of the Republican *Dayton Journal* and cut the telegraph lines. Union Major General Ambrose Burnside retaliated by ordering the suppression of the *Dayton Empire*, a Copperhead daily and ardent Vallandigham promoter, and the arrest of its editor, William Logan. The outrage spread nationwide. A protest meeting of New York Democrats, including Governor Horatio Seymour, at Albany on May 16 condemned the trial as abrogating the right to freedom of expression and the Constitution itself.

In June, Lincoln wrote a lengthy reply to the resolutions adopted in the meeting. He claimed that Vallandigham had been arrested because he tried to interfere with the raising of the troops and encouraged desertions, not because he was "damaging the political prospects of the Administration" but because "he was damaging the army." Lincoln argued that arrests such as Vallandigham's were "constitutional at all places where they will conduce to the public safety" and that "under cover of 'liberty of speech,' 'liberty of press,' and '*habeas corpus*,' [southern sympathizers] hoped to keep on foot amongst us a most efficient corps of spies, informers, suppliers, and aiders and abettors of their cause in a thousand ways." In a brilliant piece of rhetoric, he asked: "Must I shoot a simple-minded soldier boy who deserts, while I must not touch a hair of a wily agitator who induces him to desert? I think that, in such a case, to silence the agitator and save the boy is not only constitutional but withal a great mercy."[3]

In this milieu of heated discussion about freedom of expression and hated ideas, it is instructive to examine what journalists from different regional and political allegiances wrote about freedom of speech and the press as they reported and discussed the Vallandigham case, and in particular what attitudes they expressed toward freedom for the hated ideas in the context of censorship. Eleven newspapers were studied—five from the South, five from the North (including one abolitionist and one Copperhead), and one from a border state. These included the *Charleston Daily Courier* and *Mercury*; the *Richmond Dispatch, Enquirer,* and *Examiner*;[4] the *New York Times* and *New*

York Tribune; the *Chicago Tribune*; the *Boston Liberator*; the *Columbus Crisis*; and the *Baltimore Sun*.

The *Daily Courier*, the oldest newspaper in South Carolina, was an enthusiastic supporter of the Confederacy, whereas the *Mercury*, edited by Robert Barnwell Rhett, opposed the administration of Southern President Jefferson Davis but even more fervently supported secession. Of the Richmond papers, the *Dispatch* had the largest circulation and claimed political independence and devotion to "straight" news. The *Examiner*, edited by John M. Daniels, has been likened to the *New York Tribune*, for editors of both sought to direct the government (albeit in Daniels's case in a proslavery, antinorthern way). The *Enquirer*, on the other hand, was dubbed the organ of Jefferson Davis, and its editorial stance was both conservative and cautious.

Of the northern newspapers, the *New York Times*, edited by Henry J. Raymond, was generally considered more independent than other newspapers of the time, although it was still proadministration. The *Chicago Tribune*, edited by Joseph Medill, also had a staunchly Republican slant, but its record on press freedom was much more ambiguous. According to one historian, Vallandigham was "an object of special hatred" by the *Tribune*, and it is noteworthy that in 1863 Medill became president of the Union Leagues of Home Defense (secret societies affiliated with the Republican party that were the direct counterpart to the Copperhead-backing Knights of the Golden Circle).[5] The *New York Tribune*, edited by Horace Greeley, often carried overt and aggressive political commentary; Greeley had advocated mediation to end the war and had therefore come into "close relations" with Vallandigham.[6] The *Liberator*, edited by William Lloyd Garrison, was the leading organ of the abolitionist movement, but previous research showed that Garrison was not as sympathetic to press freedom issues as his own experiences with suppression might lead one to expect. Finally, the *Crisis*, edited by Samuel Medary, was with the *Chicago Times* the leading organ of Copperheadism in the Midwest during the war.

All the newspapers examined covered the Vallandigham case in great detail. The legal proceedings of the trial were extensively, when not fully, quoted in the newspapers. The news of Vallandigham's arrest and trial always made it to the front page, and very few issues in any of the newspapers in the month of May 1863 failed to carry at least a brief news update on the Vallandigham situation. With the exception of the *Baltimore Sun* and the *Charleston Mercury*, all the newspapers studied carried editorials on various aspects of the case. The reactions expressed in their editorials were generally as expected: southern editors denounced the arrest, although they expressed outrage against northern despotism in general, rather than specific approval of Vallandigham. Unanimously, they condemned his exile to the Confederacy. Northern editors' opinions were more surprising: Both Greeley and Medary showed indignation toward the case, suggesting that public outrage in this case could cross partisan lines. On the other hand, Garrison devoted relatively little space to the events but approved of Vallandigham's treatment. More unexpectedly, so did Medill and Raymond, who both supported Burnside's actions and ridiculed Vallandigham's right to free expression, suggesting very little tolerance for "hated" ideas even in such a flagrant case of unconstitutional suppression.

Because the *Baltimore Sun* did not carry editorials or editorial comment attached to its news items, one can only note which aspects of the case were covered, without inferring an opinion by the *Sun* staff. The *Sun* announced Vallandigham's arrest on May 6, as did the northern newspapers. In 16 subsequent issues, the *Sun* carried news of the Dayton riots, including the fire at the *Journal* and the destruction of telegraph lines, as well as the suppression of the *Empire*.[7] It also devoted two columns to the proceedings of the trial and nearly one column to Burnside's defense in the application for a writ of habeas corpus.[8] Considerable space was given to news of the meetings in Albany and in New York City; Vallandigham's letter "to the Democracy of Ohio" (written while awaiting trial) and Governor Seymour's letter to the Albany meeting were also printed.[9] With regard to Vallandigham's exile to the Confederacy, the *Sun* ran a short commentary from the *Cincinnati Enquirer* stating that Vallandigham was satisfied at the commutation of his sentence and an editorial from the *Richmond Sentinel* maintaining that Lincoln had no right to send "disunionists" to the South.[10] Finally, the *Sun* ran Vallandigham's address to Ohio Democrats after his exile, which read in part, "Every sentiment and expression of attachment to the Union and devotion to the Constitution—to my country—which I have ever cherished or uttered, shall abide unchanged and unretracted till my return."[11]

The same events were covered in the three northern newspapers studied (the *Crisis* and the *Liberator* will be discussed separately). The editors' opinions were clearly and passionately stated. The editorial views can be divided into two positions—the *Chicago Tribune* and, surprisingly, the *New York Times* were adamant in approval of Vallandigham's arrest, whereas the *New York Tribune* was equally adamant in denouncing it as an infringement upon the right to freedom of expression. The only overlap between the two positions was the ridicule in the *New York Tribune* and *Times* of the Copperheads' hypocrisy. Ironically unaware of their own paradox, editors of both publications noted that Vallandigham supporters railed against governmental oppression only when it attacked their own right to expression but were unwilling to criticize suppression of ideas they "hated," such as abolitionism.

Several themes can be identified in both opinions. In the *New York Tribune*, editorial comments centered upon three main arguments: Despite Vallandigham's unworthiness, his right to free speech must be upheld; Vallandigham should be freed, not sent south; his sympathizers' claims were hypocritical. Of these themes, the defense of free speech is given most attention and stands in marked contrast to the two other papers' positions. Four editorials in particular outlined Greeley's position on the rights involved in Vallandigham's case. The first appeared on May 15; although fully unsympathetic to Vallandigham, it nonetheless denounced abridging his right to free expression. Calling the orator a "pro-Slavery Democrat of an exceedingly coppery hue," the writer said that "if there were penalties for holding irrational, unpatriotic and inhuman views," then Vallandigham would be "one of the most flagrant offenders." But because the Constitution does not punish on the basis of "perverse opinions," there is nothing one can do to prevent Vallandigham from speaking.

Greeley also expressed dissatisfaction with the banishment of Vallandigham beyond Union lines. When he first wrote about the proposed exile, he called it "the worst joke Lincoln has yet made," predicting that the exile would increase Copperhead discontent and "set a dozen such tongues wagging for every one so silenced."[12] When the sentence was finally set, Greeley commented extensively on it. He had three points: Vallandigham wasn't really exiled because the country was still one, but was only sent to those whom he considered "high-minded patriots and Unionists" in the South. Secondly, if Vallandigham were able to come back from the South with a credible Union peace overture from redeemed Rebel leaders, Greeley would give it "an immediate circulation of more than two hundred thousand copies throughout every corner and at nearly every post-office in the loyal States." Thirdly, "[T]he Presidential joke is a good one" because it sent Vallandigham, "an apostle of Peace," to the part of the country where "the whole able-bodied population is in arms to defy the authority of the Government and resist the execution of the laws."[13] Even Jefferson Davis, Greeley added, had "a grim appreciation of the melancholy joke" and asked for an oath of allegiance from Vallandigham before he "let him run."[14] Greeley reiterated his disapproval of the arrest and trial because they might "establish a very dangerous precedent and open a door to the grossest abuses."[15]

Despite the clear disapproval of the Vallandigham case, Greeley expressed scorn for the protests raised by other Copperheads ("This must not blind us to the baseless assertions and monstrous sophistries whereby [Vallandigham's] liberation is commended"), including Governor Seymour's letter, a "disgrace to New York."[16] He also condemned Vallandigham's hypocrisy:

"Free Speech" is only desirable, in his view, when it is employed to decry "Abolition," and "coercion" is horrible when it precludes slaveholders
from having their way. If Mr. V. shall be permitted to hold forth to "our
Southern brethren," we will warrant him not even to attempt to show the
futility and wickedness of the war on *their* part.[17]

The *New York Times* also railed against the Copperheads' hypocritical
stance on free speech, but this is the only point on which the editors' views
coincide. Of the newspapers studied, the *Times* articulated the most extensive and detailed defense of governmental actions in the Vallandigham case,
claiming in different instances their constitutionality, righteousness, and necessity. The arguments in the *Times* revolved on several points: The people
loyal to the Union applauded the governmental stance and demanded strong
intervention against the Copperheads; the mob activities upon the arrest were
sufficient proof of its necessity; Vallandigham should be sent south. These
same themes recurred in the *Chicago Tribune.* Most importantly, the *Times*
argued that if the war was constitutional, then so was the attack on the Copperheads; moreover, free speech had to be severely limited in times of war. The
Tribune ignored the free expression problem and justified the government's
actions on the basis of military treason.

Both the *Chicago Tribune* and the *New York Times* reserved strong epi-
thets for Vallandigham—he was an "arch-schemer of mischief," a "squeezed
orange," and a "seditious wretch" in the *Times* and a "hissing Copperhead"
and "pestilent traitor" in the *Tribune.* In its earlier editorials, the *Times* focused on the harm Vallandigham was causing and the consequent right of
the government to silence him. The *Times* editor lauded the government for
striking at "the fomenters of sedition" and wished harsh penalties would
make him an example. He added Vallandigham's "malignant and lawless"
influence—his rebellion—could be seen in the mob resistance against his
arrest.[18]

The *Times* also suggested that Vallandigham be sent south "to join that
noble company of traitors whose praises he has sounded so loudly." The paper challenged Vallandigham to decry the dangers of military power among
the Confederate powers and to "suggest to the slaveholding rebels how much
rebellion has done for abolition." It predicted his exile would help the Union
because it would show "the determination of the North, which is hardening
from flint to adamant, to suppress this rebellion and to grind to powder all
those who would sustain it."[19] Most significantly, the *Times* argued that Vallandigham's trial was justified by the Constitution because he was disloyal and
abetted the enemy's cause by his speech:

The military necessity for such a procedure is obvious to any intelligent man. . . . None but a disloyal man would attempt to influence a crowd by denouncing [the order] as usurpation, and declaring his intention to disregard it. . . . He was doing just as much as any rebel of them all to break down the military strength which the Government is using to restore its rightful authority.[20]

The first editorials in the *Tribune* highlight the same themes, stressing even more the satisfaction of the loyal people in seeing the government finally act against traitors like Vallandigham. It is noteworthy that the *Tribune* had an article on Vallandigham on May 2, before the arrest, predicting Burnside's actions and even his exile:

[T]he infamous Vallandigham will be one of the first fruits of the Burnside order. This hissing Copperhead is evidently desirous of martyrdom and General Burnside will be entirely willing to begin with him. As the two parties seem thus exactly agreed, we hope to see the wretch that has so long disgraced loyal Ohio, sent where affinities may receive and welcome him. Get him ready to be sent to Dixie.[21]

The *Tribune* frequently reiterated that the government's action "has given great satisfaction here to the mass of our citizens" and "for just this have loyal men waited for many months past" because the sight of the "traitor" made "their indignant blood" "tingle to their finger tips." The newspaper also wanted "no chance for his cheap and unharmed martyrdom" but that Vallandigham "be punished in an exemplary manner."[22] Vallandigham's role as southern sympathizer and the implied necessity of the government to silence him appear to have been the *Tribune*'s main themes. The paper insisted on not treating Vallandigham differently from a Rebel soldier because he "has done more mischief than if he had commanded a rebel division in the field," and "a failure to deal with this traitor as he deserves would be equal to a reverse to our army in the field." The protests of some newspapers upon his arrest, the paper claimed, were only proof of their disloyalty.[23] The *Tribune* dismissed charges of unconstitutionality lightly; the paper wrote that the government needed "no defense except in the facts of the case" because Vallandigham "by his own confession a hundred times made, is a traitor" and thus "ought to be hung."[24] Lastly, the *Tribune* approved of sending Vallandigham south: "The enemy before [Union Major General William] Rosecrans have [sic] been reinforced by the advent of V. among them."[25]

Garrison's *Liberator* devoted less space to the coverage of Vallandigham's arrest and trial than might have been expected, considering that hardly any idea could have been more hated by abolitionists than Copperheadism. After the first news was reported in a purely factual manner,[26] almost a month lapsed before the *Liberator*'s reports were tinged with hearty dislike for the Copperhead orator. The June 12 issue carried several editorials on the Vallandigham case, with themes similar to those already discussed disparaging the Copperhead orator: Vallandigham, "if not technically a traitor . . . is so in fact and intention"; it added that those "who have such sins to answer for against the rights of their fellow citizens, against the plainest principles of justice, against the most obvious dictates of charity, ought not to whine when the hand of military law is laid on some of their own number." The *Liberator* ridiculed the "pathetic appeals in behalf of free speech and a free press" coming from "those who are identified with every mob against free speech for the past thirty years" (and who "dragged the editor of the *Liberator* through the streets of this city"); their "devilish hypocrisy" is transparent in their support of a system that "answers a free tongue with a halter." In the present crisis, "words might be more dangerous than bullets" and the Democrats must be kept from power by "the display of firmness, undaunted resolution, and fixed policy in the treatment of Northern traitors."[27]

The *Crisis* devoted a great amount of space to the Vallandigham case—decrying his treatment as the ultimate sign of Lincoln's destruction of northern liberties. Coverage continued through the eve of the Ohio Democratic convention on June 11 with the exhortation to vindicate Vallandigham with the electoral ballot. Leaving commentary on freedom of expression issues mostly to editorials copied from other newspapers (especially Republican, so as to indicate that this was not a partisan issue),[28] the *Crisis* focused on two main themes—riots are inevitable after such an outrage, and the Copperhead position is not traitorous but, on the contrary, is the one supporting the Constitution, its liberties, and the Union. The *Crisis* emphasized the unrest caused by Vallandigham's treatment, noting that "under no circumstances did we ever witness the same state of public mind. . . . Scarcely a word passes between the Democrats and the Republicans—they pass as total strangers."[29] Added the newspaper, "[W]e pray for peace, for law and for order, but we fear that our prayers are but mockeries."[30]

The *Crisis* sought to identify the Copperhead position with the Constitution and Union (perhaps in an effort to deny its status of "hated" idea and cast abolitionists as the "real traitors"). Vallandigham's Mt. Vernon speech is defined as a protest against "the violations of the Constitution, the infringements of individual rights, and the invasions of public liberties" of which "the faithless party now in power is so flagrantly guilty."[31] Copperheads "stand behind no man in our admiration, love affection, and adoration" of the Constitution; they were ready for all sorts of punishment if Burnside considered obeying the Constitution a treason. "If, on the other hand, General Burnside's purpose is to sustain the Constitution . . . he will find no safer or more sincere friend to aid him than the Editor of the *Crisis*."[32] Medary called the exile "strange and unaccountable proceedings," for "we all know that a stronger Union man does not live than Mr. Vallandigham." Sending him south signified that nobody could remain protected in the North "if by chance of conviction [he] should differ with the authorities at Washington." Finally, Medary argued that it was up to Ohio voters to "vindicate the liberty of the citizen in his person—the case is now made so broad and clear that a vote is for the life or for the death of Constitutional liberty."[33]

The southern newspapers started covering the Vallandigham case later than the northern press but rather quickly nonetheless.[34] All condemned Burnside's actions as against fundamental rights under the Constitution and mildly sympathized with Vallandigham as a victim of despotism and someone whom they despised less than other northerners. However, none of the editors expressed approval of Vallandigham or the Copperheads—on the contrary, they seemed to have used the incident to disassociate from and disparage Copperheadism in the North as not being sufficiently prosouthern. All disapproved of Vallandigham's exile and refused to accept Lincoln's treatment of the Confederacy as his own private "penal colony."

Vallandigham's arrest was seen as the ultimate sign of Lincoln's desperate despotism. For the *Richmond Enquirer*, the case exhibited "to what depth of degradation society must now be reduced amongst a people whom we once regarded as, in one sense, almost our fellow countrymen." Defeated Union generals such as Burnside, "beaten and humiliated by armed men," were seen as "naturally anxious to take revenge upon unarmed citizens." Said the *Richmond Enquirer*:

> This performance in Cincinnati is evidently the first practical opening of Mr. Seward's new campaign for consolidating all power in the hands of his Dictator, and ferociously stamping down the last murmurs and struggles of those liege subjects, who used to be citizens.[35]

The *Richmond Dispatch* wrote:

> If the Anti-Lincoln, Anti-Abolition party are contending for principle and not for party . . . now is the time for them to prove it. . . . We shall see whether [the] hawk in his swoop has struck upon a nest of eagles or has really descended upon a covey of frightened partridges, who will send away for life and leave their companion helpless in the talons of the bird of prey.[36]

The *Richmond Examiner* concurred:

> No portion of the Anglo-Norman race, however degraded and depraved, will long abide the loss of one privilege which they have hugged to their

souls since they were savages in the woods—the great privilege reasserted in all their charters, that no freeman—"*Nullus liber homo*"—shall be imprisoned, banished or put to death, except by the jury of his peers.[37]

In light of such treatment, the editors expressed sympathy for Vallandigham. The *Richmond Enquirer* called him "a foreigner who has suffered unjust persecution from the tyrant dictator of his own country."[38] Others were stronger in their approval. Vallandigham was viewed as a "brave and able defender of constitutional rights" who deserved "a great deal of respect."[39] The *Richmond Examiner* said Vallandigham had "displayed the highest courage, and the most honorable patriotism amid the wild wickedness of [his] country."[40] To the *Charleston Courier*, he was "one of the most pure and popular of Northern politicians."[41] As the *Richmond Examiner* put it, "if sympathy for an individual and an enemy were permitted, sorrow for the fate of V. would be felt by most men of heart in the South."[42]

The *Richmond Dispatch* also criticized Vallandigham's exile, not only because Lincoln had "very cool impudence" to send his prisoners to the Confederacy but also because Lincoln should be prevented from "avoiding the issue which his outrageous and unconstitutional proceedings in the case has raised before the people of the United States."[43] The *Charleston Courier* doubted precisely that the Vallandigham issue would create a sensation in the North—the editor wrote he had "so often been befooled" by northern professions of help that he doubted the riots upon Vallandigham's arrest would "occasion alarm and trouble to the Government and its bloody-minded supporters." This was the destiny of all attempts to criticize Lincoln, for "the heel of the despot is on their necks. They are bound hand and foot. Their liberties are gone."[44] The protests "are words—mere words—and are worth nothing."[45]

In contrast, northern editors based the question of constitutionality on military necessity and martial law while not directly discussing the right to freedom of expression. Only the *New York Times, New York Tribune,* and *Columbus Crisis* articulated explicit and detailed arguments on the relevance of the Vallandigham case to freedom of speech and press. Most significantly, none of the editorials advocated free expression for Vallandigham on the basis of the intrinsic worth of his speech and ideas. One *New York Times* editorial on May 15 focused on the right as applicable in times of war. Citing libel laws and instigation to unrest, the paper claimed that

> at all times the freedom of speech is a restricted right.... No human society ever did or ever should tolerate *unlimited* freedom of speech in peaceful times. Infinitely less can it be tolerated in a state of war. The true principle at all times in regard to the freedom of speech, as in regard to

the freedom of the Press, is that it may reach just so far as it can go without injury to private rights and the public interests.[46]

The *Times* added that military orders are as binding for all citizens within the lines as civil laws. Given the condition of the country, "the idea of according unlimited freedom of speech everywhere . . . can be seriously entertained by nobody, except a madman or a traitor." While a "regular civil prosecution" would be "far more agreeable," the newspaper said it was high time to learn that "there are public rights quite as valid, and just now a good deal more urgent."

Horace Greeley argued the opposite view. Before the verdict was made public, he editorialized for Vallandigham's liberation in terms of freedom of expression. He wrote that Vallandigham should not "even *wish* to assail and weaken our Government at such a crisis as this" but that he had the right to express "hated" ideas: "We consider such speeches as he makes calculated rather to strengthen the Government than to paralyze and subvert it. We reverence Freedom of Discussion—by which we mean Freedom to uphold perverse and evil theories, since nobody ever doubted the right to uphold the other sort."[47]

The *Crisis* ran two editorials from New York newspapers upholding freedom of expression after Vallandigham's arrest. The *New York World* argued that "the law has been violated not by him who suffers the penalty, but by him who declares it," and that the precedent Lincoln had set was "fraught with such fearful danger as would bind all freemen to resist it. . . . If you can break through the Constitution to infringe the freedom of speech, the people see that you can equally break through it to destroy every other right which the Constitution guarantees."[48] The other editorial, from the *New York Evening Post*, made the important clarification that Vallandigham had not "committed overt acts of treason," but only "silly babbling." Said the *Post*: "No governments and no authorities are to be held as above criticism or even denunciation," adding, "If Vallandigham's peace nonsense is treasonable, may not Greeley's be equally so?"[49]

The study of Vallandigham's arrest, trial, and conviction by military commission produced some surprising findings. With the exception of the Copperhead *Crisis*, all other newspapers studied seemed to consider Vallandigham's Copperheadism a "hated idea"—even the southern editors. All the editors who wrote about the case considered its constitutionality, mostly supporting the larger system within which they operated. Southern and Copperhead editors used the case to accuse their opponents of despotism, whereas Lincoln supporters such as the *Chicago Tribune* and the *New York Times* ridiculed Copperhead claims. Only Greeley, at the *New York Tribune*, explicitly argued the unconstitutionality of the case made against Vallandigham even though he generally despised Vallandigham's politics. The ongoing discussion of constitutional rights and freedom of expression suggests that journalists at the time were increasingly ready to reconsider which ideas—even those they might have hated—deserved being defended. This represented a significant turning point in the evolution of journalists' understanding of freedom of expression under the Constitution.

Notes

Material in this chapter appears in a different form in Hazel Dicken-Garcia and Giovanna Dell'Orto, *Hated Ideas and the American Civil War Press* (Spokane, WA: Marquette Books, 2007).

1.   John Lofton, *The Press as Guardian of the First Amendment* (Columbia: University of South Carolina Press, 1980), 10.

2.   Donna Lee Dickerson, *The Course of Tolerance: Freedom of the Press in Nineteenth-Century America* (Westport: Greenwood Press, 1990), 179–180.

3.   Abraham Lincoln, *President Lincoln's Views* (Philadelphia: King & Baird, 1863), 7–16.

4.   One editorial from the *Richmond Examiner* was reprinted in the *New York Times* and will be discussed; the available copy of the *Richmond Examiner* was missing all issues from March 1863 to January 1864.

5.   Philip Kinsley, *The Chicago Tribune: Its First Hundred Years* (New York: Alfred Knopf, 1943), 169, 267. On the Union Leagues, see James M. McPherson, *Battle Cry of Freedom: The Civil War Era* (New York: Oxford University Press, 1988), 599.

6.   Francis Brown, *Raymond of the Times* (New York: W.W. Norton, 1951), 240.

7.   *Baltimore Sun*, 6 May 1863, 7 May 1863, 8 May 1863, 9 May 1863.

8.   *Baltimore Sun*, 12 May 1863, 15 May 1863.

9.   *Baltimore Sun*, 14 May 1863, 18 May 1863, 19 May 1863, 20 May 1863. Vallandigham's letter read, in part: "I am here in a military bastile [sic] for no other offence than my political opinions, and the defence [sic] of them and of the rights of the people, and of your constitutional liberties. . . . I am a Democrat—for Constitution, for law, for the Union, for liberty—this is my only 'crime.'"

10. *Baltimore Sun*, 25 May 1863, 26 May 1863. The *Sentinel*'s sentiment, as discussed below, was common to southern editors.

11. *Baltimore Sun*, 29 May 1863.

12. *New York Tribune*, 15 May 1863.

13. *New York Tribune*, 22 May 1863.

14. *New York Tribune*, 30 May 1863.

15. *New York Tribune*, 22 May 1863.

16. *New York Tribune*, 18 May 1863.

17. *New York Tribune*, 22 May 1863.

18. *New York Times*, 8 May 1863.

19. *New York Times*, 13 May 1863.

20. *New York Times*, 15 May 1863. Calling "monstrous" Seymour's statement that if the administration sustained Burnside half of the people in the Union would

abandon the war, the editor added, "It puts it into the power of the Administration to establish the character of war, and to decide its fate. The duty of the loyal men to put down the rebellion is all made dependent upon the wisdom or the folly, the faithfulness or the unfaithfulness, of the Administration at Washington. Were the arrest of Vallandigham ten times the flagrant wrong his best friends claim it to be, it would not be a tenth part so abominable as this doctrine. This war is a war to save the nation. . . . The men in power at Washington are but dust in the balance when weighed against the destinies at stake." *New York Times*, 19 May 1863.

21. *Chicago Tribune*, 2 May 1863. The same issue also has news of Vallandigham's Mt. Vernon speech. As nearly all *Tribune* articles on the case, these were reported by a correspondent of the *Tribune*.

22. *New York Tribune*, 6 May 1863. Identical reasoning appears in a May 14 editorial arguing that "the arrest has already done good" by showing that the Government meant the "entire destruction" of Copperheads.

23. *New York Tribune*, 12 May 1863, 8 May 1863. After the sentence, the editor called any clemency "disastrous" and "dangerously misplaced." 19 May 1863.

24. *New York Tribune*, 19 May 1863.

25. *New York Tribune*, 21 May 1863.

26. *Boston Liberator*, 8 May 1863, 15 May 1863.

27. *Boston Liberator*, 12 June 1863.

28. "Every Republican paper in the city of New York opposes the arrest of Mr. V., except the *Times*. This speaks volumes." *Columbus Crisis*, 20 May 1863.

29. *Columbus Crisis*, 20 May 1863.

30. *Columbus Crisis*, 20 May 1863.

31. *Columbus Crisis*, 20 May 1863.

32. *Columbus Crisis*, 20 May 1863.

33. *Columbus Crisis*, 27 May 1863.

34. The *Richmond Enquirer* was the last, running the news of the arrest on May 15; all others ran it on May 11.

35. *Richmond Enquirer*, 15 May 1863.

36. *Richmond Dispatch*, 20 May 1863.

37. Reprinted in the *New York Times*, 20 May 1863.

38. *Richmond Enquirer*, 15 May 1863, 2 June 1863.

39. *Richmond Dispatch*, 12 May 1863, 30 May 1863.

40. Reprinted in *New York Times*, 20 May 1863.

41. *Charleston Courier*, 14 May 1863.

42. Reprinted in *New York Times*, 20 May 1863.

43. *Richmond Dispatch*, 27 May 1863, 30 May 1863.

44. *Charleston Daily Courier*, 14 May 1863.

45. *Charleston Daily Courier*, 29 May 1863.

46. *New York Times*, 15 May 1863.

47. *New York Tribune*, 18 May 1863.

48. *Columbus Crisis*, 3 June 1863.

49. *Columbus Crisis*, 20 May 1863.

CIVIL WAR SPIN

The Bogus Proclamation of 1864

— MENAHEM BLONDHEIM —

An all-out struggle between societies rather than a limited contest between armies, the Civil War affected every aspect of American life.[1] Communications was one of those aspects. The war challenged traditional practices, principles, and policies that structured the American communication environment. If it was to emerge victorious, Union leadership would have to confront the issue of wartime communication in all its military, political, and ideological implications. Although they never explicitly formulated it as a communication policy, Northern leaders developed, in the course of four years of fighting, a distinctive approach to the problem of communication and modern war. This implicit policy spanned the military, administrative, and public spheres.

The grand new scale and scope of fighting in the Civil War called for advanced means and procedures of communication. Rapid, high-volume, flexible systems of transmission were essential for effective command and control of combat. Beyond the theater of operations, novel demands were also made on the nation's civilian complex. The waging of modern warfare required all-out mobilization of manpower and resources in finance and industrial production, agriculture, and transportation. To plan, mobilize, and coordinate the unprecedented flows of men and materiel, new methods of information gathering and transmission were essential.[2]

Above all, fighting a modern war hinged on mobilizing human wills. The voluntary cooperation and sacrifice of the public were necessary for recruiting the huge economic resources necessary for carrying out the war. The millions of men called up for active duty had to be prepared to offer the ultimate sacrifice. For leadership to effectively mobilize human resources, it had to reach out to the public mind and its collective will. No one understood that better than Abraham Lincoln. "Public sentiment is everything," he acknowledged, "*with* it, nothing can fail; *against* it, nothing can succeed. Whoever moulds public sentiment, goes deeper than he who enacts statutes or pronounces judicial decisions. He makes the enforcement of these, else impossible."[3]

Mobilizing a politically divided public for heavy sacrifices would have represented a formidable challenge to any government. Particular limitations on the powers of the American government made this challenge even more serious. In other times and other places, governments could mobilize the masses through control and use of the powerful centralized media of communication and persuasion.[4] In the case of the Civil War, this path could not be taken. Government was limited by the First Amendment from tampering with the free expression of ideas. A free press and free speech were practically untouchable, not to be violated with impunity.[5]

There was one significant exception to the rule of moderation in press and speech control at the highest level of government. This was the case of the Bogus Proclamation of 1864. The incident culminated in the closing down by presidential order of two of the most prominent opposition newspapers in the nation's largest metropolis and the arrest of their proprietors and editors.

At about 3:30 in the morning of May 18, 1864, just as a foreman of the *Journal of Commerce* was about to complete typesetting that morning's edition, one of his assistants rushed into the office. "You'll have to wait; here's a holiday for you!" he exclaimed, handing the foreman several sheets of New York Associated Press flimsies (thin tissue-paper copies), just received from an Associated Press boy. The message scribbled on the sheets was a proclamation signed by President Lincoln and countersigned by Secretary of State William H. Seward. The foreman's standing orders were that once the edition was closed and the editor gone, he could make last-minute changes only in the case of news of a battle or an official order. The late dispatch definitely embodied the latter and implied the former.[6]

The presidential proclamation called for a day of fasting, humiliation, and solemn prayer—and also for 400,000 additional men for active service.[7] The proclamation's contents, as well as its solemn wording, appeared to confirm the worst apprehensions of a public anxiously waiting for news about the fate of Lieutenant General Ulysses S. Grant's forces in Virginia, which at that time were engaging the Confederates at Spotsylvania. The dramatic proc-lamation dashed the high hopes in the North that the days of the rebellion were numbered, implying the failure of the Union army in the fateful Virginia campaign. The *Journal* staff dutifully and promptly inserted the dramatic news in the morning edition.[8]

The editorial rooms of the *Journal* had expected bad news. "All the news I have," noted William C. Prime, the *Journal*'s editor and part-owner, "comes from administration sources." Prime's close friend, Union Major General George B. McClellan, in early retirement from the rages of battle and entering a new career in Democratic politics, had helped Prime and their mutual ac-quaintance, Manton Marble, editor of the antiadministration *New York World*, interpret the administration's news. This interpretation by the great expert on the Army of the Potomac was not cheerful. "Depressed and fearful," the *Jour-nal*'s editor had expected the worst. "Heaven help us all," he wrote his wife.[9]

A few blocks away, Marble's employees were inserting the same words in their edition. They too had received a set of NYAP flimsies with the president's proclamation. A third New York daily, the *Herald*, also incorporated the proc-lamation in its May 18 issue. However, while the momentous document was rapidly rolling off the fast presses, the attention of the *Herald*'s night manager was drawn to early copies of the *Times* and *Tribune* that had just reached his office. The two leading proadministration papers did not contain the dramatic news. The men at the *Herald* office found this perplexing in the extreme. Why, wondered the men at the *Herald*, had the *Times* and *Tribune* not published their copy of the presidential proclamation? They immediately stopped the presses.

A short investigation satisfied the *Herald* men that the proclamation they had received was not genuine. They found that other local newspapers had managed to discover the forgery before going to print. The first to sus-pect the authenticity of the news was a cautious clerk at the counter of the Copperhead *Daily News*. That newspaper had just marked the anniversary of its resuming publication after being suppressed for disloyalty by Postmaster General Montgomery Blair, and understandably it was on guard. The *Daily News* clerk, handed a copy of the dispatch, inquired of the messenger why it was not sent in the standard NYAP envelope. The messenger evaded the ques-tion and hurried away. Suspicions aroused, the *Daily News* made a round of inquiries and found that whereas the *Times* had received the dispatch, and apparently even typeset it, the *Tribune* had not.[10] At NYAP headquarters, the night clerk informed the *Daily News* people that the dispatch was "as false as hell." The association had not received or sent any presidential proclamation. On learning these facts, the *Herald* immediately recalled some 25,000 copies featuring the purported presidential proclamation. Few if any copies of the *Herald*'s abortive edition found their way to newsboys or subscribers.[11]

The *World* and *Journal of Commerce* were not as fortunate. It was only after their issues had been distributed that the editors discovered the proclamation they published was not an authentic NYAP dispatch. They immediately went about informing the public by means of their bulletin boards that the news was a false alarm.[12] The *World* even published an extra edition announcing that the proclamation was a hoax and offering a prize for discovering its perpetrators. Manton Marble sent a telegram giving all the facts of the matter to the NYAP for circulation over its vast news circuits from Maine to California. Daniel H. Craig, manager of the Associated Press, immediately announced a $1,000 reward for information that would lead to the discovery of the forgers who had taken the name of the NYAP in vain.[13]

While the New York newspapers victimized by the forgery were busy assuaging as much as possible of the damage, Washington was alerted to the publication of the suspected proclamation. The New York manager of the government-controlled American Telegraph Company sent the text of the proclamation, as printed in the *World*, to his superior, Major Thomas T. Eckert, superintendent of the military telegraph. Major General John A. Dix, commander of the Department of the East, informed Secretary of State Seward of the publication of the proclamation, "believed to be spurious," and requested immediate official clarification.[14]

The haste was due to the scheduled departure of the steamer *Scotia* for England that same day. Since the early stages of the war, the State Department and the NYAP had had in place a carefully devised procedure for timing the release of war news according to the scheduled departure of Europe-bound mail-bearing steamers. Reuter's agency in England collaborated with them in disseminating the news in England and Europe upon the arrival of the steamers in the Old World.[15] Should the *Scotia* leave New York with information of the purported presidential proclamation on board, Europeans were certain to believe that the Union war effort was in dire straits. The British and French governments, if convinced that momentum was with the Confederacy, were likely to make irreversible policy decisions that could significantly affect the course—and perhaps even the outcome—of the war. The Canadian owner of the *Scotia*, Samuel Cunard, notified of the emergency, agreed to delay the departure of the steamer until the affair was sorted out.[16]

It shortly was, through a brief but emphatic telegram from Seward to the NYAP. The proclamation, announced the secretary of state, was "an absolute forgery." "No proclamation of that kind or any other," he assured the public, "has been made or proposed to be made by the President, or issued or proposed to be issued by the State Department or any Department of the Government." The denial was to be conveyed to Europe by the *Scotia* and telegraphed to ambassadors Charles Francis Adams in London and William A. Dayton in Paris.[17]

Secretary of War Edwin M. Stanton, in a telegram to Dix, tersely confirmed the denial. The proclamation, said Stanton, was " a base and treasonable forgery." Stanton's wording underscored the severity with which the incident was viewed in Washington. Dix immediately launched an investigation, and early in the afternoon he met with the *World*'s Marble and the *Journal*'s Prime. Dix received from the editors a full account of the circumstances surrounding the publication of the forged dispatch.[18] The editors' explanations squared well with Dix's own findings, and he prepared a telegram for Stanton with a summary of his investigation. Dix was relieved to report that the bogus proclamation was nothing more than a "gross fraud."

Dix understood the whole affair as a simple case of wartime financial speculation. Together with all astute Americans, the general knew full well that news of a military debacle was sure to produce rapid and dramatic increases in the price of gold. By anticipating such news, let alone manufacturing it, one could make a fortune in a series of brisk speculative transactions on the exchange.[19] By finding who had bought large amounts of gold on the exchange in the preceding days, Dix could most likely detect the perpetrators of the forgery. He was confident that before long he would have the guilty party under lock and key. He conveyed this assurance to Stanton.[20]

Before Dix's telegram went out, however, he received a dispatch from Washington, signed by the president himself, which put the affair in an entirely different light. Lincoln considered the publication of the spurious proclamation no less than a premeditated act of treason, giving "aid and comfort to the enemies of the United States and to the rebels now at war against the Government, and their aiders and abettors." Accordingly, Lincoln instructed Dix to arrest and imprison the editors, proprietors, and publishers of the two offending newspapers, and to take possession of their printing establishments.

The president's order was followed by a bizarre set of instructions from Stanton. Dix was also directed to take possession of the offices of the Independent Telegraph Company, close down the four offices of the company in New York City, confiscate all the office equipment and message files, and arrest the entire personnel of the company. He was commanded to delegate his best officers to the attack on the telegraph company, to give it his personal attention, and to exercise it with "strict diligence, attention, and confidence." Dix could not possibly have understood Stanton's orders. After all, what could a telegraph line connecting New York with Washington have to do with a local forgery?

Nevertheless, he moved promptly against the telegraph company. But he procrastinated in carrying out the president's unprecedented orders to close down newspapers and arrest editors protected by the First Amendment. Expecting that before long someone in Washington was bound to realize that the affair was a small-time local swindle, Dix delayed seizing the newspapers and their editors.

Dix's delay tactics were not appreciated. Stanton, in an angry telegram, commanded him to carry out his orders forthwith and gave his longtime friend a summary lecture on the duties of a loyal officer. "How you can excuse or justify delay in executing the President's order," he snarled, "is not for me to determine." By the time Dix's guard managed to round up the editors, Washington finally retreated. Possibly influenced by pleas from the member newspapers of the New York Associated Press and from Thurlow Weed, a leading Republican political operator and acknowledged expert on New York press affairs, Dix was allowed to suspend action against the editors. But the strange operation against the telegraph was to proceed swiftly.[21]

The *Berdan*, waiting at Castle Garden to transport her cargo of imprisoned editors to Fort Lafayette, transported instead the personnel of the Independent Telegraph Company.[22] In fact, the entire work force of the young telegraph company would spend the weekend in military prison. For besides prodding and scolding Dix, Stanton kept busy that day masterminding and executing a coordinated attack on telegraph companies. First, early in the morning, Washington's provost marshal occupied the headquarters and offices of the Independent in the capital. Its operators were interrogated, then sent to the Old Capitol Prison. The company's offices and files were thoroughly searched and put under guard.[23] Then, in concert with Dix's raid on the Independent's New York offices, the commanding officers in Philadelphia, Harrisburg, Pittsburgh, and Baltimore were instructed to arrest the local managers and operators of the Independent and the Inland—another emerging telegraph network—and to send them under guard to Washington, together with all the records, documents, and instruments in their telegraph offices.

The hyperactivity in Washington did not subside with the launching of its telegraph campaign. The provost marshal soon received a further mission relating to the public communications sector. The target this time was a wire news and feature service in the process of expanding its operations out of Washington. The service, established early in 1864, was the initiative of three successful war correspondents, Henry Villard, Horace White, and Adam S. Hill. Its nightly dispatch to the country's newspapers was comprised mainly of the official reports and bulletins issued by the War and Navy Departments, the White House, and assorted other units of government. Villard was incarcerated; Hill was placed under observation; and Horace White was subjected to intensive interrogation sessions by Stanton.[24] But no explanation of how a Washington-based wire service could possibly be connected to a New York forgery was ever offered.

On May 20, two days after the publication of the Bogus Proclamation, Dix managed to put his hands on its perpetrator. Surprisingly it was Joseph Howard Jr. of Brooklyn, a prominent journalist and staunch Republican, who happened to be temporarily short on funds. Former president of the Young Men's Republican Club in Brooklyn and Henry Ward Beecher's secretary, Howard was one of the most supportive of the Lincoln administration among the so-called Bohemian Brigade of journalists. He had worked on the *Times* and *Tribune* before joining the *Daily News* and then the *Brooklyn Eagle*. Howard made a full confession: his motivation was indeed financial gain, and he was apparently unaware of the potential damage to the Union that his daring speculative sting could cause. Colonel Edward Sanford, military supervisor of the civilian telegraph, described him after his arrest as "crack brained at best," with "not wit enough to realize the enormity of his offence."[25]

Dix had been confident all along that he would find the forger by snooping in the financial sector. And indeed, his lead appears to have been a New York broker, a Mr. Kent of the firm Kent and Clapp, to whom Howard confided his scheme. Howard had assured the broker that a genuine proclamation was in the works in Washington and that it would be issued before long.[26] Other well-connected New Yorkers, such as steel merchant Charles Augustus Davis, appear to have possessed the same information.[27] Whether "crack brained" or not, Howard was onto something.

On the same day Howard was arrested, Ohio Representative Samuel Sullivan ("Sunset") Cox stunned his peace-Democrat ally, *World* editor Manton Marble, with a revelation from Washington. "The forged proclamation is based on a *fact*," wrote Cox. "A proclamation was written and similar in impact to the base and damnable forgery for which you are under ban." Cox declined to disclose his source but stated parenthetically that "it may come from Mrs. Mary Lincoln or some one." Mary Lincoln had leaked information out of the White House in the past, and Howard was known as one of her confidants.[28]

Both Joseph Howard and "Sunset" Cox were correct. On the night of May 17, President Lincoln put pen to paper and drafted a proclamation calling up 300,000 men for active duty in the fateful Virginia campaign. Lincoln had not officially issued the proclamation, possibly due to considerations of timing.[29]

This draft seems to account for the otherwise inexplicable chain of events after the publication of the bogus proclamation in New York. One can imagine Lincoln's astonishment when he discovered that a variation on his nocturnal composition was published within a few hours in New York. When news of the bogus proclamation first hit Washington, it was immediately and naturally assumed that the source of the published proclamation was Lincoln's own draft, which somehow had found its way to the opposition press—in other words, that the bogus proclamation was not bogus after all, but the genuine item.

Given this plausible, if erroneous, theory, Washington's response to the publication appears perfectly reasonable and, moreover, legally sound. Here was a sensitive state document, a state secret not intended for immediate publication leaked out of the White House, transmitted rapidly to New York, and made public there. It must have been transmitted by telegraph—no other means of conveyance would have allowed its appearance the very next morning in the New York press. Villard's start-up wire service, which unlike the NYAP was not bound to the administration, was suspected of getting hold of Lincoln's draft in Washington, then sending the contraband by telegraph to New York. The Independent, its message traffic neither regulated nor censored, was the most likely suspect for transmitting it. And finally, given the source, the *Journal* and *World* would seem responsible for knowingly making public a sensitive state secret whose timing would allow it to reach a watchful Europe with potentially disastrous consequences to the Union.

Much evidence supports this scenario. The administration's first action after it received news of the publication was to investigate whether the text of the published proclamation had passed over the wires of the War Department-controlled American Telegraph Company from Washington to New York.[30] Stanton himself telegraphed Dix that, contrary to Dix's opinion that the proclamation was a New York forgery, "the officer in charge of the investigations . . . reports that he is led to believe it originated in this city"—namely, in Washington. One of the military telegraph operators on duty in Washington wrote in his diary that the notion that the proclamation originated in Washington persisted throughout the early stages of the investigation. Accordingly, the Washington office of the Independent was the first to be seized, its files searched, and its operators questioned.[31]

But as the facts of the affair were rapidly accumulating in Washington, it became clear that the administration's working theory as to the source of the Bogus Proclamation could not be confirmed or sustained. No copy of the president's draft proclamation was found in Washington, either in the offices of the government-controlled American, the Independent, or Villard's agency. At the same time, positive proof that the Bogus Proclamation was a local—one might say innocent—New York forgery was mounting. With the collapse of its paradigm under the pressure of a critical mass of evidence, the administration began seriously considering Dix's alternative hypothesis about the source of the proclamation—and it wasn't Abraham Lincoln.

Once its scenario was disproved, the administration could have been expected to drop the case. Surprisingly, however, it did not immediately roll back its quixotic attack on telegraphs, wire services, and journalistic word-mills—far from it. Official Washington doggedly pursued its original course. It did not immediately restore the *Journal of Commerce* and *World* to their proprietors, nor did it release Villard and the personnel of the Independent and Inland or permit the immediate resumption of their operations. Although part of the delay in restoring the presses was due to negligence on the part of Dix's staff,[32] the officers and offices of the telegraph companies were not released until three full days after Howard had been placed behind bars, and Villard remained in custody for three days after Howard's confession. The slow processing of the affairs of the Independent, of the Inland, and of Villard's agency appeared both deliberate and inexplicable.

Lincoln, a temperate individual, had responded to the publication of the Bogus Proclamation with wrath. "It angered Lincoln more than almost any other occurrence of the war period," stated an eye witness.[33] Lincoln's wrath, the hyperactivity in Washington pursuant to the publication, and its persistence after the source of the proclamation was ascertained, indicated that the incident was perceived by the administration to have considerable significance. It represented much more than a bizarre coincidence and its gross misunderstanding.

To the administration, the meaning of the publication was ominous. It signaled the collapse of its public communication policy, a policy carefully crafted and nurtured during three years of war. The imagined collapse happened at perhaps the most critical period in the war and in Lincoln's political career. Both were hanging in the balance in mid-May 1864. The Union was waging its decisive battle of the war in Virginia, and the presidential nominations and election were nearing. This was a bad time for a public communication policy to self-destruct.

Lincoln and his administration clearly understood the new dynamic of recentralization that had affected America's news communication system as the Civil War was nearing. They worked effectively to harness the new tools for central control over news, focused on the telegraph and wire service, to their advantage. In fact, recentralization provided them with their solution to the wartime dilemma of public communication. The administration could live with a free press, as long as it (the administration) exercised control over the process of feeding information to that press. Through influence over the release of wartime news, over telegraphy, and over the wire service, the administration could dominate the process of providing timely hard news to the public. This would still be done by means of the nation's newspapers but over the heads of their editors.

The administration's influence over the news-providing process ran along an axis from the battlefield to the printed copy of the newspaper, its power diminishing as news progressed along the axis. The administration's power was highest at the source of the news—the battlefield—and its own newsworthy affairs, and lowest at the outlet—the newspaper. Through well-developed and orderly procedures the Union armies sent timely information up the military hierarchy and, over networks of military telegraph lines spatially paralleling this hierarchy, to the civil administration. The administration, in turn, would decide what of that news it would release to the public, when, and in what form. The reporting of timely news from the battlefield—the information that captured readers' attention—was effectively controlled by the administration.

The next step along the path from news sources to news outlets was the lines of the American Telegraph Company radiating out of Washington, and the news distribution system of the wire service hedged on that network. Government had total control over the operations of the nominally civilian American, which dominated eastern-seaboard telegraphy. This power was at first exercised by way of informal arrangements and subsequently was formalized by legislation. The legal nature of the executive branch's control over the message traffic of a nominally civilian system was murky. But however ambiguous its powers over telegraphic information flow in theory, in practice the government exercised full control over press reports transmitted by American and censored them rigorously.[34]

When it came to the national news wire service, government power and influence had no legal, nor any other formal foundation. Substantial mutual interest sustained a cozy, semiofficial liaison in which the NYAP served as a de facto organ of the administration.[35] The government provided the NYAP exclusively with its news bulletins and other information valued in the news market. It gave the wire service cart blanche to use the government-owned lines of the military telegraph and American's government-supervised telegraph networks, which transmitted its news. The administration even waived the required preapproval of press reports transmitted by American: NYAP reports went uncensored. Government had in this way a mechanism for delivering its message to practically the entire press of the country, and through those newspapers it could access and address the American public rapidly and simultaneously.

The Bogus Proclamation episode provides a revealing illustration of the contours of this masterpiece of creative communication policy. One can observe the extremely effective use of the telegraph for the management of military operations—in this case through the rapid, concerted attack on the Independent and Inland, orchestrated by the secretary of war and carried out simultaneously over a vast field, with information flowing back and forth between the War Department and the units operating on the periphery. One can witness how a self-serving wire report—in this case a bogus one—could be incorporated in the nation's newspapers over the heads of their editors. And one can see how, in its denial of the proclamation via NYAP, the administration could access the entire American newspaper-reading public (and to an extent the European public too) almost instantly.

But the Bogus Proclamation affair also sounded an alarm that the entire wartime system of public communication could collapse. New independent and uncontrolled telegraph networks—the Independent, the Inland, the United States—had entered the field of real-time transmission. A competing wire service, not bound to the administration, had established itself as an alternative system of news gathering and diffusion, and a third was organizing to enter the field.[36] The opposition press could easily recruit the multiplying telegraphic and news-gathering infrastructures to promote an antiwar and antiadministration cause. It would control what really mattered: the traffic of independent, fast news, the very commodity that an anxious American public most sought. That was what the administration believed had happened in the case of the Bogus Proclamation.

A crackdown was inevitable. It was done with authority and spanned the entire axis of news reporting, from news sources and news-gatherers, through the transmission infrastructures, and all the way to the opposition press—the First Amendment notwithstanding. Indeed, in the course of sorting out the Bogus Proclamation affair, the administration also arrested Samuel Medary, editor of the seditious *Crisis* in Columbus, Ohio, and closed down the *Transcript* in Baltimore and the *Picayune* and *Courier* in New Orleans.[37] It also semiofficially threatened the Washington press corps not to criticize the recent newspaper seizure in New York. "In these broiling days," observed the Washington correspondent of the proadministration *New York Commercial Advertiser*, "Mum's the word."[38]

The administration's actions in the aftermath of the affair thus represented no less than an emergency attempt at fixing a collapsing public communication policy. And indeed, the way the affair was ultimately settled underscored the administration's purpose in its comprehensive multimedia war. The Independent and Inland were fully restored only after a series of meetings between their presidents, John J. Speed and Theodore Adams, and Stanton. They reached an agreement to the effect that the lines of the Independent would thereafter be connected to the War Department, subject to government supervision and censorship. [39] Although the terms for Villard's release were never formally disclosed, the well-informed David Homer Bates, one of Lincoln's telegraphers, observed that thereafter the administration began supplying Villard's agency with news, including some choice exclusives. [40] Howard himself was released several months after the affair at the behest of his former employer and friend of the family, Henry Ward Beecher.

The publication of the Bogus Proclamation prompted the war administration to review the state of the Union's communication policy. The publication appeared to imply that the dynamic of centralization that had transformed the communication environment just prior to the war was reversing itself. That centralization had given the administration its power over the wartime flow of public information, and a movement toward decentralization was therefore perilous. In response to such a trend, a revision of the government's wartime communication policy appeared imperative. In a field of parallel communication infrastructures and content systems, the opposition press would inevitably develop an alternative supply of timely news that would promote its cause and appeal to the public. The opposition would thus escape the administration's stranglehold over the war news market and come to represent a clear and present danger. The administration would be deprived of the luxury of having a free press and controlling information flow, of both fighting a total war and adhering to the First Amendment.

In the end, such fears proved groundless. The perceived splintering of the communication environment was deceptive. In fact, the fracturing of the telegraph and wire service systems was merely a symptom of a process of change signaling a transition from oligopoly to monopoly in telegraphy and in wire news. Because that indeed was the trend, a free press could be safely suffered by the Lincoln administration, all the way to Appomattox and the end of the Civil War.

NOTES

An earlier version of this chapter was published as "'Public Sentiment Is Everything': The Union's Public Communications Strategy and the Bogus Proclamation of 1864," *Journal of American History* 89 (2002): 869–899.

1.   In this respect, the Civil War is widely recognized as a "modern" or even "total" war. See Edward Hagerman, *The American Civil War and the Origins of Modern Warfare* (Bloomington: Indiana University Press, 1988). For a comparative evaluation of this view, see Robert M. Epstein, *Napoleon's Last Victory and the*

Emergence of Modern War (Lawrence: University of Kansas Press, 1994), and Stig Förster and Jörg Nagler, eds., *On the Road to Total War: The American Civil War and the German Wars of Unification, 1861–1871* (Washington D.C.: German Historical Institute and Cambridge University Press, 1997).

2. Martin van Creveld, *Technology and War* (New York: The Free Press, 1989), remains an excellent introduction to the history of this aspect of warfare. Robert M. Epstein, "Patterns of Change and Continuity in Nineteenth-Century Warfare," *Journal of Military History* 56, no. 3 (July 1992): 375–388, provides a useful overview.

3. Abraham Lincoln, notes prepared for speeches after the Dred Scott decision, (21 August 1858), in *The Collected Works of Abraham Lincoln*, ed. Roy P. Basler, vol. 2 (New Brunswick: Rutgers University Press, 1953–1955), 553.

4. A comprehensive introduction to this dual process is provided in Harold D. Lasswell, David Lerner, and Hans Speier, *Propaganda and Communication in World History*, vol. 2, *Emergence of Public Opinion in the West* (Honolulu: University Press of Hawaii, 1980).

5. The literature on this problem in the context of the Civil War is vast. See, for instance, James G. Randall, *Constitutional Problems under Lincoln* (New York: D. Appleton and Company, 1926), and Mark E. Neely Jr., *The Fate of Liberty: Abraham Lincoln and Civil Liberties* (New York: Oxford University Press, 1991).

6. *Journal of Commerce*, 26 March 1870. The *Journal*'s account is also quoted in full in Frederic Hudson, *Journalism in the United States, from 1690 to 1872* (New York: Harper & Brothers, 1873), 374–376.

7. *New York World*, 18 May 1864, and *New York Journal of Commerce*, 18 May 1864.

8. *New York Tribune*, 10 May 1864.

9. William C. Prime to Mary Trumbull Prime, 11, 12, and 13 May 1864, letters in the possession of the family transcribed in Alice Scoville Barry, *Why Did President Lincoln Suppress the Journal of Commerce?* (New York: Twin Coasts Newspapers, Inc., n.d.), 2–3.

10. It may be that the *World* and *Journal of Commerce* received their copies in NYAP envelopes. Craig to Bangs, 18 May 1864, Marble papers, LC. The *New York Times*, 19 May 1864, claimed to have suspected the proclamation upon its receipt due to its awkward wording and claimed the credit for initiating and making the inquiry at the NYAP offices and exposing the hoax. This version was elaborated in the *Times*'s jubilee supplement, 18 September 1901. However, William C. Prime, editor of the *Journal of Commerce* stated that the *Times* in fact had typeset and stereotyped the proclamation. William C. Prime to Mary Trumbull Prime, 20 May 1864, letter in the possession of the family transcribed in Barry, 22.

11. *New York Daily News*, 19 May 1864; *New York Times*, 19 May 1864. William Prime to Mary Prime, 20 May 1864, op. cit. The *New York Daily News*, 19 May 1864, stated that one of the German language NYAP client newspapers in the city also published the proclamation. No steps, however, are known to have been taken against it.

12. The *World* stopped over-the-counter sale of the edition at 8:00 a.m. The employees of both newspapers were dispatched to retrieve as many copies as possible

of the morning edition. Morgan Dix, *Memoirs of John Adams Dix* (New York: Harper & Brothers, 1883), 98–99.

13. Marble to Craig, 18 May 1864; Craig to Marble [18 May 1864], Marble papers, LC. Craig to the proprietors of the *New York Journal of Commerce, Sun, Herald, Express, Tribune, World,* and *Times,* 18 May 1864, Manton Marble papers, LC.

14. The entire correspondence is available in the collection of "Telegrams Collected by the Office of the Secretary of War, 1861–1882," RG 107, Records of the Office of the Secretary of War (M-473), National Archives. Quotations from the official correspondence in the text are from this record. Much, but not all, of the official correspondence was reproduced in Robert N. Scott, ed. *War of the Rebellion*, ser. 3, vol. 4 (Washington, D.C.: Government Printing Office, 1900), 386–395, and in Harold L. Nelson, ed., *Freedom of the Press from Hamilton to the Warren Court* (Indianapolis: Bobbs Merrill, 1967), 232–247.

15. As early as October 1861, the War Department adjusted the publication of news via the NYAP to the schedules of trans-Atlantic steamers so as to impact the shaping of policy in Europe. See, e.g., Thomas A. Scott to D. H. Craig, 31 October 1861, *War of the Rebellion*, ser. 3, vol. 1, 612. An elaborate attempt to spin war news for the European public, featuring the interception of a London-bound steamer at Cape Race, Newfoundland, by NYAP yachts and providing it with late news transmitted by telegraph and cable is documented in *War of the Rebellion*, ser. 2, vol. 2, 1,093. For the general features of the cooperation between the State Department, the NYAP, and Reuter in reporting war news to Europe, see Reuter to Craig, 24 January 1863; Craig to Gobright, 16 February 1863, and 11 March 1863, William Henry Seward papers, LC.

16. The delay, however, was brief. At 2:30 p.m. official Washington was notified by the Associate Press that the *Scotia* had sailed with the official contradiction of the Bogus Proclamation aboard. Philadelphia Associated Press to William Henry Seward and Edwin M. Stanton, 18 May 1864, Seward papers, LC. The source suggesting that Samuel Cunard was personally involved in the episode is Morgan Dix, *Memoirs of John Adams Dix*, vol. 2 (New York: Harper & Brothers, 1883), 99.

17. The denial and orders for forwarding it to Adams and Dayton were sent from Washington at noon. The *Journal of Commerce* editors informed Seward directly that they had authorized a denial to be sent by the steamer. See Prime, Stone, Hale, and Hallock to Seward, 18 May 1864, Telegrams Collected.

18. W.C. Prime to Mary Prime, 18 May 1864, reproduced in Barry, 7.

19. Gold, however, rose by only 5 percent on the morning of the publication of the Bogus Proclamation, from 177 to 184. *New York Times,* 17 May 1864, 19 May 1864.

20. By then Dix apparently had been advised by a New York broker of the inquiries of a journalist on the potential market effect of the publication of a proclamation calling up 300,000 additional troops.

21. NYAP editors to Lincoln, 19 May 1864, Lincoln papers, LC. The appeal to the president was the initiative of the *Herald's* Frederic Hudson: Craig to Marble, 19 May 1864, Marble papers, LC. Weed to Stanton, 18 May 1864 (received 5:00 p.m.), Telegrams Collected. On Weed's assurances see W.C. Prime to M. Prime, 19 May 1864, and cf. W.C. Prime's earlier letter on the same day, both reproduced in Barry, 11, 15; Weed to Stanton, 19 May 1864, Telegrams Collected.

22. (Robert Morton), "A Reminiscence of the Arrest and Incarceration of Five New York Telegraphers, Charged with Conspiracy against the Government in 1864," *Telegraph Age* (February 1905), 56–57. One of the prisoners was former governor Edwin B. Morgan's brother. Morgan appealed to Seward upon the transfer of the Independent's New York staff to Washington. Morgan to Seward, 19 May 1864, Seward papers, LC.

23. Order to Superintendent of the Old Capitol Prison for receiving and confinement of J.N. Worl, J.M. Lock, and others, 18 May 1864, Union Provost Marshals' File of Papers Relating to Two or More Civilians, RG 109 (M416), National Archives; Thomas T. Eckert to Stanton, 18 May 1864 (received 2:15 p.m.), Telegrams Collected; "Reminiscences of the Forged Proclamation Incident during the Civil War," *Telegraph Age* (March 1905), 117–120.

24. David Homer Bates, *Lincoln in the Telegraph Office* (New York: Century Co., 1907), 242.

25. Sanford to Stanton, 21 May 1864, Telegrams Collected. Robert Harper suggests that Dix had arrested Howard on the day the proclamation was published. Robert S. Harper, *Lincoln and the Press* (New York: McGraw-Hill, 1951), 293. This plausible theory, however, conflicts with most of the primary-source evidence.

26. *New York Daily News*, 22 May 1864; *New York Times*, 22 May 1864; *Brooklyn Eagle*, 22 May 1864; *Washington Star*, 24 May 1864. Howard consulted Kent as to the anticipated effect of a proclamation announcing the draft of 300,000 men— the exact number as in Lincoln's draft. Howard claimed to know of the draft "through secret channels of intelligence at Washington."

27. Charles Augustus Davis to Seward, 19 May 1864, Seward papers, LC. In fact, the *New York Evening Post* and the *New York Commercial Advertiser* had reported that same morning that "it has been determined" to call up 300,000 more troops. Although there was no "official promulgation" of the fact, it was based on confidential assertions by "leading Congressional friends of the administration." *New York Evening Post*, 18 May 1864, and see "The Forged Proclamation," in the same issue; *New York Commercial Advertiser*, 18 May 1864.

28. Samuel Sullivan Cox to Marble, 20 May 1864, Marble Papers. On May 18, Lincoln told the *Tribune*'s James Gilmore that he had signed a proclamation calling up 300,000 men the night before but did not intend to publish it until July. James Gilmore to Sydney Howard Gay, 18 May 1864, Gay Papers.

29. Abraham Lincoln, draft order, 17 May 1864, Lincoln Papers, Lincoln Museum, Fort Wayne, Ind.; *The Collected Works of Abraham Lincoln*, Roy P. Basler, ed., vol. 7 (New Brunswick: Rutgers University Press, 1953), 344; Lincoln to Salmon P. Chase, 18 May 1864, ibid., p. 347. On timing considerations, see Thurlow Weed to Stanton, 10 May 1864, Lincoln papers, LC; Stanton to Seymour, 22 May 1864, Telegrams Collected.

30. B.P. Snyder to E.S. Sanford, 18 May 1864, Telegrams Collected. Snyder, after confirming that he found no such message also informed Sanford that he understood that the "Independent line sent dispatch stating 400,000 men were called for and president had asked for day of fasting and prayer."

31. David Homer Bates diary, 20 May 1864, Bates Collection, Library of Congress. Cf. Morton, "A Reminiscence," and "Reminiscences of the Forged Proclamation."

Earlier in the war the Independent had transmitted a bogus telegraphic report of Union victories in the interest of gold speculators. The dispatch was blocked by censorship from passing over the lines of the American. J. Cutler Andrews, *The North Reports the Civil War* (Pittsburgh: University of Pittsburgh Press, 1955), 371. This precedent may have helped condition the administration's response.

32. W.C. Prime to M. Prime, 22 May 1864, transcribed in Barry, 27.

33. F.A. Flower to C.F. Gunther, 14 February 1904, quoted in James G. Randall and Richard N. Current, *Lincoln the President: Last Full Measure* (New York: Dodd, Mead & Company, 1955), 156, and in Shelby Foote, *The Civil War: A Narrative* (New York: Random House, 1974), 376.

34. General Order No. 10, 4 February 1862, *War of the Rebellion,* ser. 3, vol. 1, 879; and see report of debate in the Senate on this issue: *New York Times,* 30 January 1862; E.S. Sanford to B.P. Snyder and G.H. Burns, 9 August 1861; War Department Order, 25 February 1862, *War of the Rebellion,* ser. 3, vol. 1, 394–395, 899.

35. Menahem Blondheim, *News over the Wires: The Telegraph and the Flow of Public Information in America, 1844-1897* (Cambridge: Harvard University Press, 1997), 132–137.

36. Francis O.J. Smith to Executive Committee, United States Telegraph Company, 16 August 1864, Francis O.J. Smith papers, Maine Historical Society.

37. "Freedom of the Press," *American Annual Cyclopedia and Register* (New York: Appleton, 1965), 394; Harper, 298.

38. Quoted in Harper, 298.

39. Edwin M. Stanton, Order, 23 May 1864; John J. Speed and Theodore Adams, Statement, 23 May 1864, Stanton papers, Library of Congress.

40. David Homer Bates diary, 21 May 1864; Bates, *Lincoln,* 243.

Part III

"The Union Forever"

Journalism in Civil War Indiana

The Party Press and Free Expression

— David W. Bulla —

The period of 1861–1865 was a transitional phase for journalism in the Hoosier State. The party press of the 1820s and 1830s was gradually being replaced by a new type of journalism that was still partisan in nature but also was becoming increasingly personal. The editor's personality was a central feature of the paper, and he interpreted the news in terms of his own political beliefs. Political ideology played a large role in the transitional party-personal press in Civil War Indiana. Democrats in the state worried about the expansion of federal powers, particularly those of the president. The Democratic editors represented the middle ground between what they saw as two radical groups: the secessionists in the South, who had no desire for reunion, and the radical abolitionists in the Northeast, who wanted to destroy slavery while forcing reunion. Although some Hoosier Democrats believed "the war was a mistake and that there was no way that it could be won," as newspaper historian George Douglas has observed, most Democrats in the state supported the war but upheld their right to criticize the prosecution of the war.[1]

The U.S. Constitution was central to the political ideology of Indiana's Democrats, who tended to read it much more literally than their Republican counterparts, especially the sections that dealt with the powers enumerated to the states. For the Democrats, the Constitution gave shape to the American Revolution. It was prescriptive, and its core was passed down from

previous generations. Indiana's Democrats believed the Constitution protected them from martial law during the war. As strict constructionists of
the Constitution, Democrats construed the Bill of Rights literally and ignored
the "responsibility-for-abuse" clause of the Indiana Bill of Rights. John W.
Dawson's Fort Wayne newspaper published key civil liberties passages from
the constitutions of the original 13 states. Dawson was fond of quoting a particular sentence that appears in several New England state constitutions: "The
liberty of the press is essential to the security of freedom in a State."[2] Democratic editors in Indiana conveniently did not refer to the press responsibility
clause in their own state's constitution.

By 1861, most newspapers in Indiana were aligned with either the Republicans or the Democrats, although a few Free Soil, Peoples Party, independent, religious, and one-issue papers existed too. Almost every town had a
least one Republican newspaper and one Democratic paper. Many had more
than one for each party. Hoosiers were intent on maintaining politics as usual
during the war. According to Indiana historian Gilbert R. Tredway, this was
because each party refused "to put the country's interests above party advantage. The 1860s featured political vituperation and personal journalism to a
degree astonishing to the twentieth century mind."[3]

The practice of politics as usual came under fire in April 1863, the mid-
way point of the Civil War. That month, Brigadier General Milo Hascall, the
commander of the District of Indiana and the de facto head of its shadow
federal government, would suspend publication of 11 Democratic newspapers
in the state.[4] Those 11 cases of press suppression in Indiana during 1863 represented the highest single-year total of the war.[5] The overwhelming majority
of those cases came while Hascall was in office and Democrats were rallying
against what they now considered to be an abolitionist war. When Indiana
Governor Oliver P. Morton effectively closed down the general assembly to
prevent its planned entreaties to the South for a peace conference and raised
money privately to run the state government, the role of the federal military
shadow government increased dramatically. Indiana was a state in turmoil,
and Hascall, serving as Department of the Ohio Commander Major General
Ambrose Burnside's proxy, worked to stifle the Democrats as the war news
took a turn for the worse.

The political nature of Civil War journalism is best seen in the fact that
Hascall targeted editors primarily in the more Republican northern part of
the state. All of these papers were near his home of Goshen, which suggests
that he felt confident he could intimidate the Democratic editors of Plymouth, South Bend, Warsaw, Bluffton, Columbia City, Winamac, Huntington,
Rushville, Hartford City, Franklin, and Knox because he was close to the Re-

publican political leaders in those towns. Furthermore, the general bypassed the Democratic editors in the area's largest city, Fort Wayne, precisely because he knew that the Democrats were stronger there and the press was more sophisticated in Allen County. He also did not threaten editors in Indianapolis, which was evenly split between Republicans, who had control of the executive branch, and Democrats, who had the majority in the legislature. Nor did he go after Democratic editors in the southern part of the state, where anti-Lincoln, pro-Confederate sentiment was strongest.

From 1861 to the late summer of 1862, the Civil War had tended to unify the press in Indiana. After Lincoln announced the Emancipation Proclamation on September 22, 1862, however, such unity disappeared. Democrats began to become more and more critical of the war, whereas Republicans dug in and began to see the political battle in terms of loyalty and disloyalty. The generally muddy war news of the first two years of the conflict intensified the divide, as did Democratic concerns about forced conscription and their economic future in a nation of freed slaves and dispossessed slave owners. In a sense, both Democratic and Republican editors began to dabble in the politics of fear. Hascall's edict added fuel to the fire. Republican editors cheered Hascall. Democrats cursed him, while still swearing loyalty to the Union.

The limits of free expression in the Hoosier State would undergo public debate after Hascall promulgated General Order No. 9 on April 25, 1863. The order made it a crime punishable by a military commission for citizens, especially political orators and newspaper editors, to encourage resistance to the draft; disparage any law passed by Congress as a war measure; criticize the war policies of President Lincoln, his cabinet, and military leaders; or express words that in effect gave aid and comfort to the enemy. Hascall said further that he intended to enforce General Order No. 38, enacted by Burnside 12 days earlier. Burnside, also a native of Indiana, was a man who had a keen interest in the press. In 1862 he had established a pro-Union newspaper in New Bern, North Carolina, after he led conquering forces in much of the eastern part of that state.[6] In December of that year, he had become the subject of ridicule in papers throughout the North after he was made the commander of the Army of the Potomac and led his men to a disastrous defeat at Fredericksburg, Virginia.

Burnside's order outlawed public criticism of the Lincoln administration's war effort in the Department of Ohio, which included Ohio, Kentucky, Indiana, Illinois, and Michigan. General Orders No. 38 also stated, "The habit of declaring sympathies for the enemy will not be allowed in this department."[7] Burnside added: "Treason expressed or implied will not be tolerated."[8] Elsewhere, Burnside said public discussion of war policy should be done at "a proper time," although he did not express when that time might be. "My duty requires me to stop licensed and intemperate discussion which tends to weaken the authorities of the Government and army," he said.[9] This meant any expression, written or spoken, that opposed the Lincoln Administration, the war itself, or the ongoing war effort, including the Emancipation Proclamation, which was wildly unpopular in many parts of the Midwest. Burnside's department coexisted with the already existing state and local civilian governments in the Ohio Valley, something that was not lost on the legal minds on the Democratic side.

Hascall, who had seen action in West Virginia, Tennessee, and Mississippi, had been brought to Indiana to seize Union Army deserters and to help slow the escape of Confederate prisoners from camps in the Hoosier State and to make it less attractive to anti-Lincoln southerners migrating North.[10] Intelligence information raised suspicions of some Peace Democrats as aiding and abetting these escapees.[11] Burnside had placed Hascall in charge in Indiana because of his tenacity at policing just such problems. Burnside may have been eager, as well, to make his mark on the war in the aftermath of his well-publicized failures in the past. If so, he needed tough-minded subordinates like Hascall to help him prove he could be an effective leader.[12]

Hascall's order was soon challenged by Tenth District Congressman Joseph Ketchum Edgerton, a Fort Wayne attorney and businessman who had made much of his money on the railroads. Edgerton, who earlier had published a letter in northeast Indiana newspapers denouncing the Conscription Act, argued that the Constitution was not suspended by war and that the necessary civilian governments were in place to keep the peace and run municipal governments of the state. A dedicated Jeffersonian who believed in limited government, Edgerton maintained that the Bill of Rights was the law of the land and that no military leader had the right to squelch free expression. He also predicted that Hascall's policy would mobilize Democrats.

One week after Hascall's April 25 order was made public, Edgerton, a resident of Allen County, sent a letter to Hascall that was published in dozens of newspapers in the state. In it, Edgerton tried to express a civil tone, saying that Hascall's intentions in enacting the order seemed to be patriotic. "It seems to recognize the fact that opposing political parties may still be permitted to exist," Edgerton writes, "and yet co-operate to restore harmony and good feeling in the State."[13] However, the congressman had questions about the general's new policy regarding civil rights. Edgerton, as a politician, wanted Hascall to clarify exactly what he meant when he wrote that all newspaper editors and public orators who "endeavor to bring the war policy government into disrepute" and are "actively opposed to the war policy of the administration" would be subject to incarceration and trial by a military commission.[14]

Hascall responded with a private letter to Edgerton on May 5 that was sent to newspapers in the state, apparently by Edgerton's brother, Alfred P. Edgerton.[15] In the letter, the Union military leader defined loyalty as practical loyalty, not in legal or theoretic terms. He wrote, "You know as well as I, that practically, during the next two years, there is no difference between the Administration and the Government. You cannot destroy or impair the one without effecting [sic] the other similarly."[16] Because of the federal election schedule and the war powers of the president granted by the Constitution, the Lincoln administration, with a Republican majority in both houses of Congress, was in fact the federal government for the next two years—until the 1864 elections. Lincoln had a mandate until March 1865. This was a constitutional issue that the Democrats could do nothing about.

In a larger sense, however, Hascall was off the mark: although the Democrats were effectively out of power and had at best minimum input on war policy, they certainly had the right to criticize government and to use their criticisms to build a base of power to oppose Lincoln in 1864. Nothing in the Constitution prohibits the party out of power from campaigning and devising alternate political strategies during war. Just because the Republicans had the upper hand in the federal government, especially with control of Congress and the executive branch, they did not dominate all state and local political institutions in the North. In many locales, Democrats still held the majority. If they had different war policies and objectives, including a negotiated peace, there was nothing that Lincoln and the Republicans could legally do about it. A democracy allows for a diversity of policies and policy positions.

Furthermore, Hascall had propounded an either-or argument that flew in the face of a two- or multiparty system: either you were for the Republicans or you were against the government and therefore in favor of the Confederacy. This meant that a citizen who might be against war based on conscience—as some Quakers were—would, in Hascall's reasoning, be a traitor. Clearly, this was a perilous rationale for a military governor to be making, particularly in an area of a state not under attack or anywhere near a battlefield. It clearly upset Indiana Governor Oliver Morton, who had not been thrilled about Hascall's rise to power from the start.[17]

Hascall wrote that it was appropriate to carp about government policy and action during peacetime but that such inveighing is inappropriate during wartime. The general went on to say that Democratic resolutions finding fault with the Republicans were "evil" and implied that they were intended to wreak havoc on the Union war effort. "The only practical effect, then, of allowing newspapers and public speakers to inveigh against these measures is to divide and distract our own people, and thus give material 'aid and comfort' to our enemies," Hascall wrote.[18] This argument was frequently cited by Republican editors, politicians, and Union military officials. War, they maintained, creates a special circumstance, and harmony is essential to fighting such a war effectively. It would be awful, in their opinion, if the North lost the war because its citizens were fragmented. In the back of the Republicans' minds was the belief that the nation's history was in the balance, that the still relatively young nation could be torn apart by secessionism, and that the British or some other foreign power might use the conflict to further divide the country. That the South courted the British and French for official recognition throughout the war was not lost on Union military leaders.

Hascall lumped Edgerton with Terre Haute Congressman Daniel Wolsey Voorhees, a leading Peace Democrat and close ally of former Ohio Congressman Clement Vallandigham, whom Burnside had thrown in jail on May 1 for a speech that criticized Lincoln and called the president a despot, even though Vallandigham had advised his listeners that the only way to make changes was through the ballot box. Hascall added that he would hold Edgerton responsible for any violence or mob activity that took place in Fort Wayne as a result of antiwar rhetoric. "I take deep interests in you for more reason than one," Hascall concluded.[19] Hascall, in effect, was setting up a sort of police state and keeping political intelligence on Democrats, something that Morton had neither the time nor the resources to undertake. Hascall made it clear that he wanted to go after political leaders, including newspaper editors, because they were the ones inflaming ordinary citizens and potential soldiers. He added, in his best line of the exchange, "To kill the serpent speedily it must be hit on the head."[20]

Edgerton, who was on his way to England while Congress was in recess, replied to Hascall on May 12, having read Hascall's May 6 letter in the *New York Evening Express*. Edgerton said that any intelligent Hoosier would construe General Order No. 9 to mean that free speech and press were suppressed under Hascall's military administration in the state. Edgerton questioned whether or not the order would promote Hascall's stated intent to "restore harmony and good feeling in the State."[21] Edgerton said that Hascall should "recede as soon as gracefully as you can from the arbitrary purpose you have indicated." Edgerton, who had studied law under William Swetland in Plattsburg, New York, when he was 16, said there would be no disturbance of the peace in Indiana as long as Hascall did not constrain the constitutional rights of Indiana citizens.[22] Edgerton warned that the order would be ignored by Indiana's citizens. "It is not in rebellion, nor in a state of war, nor 'disloyal.' It has a constitution and laws of its own, all accordant with the constitution of the United States. . . . Among the civil rights of the people of Indiana are the rights of free speech, free press, and free courts. The people of Indiana have done nothing to forfeit these rights. They cannot forfeit them, for they are inherent and inalienable."[23]

Edgerton predicted that General Order No. 9 would not survive the ordeals of judicial review and popular defiance. Then he launched into rhetoric that was popular with his largely Democratic constituents in Fort Wayne: "The people of Indiana are not slaves—they are freemen. They will read and think; they will assemble and make and hear speeches; they will freely discuss public affairs, and freely resolve and vote upon them, and they organize political parties, some opposed to, some favoring the Administration, and you cannot prevent it."[24] Edgerton said neither the federal government nor the Republicans had the power to stop freedom of expression. "You may attack it and temporarily abridge or trammel it, but you can not subvert it."[25] Rather, attempts at suppression would only lead to Republican losses at the polls.

Edgerton maintained that he was for peace, prosperity, and the restoration of the union, although he preferred to suppress the rebellion by nonmilitary means. He also said he opposed such federal laws as emancipation and confiscation. "I believe the administration has justly forfeited the confidence of a large majority of the people, even in the States faithful to the Union." He said that change in the administration must come at the ballot box and that such change could only occur if politicians could freely express themselves as is guaranteed by the Constitution. Edgerton added that his criticisms of Lincoln resonated with a majority of the Tenth District, who had voted Edgerton into office the previous fall. "I shall support the war policy or any other public policy of the administration when I think it entitled to support, and I will oppose it before the people and Congress when I think it ought to be opposed . . . I will never, as long as life and intelligence remain, surrender my constitutional right to freely discuss, approve or condemn, in a constitutional way, and as I think the public good my demand, any policy or measure, be it for peace or war, of any administration, State or national."[26]

In the midst of the Edgerton-Hascall debate, the general sent a letter to the *New York Express*, which had criticized General Order No. 9 in an earlier editorial. James Brooks, the editor of the *Express*, decided to publish Hascall's reply to the editorial. Hascall called Brooks's editorial "exceedingly witty and smart"; the order had been promulgated only after "mature deliberation and consultation."[27] Then Hascall added, "It is fortunate for you that your paper is not published in my District."[28] Brooks countered that it was fortunate for Hascall that "this threat is not uttered in 'my District,' for if it were, the Grand Jury would indict you for threatening to disturb the peace and the least punishment you could hope for would be 'bound over,' with sureties, 'to keep that peace.'"[29]

Brooks said that Hascall was delusional like many military men, believing that the war policy of the Lincoln administration was the law of the land: "It would be safe to labor under the delusion in Indiana just now, but it would not be safe to be deluded by it, in New York."[30] Brooks warned that if Hascall tried to do anything to interfere with publication of the *Express* he would have the Hoosier general arrested. Brooks reminded Hascall that the supreme military leader in New York was Governor Horatio Seymour, a Democrat who sided with the press in its conflicts with the Lincoln Administration. He also wondered why Union military leaders were only arresting Democratic editors when abolitionists in New York frequently chided the president and his war policy. He finished by wondering why talented Union soldiers were not off fighting the Confederates instead of imposing unnecessary federal power on the denizens of the Hoosier State. This was a direct shot at Hascall's manhood.

The problem with Hascall's order was its extremity. He made an argument for shutting down civil liberties, saying they were conditional and based on loyalty to the Republican administration in Washington. This is where he most overstepped his authority: Hascall made it an offense to endeavor to "bring the war policy of the government into disrepute." That is, even if a citizen made legitimate criticisms of the government's prosecution of the war, he was subject to military arrest and imprisonment. In effect, any opposition of the Lincoln administration amounted to treason. This would have made it impossible to have a democratic dialogue. Although many aspects of the war effort probably did not need exhaustive debate, such major issues as conscription and funding it did. Democratic speakers and writers felt that they had the right to express themselves freely. In essence, Hascall was saying that the Lincoln administration could act like a dictatorship and demand loyalty of all. He gave no room for a loyal opposition or minority rights. He could not conceive of the Union in any other terms than the successful prosecution of the war by Lincoln and the Republicans.

The Republican newspapers in the 19th State supplied the arguments in favor of the criticism-is-treason approach. As a Republican paper in Indianapolis wrote, Hascall's "determination to crush the budding disloyalty which, in the name of Democracy, has so nearly ripened into treason, is so manifest from his order, that no one can mistake his meaning. In this work he has the hearty cooperation and confidence of all loyal men."[31] Republicans deluged Hascall with intelligence about "disloyal" Democratic editors.[32]

Military leaders like Burnside and Hascall argued that silencing Lincoln's critics would stymie any signals the South might be getting that the northern states were in political disharmony. Meanwhile, soldiers as well as civilians who favored the Republicans tended to take their orders to mean that intimidation of Democratic free expression was acceptable. In fact, a strong case could be made that Lincoln and his generals gained much more by not systematically suppressing free speech but by looking the other way or not vigorously prosecuting mob intimidation of Democratic newspaper editors and Democratic public speakers. One scholar has observed that although there were at least 11 cases of Hascall's trying to suppress newspapers in Indiana in 1863, there were many more cases of intimidation during the course of the war. One such example had occurred only a month before Hascall took control when Union troops returning from the South ransacked the office of the *Richmond Jeffersonian*.[33]

The military leaders operated under a different system within the military. It was hierarchical, not democratic—orders came from the top down. Soldiers had given up certain freedoms and privileges when they entered the military. Officers and soldiers accustomed to fighting in a long and bloody war understandably were more concerned with personal survival than with peacetime rights. If anything, including Democrats' words, was helping the Southern war effort, it was simultaneously hurting the Northern war effort. Information that might directly lead to one's death was certainly treasonous; information or opinions that might indirectly help the enemy was not much better in the military's eyes.

In another sense, Hascall had on his mind the wives, children, parents, and siblings of the soldiers. This was by far the bloodiest conflict in American history, eventually claiming 625,000 deaths. Hascall, a West Point graduate, knew that such killing caused tremendous damage to society, and he did not want Indiana to contribute any more to the suffering than was necessary. It was at heart a humanitarian argument, and perhaps his best. Hascall wrote: "As I value the lives of our hundreds of thousands of gallant soldiers in the field, as I regard the feelings of bereavement, and sufferings of their anxious families and friends at home, and as I regard the true interests of our State and nation, I am going to see to it that in Indiana, at least, such [disloyal] men have no abiding place."[34]

These were strong arguments because the war was so central to the political shape the country was assuming as it expanded across the continent. Yet Hascall did not answer Edgerton's key charge: why should the military government supersede the civilian government? Governor Morton, the legislature and state courts were still running the state, and were they not sovereign? James Elder, the editor of the *Richmond Jeffersonian*, provided an argument similar to Edgerton's in a late April editorial. Elder noted that the Constitution was the supreme law of the land. "There can be no other just test of loyalty but fidelity to the Constitution."[35] Elder went on to say that Democrats should obey the law; indeed, such obedience was a Democrat's duty. "A man is no longer a Democrat when he fails this duty." Likewise, Elder found a hole in Hascall's argument that the Lincoln administration was the government. He wondered what would happen if Lincoln lost the election in November of 1864. Would that not mean that another political leader and his party could use different policies and measures to prosecute the war and save the Union?

Hascall's general order had a chilling effect in northern Indiana. A total of 11 Democratic newspapers were suppressed by Hascall in the six weeks he served as the Union military leader in the state. Edgerton thought Hascall's General Order 9 was close to military despotism, yet the congressman stopped short of saying that what Hascall had done was dictatorial. He urged Democrats in Indiana not to counter Hascall's heavy hand with revolutionary or incendiary means. Instead, he counseled "peaceful opposition through the press—through free public and private speech—through the courts and through the ballot box."[36] If the order was truly unconstitutional as Edgerton thought, then the courts would decide its fate. To Edgerton, continued civic peace in Indiana was worth more than any political argument.

At any rate, Hascall's reign in Indiana was short-lived. A petition went out May 14 asking Lincoln to replace Hascall with his predecessor, Henry B. Carrington.[37] Two weeks later, Governor Morton, who was closer to Carrington anyway, was able to get Secretary of War Edwin M. Stanton to sack the Goshen attorney. Hascall's shadow, however, was a long one. Press suppression did not end with Hascall out of the way. Ten more cases of suppression would occur in 1864, when the Union war effort reached another low point.[38] Only in 1865, when it became more apparent that the Union would survive, did the number drop to a single instance.[39] As the stress on the government began to recede, so the need for suppression and intimidation decreased. More importantly, Democratic editors endured a chilling effect on free expression when Hascall was in charge in Indianapolis. As Stephen Towne has observed, "Several outspoken [Democratic] editors refrained from their usual vitriolic condemnation of federal war policy and measured their words carefully."[40]

Military men like Hascall and Burnside lived in a world where control was the governing principle. The structure of power was top-down. Action, once undertaken, must be decisive. Politicians like Edgerton lived with a very different governing principle. Edgerton believed in dialogue, compromise, and slow, deliberate action. He and the Democrats of the Midwest respected the rule of law and tried to impose their understanding of the Constitution on their society. The two governing principles came into direct conflict in the Hoosier State in the spring of 1863. Hascall wanted the Democrats to stop criticizing Lincoln and the war effort, equating criticism with treason. Some

Democrats in Indiana were certainly near or over the line of treason, but most were simply expressing an opposing point of view. Democratic editors and politicians who used constitutional arguments against emancipation, conscription, and the income tax were not being seditious. They were functioning as the loyal opposition, even if their position on emancipation, in particular, seems immoral and unjust to subsequent generations.

In the end, Morton and Stanton stopped newspaper suppression in 1863 by firing Hascall for agitating "the public mind."[41] Stanton thought Hascall had gone too far in trying to intimidate the Democratic editors and had needlessly upset the already tense political atmosphere in Indiana.[42] The secretary of war wanted the next leader of the District of Indiana to work more closely with Morton and other state officials.[43] In this sense, it can be said that Edgerton's verbal counterattack had already "softened" the government's attitude toward taking further action against the Democratic editors, although Hascall's removal did not end press tensions altogether. As had been noted, intimidation of the Democratic press would continue in 1864—with most of the antipress violence coming from mobs of current or former Union soldiers—but no longer was the chilling effect coming from a written policy of the federal government or from the zealous pursuits of a politically insensitive brigadier general.[44]

NOTES

1. George H. Douglas, *The Golden Age of the Newspaper* (Westport, CT: Greenwood Press, 1999), 62.
2. *Dawson's (Fort Wayne, Indiana) Daily Times and Union*, 2 June 1863.
3. Gilbert R. Tredway, *Democratic Opposition to the Lincoln Administration in Indiana* (Indianapolis: Indiana Historical Bureau, 1973), 41.
4. Stephen E. Towne, "Works of Indiscretion: Violence against the Press in Indiana during the Civil War," *Journalism History* 31, no. 3 (Fall 2005): 142.
5. Jon Paul Dilts, "Testing Siebert's Proposition in Civil War Indiana," *Journalism Quarterly* 63, no. 1 (Spring 1986): 365–368.
6. Richard H. Abbott, "Civil War Origins of the Southern Republican Press," *Civil War History*, 43, no. 1 (March 1997): 41.
7. Russell A. Alger, ed., *War of Rebellion: A Compilation of the Official Records of the Union and Confederate Armies*, ser. 2, vol. 5 (Washington, D.C.: Government Printing Office, 1899), 480.
8. Alger, ser. 2, vol. 5, 480.
9. *Indiana Daily State Sentinel* (Indianapolis), 19 May 1863.
10. Olin Dee Morrison, *Indiana at Civil War Time* (Athens, OH: E.M. Morrison, 1961), 132. Morrison says that many wealthy southerners fled to Indiana during the war, sought citizenship, and voted against the Republicans.
11. So convinced was the government that such activity was occurring that by the final stages of the war the Lincoln administration would attempt to prove that a

DAVID W. BULLA

conspiracy of Southern sympathizers including Columbus, Ohio, Peace Democrat editor Samuel Medary was freeing Confederate soldiers in the Midwest. That
trial would never take place because Medary died before it started.

12. Edward Conrad Smith, *The Borderland in the Civil War* (New York: AMS Press,
    1970), 342.
13. *Columbia City (Indiana) News*, 21 May 1863.
14. *Columbia City (Indiana) News*, 21 May 1863.
15. *Indiana Daily State Sentinel* (Indianapolis), 6 May 1863.
16. *Indiana Daily State Sentinel* (Indianapolis), 13 May 1863.
17. Stephen E. Towne, "Killing the Serpent Speedily: Governor Morton, General
    Hascall, and the Suppression of the Democratic Press in Indiana in 1863," *Civil
    War History* 51, no. 1 (2006): 48.
18. *Columbia City (Indiana) News*, 21 May 1863.
19. *Indiana Daily State Sentinel* (Indianapolis), 13 May 1863.
20. *Columbia City (Indiana) News*, 21 May 1863.
21. *New York Times*, 18 May 1863.
22. *Valley of the Upper Maumee River, with Historical Account of Allen County and
    the City of Fort Wayne, Indiana. The Story of Its Progress from Savagery to Civili-
    zation,* vol. 2 (Madison, WI: Brant and Fuller, 1889), 63–66. Edgerton's law back-
    ground was more impressive than Hascall's. Edgerton's father, Bela Edgerton,
    had been educated at Middlebury College and served as an attorney and mag-
    istrate in Clinton County, New York. Joseph K. Edgerton attended the public
    schools of Clinton County and then Plattsburg Academy. In addition to reading
    law with William Swetland in Plattsburg, he later became "a student in the law
    office of Dudley Selden and James Mowatt" (64) in New York City and was ad-
    mitted to the New York bar in 1839. He practiced law in New York for five years
    before moving to Fort Wayne in 1844.
23. *Indiana Weekly State Sentinel* (Indianapolis), 18 May 1863.
24. *Dawson's Daily Times and Union* (Fort Wayne, Indiana), 18 May 1863.
25. *Dawson's Daily Times and Union* (Fort Wayne, Indiana), 18 May 1863.
26. *Dawson's Daily Times and Union* (Fort Wayne, Indiana), 18 May 1863.
27. *Indianapolis (Indiana) Daily State Sentinel*, 19 May 1863.
28. *Indianapolis (Indiana) Daily State Sentinel*, 19 May 1863.
29. *Indianapolis (Indiana) Daily State Sentinel*, 19 May 1863.
30. *Indianapolis (Indiana) Daily State Sentinel*, 19 May 1863.
31. *Indianapolis (Indiana) Daily Journal*, 28 April 1863.
32. Tredway, 27.
33. Towne, 2005, 142.
34. *Columbia City (Indiana) News*, 21 May 1863.
35. *Richmond (Indiana) Jeffersonian*, 30 April 1863.
36. *Columbia City (Indiana) News*, 5 May 1863.
37. Craig D. Tenney, "Major General A.E. Burnside and the First Amendment: A
    Case Study of Civil War Freedom of Expression" (PhD dissertation, Indiana Uni-
    versity, 1977), 132.
38. Dilts, 367.

39. Dilts, 367.
40. Towne, 2006, 53.
41. Jeffrey A. Smith, *War and Press Freedom: The Problem of Prerogative Power* (Cary, NC: Oxford University Press, 1999), 117.
42. Smith, 116.
43. Smith, 116.
44. Dilts, 367.

Damning Voices

The Press, the Politicians, and the Mankato Indian Trials of 1862

— Brian Gabrial —

On December 26, 1862, the largest public mass execution ever in the United States took place in Mankato, Minnesota, when the United States military hung 38 Dakota[1] men for their part in the so-called Sioux Outbreak of 1862. It began in August, leaving approximately 358 white men, women, and children dead, as well as 29 Dakota warriors.[2] Just over a month later, the Dakota surrendered and returned their white captives. News accounts of the massacres as well as the "proclamations" of state leaders so inflamed the passions of Minnesota's white population that only one response—revenge—seemed appropriate. Yet, short of another war or outright extermination of the Dakota, the only available recourse for revenge was apparently legal. Minnesota public opinion, shaped in part by the attitudes of its civil and military leadership was squarely against mercy for the Dakota. For many white Minnesotans, their only knowledge of the events came from local newspapers, which published correspondence, opinions, and proclamations regarding the "atrocities" (many proved unfounded).[3] Minnesotans learned about the Dakota's military trial from Isaac Heard, whose accounts appeared in newspapers and in the first published book about the uprising.[4] What emerges from Heard's handwritten trial transcripts, his newspaper accounts, and his book is a lack of regard for the Dakota on trial and a lack of a desire for their justice.

As for Minnesota's leadership, some, including the governor and leading military commander, may have had more than civil or military interests at stake when they argued for the prisoners' death sentences—namely Minnesota land and federal money.

The outbreak began on August 17, 1862, near Acton, Minnesota, when four Dakota hunters came across five settlers and killed them.[5] Although what sparked the murders was not clear, they began a chain reaction. The next day several bands led by Chief Little Crow attacked white settlements, including the Redwood Agency near Mankato on the Minnesota River.[6] Throughout the week, the bands continued assaults on settlements along the river, although with limited success.

Many Minnesota newspaper editors, preoccupied with news about the Civil War, failed to grasp the outbreak's serious nature. The *St. Paul Pioneer and Democrat* (later the *St. Paul Pioneer*) reported the first murders on August 20 with this call for action: "[T]he miscreants deserve such a measure of vengeance, as they have never yet received." A day later, its editorial staff retreated from sounding a general alarm. "We might fill our paper with the rumors of wholesale massacres and devastation," one editorial said. It added, "we are convinced they have no foundation than the facts already published."[7]

But all was not well on the frontier, and the frantic Indian agent, Thomas Galbraith, wrote to Minnesota Governor Alexander Ramsey, saying that he could not "go into the horrible details of the wholesale massacre," adding, "It is worse than your imagination can picture."[8] Ramsey, who appointed former governor Brigadier General Henry Sibley to end the outbreak, issued a proclamation on August 22 calling for its suppression "in such a manner as will forever prevent its repetition."[9] Following several skirmishes, Little Crow and his followers realized by mid-September they could not defeat Sibley's army. Legal historian Carol Chomsky notes that "77 soldiers, 29 citizen-soldiers, approximately 358 settlers, and an estimated 29 Dakota soldiers" died during the outbreak.[10] In addition, the Dakota took approximately "269 whites and half-breeds" captive.

Ramsey issued another proclamation to the state legislature; it appeared in the September 10 *St. Paul Pioneer and Democrat*, embellishing his rhetoric with sensational language:

> Infants hewn into bloody chips of flesh, or nailed alive to door posts to linger out their little life in mortal agony, or torn untimely from the womb of the murdered mother . . . rape joined to murder in one awful tragedy; young girls, even children of tender years, outraged by their brutal ravishers till death ended their shame; women held in captivity to undergo the horrors of a living death.[11]

The governor warned that the state has been "awakened" by a "treacherous" foe . . . whose first warning of hostility was the indiscriminate massacre of men, women and children." Ramsey made clear what the final outcome of the outbreak should be: "The Sioux Indians of Minnesota must be exterminated or driven forever beyond the borders of the State. . . . They have themselves made their annihilation a social necessity."[12] Sibley, who agreed with Ramsey, assured the governor he would crush "these miserable wretches, who, among all devils in human shape, are among the most cruel and ferocious." He added, "My heart is steeled against them, and if I have the means, and can catch them, I will sweep them with the [broom] of death."[13]

Leading voices across the state also wanted to see an end to the Dakota presence in Minnesota. Articles and editorials called for the Dakota's extermination. On August 22, for example, the *Pioneer and Democrat* published the comments of the Brown County Sheriff, who said, "There are only two ways to keep up our settlements, either to have a strong force detailed to the county, to hold Indians on their reservations, or kill them all at once, AND THAT WOULD BE BEST."[14]

An item in the August 29 *Mankato Independent* said, "Extermination is the word! . . . War, bloody, relentless war, until the last of the Sioux race is exterminated or driven beyond the border of the State."[15] Almost a month later, the newspaper editorial staff explained its dearth of content by informing readers that the editor had joined "volunteer companies formed for the extermination of Indians."[16] Similarly, an editorial in the *Stillwater Messenger* suggested, "The [Sioux] race must be annihilated—every vestige of it blotted from the face of God's green earth . . . ANNIHILATION:—That is the word."[17]

By 1862, the Dakota had much to be angry about. Eleven years before, they had signed away much of their land in Minnesota. As first proposed, the Treaty of 1851 gave the Dakota a 10-mile-wide strip of land north and south of the Minnesota River, but by the time Congress revised the treaty, the tribes were restricted to a tract along the southern side of the river.[18] The Dakota were guaranteed ten cents an acre or $550,000 in annuities.[19] However, the very day the Dakota signed the treaty, they also signed a second set of documents known as the Trader Papers, which, as described by Minnesota historian Marion Satterlee, were "acknowledgement on the part of the Indians of the justice of the claims of the traders."[20] So before the Dakota could receive their annuities, they had to pay all monetary claims against them, which amounted to $431,735.78. These alleged claims, which were never proved legitimate, left the tribe with just under $120,000 in annuities.[21] Among those receiving monies for claims were then-Indian Agent Alexander Ramsey, who received $25,000,[22] and then-Governor Henry Sibley, who submitted claims of $144,984 and received $66,549.[23] (The U.S. Senate later exonerated Ramsey from any culpability.[24])

As Indian agent or governor, Ramsey's behavior toward the Dakota did not change. He ignored the Dakota's plight, instead, accusing them of breaking the 1851 treaty. In his September 10 message to lawmakers, he said the Dakota had been dealt with fairly, claiming, "In return for their lands . . . which they had voluntarily relinquished . . . a home had been given them in the western part of the State, and magnificent provisions made for their comfort, education, and reclamation to civilized pursuits."[25]

In 1862, the annuities promised for June did not arrive until August,[26] causing great hardship among the Dakota bands along the Minnesota River. The Indian agent in charge, Thomas Galbraith, who in Satterlee's words was a "political appointee, unacquainted with Indians or their government,"[27] refused to issue any food stocks. According to Satterlee, many Dakota decided they might as well "die fighting as to be starved to death by the whites."[28] Satterlee told the story of Andrew Myrick, a store owner and Sioux trader, who refused to give the tribes supplies unless they paid first. Satterlee quoted Myrick as saying, "So far as I'm concerned, they can eat grass or their own dung." Satterlee noted later that the store owner was killed during the uprising and his body found with his "mouth stuffed with grass."[29]

Not everyone agreed with Ramsey's view. An editorial in the *Pioneer and Democrat* held the governor accountable for the outbreak because he was the "Superintendent of Indian Affairs, who paid most of this money to traders—in disregard of the protest of many of the Indians."[30] And Bishop Whipple, the head of the Episcopalian Church in Minnesota, understood the gravity of the Dakota situation. In a letter published in the *New York Evening Post* and the St. Paul newspaper, he wrote that the cause of the outbreak was believed to be "the fault of a system which thwarts the kind intentions of the government, leaving the treaty Indians without protection of Law, and subject to the frauds and dishonesties of unscrupulous men."[31]

By September 23, the Dakota were willing to surrender and return their white captives to Sibley. Three days later Sibley set up Camp Release on the Minnesota River where he could receive the captives and formally end the hostilities. Once he gained custody of the whites, he and his troops proceeded to arrest 1,200 Dakota men.[32] Following that, according to Folwell, "individual Indians and small parties came in and gave themselves up."[33] Days later, Sibley sent runners throughout the villages, urging others to come in "under a flag of truce." Sibley promised "protection to all who were innocent."[34]

In Folwell's account, Sibley and his commission went to great lengths to arrest Dakota men and bring them to "justice." Interpreters were ordered to tell tribal members they needed to report to the camp and be "counted" in order to get their annuities:

> The families came up, were counted, and were motioned to pass on. As they came to the doorway, the men were told to step aside to be counted for extra pay. As they entered, they were asked to give up their arms upon a promise they would receive them back "shortly." 236 of Little Crow's warriors were thus safely placed in custody and were presently "fixed" (chained) in the same way as their comrades at Camp Release.[35]

Nearly two thousand Indians voluntarily gave themselves up to Sibley on his promise of protection, according to John Beeson's account in the *National Intelligencer* on June 1, 1864.[36]

On September 28, Sibley appointed a five-member commission to conduct the trials,[37] which began that day and ended on November 3, 1862, with the conviction of 303 Dakota men.[38] The trials were conducted with celerity, according to Isaac Heard's account in the *St. Paul Pioneer* on November 15.[39] According to trial transcripts, each defendant was charged in the "participation in the murders, outrages and robberies . . . on the Minnesota frontier."[40] Each charge outlined the nature of the accusations. Those on trial represented "all ages . . . from boyish fifteen up to old men scarcely able to walk or speak."[41] The commission gave each defendant an opportunity to answer the charges and gave witnesses a chance to testify. The commission then cleared the room to determine guilt or innocence. Folwell, who studied the transcripts, concluded: "The whole proceeding was a disgraceful travesty on justice. . . . Most of the witnesses were plainly biased by circumstances of the massacre or personal interest,"[42] adding that a prisoner's sole defense was "his own story in broken English without interpreter."[43] Few of the Dakota defendants understood English, and not one of those eventually executed admitted to killing anyone.

Three hundred and ninety existing trial transcripts reveal how little evidence was required to condemn the prisoners.[44] They illustrate how the commission used witnesses who provided mostly hearsay evidence that often consisted of the witness's saying the defendant admitted committing an act of violence or being present at battle. For example, in the case of Wa-Kan-Tanka, the only witness against him said that Wa-Kan-Tanka "took out his knife and showed it to me and said his brother had died recently, and he had now avenged his death."[45] This witness did not see the defendant kill anyone. Other transcripts revealed the defendants' limited understanding of the court procedures and charges. One defendant, Ta-tay-hde-don, told the commission:

> I never did anything bad in my life except a good while ago when I ran after a chicken at Mendota and couldn't catch it. . . . I went to church when I was young. I was in two battles with arrows, a cannonball bounced and

scattered the earth near me, and I ran. . . . I ran a coward and kept out of danger.[46]

Most defendants simply answered with a brief, "I have not killed or shot a white man." However, some prisoners tried to reason with the commission. One said that if had he killed "a white man," he would be with Little Crow now and would never have given himself up to Sibley.[47] Another defendant, after declaring his innocence, stated, "All of the Dakota have killed whites. If all the guilty are punished, there will be none left."[48]

If a defendant admitted guilt, he usually included mitigating circumstances, as the testimony of Hypolite Ange shows.

> I fired last—after he fell—the white man was standing when I fired—I was running towards the man when I fired. That is all I did. . . . My sister was here and that is the reason I didn't run away from the Indians. I wanted to be killed with her if she was killed.[49]

As for the two defendants charged with rape, one of them, Te-he-hdo-ne-cha admitted he "did bad towards" the victim once. But in his "final confession," printed in the Mankato and St. Paul newspapers, he admitted only to taking "some women captives."[50] The other defendant probably did not understand that he was assuring his death sentence when he admitted he "ravished" a woman named Mattie Williams, but he added he desisted when she "was not willing."[51] In his "final confession," he said he thought "he did a good deed" in saving the woman.[52]

As the official court recorder, Heard created the only surviving record of trial events and testimony. He also provided Minnesota readers with the only newspaper account of what happened at the trials. Throughout his accounts, Heard remained a strong defender of the trials, their outcomes, and their legacy. On November 15, 1862, nearly two weeks after the trials ended, the *St. Paul Pioneer* published Heard's unsigned account.[53] According to Heard, once the fighting ended and the return of the white captives was assured, the U.S. military acted with great restraint by not killing all the Indian men, women, and children held in custody.[54]

Heard could barely contain his contempt for the defendants, regardless of their age, as the following excerpt from the *St. Paul Pioneer* indicates:

> An old man, shriveled to a mummy, one of the criers on the Indian camp, was also tried, and two little boys testified against him. . . . The old wretch was made to stand up, looking cold and impassable, the boys [witnesses against him] likewise standing, placed opposite, gazing at each other for a moment, when one of the boys said, "I saw him shoot my mother."[55]

Heard also provided interesting insight into the commission's attitude toward the trials' star witness, the "half-breed" named Godfrey. According to Heard, Godfrey (whose Indian name, O-ta-cle, means "he that kills many") was considered the "most brutal in atrocity." Heard observed that Godfrey, under more normal circumstances because of "the natural prejudice against his color, to a white heart . . . would have been lynched." However, his testimony proved too important. Heard told readers, "It was a study to watch him, as he sat in Court, scanning the face of every culprit who came in, with the eye of a cat about to spring."[56]

Heard praised the commission's "elaborately conducted" trials, which could have been conducted in "five minutes"[57] because all that was required to condemn a prisoner was admission he participated or a witness's testimony. Heard boasted, "As many as forty were sometimes tried in a day,"[58] adding that "each case need only occupy a few minutes" because all that was really needed was the prisoner's admission of participation in the battles.[59]

In the November 15 article, Heard dismissed the defendants' alibis and claims of innocence. He wondered to readers how commission members could believe, for example, the elderly defendants who claimed they could not go into battle when they were in the "vigor of manly strength," or how they could believe a "fiery-looking warrior" who claimed he "felt so bad . . . to see the Indians fire on the whites" that he went to sleep and did not wake up until the fighting ended. He described one defendant in this manner:

> Another weazen faced, shaggy haired lank specimen of many winters, with green goggles, looked more like the Devil, than any thing human; I should have run from him in the night had he been a "good Indian" in times of peace, in a reasonable probability he was Satanic—horns and a tail were all that were necessary to make the personification.[60]

Three hundred and three men were condemned to die. Sibley, the commission, the governor, and Minnesotans hoped their executions would take place post haste. However, Lincoln immediately interceded and told Sibley's immediate commander, Major General John Pope, to instruct his subordinate that "no executions be made without his sanction."[61] Minnesota's congressional delegation was outraged by Lincoln's interference. M.S. Wilkinson, Cyrus Aldrich, and William Windom sent the president a letter that focused on the captive white women's ordeal and alleged gang rapes, pointing out that the Dakotas were rightly "condemned . . . upon the testimony of women whom they had carried into captivity . . . and who were treated with a brutality never known in this country, nor equaled in the practices of the most barbarous nations."[62] One

excerpt from the letter described in horrific detail the rape of a young teenaged
girl and her mother:

> [T]hese fiends incarnate...took her little girl...removed all of her
> clothes, and fastened her back upon the ground. They then commenced
> their work of brutality upon the body of this young girl. One by one, they
> violated her person, unmoved by her cries . . . until her Heavenly Father
> relieved her from suffering.[63]

The delegation's letter also described the ordeal of an 18-year-old girl,
"as refined and beautiful a girl as we had in the State": "She was taken, her
arms were tied, behind her, she was made fast to the ground, and ravished by
some eight or ten of these convicts."[64] The letter noted that "[W]ithout being
more specific, we will state that all or nearly all the women who were captured
were violated in this way."[65]

A letter from St. Paul's "citizens" to the president reiterated the congressional delegation's message, noting that the "Indian's nature can no more be
trusted than the wolf's. Tame him, cultivate him, strive to Christianize him
as you will, and the sight of blood will in an instant call out the savage, wolf-
ish, devilish instincts of his race."[66] It added that it was in the best interest of
Minnesota (being the "best farming State in the Union") and of the Union to
execute these Dakota and expel them from the state.

Ramsey, angered by the executions' delay and possible pardons, wrote in
his "Proclamation to the People of Minnesota" on December 7:

> The captured Sioux, instead of being indiscriminately slaughtered in the
> heat of passion, as might have been expected, were conceded an impartial
> trial by a military tribunal. . . . Our people indeed have had just reason to
> complain, of the tardiness of executive action.[67]

Lincoln, who respectfully read the letters, told the Senate on December 11
that he was "anxious to not act with so much clemency as to encourage another
outbreak, on the one hand, nor with so much severity as to be real cruelty."[68]
But after reading the trial transcripts, Lincoln could not, in good conscience,
condemn all 303 men and dismissed the congressional delegation's claims of
rampant gang rape, noting that their letter "contained some statements of fact
not found in the records of the trials." Although Lincoln initially wanted to
execute only those who had violated women, he discovered, "Contrary to my
expectations, only two of this class were found."[69] (The cases involved Te-he-
dno-ne-cha and Tazoo. Another prisoner, Do-wan-sa was condemned too because of his "design to ravish" a young girl.[70]) Lincoln focused on those "proven
to have participated in massacres, as distinguished from participation in battles" and thus ordered the December 19 execution of 40 Dakota men.[71]

Despite Lincoln's pardon of 263 Dakota men, some Minnesotans believed justice had not been served. Both the Reverend Stephen R. Riggs and Bishop H.P. Whipple questioned the trials' fairness. Riggs, who later translated the final "confessions" of the prisoners, said, "A military commission where the cases of forty men are passed in six or seven hours, is not the place for the clear bringing out of evidence and securing a fair trial."[72] While Whipple referred to the Dakota as a "wretched people" and blamed the troubles on their alcohol use, he noted that the Dakota had "been more sinned against than sinning" and that they were driven by "grievances and temptations" that "would drive civilized people to madness."[73] His letter in the December 5 *St. Paul Pioneer* said, "It is due justice that every fact connected with that trial should have been such as to secure the condemnation of none save the really guilty."

Most Minnesotans were in agreement with Isaac Heard's unsigned editorial in the December 11 *St. Paul Pioneer*. Heard explained to the readers that he was at the trials and knew firsthand that the military commission was headed by men who were "well known to the community as respectable and humane citizens" and "of more than average intelligence." In addition, Heard observed that during the outbreak "all of the Indians went on the war path." In defense of the commission, he observed that it had no interest in thwarting justice because the members lost no family members or property during the uprising. Procedurally, he argued that the commission ran a proper hearing and that the convictions met the minimum requirement of eyewitness testimony or confessions.[74] Heard attacked Riggs's sincerity. After all, according to Heard, it was Riggs who helped determine who stood trial:

> He [Riggs] was in fact the Grand Jury of the Court. His long residence in the Indian country and extensive acquaintance with them, his knowledge of their character—what Indians would be likely to be implicated and what ones not . . . eminently fitted him for the position.[75]

Lincoln directed Sibley to erect the gallows on a levee in front of the quarters to afford "ample opportunity to every person to witness the execution."[76] The originally scheduled date of execution changed from December 17 to December 26 because Sibley did not receive necessary instructions in time. Apparently, the messenger carrying them was delayed, arriving "too late to make the requisite preparations for the execution."[77] But soon thereafter, preparations began. The gallows were built in a square where ten prisoners could be hung from each of the four sides.[78]

At the request of Mankato citizens worried about "some disturbance occurring,"[79] martial law was declared on December 24, 1862. Colonel Miller also forbade the "use of intoxicating liquors, about the time of the approaching

Indian execution" because it "may result in a serious riot or breach of the peace."[80] The Dakota prisoners were kept in a "back room on the first floor of Leech's stone building, chained in pairs and closely and strongly guarded."[81] According to the *Mankato Weekly Record*, Miller, with Riggs acting as interpreter, read to them the president's order. Miller instructed Riggs to tell them to look toward the Christian God to provide "their only remaining source of consolation." Each Dakota man was given the option of receiving a Christian "minister of his choice."[82] Two days before the Wednesday execution, the condemned men could send for "two or three" of their relatives and friends and send messages to others. According to an item in the December 26 *Weekly Mankato Record*, "each Indian had some word to send to his parents or family. When speaking of their wives and children almost every one was affected to tears."[83]

On the day of the execution, the crowds gathered at the appointed spot, where according to the *St. Paul Pioneer* reporter, they did so not out of curiosity but out of a "duty, to witness the death of a portion of a horde of savage fiends who had desolated a whole frontier."[84] Shortly before 10:00 a.m., the condemned men "set up a death-dance and kept it up on the platform." At precisely ten after ten, the signal was given, and the platform gave way. According to the *Mankato Independent*, "37 Sioux murderers hung by the neck."[85] However, the 38th prisoner "fell to the ground, but his neck had been broken in the jerk and fall. He was instantly strung again."[86] According to the *Mankato Independent*, "The falling of the platform was a splendid success, it reflects the high credit on all concerned."

Other newspapers reported that a cheer rose from the crowd when the prisoners fell through the platform. The *St. Paul Pioneer* editor added this affecting account to that paper's coverage:

> The most touching scene on the drop was their attempt to grasp each other's hands . . . They were very close to each other, and many succeeded. Three or four in a row were hand in hand, and all hands swaying up and down with the rise and fall of their voices. One old man reached out each side, but could not grasp a hand. His struggles were piteous and affected many beholders.[87]

Almost immediately, soldiers removed the bodies and buried them in a mass grave in a "sand bar in front of the city."[88]

One Chicago doctor made an immediate request following the executions. In a January 2, 1863, *Mankato Independent* item headlined "A New Article of Commerce," the doctor offered a "good price" for the Dakota bodies because he needed them for his medical students. He explained the executions could turn a profit for the county. His request was denied.

During the course of the trials and subsequent executions, Minnesota's congressional delegation sought to move the Dakota out of Minnesota. Senator Wilkinson, one of the signers of the letter to Lincoln, introduced a bill "to remove the Sioux Indians to the Missouri River" and asked for $100,000 to carry out that plan.[89] Eventually, most Minnesota Dakota tribes were removed.

No doubt many innocent men, women, and children died during the Sioux outbreak of 1862. Most likely, some of those Dakota men executed in Mankato were guilty of taking part in the outbreak and of killing whites. Admittedly, the voices most notably absent were those of the whites killed. However, the voices of the Dakota executed were barely audible either. In the newspaper accounts, the loudest voices came from the seats of Minnesota power, notably Governor Ramsey and General Sibley. These powerful voices may have combined to shape or at least maintain an unfavorable public opinion about the Dakota. They contained such a high degree of animosity that not even the president of the United States dared to thwart them.

NOTES

1. The term *Dakota* will be substituted for *Sioux* whenever possible. The term *Sioux* is considered pejorative and derives from the French word Nadouessioux, which, in turn, is derived from the Chippewa word meaning enemy. The eastern tribes of the Sioux called themselves Dakota and included the Santee tribes: the M'dewakanton, the Wahpteton, and the Sesseton.

2. Carol Chomsky, "The United States-Dakota War Trials: A Study in Military Injustice," *Stanford Law Review* 43 (November 1990): 13. The number of whites killed during the outbreak varies with some estimates as high as 800.

3. Chomsky indicates, "Wild stories of mutilation by the Dakota in these encounters spread among the settlers, but historians have concluded that these reports were probably exaggerations of isolated instances of atrocities." Chomsky, 20.

4. Heard's *History of the Sioux War and Massacres of 1862 and 1863* was published by Harper and Brothers in 1863. The book contains several passages similar to what Heard wrote in his newspaper articles.

5. Gary Anderson, *Through Dakota Eyes* (St. Paul: Minnesota Historical Society Press, 1988), 13.

6. Ibid., 13. Speculation exists that the bands may have decided it was an opportune time to attack because they knew that many white men had gone to fight the Civil War.

7. *St. Paul Pioneer and Democrat*, 21 August 1862.

8. Reprinted in the *St. Paul Pioneer and Democrat*, 22 August 1862.

9. Ibid.

10. Chomsky, 13.

11. "Governor's Message," reprinted in the *St. Paul Pioneer and Democrat*, 10 September 1862. Later, similar rape accounts would be used by the congressional delegation in an attempt to persuade President Lincoln against granting clemency.

12. Ibid.

13. William Folwell, *A History of Minnesota*, vol. 2 (St. Paul: Minnesota Historical Society Press, 1924), 191.

14. Reprinted in the *St. Paul Pioneer and Democrat*, 22 August 1862.

15. *Mankato Independent*, 29 August 1862.

16. *Mankato Independent*, 20 September 1862. The article further adds that "General Pope has arrived at Saint Paul, and promises immediate and in vigorous [action] for the extermination of the Sioux race." On October 10, the editor assured his readers that he and members of his staff were once more "at our post in the Sanction of the *Independent*."

17. Reprinted in the *St. Paul Pioneer and Democrat*, 4 September 1862.

18. Marion Satterlee, *A Detailed Account of the Massacre by the Dakota Indians in Minnesota in 1862* (Minneapolis: n.p., 1923), 4. Anderson noted in *Through Dakota Eyes* that the Dakota did not lose ownership of the northern tract of land until the treaty was renegotiated in 1858. Anderson, 8.

19. Satterlee, 4.

20. Satterlee, in William Watts Folwell et al., *The Court Proceedings in the Trial of Dakota Indians Following the Massacre in Minnesota in August 1862* (Minneapolis: Satterlee Print Co. 1927), 76.

21. Ibid., 4. Satterlee added that tribal members had little discretion in spending the remaining annuity money. Instead, a large sum went to schools "and other purposes repugnant to Indians."

22. Ibid., 5.

23. Folwell, *Court Proceedings*, 77.

24. Ibid. However, in his 1863 history, Isaac V.D. Heard, who had served as a court reporter for the trials and who thought highly of Ramsey, wrote that the Senate decided that "Governor's Ramsey's conduct was not only free from blame, but also highly commendable." See his *History of the Sioux War and Massacres of 1862 and 1863* (New York: Harper, 1863), 41.

25. "Governor's Message."

26. Satterlee, *Detailed Account*, 7. During the 1850s, the Dakota endured delays in receiving payment on the remainder of the annuities. One delay occurred in 1857 after a Dakota band massacred several whites at Spirit Lake, Iowa. The military wanted them found, and the government would not make payment until that happened. Satterlee, *Detailed Account*, 6.

27. Satterlee, *Detailed Account*, 7. Isaac Heard would describe Galbraith as "energetic and faithful." See Isaac V.D. Heard, *History of the Sioux Wars* (New York: Harper and Bros., 1864), 25. Antoine Frenier, who acted as a government interpreter during the trials, called him the "most honest and upright Agent the sioux have had since 1851." See "Antoine Frenier's Statement," *Mankato Weekly Record*, 20 December 1862.

28. Satterlee, *Detailed Account*, 7.

29. Satterlee, *Detailed Account*, 8–9.

30. *St. Paul Pioneer and Democrat*, 10 September 1862.

31. *St. Paul Pioneer and Democrat*, 28 October 1862.

32. Chomsky, 21.
33. Folwell, 192.
34. Ibid.
35. Ibid., 194.
36. John Beeson, "The Savages Par'doned," *National Intelligencer*, 1 June 1864.
37. Chomsky, 23. According to Chomsky, all of the members had, at some point, fought the Dakota.
38. Folwell, 3.
39. "The Indian Expedition," *St. Paul Pioneer*, 15 November 1862.
40. Folwell, 1.
41. Heard, 258.
42. Folwell, 79. Folwell noted that his "Trial record is not published to malign those concerned, their acts can be left to the Almighty, but to show that history is far from just to the Indian people, whose land have been taken, by force, fraud and deceit, whose demoralization and destruction as a race is due to the advent of the white man. The record is a living picture of their treatment." Folwell, 3.
43. Folwell, 76.
44. Most of the transcripts contained more procedural information than actual testimony.
45. Trial Transcript 210, the case of Wa-Kan-Tanka.
46. Trial Transcript 279, the case of Ta-tay-hde-don.
47. Trial Transcript 12, the case of Wa-Ho-Hud.
48. Trial Transcript 11, the case of Wah-pa-du-te.
49. Trial Transcript 175, the case of Hypolite.
50. *Mankato Weekly Record*, 26 December 1862.
51. Trial Transcript 4, the case of Ta-zoo.
52. *Mankato Weekly Record*, 26 December 1862.
53. The *Mankato Weekly Record* reprinted the St. Paul paper's account on November 22, 1862. In general 19th century newspapers did not provide bylines for writers. In this, and a later article, they are signed "H." It was determined that these articles could be attributed to Heard because almost identical passages are published in Heard's 1863 history.
54. Isaac V.D. Heard, *History of the Sioux Wars* (New York: Harper and Bros., 1864), 187.
55. "The Indian Expedition," *St. Paul Pioneer*, 15 November 1862.
56. Ibid. Godfrey was sentenced to die, but the commission commuted his sentence because of testimony he provided.
57. Heard, 254.
58. Heard, 257.
59. Heard, 267. In his letter to the Senate, Lincoln reasoned that only those participating in massacres should be executed.
60. "The Indian Expedition," *St. Paul Pioneer*, 15 November 1862.
61. Quoted in Chomsky, 27.
62. "Letter to the President of the United States," also printed in the *Mankato Weekly Record* under the headline of "The Sioux War," 20 December 1862.

63. Ibid.

64. Ibid.

65. Ibid.

66. "Memorial," letter from St. Paul to president. The letter was also published in the *St. Paul Pioneer* on November 27, 1862. In addition the *Mankato Weekly Record* on December 20, 1862, printed a response from Antoine Frenier, who acted as an interpreter during the trials. He said the "Indians convicted of implications in the late *outrages*, and many others, should suffer death."

67. "Proclamation to the People of Minnesota," *St. Paul Pioneer*, 7 December 1862.

68. "Message of the President of the United States," 11 December 1862.

69. Ibid.

70. Executive order dated 6 December 1862 addressed to General Sibley.

71. "Message of the President of the United States," 11 December 1862.

72. "Trial of the Indian Prisoners—Another Letter from Bishop Whipple," *St. Paul Pioneer*, 5 December 1862.

73. Quoted in the *New York Observer*, 18 December 1862. The paper further quoted Whipple as saying, "Who is guilty of the causes which have desolated our borders? At whose door is the blood of these innocent victims? I believe God will hold the nation guilty."

74. "The Indian Trials," *St. Paul Pioneer*, 11 December 1862.

75. Ibid.

76. Lincoln's letter to Sibley, reprinted under the headline "Indians to Be Hung," *Mankato Weekly Record*, 20 December 1862.

77. Ibid.

78. *Mankato Record*, 20 December 1862.

79. "Letter to Stephen Miller, Col. 7th Reg't Minn. Vols.," reprinted in the *Weekly Mankato Record*, 26 December 1862.

80. Colonel Miller's "General Order No. 21," reprinted in the *Mankato Weekly Record*, 26 December 1862.

81. *Mankato Weekly Record*, 26 December 1862.

82. "Reading of the Death Warrant," *Mankato Weekly Record*, 26 December 1862.

83. "An Affecting Interview," *Mankato Weekly Record*, 16 December 1862.

84. *St. Paul Pioneer*, 28 December 1862.

85. *Mankato Independent*, 26 December 1862.

86. *Mankato Weekly Record*, 26 December 1862.

87. *St. Paul Pioneer*, 28 December 1862.

88. Ibid.

89. "Senator Wilkinson and the Sioux," *Mankato Weekly Record*, 20 December 1862.

African Americans and the Civil War as Reflected in the *Christian Recorder*, 1861–1862

— Hazel Dicken-Garcia and Linus Abraham —

After the attack on Fort Sumter on April 12, 1861, northern black men inundated the Lincoln administration with offers to join the army effort. Anticipating objections, several suggested using able white officers to lead black troops, a suggestion intended to help whites accept them as soldiers. The government, however, continued to reject black soldiers for another 16 months, and blacks who secretly joined the Union Army were removed when discovered. The Militia Act of July 17, 1862, empowered the president to use blacks for any military or naval service for which they were found competent. Five days later, although still reluctant to use black soldiers, Abraham Lincoln directed Brigadier General Rufus Saxton to raise a black regiment in South Carolina (Thomas Wentworth Higginson's soon-to-be-famous First South Carolina Infantry) and allowed Major General Benjamin Butler to muster black militiamen in New Orleans into Federal service.[1]

Of the many books published about African American participation in the war, few have told African Americans' experiences in their own words.[2] The *Christian Recorder,* an African Methodist Episcopal (AME) Church publication, provided a forum where many blacks wrote of their experiences. This weekly newspaper was filled with lengthy essays and reports on church activities and religious issues from across the country.[3] As the war wore on, news and commentary increased, including letters from black soldiers, army chaplains, and other African Americans. Regular columns, typically headed "Domestic News" or "Our Country," reported war news, including items from other newspapers at home and abroad. Religious themes continued to dominate. Recurring topics were Christianity and war, the importance of remaining steadfast in faith, and not allowing the inevitable distractions of war to deter believers from remembering the Sabbath.

The newspaper's religious commitment and existence as an African American newspaper in the Civil War created a dynamic of conflicting interests and ideological positions that make its representation of the war historically significant. Calling duty to one's country second to duty to God, the paper always emphasized the former. One writer said he had felt a duty "to plead with all our power [for] support of a government like ours; for the maintenance of the majesty [of] the freest and most beneficent Constitution and laws . . . the world ever saw," and "for the perpetuity of the American nation against the plots of traitors, at any and every cost." War to maintain the government meant "salvation from the anarchy" threatening the North that was exemplified in "Baltimore on last Friday."[4] No citizens who wanted to "transmit the priceless blessing of a good government to their posterity" would shrink from any duty the crisis might bring.

Contributors to the newspaper located the war's cause in immoral behavior, particularly by southern leaders. Broken promises and treasonous activities, among other southern sins, were frequently cited. To negotiate the conflict between serving blacks' interests and Christian principles, the paper's editor and contributors cast the crisis in moral terms. This allowed for a moral evaluation of the problem that justified support for the war. Immoral behavior should not be left unchecked; the war had a righteous cause. A northern victory would serve blacks' interest, and all stood ready to fight.

Slavery drove virtually all discussion of the war. The first notice found of the war's outbreak, eight days after the firing on Fort Sumter, alluded to slavery as the war's cause. The writer blamed the South while commending the patriotic response to Lincoln's war preparations and predicting the inevitable bloodletting of American by American. "At last," he wrote, "the WAR has burst forth like a mighty tornado. What will become of the country?" Perhaps fearing that the nation would turn on blacks for causing the war, the writer pointed to other causes. "[W]hat is the cause of all this tumult? Is it really the Negro?" With an emphatic "No," he wrote that, although "many of our white friends" erroneously believed they were "fighting about the negroes," they were really "fighting about the Territories." Calling the tumult simply a North-South dispute, he said that neither side wanted the other "to intrude one inch on their territory, and on such portion of the Territories as they think they ought to be in possession of."[5]

More than a year later, another correspondent predicted that the "plagues on this nation" would never end until "slavery and oppression shall be foiled [and] right, equity, and justice shall be seen in all its grand regalia, leading on in triumphant conquest the victories of humanity." Slavery, not treason, was the real problem, he stressed.[6] Approximately a month later, T. Strother, writing from Terre Haute, Indiana, also identified slavery as the problem. "This rebellion will never be crushed until the nation agrees in its sovereign capacity to make restitution to the colored people of this country," he observed, and to restore "their God-given rights, of which they have been now so long robbed."[7]

As a solution to the problem of slavery, schemes to colonize African Americans outside the United States began formally in 1816 with formation of the American Colonization Society. Although more than 3,000 African Americans convened in Philadelphia the following year and went on record as opposing the society, colonization plans continued well into the Civil War. A plan spearheaded in the late 1850s by James Redpath encouraged blacks to immigrate to Haiti.[8] During the war, blacks were urged to go to different places, wrote the Reverend W.R. Revels, because the United States would not "at some future day, contain us." But the "Haytien scheme," he said, "panders to the vile spirit of negro hate by urging the expediency of a white Haytien representation at Washington, and of white Haytien consuls."[9] On August 14, 1862, the paper reported that Lincoln had told a committee of black men at the White House that Congress had appropriated and placed at his discretion funds to aid the colonization of people of African descent. Addressing why blacks should be colonized and leave the country, Lincoln said that blacks and whites had "broader difference" than other races. There was no need to discuss whether this was right or wrong, he said, "but this physical difference is a great disadvantage to us both" because many blacks "suffer very greatly . . . by living among us," while whites suffer from blacks' presence. "In a word," Lincoln said, "we suffer from each other," and the races "should be separated."[10] The forced "existence of the two races on the continent" had "general evil effects on the whites," he continued, adding:

> See our present condition!—the country engaged in war—our white men cutting each other's throats, none knowing how far it will extend—and then consider what we know to be the truth. But for your race among us

there could not be war. Although many men engaged on either side do not care for you one way or the other, nevertheless, I repeat, without the institution of slavery and the colored race as a basis, this war could not have an existence. It is better for us, therefore, to be separated.[11]

Strong reaction followed the meeting. Through the *Christian Recorder,* "Cerebus" appealed to people of color to "use every effort to defeat, contravene and oppose this most unreasonable edict that would forcibly eject us from the country for which our ancestors fought, bled and died." Blasting the very idea of the meeting, he wrote that most of "the most intelligent and influential men of the city are highly incensed and greatly exasperated with the pastors' under-handed work because they did not consult nor let the people know anything about it but a few selected ones, (assembled, we suppose, at the request of Rev. Mitchell,) and chose a *bogus* committee to wait on the President." Cerebus said he would "like to know *who* gave *that committee* authority to act for us, the *fifteen thousand* residents of color in this District—and who requested them to represent the interests of the *two hundred and ten thousand* inhabitants of color in the Free States!" "Was it," he asked, because they had "no intelligence, or [were] incapable of acting for" themselves? "Or was it too great a condescension for the *distinguished* committee to consult our views relative to the all-important proposition which they had under consideration?" Making their doings more regrettable, *"this bogus party* [was] *ready to give the President an answer for the two hundred and twenty-five thousand Anglo-Africans in the District and in the States*—in fact, had written their reply to him *before* they started for the [White House]."[12]

Compounding such indiscretions, Cerebus continued, were reports of a colony being raised in Washington, "to settle in that cheerless wilderness of Central America." Those joining had signed and legalized an agreement to immigrate to the settlement proposed by Lincoln. By such means, Cerebus wrote, "our own color was driving us from the land of our nativity." Colonization would come soon enough without blacks rushing it, he said. Congress had already appropriated funds for voluntary emigration," which he called "simply the stepping stone to *compulsory* expatriation!" Congress knew full well that blacks were generally antiemigrationist, and it was unnatural to suppose that they would voluntarily leave the land of their birth to go "live in the desolate wastes of Central America, or under the scorching rays of Liberia's sun, or with the bigoted and prejudiced Haytiens." He called the idea "absurd and ridiculous; and only a legislative dodge or a Congressional scheme, fraught with the most contemptible, lowest, rottenest craftiness and chicanery susceptible of contemplation. It is high time for us to arise from this criminal lethargy and suicidal enervation which enthralls us, for ostracism and expatriation under the new name of colonization is just ahead."[13]

Frances Ellen Watkins Harper, who said she had been asked for her thoughts on the war, wrote in the September 27 issue of Lincoln's plan: "If Jeff. Davis does not colonize Lincoln out of Washington, let him be thankful. The President's dabbling with colonization just now suggests . . . the idea of a man almost dying with a loathsome cancer, and busying himself about having his hair trimmed according to the latest fashion."[14] Harper envisioned no trouble for blacks from the new movement, but said the president should "be answered firmly and respectfully, not in the tones of supplication and entreaty, but of earnestness and decision." He should be told that, although blacks admit every man's right "to choose his home," they saw "neither the wisdom nor expediency" of their "self-exportation" from a land "enriched by [their] toil for generations," until they had "a birth-right on the soil, and the strongest claims on the nation for that justice and equity" withheld from them for ages. Even if blacks were willing to emigrate, could the country afford to "part with" "four millions of its laboring population?" Harper asked. Would not the country want blacks' labor to help rebuild the country if and when it should "emerge from this dreadful war?"[15]

Another strong reaction to the colonization meeting came from T. Strother, who wrote that, although he "never liked much to hear [colonization] mentioned," he had considered carefully what had been said about it and was "unwilling to subscribe much in favor" of it. He believed that "every white person in the nation" who favored colonization did so "from deep-seated prejudices . . . against the colored man [and] not because he is so deeply interested in our welfare." Lincoln, he said, "may have uttered the convictions of his mind honestly in his address to the colored committee," but he did not believe Lincoln "came honestly by such convictions." Strother could not understand "how . . . the colored people of this country are the cause of the present great rebellion and war." While he believed the existence of slavery brought the war about, he was certain that blacks were not the authors of slavery; therefore, the charge was "incorrect, and a slander, and . . . a perfect outrage. I cannot conceive how the colored people have caused the war any more than I could conceive how slavery could be the author of its own existence." He was "contumaciously opposed" to any scheme of colonization because this was his native country and his "sires and race" had "shed a great deal of blood in defence [sic]" of its liberties.[16]

The Emancipation Proclamation appeared without comment in the September 27, 1862, *Christian Recorder.* Less comment than one might expect appeared in the ensuing two weeks, and in fact, one person (likely a member of the committee that had met with Lincoln) wrote both of the two items about the Proclamation in the October 4 issue. In them, the writer wrestled with reconciling Lincoln's colonization proposal with the proclamation. Saying the proclamation "gives freedom to so vast a quantity of our people,"[17] the writer said he believed—unlike many blacks—that the president had acted in good faith. The proclamation proved that the president's policy was "to wage the war in favour of freedom, till the last groan of the anguished heart slave shall be hushed in the ears of nature's God," the writer said, adding:

> This definition of the policy bids us rise, and for ourselves think, act, and do. We have stood still and seen the salvation of God, while we besought him with teary eyes and bleeding hearts; but the stand-still day bid us adieu Sept. 22, 1862. A new era, a new dispensation of things, is now upon us—*to action, to action*, is the cry. We must now begin to think, to play, and to legislate for ourselves, for the time has arrived in the history of the American African, when grave and solemn responsibilities stare him in the face. The time for boasting of ancestral genius, and prowling through the dusty pages of ancient history to find a specimen of negro intellectuality is over. Such useless noise should now be lulled, while we turn our attention to an engagement with those means which must, and alone can, mould [sic] out and develop those religious, literary, and pecuniary resources, adapted to the grand expediency now about to be encountered.[18]

In the October 11 issue, editors reported southern reactions to the Emancipation Proclamation with items taken from the *Richmond Whig*, where the proclamation was called "a dash of the pen to destroy four thousand millions of our property, and a bid for the slaves to rise in insurrections, with the assurance of and from the whole military and naval power of the United States." Confederate Senate reactions included a joint resolution that the proclamation was "a gross violation of the usages of civilized warfare, an outrage on the rights of private property, and an invitation to an atrocious servile war, and therefore should be held up in the execration of mankind, and counteracted by such severe retaliatory measures as in the judgment of the President may be best calculated to secure its withdrawal or arrest its execution."[19]

Perhaps in response to those southern views, a column in the same issue discussed the proclamation in relation to southern blacks. Many in the "so-called 'free North'" favored "Slavedom" and were using "every means to work upon the animal passions of those who may not understand [the proclamation's] righteous intentions—to incense and enrage, or arouse a sense of fury and indignation against the colored people," the writer said. They were "trying to kindle a fire of untruthful, unrighteous and un-God-like indignation against the poor, oppressed slaves," and "using every effort to take their spite out [on] the free colored people here in the North," on grounds that the proclamation would cause slaves to revolt, "slay, and kill men, women, and children." Slaves were human beings, he wrote, and, "as bad as the slave has been treated, he would not be as brutal as some portions of the rebel army have proved themselves to be, with all their instinct and intelligence, towards white Union men, women and children."[20]

Even before Lincoln met the committee of African American men and before he issued the Emancipation Proclamation, blacks debated serving in the war. Editorials in the first months of the war argued that African Americans should not offer to fight in the war because, despite having served in the War for Independence and the War of 1812, they were still denied citizenship rights. When and if rights were accorded and they were called for military service, then—and only then—should they fight. One editorial said that in 1861 "not only our citizenship, but even our common humanity is denied," and "[t]he same cruel prejudice which excludes us from the halls of science, also repels us from the militia and the standing army. To offer ourselves for military service now, is to abandon self-respect, and invite insult."[21]

The Federal move toward using African American troops also met initial resistance in the newspaper. The appeal for black soldiers was too late, one writer said, after implying that northern troops' hearts were not in the war effort because they did not care about the lot of blacks: "Many of the [white] officers and soldiers stated . . . that if they thought their fighting the so-termed rebels would be the means of freeing the colored people, they would throw down their arms." They would have aided southerners in squelching any slave insurrection, the writer charged. But, "Now, that same people want the slaves to rise up and fight for their liberty. . . . Rise against what?" Black men had "too much good sense" to do anything of the kind, he wrote, and then, seemingly addressing the northern government, added: "Since you have waited till every man, boy, woman and child in the so-called Southern Confederacy has been armed to the teeth, 'tis folly and mockery for you now to say to the poor bleeding and down-trodden sons of Africa, 'Arise and fight for your liberty!'"[22]

Following the July 17, 1862, Militia Act, an editorial announcing that Congress had approved colored soldiers said that was "all good enough and right." But, "What provision has Congress made" for "guarantying [sic] to the colored people . . . full protection from her laws and the privilege of enjoying all the rights accorded to other human beings in the United States of America?" Given such protection, the writer said, "no class of people . . . are or will be more loyal in every sense of the word or will do as much service and honor to this—the country of their BIRTH! Every true, honest-hearted and patriotic man and woman who knows anything about the history of this country must acknowledge that the blacks are loyal, and did most positively shed blood, and freely, too, to gain the independence of America." History shows that blacks had fought "like heroes" in earlier wars and "for their services were promised their freedom and all the rights that white men enjoyed." But the promise had not been kept.[23]

The first item that forthrightly endorsed black soldiers was signed "Aleph" and dated July 23, 1862. Calling slavery the "bone and sinew of the rebellion," Aleph urged, "Remove it by proclamation—invest the slaves with their natural rights—take them in the army—employ them as other men, and soon the cotton lords of the lash will be compelled to yield to coercion—the only thing they will ever submit to." Americans must mark, he wrote, that "the men whose fathers fought in State Street, Boston, at Bunker Hill, on Lake Erie and at New Orleans . . . are now abused—abused by secession-sympathizers— now attacked by rebels." "Mark the fact," Aleph wrote, "that, when the present raid against the UNION first broke out, colored men were among the first to offer their services to the country," an offer met with threats of mob violence and being "politely informed" by "our patriotic officials" "that this was a *white man's war* and that the *niggars* had nothing to do with it."[24]

The same issue reports that Lincoln and the secretary of war had authorized Senator James Henry Lane of Kansas to recruit troops, "irrespective of party or color," and that Lane expected "to have one white and two black regiments in the field" three weeks after "reaching his destination."[25] Also in the same issue, the editor refutes claims in an Allentown, Pennsylvania, German newspaper, *Weltbote*, that a black brigade in Port Royal, South Carolina, had run away from army service. To show the claim had no foundation in truth, the editor published a letter from a *New York Independent* correspondent who said he rode out to see the regiment drill and was astonished by "[t]he proficiency of these men in the manual of arms and marching, after so short a practice. No white recruits in service for the same length of time could do better. Their improvement has been wonderful, and exceeds the expectations of their most sanguine friends."[26]

A week later, another writer criticized divided northern opinion about blacks as soldiers and the general mistreatment of blacks, implying that this rendered the North weaker than the South. The writer emphasized blacks' contributions in previous wars and guaranteed that they would give their all in the war when given their just rights as citizens. "Their forefathers have helped to gain the Independence of America, and the first blood ever spilt for that cause was that of a colored man." He added that, although "no class of people in this country" had "been treated half so meanly . . . yet we have borne it all," and were "sensitive of the wrong" and "willing to endure it." No blacks wanted to lose their lives, he said, but, "If the Union wants our aid, as citizens of the United States, and gives us the rights of men, there is not a colored man but what will readily shoulder his musket, and this Rebellion will soon cease—universal liberty proclaimed to all men, and the Union restored."[27]

A letter in the August 30, 1862, issue that described Baltimore as "all excitement and confusion" because of soldiers' continual arrival, reveals pride, sadness, and patriotic defiance regarding black soldiers:

> When we look upon the newly arrived men as they file through our city, and watch their steady and measured tramp, and skillful evolutions, and see how every face seems to beam with joy and gladness, and every heart swelling and pulsating with animation, as if they were going to participate in a holiday parade or in a grand review, and not in the stern realities of an awful fratricidal war when we look on these things, it fills our hearts with sorrow and sadness; and when we think of the dangers which they are subjected to, and how many will see their wives and little ones no more forever, it causes us, notwithstanding all the infamous State laws, unrighteous Congressional edicts and God-hating ordinances . . . enacted to oppress us, we find ourselves offering voluntarily a prayer and a willing [appeal] to God to bless this nation, sustain its defenders and let defeat, discomfiture and destruction be the lot of the traitors who seek its overthrow.[28]

Two weeks later, a writer said it was not known if Massachusetts would have a draft, but if so, it was "generally believed that . . . colored men will have to take their chances with the rest, except in Boston," where the mayor had implied that the draft would accord with the state militia law, "which are the only laws in that State that proscribe men on account of their color." An excerpt of a letter followed, in which John S. Rock had written to the Boston mayor:

> We are willing to bear our proportion of the National burden; and though debarred the privilege of being soldiers . . . we are not behind others in the proportion of men we have contributed to the war; some . . . have gone as servants, but the greater portion have enlisted in the navy. We are not surprised that when there were large bounties, and provisions made for the families of the soldiers, we were not permitted to volunteer; but when it is universally known, that, up to this time, the national Government has not recognised [sic] us as soldiers, and the State has declined to accept us as volunteers, we do not understand why . . . we are prohibited from going out of the State, unless we make oath that we are not leaving to avoid the draft! If we are to be drafted in this city, your Honor will please inform us, so that if any desire it, they may avail themselves of the legal privileges granted to others.[29]

While the core issue about black soldiers concerned their use on behalf of the Union, writers conveyed the ambivalent position that blacks stood ready to fight for their country but were reluctant to do so, doubting that such efforts would be rewarded (or even recognized). Rejection of black soldiers in the war was considered a problem of racism and prejudice. While condemning the Union government's reluctance to enlist blacks in the military, the *Christian Recorder*'s writers used the historical record to justify a "fight-only-with-rights" solution. Noting blacks' exemplary performance and many sacrifices in helping to win American independence, as well as subsequent generations of blacks' labor in building the nation, the *Christian Recorder* in the first 18 months of the Civil War, while condemning the war as unchristian, still suggested that it served black interests by eradicating slavery and affirmed that blacks stood ready and willing to fight for the nation—but not without guarantees of their full civil rights in years to come.

NOTES

1. Joseph T. Glatthaar, *Forged in Battle: The Civil War Alliance of Black Soldiers and White Officers* (New York: The Free Press, 1990), 5–6; Benjamin Quarles, *The Negro in the Civil War* (Boston: Little, Brown, 1953), 31–32.

2. Some important sources are Ira Berlin, Barbara J. Fields, Thaviola Glymph, Joseph P. Reidy, and Leslie S. Rowland, eds., *Freedom: A Documentary History of Emancipation, 1861–1867* (New York: Cambridge University Press, 1982), and Edwin S. Redkey, ed., *A Grand Army of Black Men: Letters from African-American Soldiers in the Union Army, 1861–1865* (Cambridge: Cambridge University Press, 1992). Of invaluable help in identifying sources were compilations by Katherine Hawkins, "Bibliography Highlighting U.S. Colored Troops," *USCT Civil War Digest* 2 (May 2000): 4–5, and by Harry Bradshaw Matthews, "Editor's Choice for Family Research," *USCT Civil War Digest* 2 (May 2000): 2.

3. For general history of the *Christian Recorder*, see Gilbert A. Williams, *The "Christian Recorder," Newspaper of the African Methodist Episcopal Church: History of a Forum for Ideas, 1854–1902* (Jefferson, N.C.: McFarland, 1996). Gilbert A. Williams, "The Role of the *Christian Recorder* in the African Emigration Movement, 1854–1902," *Journalism & Mass Communication Monographs* 111 (April 1989).

4. *Christian Recorder*, 20 April 1861. This refers to the April 18, 1861, attack on Union soldiers marching through Baltimore to defend Washington, D.C.

5. Ibid.

6. Ibid., 30 August 1862.

7. Ibid., 27 September 1862.

8. Tracee Mason, who discusses colonization plans and African Americans' attitudes toward them, says that the *Anglo-African*'s founder-editor bought the magazine back from Redpath after learning he was using it to promote Haitian emigration. See "To Encourage the Now Depressed Hopes of Thinking Black Men: The Anglo-African, 1859–1860" (master's thesis, University of Minnesota, 2002). Other sources on the African emigration movements before and after the Civil War include Carl Patrick Burrowes, "Modernization and the Decline of Press Freedom: Liberia, 1847 to 1970," *Journalism and Mass Communication Monographs* 160 (December 1996): 1–35; Robert G. Athearn, *In Search of Canaan: Black Migration to Kansas, 1879–1880* (Lawrence: Regents Press of Kansas, 1978);

Nell Irvin Painter, *Exodusters: Black Migration to Kansas after Reconstruction* (New York: Alfred A. Knopf, 1977); and Edwin S. Redkey, *Black Exodus: Black Nationalist and Back-to-Africa Movements, 1890–1919* (New Haven: Yale University Press, 1960).

9. *Christian Recorder*, 5 July 1862.
10. Ibid., 14 August 1862.
11. Ibid.
12. Ibid., 30 August 1862.
13. Ibid.
14. Ibid., 27 September 1862.
15. Ibid.
16. Ibid.
17. Ibid., 4 October 1862.
18. Ibid.
19. Ibid., 11 October 1862.
20. Ibid.
21. Ibid., 4 May 1861.
22. Ibid., 28 June 1862.
23. Ibid., 19 July 1862.
24. Ibid., 2 August 1862.
25. Ibid.
26. Ibid.
27. Ibid., 9 August 1862.
28. Ibid., 30 August 1862.
29. Ibid., 3 September 1862.

Independent or Compromised? Civil War Correspondent Sylvanus Cadwallader

⸺ William E. Huntzicker ⸺

Sylvanus Cadwallader, the newly minted war correspondent for the *Chicago Times*, must have had mixed feelings when he arrived to cover Major General Ulysses S. Grant's command along the Mississippi River during the siege of Vicksburg in the spring of 1863. Cadwallader was in a tough spot: he had to consider the feelings of at least three other people—his demanding editor, Wilbur F. Storey, who lived to taunt the Republican establishment; his immediate predecessor, Warren P. Isham, whom Grant had just sent off to jail for getting out of line; and the general himself, who was notably reticent and not given to public utterances or private confessions. Treading a thin line between the editor and the general would provide plenty of challenges for any reporter eager to walk a careful, credible path and send back stories based on his own firsthand observations.

Cadwallader's new editor, Storey, was among the most colorful Copperhead editors. His purpose in the Democratic papers he had edited in Indiana and Michigan, as well as in Chicago, was to "print the news and raise hell!" Vituperation, occasionally leading to street brawls and duels, was not unique to Storey in 19th-century partisan journalism, but Storey practiced it with a particular vengeance. In 1838 at the age of 18, Storey turned around a previously unprofitable Democratic paper in the predominately Whig county of La Porte, Indiana. In the process, he labeled his Whig opponents as "black-hearted falsifiers," "ignorant brawlers," "long-faced hypocrites," and "foul-mouthed slanderers." He detested abolitionists, who, he said, were "too indolent to earn their bread honestly."[1]

In 1846, Storey married Maria Parsons Isham, a graduate of a female seminary and daughter of a Congregational minister who had edited an Ohio newspaper and later contributed newspaper articles throughout his ministerial career. Maria's younger brother, Warren, went into the field for Storey in 1862 and literally created news. "He was a slender, handsome young fellow, and noticeable from the fact that he was stylishly dressed, and looked very much out of place in the roughness and uncleanliness of the surroundings," wrote Franc Wilkie, a *New York Times* correspondent who later joined the *Chicago Times*. "I saw him but for a moment, and it was the only time I ever met him."[2] When Isham was in Memphis, the Federal post commander retreated from Confederates, allegedly in his underwear. Wilkie continued the story:

> Isham wrote up the occurrence in a manner which, if possible, added to the real absurdity and ludicrousness of the situation. It was a communication which set the entire North in roars of laughter. The fugitive with the single garment, and his frantic, headlong rush, became the butt of universal ridicule.
>
> The offense of Isham was too serious to be condoned. It exposed the legs of a mighty brigadier-general scurrying through the streets of Memphis, with a slender, sail-like appendage flapping swiftly in his rear.
>
> The dignity of the Federal arms—perhaps legs is a better word—had been insulted, and stern and swift, like the flight of the fugitive, must be the punishment of the insolent offender. A court-martial was convened, and at the termination of the trial he was sent to the penitentiary at Alton.
>
> He remained there some months. I have never heard that Mr. Storey ever made an effort to get the prisoner released, or gave him the slightest attention. It may be that he was pleased at Isham's seclusion, as it relieved him of a brother-in-law whom he appears to have profoundly hated.[3]

Isham's sins were a bit more complex than Wilkie let on. The Chicago correspondent had spent some previous time in the guardhouse, and this time he was not released until he received a personal reprimand from Major General Henry Halleck, commander of the Union armies in the western theater. Grant, too, had warned Isham to "stop your cock-and-bull yarns from Memphis." But the last straw hit Grant when he picked up the *Chicago Times* to find under the Memphis dateline a complete story by "W.P.I." about a fictitious fleet of Confederate ironclad ships at Pensacola, Florida. That did it. Grant wrote to Memphis commander William T. Sherman, himself no fan of correspondents, saying that because Isham's piece "is both false in fact and mischievous in character, you will have the author arrested and sent to the Alton Penitentiary . . . for confinement until the close of the war, unless sooner discharged by competent authority." To Sherman's delight, Isham went to the penitentiary, but Grant released him after three months.[4]

The following summer, Isham took a vacation on the steamer *Sunbeam*, which ran between Chicago and Ontonagon. After leaving Ontonagon, the ship ran into a storm and sank, killing all thirty people on board. Isham's death created an opening for an assistant editor of the *Times,* the position that Wilkie soon obtained. Strangely, Storey waited one full month before he published the following obituary:

> In the midst of war, when thousands are falling daily, it is not much that *one* should have sunk in the waves of Lake Superior, and through them into the dark and illimitable ocean which "rolls all round the world." But there is here a desk claiming his presence, on which he communicated daily with thousands. Some of these thousands, at least, were moved by his gentle humor to rejoice with him when he did rejoice, and some have felt their hearts beat faster as he struck answering chords of sympathy. To them this slight and imperfect tribute to his merits and memory, even in the midst of events "big with the fate of nations," and of columns crowded with their rehearsal, will not be without interest."[5]

When Storey subsequently sent Wilkie to cover Major General George Thomas's Union army in Tennessee, he gave him a now-famous instruction: "Telegraph fully all the news, and when there is no news, send rumors."[6] Wilkie described a confrontation between Storey and four drunken Union soldiers who had decided one morning to punish the traitorous editor:

> They were talking very loudly, albeit somewhat incoherently and huskily, of "copperhead," and the like, and shaking their fists at the frightened clerks, when Mr. Storey entered the door from the street and walked rapidly along the passage-way in the direction of his room in the rear. He paid no attention to the patriots, and was passing through them, when the corporal staggered against him.
>
> "Who you a-pushin', you damned old secesh son of a —— ?" said the gallant patriot in blue.
>
> As quick as a flash of light Storey turned, seized the corporal by the throat, and pushed him backward until they reached the window, through which the patriot went, head and shoulders, carrying a considerable portion of the sash and glass with him into the street. This done, Storey, without a glance at the other loyalists, who were rapidly falling back toward the sidewalk, went to his room, not having uttered a word during the occurrence.[7]

In Ulysses S. Grant, Cadwallader faced a young general whose unassuming demeanor can be seen in a story that *New York Herald* correspondent D.B.

Randolph Keim told about his own arrival to Grant's camp. Keim approached a "plain-looking man" standing outside Grant's tent wearing a cheap shirt and chewing a large cigar. "I am a newspaper correspondent, have just arrived in camp, and I want to see Gen. Grant," he announced. "This is the general's headquarters," the man told him, "and if you will come here tomorrow morning I am sure the general will be glad to see you." Early the next morning, Keim discovered that he had already met the cigar-chewing general in that brief encounter.[8]

Grant said little about his regard for newspapers. In his memoirs, written late in life, Grant recalled that his father, who operated a tannery at Point Pleasant, Ohio, was a constant reader who learned rapidly; he read every book he could borrow from neighbors. "Even after reading the daily papers—which he never neglected—he could give all the important information they contained," Grant recalled.[9] A West Point graduate, Grant had served under Whig generals Zachary Taylor and Winfield Scott in the Mexican War, distinguishing himself in battle. He resigned his commission in 1854 because of loneliness and drinking problems while stationed in California. In 1860 he moved to Galena, Illinois, to work in his father's leather store.

Grant must have had some curiosity about the press after seeing how correspondents covered the indecisive Battle of Belmont, which had an important bearing on Grant's ongoing effort to open the Mississippi. Newspaper coverage in St. Louis, Chicago, and New York described the battle as everything from a victory to a defeat.[10] Grant became annoyed at correspondents who made up stories, and he would later have serious personal reasons to be annoyed at newspapers. "There never was a more thoroughly disgusted, disheartened, demoralized army than this is," a Cincinnati correspondent wrote to his publisher in a letter forwarded to Secretary of the Treasury Salmon P. Chase in early 1863. The publisher, Murat Halstead of the *Cincinnati Commercial,* sent a note vouching for this dismal but inaccurate picture that blamed defeats, disease, and demoralization on Grant's drinking.[11]

After the initial fighting in early 1863, Grant settled in for a long, troublesome siege of Vicksburg, Mississippi, an action that drew criticism from many quarters as indecisive, but one that Grant defended, noting that a failed attack or withdrawal would have been worse:

> At this time the North had become very much discouraged. Many strong Union men believed that the war must prove a failure. . . . It was my judgment at the time that to make a backward movement as long as that from Vicksburg to Memphis, would be interpreted by many of those yet full of hope for the preservation of the Union, as a defeat, and that the draft would be resisted, desertions ensue and the power to capture and punish

deserters lost. There was nothing left to be done but to *go forward to a decisive victory*. This was in my mind from the moment I took command in person at Young's Point.[12]

Cadwallader joined Grant during the Vicksburg siege. Given what had happened to his predecessor, Cadwallader was understandably apprehensive when he reported to Grant's command. The sheepishness that Wilkie perceived may have been related more to Cadwallader's low opinion of his profession and colleagues than to his own newspaper. "At that time nearly all army correspondents were in bad odor at all army headquarters, and were always secretly held to be a species of nuisance that needed abating," Cadwallader recalled in a memoir years later. The officers, especially West Pointers, despised the correspondents, often with good reason, Cadwallader wrote, adding:

> Candor compels the admission that as a class, the first installment of correspondents sent to the armies deserved no high rank in public or official estimation. Some unduly magnified their importance as the representatives of the leading metropolitan daily newspapers. Some were so lacking in conventional politeness as to make themselves positively disagreeable wherever they went. Others were base enough to make merchandise of personal mentions in their correspondence. Others almost unblushingly took the contract of "writing up" some Colonel to a Brigadier Generalship, for a specified consideration in dollars. And still others were sufficiently ignoble to fasten themselves upon some Colonel or Brigadier, and pay their bills, whiskey bills and horse hire, by fulsome and undeserved praise of their patrons and protectors in every communication sent back for publication.
>
> There was also still another class, more despicable if possible than those already mentioned, who would purloin papers and orders, hang around officers' tents secretly at night hoping to overhear conversation that could be used by their papers. . . . A small proportion only of the whole number possessed the rudimentary qualifications of common honesty, tact, and the ability to discriminate between legitimate and illegitimate news from the seat of war. In the end, "the survival of the fittest" corrected all this. At the close of the war, good standing at Army headquarters equaled a patent of nobility.
>
> In view of this status of army correspondents, I resolved upon an entirely new line of procedure. This was first to sustain my own self respect and secondly, to so govern my intercourse with military men in the Dept. as to deserve theirs. I decided to procure my own outfit, to ride my own horses and pay my own expenses liberally rather than parsimoniously. That if the exigencies of the service required me to enter a military 'mess,' to pay my full *pro-rata* share of all its expenses and to accept no hospitalities on any other conditions. I also decided to make all calls at

Regimental, Brigade, and Division, Corps & Army headquarters rather formal than otherwise at the outset; to make them brief, and never to allow them to interrupt official business.[13]

Cadwallader said he soon learned that if he did not impose himself, he received more access and a friendlier reception. One evening in November, an officer called him aside and asked if he were interested in seeing an active campaign. If so, he said, Cadwallader should board a nearby car with locomotive attached on which the general would leave for the front the next morning. The officer, Colonel R.L. Dickey, then advised him to get a horse and be ready for an early morning start. To his surprise, when Cadwallader went to the hotel dining room for breakfast and encountered Grant and his staff already there, the general invited him to join them.[14]

Politeness paid well for Cadwallader, but his apprehension grew when he wrote an article criticizing Grant's troops for their unnecessary destruction of civilian property and the general for his failure to control them. The correspondent recalled walking by Grant's room and being summoned by the general, who inquired whether he had written the article in the *Times*. After acknowledging that he had, Cadwallader said, Grant admitted that his troops had behaved badly on the march and in violation of orders, but he said he had been too busy on the march to stop and establish courts of inquiry and courts-martial. If men were caught looting, though, he said he would have them punished. The general then told Cadwallader "that if I never wrote more untruthfully than this, he and I would never have any difficulty concerning my correspondence." Grant said he was too engrossed with his own affairs to censor Cadwallader's dispatches.

Without a hint of contradiction, Cadwallader responded quite differently when a woman came running after three cavalrymen she said were stealing her chickens and complained that soldiers had been stealing them all day. "I suggested that the loss of a few chickens cut little figure in the war, and advised her to make up her mind to lose them all, and everything else good to eat, that was not securely guarded," Cadwallader remembered.[15]

The Chicago reporter developed a special relationship with the general from Galena, Illinois. Colleagues speculated about their relationship, and Cadwallader never commented on it during their lives. In his unpublished memoir, however, the reporter attributed the relationship to his special tact about the general's drinking. He claimed to have discovered Grant once after he had been drinking heavily aboard a steamship used during the Vicksburg siege. At one point, he said, Grant mounted a spirited horse owned by another officer and went galloping through the bayou and sloughs, charging through people's camps and disrupting them. Fortunately, no one saw who he was, and when

Cadwallader caught up with him, he unsaddled the horse and persuaded the general to lie in a thicket and go to sleep using the saddle as a pillow. Cadwallader obtained a wagon and quietly took him back to the boat. The incident was never mentioned, except to Brigadier General John Rawlins of Grant's staff, who kept his commander away from alcohol. Grant vowed never to drink again, and he avoided liquor for months at a time. "The truth was Gen. Grant had an inordinate love for liquors," Cadwallader wrote. "He was not an habitual drinker. He could not drink moderately." As a result, contradictory rumors arose about Grant's drinking. Lincoln was under so much pressure about Grant's drinking that he sent Charles A. Dana, former managing editor of the *New York Tribune*, to the western front to monitor Grant's activities. Dana's reports to Lincoln and Secretary of War Edwin Stanton amounted to news stories from the front. Like Cadwallader, Dana grew to respect Grant's military talent.[16]

Cadwallader's standing with the general grew, and he seemed to get special attention. Cadwallader had become a staunch defender of Grant by the time *Cincinnati Commercial* reporter Murat Halstead attacked the general as a drunk and began a campaign to have him removed.[17] Cadwallader became one of the most reliable war correspondents, especially among Democratic papers. During the eastern campaigns, colleague Franc B. Wilkie wrote, "He was the chief of 'The New York Herald' staff of army correspondents,—a position he filled with surpassing ability."[18] With Cadwallader in the field, the *Chicago Times* beat its competitors covering events in Missouri, Tennessee, and the lower Mississippi. By spring 1863, Cadwallader had become so well known that editors and politicians throughout the country looked to the notoriously Democratic *Chicago Times* for the most reliable accounts of the Republican Grant's command.[19]

In his personal correspondence, Cadwallader shared some of his life as a correspondent in pencil-written letters to his eight-year-old daughter. "You would be amused if you see me writing this letter," he wrote in a revealing letter about camp life. He continued:

> I am sitting on the side of an army cot, or bedstead, a little higher than your trundle bed with a pillow in my lap for a writing table. . . . Our cots reach from the front to the back of the tent, and there is just room enough between each cot, for us to walk in. A rope is stretched across overhead on which we hang our clothes, or other things not in use. Our saddles and bridles are stowed under our cots each night for fear they might be stolen if left outside. You can imagine by this description that we have no room to spare. We have a fire built in front of the tent, and sit outside unless it rains. . . . Droves of mules and horses pass through the streets at all hours of the day; and long strings of wagons with six mules to each and driven by negroes, go to the country daily and return loaded with corn and fodder for the horses of the army. Not less than 100 wagons go out every day.

When we first came here they could get corn near by, but this is used up, and they now have to go several miles. A company of soldiers is detailed to go with each train of wagons, for fear the rebels might capture them. These soldiers catch all the turkeys and chickens on the farms they go to, and carry them to camp for their own use. They also dig all the sweet potatoes they can find and carry off everything they want. The farmers are afraid to resist the soldiers, lest they should be shot. The soldiers behave so badly Gen. Grant issued orders a week ago to have everyone punished severely who stole from the farmers. One of Gen. Hamiltons soldiers stole a very handsome pony 8 miles from here. I bought it for a few dollars, and used it nearly a week. The soldier said he bought it from near Corinth, or I would not have purchased it. Yesterday a little boy living here, going to school, stopped me in the street and said I was riding his pony. I went to his boarding house, found out who he was, went to parties that knew the pony to be his, and returned it to him. He was wonderfully pleased I assure you; and I lost nothing, for I gave no more for it, than the hire of a horse would have cost me while I used it. I gave the soldiers name and regiment to the Provost Marshal, and hope he will be punished for stealing it. Not liking to be stopped in the street and suspected of horse stealing I have taken another and better method of getting a horse to ride.

All the negroes here were slaves before we came; They call themselves free now, but have only changed masters. A great many have left their masters farms, and came into camp. Our soldiers make them chop wood, wash, cook, and do the camp work instead of doing it themselves. Last night one of the old darkies got a "fiddle," and all the others danced while he played. It was a funny sight to see a whole lot of them dancing by the firelight.[20]

In 1864, Cadwallader joined the *New York Herald* and eventually became chief of the *Herald's* correspondents. Managing editor Frederic Hudson sent him letters complimenting him for his organization and urging him to beat the competition. "When Richmond falls we desire not to be beaten I feel that we shall not be," Hudson wrote in March 1865. "The *Herald* was a newspaper this morning," he wrote a month before the war ended. "Our accounts of the battle of Saturday surpassed all others in quality and quantity and time. . . . I wish you would thank the correspondents for Mr. Bennett for the promptness and ability shown in the affair. You have the corps well arranged and your plans work efficiently."[21]

Given the western generals' less than cordial attitudes toward correspondents, little would have been known about their operations without the Grant-Cadwallader relationship. Working together instinctively, Grant and Cadwallader developed a successful professional relationship in which Cadwallader asserted his right to evaluate critically Grant's battlefield performance. Cadwallader's reports for the *Chicago Times* and later the *New York Herald* were certainly not what would be today called objective journalism.

At least once, Cadwallader found it in the national interest to ignore Grant's drinking in print. Nevertheless, Cadwallader and Grant informally defined an important independent role for journalists.

NOTES

1. Justin E. Walsh, *To Print the News and Raise Hell! A Biography of Wilbur F. Storey* (Chapel Hill: University of North Carolina Press, 1968), 4, 19, 21, 23, 26, 29.

2. Franc B. Wilkie ("Poliuto"), *Personal Reminiscences of Thirty-Five Years of Journalism* (Chicago: F.J. Schulte & Company, 1891), 94–95.

3. Ibid., 95–96.

4. Walsh, 176–177. Louis M. Starr, *Bohemian Brigade: Civil War Newsmen in Action* (1954; repr., Madison: University of Wisconsin Press, 1987), 278–279.

5. *Chicago Times*, September 1863, reprinted in Walsh, 179–180.

6. Wilkie, 114.

7. Wilkie, 115–116.

8. J. Cutler Andrews, *The North Reports the Civil War* (Princeton: Princeton University Press, 1955), 374.

9. U.S. Grant, *Personal Memoirs of U.S. Grant,* ed. E.B. Long (New York: Da Capo Press, 1982), 7.

10. Andrews, 119.

11. Ibid., 119, 384.

12. Grant, 231.

13. Benjamin P. Thomas, ed., *Three Years with Grant as Recalled by War Correspondent Sylvanus Cadwallader* (New York: Alfred A. Knopf, 1955), 11–12.

14. Ibid., 16–17.

15. Ibid., 28.

16. Ibid., 103–112. Franc B. Wilkie, *Pen and Powder* (Boston: Ticknor and Company, 1888), 205–208. William S. McFeely, *Grant: A Biography* (New York: W.W. Norton and Company, 1985), 131–138. In his introduction to a more recent edition of Cadwallader's memoir, Brooks D. Simpson challenged the reporter's story about discovering Grant on a binge. Instead, claimed Simpson, Grant probably had a stiff drink for an illness he suffered at the time, and Dana probably recognized the problem. "In contrast," Simpson wrote, "Cadwallader's account strikes one as a tall tale told to impress others, a story hard to reconcile with the available evidence." Simpson, introduction to *Three Years with Grant*, Bison Books (Lincoln: University of Nebraska Press, 1996), xiii–xv.

17. Cadwallader, 112–119. For his part, Lincoln said, "I can't spare this man; he fights." David Herbert Donald, *Lincoln* (New York: Simon & Schuster, 1995), 349.

18. Wilkie, *Pen and Powder,* 208.

19. Walsh, 176.

20. Sylvanus Cadwallader to his daughter Carrie, Cadwallader Papers, Library of Congress, Personal and Family Correspondence folder 1849–1897.

21. Hudson to Cadwallader, 18 March 1865; Hudson to Cadwallader, 28 March 1865; Hudson to Cadwallader, 6 April 1865; Cadwallader Papers, Library of Congress, General Correspondence folder 1865–1882.

Abraham Lincoln's Relationship with James Gordon Bennett and Horace Greeley during the Civil War

— Gene Murray —

During his forty-nine months in the White House, Abraham Lincoln had no formal method of dealing with the press. Instead, Lincoln dealt with certain leading journalists in person and at length. Much more accessible than previous presidents, Lincoln welcomed all reporters and often talked freely with them in his chambers. One of his favorite questions to ask reporters was: "What news have you?" The two journalists with whom Lincoln was most concerned were James Gordon Bennett, editor-publisher of the *New York Herald*, and Horace Greeley, editor-publisher of the *New York Tribune*. He assiduously cultivated their relationships, even though the editors' support of his presidential policies was somewhat erratic throughout the Civil War.

Bennett, who came to America in 1819 and worked in Boston and South Carolina before settling in New York, was described as a "Scottish-born prodigy of journalism" who was "tall and might have looked distinguished except for a strabismus, a persistent squint in one eye,"[1] He was cynical, impudent, purposeful, and vulgar. Bennett usually is credited by historians as being responsible for placing news first in his paper. A pioneer in the use of Washington correspondents, Bennett originated the "money article" and conducted some of the first interviews. He also organized the first newsroom and reporting staff, hiring reporters and sending them out on rounds to gather information for the readers.[2] Founded as a politically independent paper, the *Herald* had a sizable circulation and a considerable circulation in the South.

Bennett's fiercest rival, Horace Greeley, looked "like some medieval philosopher, oblivious to the shouts of omnibus drivers, wrapped in thought, his benign face framed in a fringe of light scraggly whiskers. His long coat flapped around his ankles. Pockets bulged with papers, scrawled notes, reminders, and editorial paragraphs for his *Tribune*."[3] Although often beaten by Bennett to a news story, Greeley concentrated on the editorial page, supporting a variety of causes with vigor. Politically, Greeley supported the Whigs and later helped organize the Republican Party. The weekly edition of the *Tribune* was deeply detested throughout the South.

Greeley and Bennett met sometime in the 1830s in New York, where they both worked for newspapers. In 1834 Bennett with about $500 asked Greeley to enter a partnership to establish the *Herald*, but Greeley refused. However, Greeley did advertise his weekly *New Yorker* in Bennett's *Herald*. The *Herald*'s treatment of the sensational 1836 Jewett murder trial helped establish the newspaper's reputation. Bennett thoroughly covered the case of Richard P. Robinson, a clerk accused of killing reputed prostitute Ellen Jewett. The public responded so well to the coverage that Bennett decided to carry in each issue some stories about crime, violence, sex, and adventure in order to sell more newspapers. When the *Tribune* appeared in 1840, Greeley wasted little time in criticizing the detailed trial coverage by the *Herald*. "The moral guilt incurred and the violent hurt inflicted upon social order by those who thus spread out the loathsome details of the most damning deed," he complained, "are ten-fold greater that those of the miscreant himself."[4]

Bennett responded angrily. "Horace Greeley is endeavoring, with tears in his eyes, to show that it is very naughty to publish reports of the trial, confession and execution of Peter Robinson," he wrote. "Now this Horace Greeley, BA and ASS, is probably the most unmitigated blockhead connected with the newspaper press. Galvanize a large New England squash, and it would make as capable an editor as Horace."[5] Regardless of his rival's stated opinions, Greeley started the *New York Tribune* in 1841 as an instrument to fight social ills. A war of words had begun and would continue for the next 30 years. An example appeared in 1843, when Bennett wrote about a Greeley lecture, "Horace had better stay at home and look after his newspaper."[6] On another occasion, Greeley wrote, "Don't cowhide Bennett if the *Herald* slander you. You cannot make him a gentleman—it has been tried a hundred times—but you may make yourself a blackguard."[7]

In 1846, Bennett and Greeley were involved in a race for news from Europe about the pending Oregon treaty. Bennett made arrangements with the captain of the trans-Atlantic steamer *Cambria* in order to beat the *Tribune* and several other newspapers with the news. After beating Greeley by five hours, Bennett sent Greeley a complimentary note for his efforts. Two years later, the *Tribune* challenged the circulation figures of the *Herald*. The $200 wager was to be donated to New York City's orphanages. Counting all editions, the *Herald* won, 28,946 to 28,195. According to Greeley, the major portion of the *Herald*'s circulation was in "houses of infamy, in gambling halls, and in grog shops and drinking saloons of the lowest character."[8] Bennett interpreted this remark to mean that he was reaching the common man.

The *Herald* came closest of the leading New York papers to supporting the views of the South. It supported the Kansas-Nebraska Bill of 1854, which called for popular sovereignty to determine the makeup of new territories entering the Union. Bennett represented the Democratic party's and the South's view of states' rights. When Greeley supported a Republican platform in 1855, Bennett attacked the "niggerizing" program. Bennett referred to his rival as "Massa Horace."[9] Perhaps by coincidence, biographies of the two publishers appeared in 1855, Greeley's in the spring and Bennett's late in the year. Greeley's life story was written by Englishman James Parton, and Bennett's by Isaac C. Pray, a former *Herald* staffer who signed the book merely as "a journalist." The Bennett book supposedly was written without his cooperation.

A temporary peace was reached between Greeley and Bennett in 1856, when both rallied behind the Republican candidate for president, John C. Frémont. After Frémont's defeat, Bennett returned to the Democrat ranks. Bennett and Greeley also agreed that the states wishing to secede should be allowed to go in peace. Before the Civil War began, Bennett suggested that the North and South separate, with the South annexing Mexico and the North seizing Canada.

During the 1858 senatorial campaign between Abraham Lincoln and Stephen A. Douglas, Greeley at first supported Douglas in hopes that he would switch to the Republican stance but later supported Lincoln. Bennett more or less ignored the entire campaign, printing little about it. Both newspapers covered Lincoln's Cooper Union Institute speech in February 1860. The *Herald* remarked that Lincoln was "unsteady in his gait" and had a "comical awkwardness and remarkable mobility of features."[10] Greeley covered the speech and reprinted it in pamphlet form.

Greeley played an instrumental role in Lincoln's 1860 presidential nomination. Although he originally went to Chicago with plans of backing lawyer Edward Bates of Missouri, the publisher took a stand to prevent his former crony, U.S. Senator William Seward, from winning the nomination.

Despite fears that Lincoln was too inexperienced in national affairs, Greeley persuaded other delegates to support Lincoln's bid.

Lincoln and Greeley had met in Chicago in 1847, and Greeley had written: "In the afternoon Hon. Abraham Lincoln, a tall specimen of an Illinoisan, just elected to the Congress from the only Whig district in the state, was called out, and spoke briefly and happily."[11] Later in an 1847 article on Congress, Greeley counted Lincoln insignificant. In late 1848 and early 1849, Greeley was appointed to a three-month term in Congress and served with Lincoln. He described the Illinois representative then as a "quiet, good-natured man" who "did not aspire to leadership and seldom claimed the floor."[12] Lincoln, according to Greeley, claimed too much travel mileage, and his excess expenses of $676.80 were included in a Greeley exposé.

Immediately after Lincoln's nomination for president, the *Tribune* began to laud him as an able statesman who had struggled from the impoverished surroundings of a log cabin to command the respect of the nation. Lincoln was painted as the true political descendant of the revolutionary fathers and as a man of the people who would sustain the Union as Andrew Jackson and Zachary Taylor had done before him.[13] Meanwhile, Bennett penned editorials filled with malice and hostility toward the candidate but also published some lengthy articles favorable to Lincoln.

Greeley scoffed at the spreading secession movement, saying that the "overawed, gagged, paralyzed majority" of southerners would refuse to follow the desperate minority. It would be better to have a Union with the South, Greeley wrote, than a Union submissive to slaveholders. Bennett, on the other hand, editorialized that North America had room for both the U.S. and Confederate governments. Greeley sent the president-elect a letter in December 1860, suggesting that he make no compromises with the South. Greeley visited with Lincoln in Springfield, Illinois, during a lecture tour in February 1861 and reaffirmed his no-compromise stand. Before the inauguration, Bennett suggested that Lincoln return to Illinois and allow someone more acceptable to both North and South to assume the presidency.

During the prewar days of 1861, neither newspaper was very critical of Lincoln. Greeley tried to secure Lincoln's support in his Senate race for the seat vacated by Seward's appointment as secretary of state, but Lincoln remained neutral. Bennett ridiculed Lincoln's inaugural address, claiming it was filled with vague generalities. Greeley found the language conciliatory yet firm.

Greeley's contact with the president was more direct and less formal than Bennett's. Lincoln tried unsuccessfully in 1860 to obtain Bennett's support by sending Joseph Medill as a spokesman, but Bennett remained a Democrat and resolutely prosouthern. Until mid-April 1861, the *Herald* argued: "A

Civil war . . . what for? To show we have a government? . . . A wall will only widen the breach and enlarge and consolidate the Southern Confederacy."[14] After Fort Sumter was threatened, Bennett wrote that "our only hope now against civil war of indefinite duration seems to lie in the overthrow of the demoralizing, disorganizing and destructive sectional party of which 'Honest Abe' Lincoln is the pliant instrument."[15] As hostilities mounted, Greeley called Bennett a "yellow-bellied secessionist" and "hero of the South" who should be hanged.[16] After a mob visited Bennett's proslavery office, he quickly hoisted the proper colors and changed his tune to pro-Union. He viewed the war as a tremendous news opportunity, whereas Greeley saw it as a great moral issue. While Bennett was issuing a four-page *Herald* war extra, Greeley was busily writing an editorial stating that right would eventually prevail. He demanded that the war be carried out with the utmost rapidity and efficiency.

"Forward to Richmond!" became the battle cry of the *Tribune*. Greeley was absent from his office when that notorious editorial campaign was begun by Washington correspondent Fitz Henry Warren under the direction of managing editor Charles Dana. The "Forward to Richmond" campaign was quickly followed by a Greeley editorial titled "Just Once," in which he acknowledged his overall responsibility for the contents of his newspaper. He wrote, "Henceforth I bar all criticism in these columns of Army movements, past or future. Correspondents and reporters may state fact, but must forebear comments."[17]

Through correspondent Henry Villard, who had developed a close working relationship with Lincoln during the 1860 campaign, Bennett relayed a message to Lincoln that the *Herald* would support the administration. Bennett offered the use of his son's yacht to the government in return for a Coast Guard commission for the younger Bennett. In a separate interview, Lincoln told a *Herald* reporter that Bennett was a great editor, "the greatest in the country, perhaps, if my good friend Horace Greeley will allow me to say so."[18] Although Bennett pledged support for the war effort, he looked upon the president as a conservative misled by a group of radicals.

An example of Lincoln's letters to Bennett is one concerning a rejected pass for a *Herald* reporter in which Lincoln wrote, "I write this to assure you that the administration will not discriminate against the *Herald*." In a separate memo to Secretary of State Seward, Lincoln stated that the *Herald* must be humored. On other occasions, Lincoln addressed private letters to Bennett, expressing thanks for his support and clarifying possible misinterpretations. The president sent Thurlow Weed as an emissary to seek Bennett's support, and Weed went to New York, although he and Bennett had not spoken for 30 years. Lincoln sensed an improvement in the *Herald*'s coverage after the Weed visit. Medill had told Lincoln earlier that Bennett was too rich for favors—he would just like some attention.

Unlike Bennett, who chose to deal with the president from a distance and not to give him advice, Greeley wrote pleading letters instructing Lincoln how to better run the country. In July 1861, following an attack of brain fever possibly brought about by Union war losses, Greeley wrote, "I will second any movement you may see fit to make. But do nothing timidly or by halves. Send me word what to do. I will live till I can hear it, at all events. If it is best for the country and for mankind that we make peace with the rebels at once, and on their terms, do not shrink even from that."[19] Lincoln tucked away the letter until the war was almost over before showing it to anyone.

In an effort to pacify Greeley, Lincoln wrote a letter to another man late in 1861 but intended to reach Greeley indirectly. "I need not tell you that I have the highest confidence in Mr. Greeley," the president told the former Kansas governor, George M. Beebe. "He is a great power. Having him firmly behind me will be as helpful as an army of 100,000 men. . . . If he ever objects to my policy, I shall be glad to have him state to me his views frankly and fully. I shall adopt his if I can. If I cannot, I will at least tell him why. He and I should stand together."[20]

In December 1861, Lincoln went to the Smithsonian Institution to hear Greeley lecture. Looking directly at Lincoln, Greeley remarked that the primary objective of the war was the destruction of slavery. Several audience members cheered, but Lincoln remained silent and looked uncomfortable. Perhaps Greeley's most effective and impressive message to Lincoln was his "Prayer of Twenty Millions," an open letter to the president published in the *Tribune* on August 20, 1862. Speaking as the voice of the masses, Greeley argued: "What an immense majority of the loyal million of your countrymen require of you is a frank, declared, un-qualified, ungrudging execution of the laws of the land, more especially the Confiscation Act. That act gives freedom to the slaves of rebels coming within our lines, or whom those lines may at any time enclose—we ask you to render it due obedience by publicly requiring all your subordinates to recognize and obey it."[21]

Lincoln replied on August 22 in a letter in the *National Intelligencer,* "My paramount object in this struggle is to save the Union, and is not either to save or destroy Slavery. If I could save the Union without freeing *any* slave, I would do it; and if I could save it by freeing *all* the slaves, I would do it; and if I could do it by freeing some and leaving others alone, I would also do that." He added that "I shall correct errors when shown to be errors, and I shall adopt new views so fast as they shall appear to be true views. I have here stated my purpose according to my view of *official* duty, and I intend no modification of my oft-expressed *personal* wish that all men, everywhere, could be free."[22]

Greeley's reply to Lincoln urged "that you may promptly and practically realize that slavery is to be vanquished only by liberty—is the fervent and anxious prayer of HORACE GREELEY."[23] Perhaps partially as a result of Greeley's pleading, Lincoln issued the Emancipation Proclamation on September 23, 1862, to become effective the following January 1. The *Tribune's* headlines screamed "GOD BLESS ABRAHAM LINCOLN!" On the other hand, Bennett seemed to feel that Lincoln was yielding to the radicals. Bennett attacked Greeley as a "seditionist, a disunionist, a political cheat, and a hypocrite." Lincoln was simply "an imbecile joker."[24]

During the summer of 1864, Greeley was a prophet of doom, saying that the South could never be defeated and that the North must compromise. He sent Lincoln the message that "our bleeding, bankrupt, almost dying country . . . longs for peace—shudders at the prospect of fresh conscriptions, of further wholesale devastation, and of new rivers of human blood.[25] Hoping to aid the peace effort, Greeley traveled to Niagara, Canada, to meet with some southern representatives in 1864. After his aborted mission, Bennett attacked Greeley as "cuddling with traitors" and jeered his "meddling, bungling" and willingness to compromise the U.S. government.[26] Bennett referred to him as "poor Greeley that nincompoop without genius."[27] Greeley tended to take out his frustrations on the chief executive, causing Lincoln to say, "You complain of me—what have I done, or omitted to do, that has provoked the hostility of the *Tribune?*"[28]

Meanwhile, the war dragged on, and the possibility of Lincoln's seeking reelection was discussed. In March 1864, a Washington correspondent for the *Tribune* wrote that although a majority of Republican leaders seemed averse to Lincoln, the people supported him. Greeley offered four choices as good replacements for Lincoln—Salmon Chase, John C. Frémont, and Union Generals Benjamin Butler and Ulysses Grant. "As to the Presidency, I am not at all confident of making any change but I believe that I shall make things better by trying," Greeley wrote. "He will be a better President, if re-elected, from the opposition he is now encountering."[29]

When the Republicans held their national convention in Baltimore in the summer of 1864, Bennett wrote a vicious editorial critical of the "Ghoul convention" and calling Lincoln the chief ghoul in Washington. The *Herald* at first advocated Union Major General George McClellan on the Democratic ticket and later mentioned Grant as a possibility. In order to win the favor of the two most influential editors, Lincoln pulled some strings. He circulated a rumor that he thought of Greeley as another Benjamin Franklin and was considering appointing him postmaster general if he was reelected. Although he called the offer a lie, Greeley eventually came out in support of Lincoln.

To Bennett Lincoln offered the ambassadorship to France, which Bennett promptly refused, explaining that at his age (almost 70), he would be more useful to his country by remaining at the *Herald*. Calling Lincoln the lesser of two evils, Bennett also came out in support of the president's reelection. He finally had gotten the attention he wanted.

Although he, too, supported Lincoln's reelection, Greeley did not slack off much in his efforts to end the war. His theme throughout the winter of 1864–1865 was peace with mercy and general amnesty. Attending the second inaugural, Greeley wrote that Lincoln seemed "Weather-beaten." In an editorial a few days later, Greeley wrote that "his usefulness, his strength, his popularity grew out of the fact that he accurately collects, comprehends, embodies the average sentiment of the American people." Greeley added, almost prophetically, that "his death or a permanent disability now would be a calamity—very generally and justly deplored."[30]

Even though he thought the president was weary, Greeley on March 22, 1865, outlined several ultimatums that Lincoln should give the Confederates in order to cause a peace settlement. But the ultimatums proved unnecessary when Confederate General Robert E. Lee surrendered to Grant at Appomattox Court House on April 9. "MAGNANIMITY IN TRIUMPH" proclaimed a *Tribune* banner headline, and Greeley wrote editorials urging amnesty and rebuilding.

The war's end was followed closely by Lincoln's assassination on April 14. Greeley wrote that Lincoln

> was not a born king ... but a child of the people, who made himself a great persuader, therefore a leader, by dint of firm resolve, patient effort and dogged perseverance. He slowly won his way to eminence and fame by doing the work that lay next to him—doing it with all his growing might—doing it as well as he could and learning by his failure, when failure was encountered, how to do it better. He was open to all impressions and influences, and gladly profited by the teachings of events and circumstances, no matter adverse or unwelcome. There was probably no year in his life when he was not a wiser, cooler and better man than he had been the preceding.[31]

The South had lost a friend who represented "the triumph of the democratic principle over the aristocratic," wrote Bennett. His *Herald* editorial stated:

> He may not have been, perhaps was not, our most perfect product in any one branch of mental or moral education; but, taking him for all in

all, the very noblest impulses, peculiarities and aspirations of our whole people—what may be called our continental idiosyncrasies—were more collectively and vividly reproduced in his genial and yet unswerving nature than in that of any other public man of whom our chronicles bear record.[32]

Following Lincoln's death, the two aging editors did not quarrel as much as they had done in the past. Bennett gradually went into semiretirement while Greeley continued to chase causes, but his old rival was not around to see Greeley fight his last big battle. Bennett died in 1872 a few weeks before Greeley was nominated to run for president. Greeley wrote an editorial somewhat laudatory of Bennett and served as a pallbearer at his funeral. Before the year ended, Greeley joined him in death.

The two most influential editors in American journalism in the 1860s grew to respect the abilities of Abraham Lincoln. They supported him when he desperately needed it, although that support was somewhat irregular and, where Greeley was concerned, inconsistent. Lincoln, in turn, was well aware of the power of the pens of Greeley and Bennett and was grateful for their support. In their editorials upon the occasion of Lincoln's death, the editors reflected regret that they had not aided him more.

NOTES

1. Emmett Crozier, *Yankee Reporters, 1861–1865* (New York: Oxford University Press, 1956), 17.
2. John Vivian, *The Media of Mass Communication* (Boston: Allyn and Bacon, 1999), 261.
3. Crozier, 16.
4. Harvey Saallberg, "Bennett and Greeley, Professional Rivals, Had Much in Common," *Journalism Quarterly* 49 (1972): 541.
5. Henry Luther Stoddard, *Horace Greeley: Printer, Editor, Crusader* (New York: G.P. Putnam's Sons, 1946), 65.
6. Ibid., 137.
7. Glyndon Van Deusen, *Horace Greeley: Nineteenth-Century Crusader* (New York: Hill and Wang, 1953), 56.
8. Oliver Carlson, *The Man Who Made News: James Gordon Bennett* (New York: Duell, Sloan and Pierce, 1942), 238.
9. William Harlan Hale, *Horace Greeley: Voice of the People* (New York: Harper & Brothers, 1950), 171.
10. Carlson, 296.
11. Herbert Mitgang, *Abraham Lincoln: A Press Portrait* (Chicago: Quadrangle Books, 1971), 50.
12. Ibid., 52.
13. Jeter Allen Isley, *Horace Greeley and the Republican Party* (Princeton: Princeton University Press, 1947), 296.

14. Hale, 243.
15. Robert Harper, *Lincoln and the Press* (New York: McGraw-Hill, 1951), 101.
16. Crozier, 46.
17. Louis Starr, *Bohemian Brigade* (New York: Alfred A. Knopf, 1954), 53.
18. Ibid., 57.
19. Hale, 249.
20. Ibid., 256.
21. Mitgang, 300.
22. L.D. Ingersoll, *The Life of Horace Greeley* (Philadelphia: John E. Potter and Co., 1847), 400.
23. Ibid., 406.
24. Hale, 265.
25. Ibid., 281.
26. Ibid., 284.
27. Van Deusen, 308.
28. Edwin Emery, *The Press and America: An Interpretative History of the Mass Media* (Englewood Cliffs, N.J.: Prentice-Hall, 1972), 233.
29. Stoddard, 244–245.
30. Harper, 345.
31. James H. Trietsch, *The Printer and the Prince* (New York: Exposition Press, 1955), 297–298.
32. Ibid.

"No Turning Back"

The Official Bulletins of Secretary of War Edwin M. Stanton

— Crompton Burton —

In earlier days, the room had served as a library adjacent to the chambers of the secretary. Now, in the fourth summer of the Civil War, it had been transformed into the telegraph office for the War Department. It was not unusual for President Abraham Lincoln and Secretary of War Edwin Stanton to spend long hours in the office or with the cipher operators in an adjoining room, anxiously awaiting dispatches from the front. They were there again late in the evening of May 6, 1864, when word from the Army of the Potomac made its way through the tangle of the Virginia Wilderness as the telegraph clicked to life with electrifying news.[1]

Addressed not to Lincoln or Stanton, the message was directed instead to an assistant War Department secretary, Charles Dana. It said simply that the sender had left the headquarters of General Ulysses S. Grant early that morning and wanted to communicate to the department.[2] Stanton was suspicious. "Who are you and what is your message for Dana," he wired back. "Where did you leave Grant?" On the other end, in a small telegraph office at the depot of Union Mills, more than 20 miles from the capital, the answer was dictated immediately to the operator. "Tell him I am Henry Wing of the New York *Tribune*. I have just come from Grant's headquarters and would like to send a brief report to my paper. Only one hundred words."

The cheek of the young reporter irritated Stanton, who had forbidden the use of the military telegraph by the newspapers. He repeated his demand that Wing immediately send his news of Grant and the army or be arrested for a spy. Wing refused. An impasse seemed certain until the operator in Union Mills handed another message to Wing: "This is the President. Mr. Stanton tells me you have news from the Army. Will you give it to me? We are anxious here in Washington to learn developments at the front." It was signed simply, "A. Lincoln." Despite having left Grant's headquarters at Wilderness Tavern that morning at 4:30 a.m. and walking more than 24 miles after abandoning his horse, Wing proceeded to press for the right to send his dispatch to New York. Lincoln assented, and for the next 20 minutes Wing shared with an anxious nation the first news of the bitter fighting between Union and Confederate forces south of the Rapidan River.

More drama soon followed. Eager for additional news, Stanton dispatched a train to Union Mills to carry Wing to Washington to repeat the briefing in the White House. Shortly after midnight, the engine, baggage car, and coach pulled into the railroad station in Washington, where they were met by a carriage whisking Wing to an early-morning audience with Lincoln and his cabinet. In front of the president, Stanton, Secretary of State William Seward, Secretary of the Treasury Salmon P. Chase, and Secretary of the Navy Gideon Welles, Wing repeated his account. Dawn was breaking as he concluded, but when the others left the room, the young reporter attracted Lincoln's attention. "Mr. Lincoln, I have a personal word for you." Lincoln bent down and asked, "What is it?"

Given the message personally from Grant more than 24 hours before, Wing delivered the words that Lincoln and the Union were desperate to hear. "General Grant said to tell you, no matter what happens, he will not turn back." The careworn figure of the president loomed over Wing. So great was his relief that, as they parted, Lincoln leaned down and gently kissed the reporter on the forehead. The moment is legend, transcending both the military and the political histories of the conflict. In one poignant moment, Wing had delivered all the power and grim resolve of Grant and the Union to press home resolution of the conflict.

Whereas Henry Ebenezer Wing, the Union Army veteran-turned-reporter, occupies the imagination of the student of Civil War journalism, less attention has been paid the passenger who rode the cars out to Union Mills on the night of May 6, 1864. The story behind his journey and the mission he was to carry out constitute an important, albeit abbreviated, example of Civil War journalism during the summer of 1864, one that witnessed government attempts at censorship take a turn toward a more aggressive and progressive approach to news management than at any other time during the rebellion.

The passenger riding the rails out to Union Mills was the same assistant secretary of war whom Wing had been trying to raise by telegraph earlier in the evening, Charles Dana. Himself a former newspaperman of significant reputation, having served at one time as editor of the same *New York Tribune*, Dana already had furnished great service to both Stanton and Grant, providing updates and observations from Vicksburg, Mississippi, in the spring and summer of 1863 and again at Chattanooga, Tennessee, that fall. His relationship with Grant was strong and enduring, and Stanton trusted him to provide unvarnished views of a campaign's progress. He was a known quantity, able to earn the trust of officer and correspondent alike. Not prone to offering either gratitude or praise, the shrewd Stanton was almost effusive in thanking Dana for his work in Mississippi, indicating that his reports were anticipated with "deep interest" and adding, "I can't thank you as much as I feel for the service you are now rendering."[3]

Dana was not present at the War Department when Wing's message was received by telegraph. In fact, he had been at a reception and was summoned to Stanton's office in evening dress. Lincoln quickly got to the point. "Dana, you know we have been in the dark for two days since Grant moved," he said. "We are very much troubled and have concluded to send you down there. How soon can you start?"

"In half an hour," Dana replied and was off to change into his camp clothes, grab a toothbrush and cavalry escort, and fire up a locomotive at Alexandria. Riding the outbound express, he crossed paths with Wing. By seven o'clock the next morning, he was with the rear guard of the Army of the Potomac and poised to perform another great service to the Union cause.[4]

Upon his arrival at Grant's headquarters, Dana began to route a steady stream of telegrams to Stanton at the War Department in Washington. These updates on the campaign served, in turn, as the basis for the issue of dispatches under Stanton's signature to Major General John A. Dix, commander of the Department of the East, in New York. Their true destination was not really the desk of the aging volunteer officer on garrison duty in the northeast but rather the Associated Press, to which they were distributed directly. These dispatches were issued almost daily throughout the course of Grant's grinding overland campaign in Virginia that hot, dusty summer of 1864. Picked up by newspapers across the Union, they became a staple of the papers' coverage of the Army of the Potomac's progress from the Wilderness to Spotsylvania and on to Cold Harbor and Petersburg.[5]

To fully appreciate the departure that Stanton was willing to pursue in his communications, one must explore in greater detail the nature of Union censorship throughout the course of the war and Stanton's own dealings with the press during his tenure as secretary. From the outset of the conflict, the relationship between newspaper correspondents and the government had been inconsistent at best. First attempts to regulate the flow of information to the composing rooms of the great metropolitan sheets of the day had been instituted as early as April 1861 when then-Secretary of War Simon Cameron sought to seize control of the telegraph lines out of Baltimore a mere eight days after the fall of Fort Sumter. Tight control of the telegraph was an instrument of censorship that the government would revisit again and again, and a technique that Stanton himself would institutionalize by the time Grant's army stepped across the Rapidan in May 1864.

As early as February 1862, Stanton already had positioned the War Department to intercede and attempt a comprehensive approach to censorship. Just 24 hours after Stanton was sworn in as secretary, he issued an order to invoke the act that gave the government control of telegraph traffic and the railroads, effectively clamping down on the flow of information from the front lines. The consequences of violating this edict were clear. Any newspaper publishing unauthorized military information, no matter the source, could not use the telegraph or transport its dispatches via rail. Stanton appointed E.S. Sanford, head of the American Telegraph Company, as supervisor of telegrams and threatened any newspaper correspondent crossing his brand new colonel on the issue of censorship with loss of mail privileges as well.[6] In theory, the directives were effective methods to staunch the stream of potentially compromising dispatches from correspondents embedded in the headquarters of commanding generals. In practice, however, the approach was badly flawed. Even as Stanton restricted the issue of credentials to journalists seeking to accompany the Army of the Potomac, Lincoln himself distributed passes allowing reporters to move forward into the Wilderness.[7]

Stanton pondered how best to effectively provide news of the campaign's progress while at the same time preventing false and dangerous accounts from making their way into print. Newspapers without correspondents at the front, such as the *New York Sun* and the *New York Express,* whined incessantly that daily bulletins should be issued so that the public might have news during the coming campaign of 1864.[8] It is difficult to imagine that Stanton, so impervious to such demonstrations, would have acquiesced on the force of their demands alone. Nonetheless, the die was cast. Supplanting false and misleading newspaper accounts with official bulletins from the War Department was the course that Stanton set. His first dispatch to Dix in New York, datelined

"Washington, D.C., May 7, 1864—7.10 p.m.," contained precious little information on Grant's progress in the Wilderness, but it did provide clear insight into the cautious approach taken by the secretary even after Wing's report had been published in the *Tribune*:

> We have no official reports from the Army of the Potomac since Wednesday's dispatch from General Grant announcing his crossing of the Rapidan. There is no telegraphic or railroad communication within thirty or forty miles of his headquarters. It is certain, however, that the Army of the Potomac and Lee's forces came in collision Thursday and an indecisive action was fought yesterday. The report of the Tribune correspondent, published this morning and forwarded from here last night, is the substance of all that is known here at this hour."[9]

With this first tentative step, the summer series of official bulletins was instituted.

Papers such as the *New York Herald* were slow to pick up the dispatches from the Associated Press via Dix. On Sunday, May 8, newspaper publisher James Gordon Bennett and his editors were lamenting the absence of information from reliable sources, complaining that "up to midnight the government had no official intelligence from the front either confirming or denying the reports current in Washington."[10] The next day, Stanton's dispatches were beginning to find play in the columns of the *New York Times*. Dated at nine in the morning the day before, his update was given adequate space to detail the absence of official reports from the front and included an alert from the army's medical director that wounded numbering between 6,000 and 8,000 were being sent to Washington. Stanton concluded the dispatch by encouraging Dix to "give such publicity to the information transmitted as you deem proper." Stanton added a statement of purpose for his upcoming dispatches: "It is designed to give accurate official statements of what is known to the department in this great crisis, and to withhold nothing from the public."[11]

It is telling that at this early stage, Stanton's bulletins were failing to outstrip the very newspaper accounts he sought to supersede in the columns of the nation's journals. Even as he cautiously used correspondence from the medical corps as the foundation for guarded optimism, the *Times* was presenting its own special dispatches from its correspondents at the front and their accounts of the savage fighting of the previous Thursday and Friday. The level of detail included the identification of Major General Winfield Scott Hancock's Union corps and its encounter with forces under the command of Confederate Lieutenant General A.P. Hill.[12] Special dispatches to the *Chicago Tribune* mirrored the *Times,* and even as Stanton's hesitant bulletins began to find play with editors throughout the Union, reports reached the upper

Midwest describing in significantly greater detail "the most terrific battle yet fought by the Army of the Potomac."[13]

Finally, on the morning of May 9, Stanton felt confident enough of his information and its reliability to issue a more definitive dispatch in which he abandoned the caution of the previous bulletins. Despite his disclaimer that his updated information came from scouts direct from the Army of the Potomac rather than official reports, he proclaimed, "The general results may be stated as a success to our arms. The fighting on Friday was the most desperate known in modern times." Running in newspapers like the *Chicago Tribune* the next day, the bulletin also hinted that something was afoot south of the Rapidan. Said Stanton, "At last accounts Hancock was pushing forward rapidly by the left for Spotsylvania Court House and yesterday heavy cannonading was heard at Aquia Creek from that direction."[14]

Stanton and newspapers such as the *Philadelphia Inquirer* were quick to make the transition from the savage engagement near Wilderness Tavern to the footrace to Spotsylvania. One week after Grant's army had tramped across pontoon bridges to open the campaign, the two armies once again confronted one another. As Philadelphians read their journal on the morning of May 10, they noticed that the official war bulletin from Washington issued earlier that day dwelled not upon casualties from the Wilderness, but rather noted, "The enemy made a stand at Spottsylvania [sic] Court House and there was some hard fighting, but no general battle had yet taken place there." In seeking to determine how reliable the bulletins from the government proved to be, the readers were assisted by the editor's note, "The news, especially that which comes from the War Department, and can therefore, no doubt, be relied upon, is most cheering, and promises a full and triumphant success to the Union arms."[15]

Those lingering over their copies of the *Inquirer* late into the afternoon could not have been aware that by day's end one of the classic infantry assaults of all time would be attempted by Union forces and that within another 24 hours the single most-quoted dispatch of Stanton's series would be issued on the basis of Dana's telegram from the front. In an effort to break the stalemate at Spotsylvania, Union forces were marshaled for an assault on the Confederate works. Command of the operation was given to Colonel Emory Upton. A successful and aggressive brigade commander, Upton devised an innovative strategy to break the Rebel line. Arranging his twelve regiments in four tightly packed ranks of three, he instructed his infantrymen to hold their fire until they reached the enemy entrenchments. Shortly after six in the evening of May 10, his assault rocked Confederate lines. A major breakthrough appeared possible. Unsupported with additional troops however, Upton's force eventually was repelled, and disappointment at the prospect of a long siege threatened to stall Union momentum.[16]

Dana went to work immediately. With a correspondent's flair for the dramatic, he composed his first dispatch on May 11 and sent it singing along the telegraph wires at eight in the morning. For whatever reason, it was not distributed to Dix and the Associated Press until almost midnight. When it finally hit newspapers the next day, its impact was sensational. Forced to occupy space on page eight because of the lateness of its receipt, the dispatch appeared under decked headlines, "Latest Official Gazette," and "Official Despatch [sic] from Sec'ry Stanton."[17] The dispatch quoted Grant as saying that after six days of heavy fighting and despite heavy casualties, the situation favored the Union cause. The general continued, "We have taken over five thousand prisoners in battle, whilst he has taken from us but few except stragglers." Following in all upper case was the soon to be famous proclamation, "I PROPOSE TO FIGHT IT OUT ON THIS LINE IF IT TAKES ALL SUMMER."[18]

Even though the horrors of the assault on the Bloody Angle lay ahead later that same day, the impact of Stanton's dispatch cannot be overestimated. Maintaining the offensive and pressing Robert E. Lee was critical to the war effort on both the front lines and the home front. An anxious populace facing daunting casualty lists in the pages of its newspapers required the sort of resolve demonstrated by Dana's telegram. At Spotsylvania and shortly thereafter, as Lee retreated across the North Anna River, editorial comment on the quality and frequency of Stanton's dispatches began to come in from all corners of the Union. The *Chicago Tribune* was grudging in its admiration. On May 9, its columns featured a reprise of the deception practiced upon its readers by the War Department during Major General Joseph Hooker's disaster at Chancellorsville, Virginia, exactly one year earlier. Going so far as to actually repeat the dispatches from May 1863, the *Tribune* warned, "Let us hope that whatever may be the result of the present struggle between Grant and Lee, that no such deception will this time be practised [sic] by the War Department on the loyal people of the Union."[19]

Two days later, the *Tribune* once again pointed to the Chancellorsville debacle to admonish Stanton, "It must have got through the brain of the War Department by this time, that it is just as well to tell the truth in the first place as amuse the public for a week with falsehoods, to be obliged to swallow them all at week's end." The editors concluded, "We apprehend, therefore, that the public need not fear a repetition of the sort of stories which were sent on after the battle of Chancellorsville last year."[20] Five days later, the conversion of the *Tribune* remained a work in progress. Praising Stanton's "new and commendable policy of publishing to the country the official news of army operations as soon as received by the War Department," the Chicago newspaper closed with yet one more warning. "Let the War Department realize, as they have in this campaign, that this is the people's war," advised the *Tribune*. "The soldiers who are falling in it are of the people, their sons and brothers, and that all the people want to know is the truth, whether the tide of battle is with or against them."[21]

The *New York Times* offered its readers its own analysis on the worth of the Stanton bulletins, editorializing: "The War Department dispatches have thus far been very reliable. They have been quite free from exaggeration, swagger or prophecy." The newspaper concluded its comments by advocating for the continuation of this newfound practice: "We trust these reports from the War Department to the country will be continued till the close of the campaign, and will be resumed whenever events of great moment are in progress."[22] The *Times* chimed in again only days later to once again offer praise for the bulletins, exclaiming:

> The general result is a clear and unmistakable gain on the side of truth. The public taste, too apt to crave for sensational food at times like these, is corrected and purified; and people begin to acquire the discreet and becoming habit of hearing indifferent news with fortitude, and news of victory with subdued and sober satisfaction.[23]

The *Times* was not alone. Even the usually skeptical *New York Herald* joined in the chorus of approval going so far as to offer Stanton praise beyond that of a mere conduit for information:

> We are satisfied from these bulletins that he would make an excellent war correspondent of the Herald, and so, "when this cruel war is over," if he is not otherwise engaged, he may expect us to call upon him to serve as one of the corps we shall require to write up for the Herald the campaigns of our armies in Mexico, which will inevitably be the next thing in order in the settlement of our American affairs.[24]

For all the accolades, not every newspaper was convinced of either the bulletins' value or accuracy in portraying activities at the front. Charles Carleton Coffin of the *Boston Journal*, for one, remained to be convinced of their utility in rendering a true picture of troop movements. In a letter published in the *Journal* on May 24, Coffin criticized Dana's telegram of May 13 in which the assistant secretary had indicated that Lee was in retreat. Countered Coffin: "My information was second hand, but I obtained it at headquarters from an official who ought to have known. . . . Instead of retreating as the Assistant Secretary telegraphed, and instead of being five miles beyond the Court House, the army has merely swung round to a new position."[25]

By summer's end, the partisan politics began to erode some of the early enthusiasm for Stanton's official bulletins, and renewed sniping came from all corners of the Union. From faraway Maine, in the columns of the *Machias Union*, Stanton took fire for the practice of issuing daily updates. The newspaper's editor, G.W. Drisko, barked, "The 'bogus' trash called 'war news' sent North from Washington daily by men in official statien [sic], by men who know that they are communicating falsehood to the public for the basest of purposes ought to be stopped." Drisko pressed home the attack, "For eight weeks one E.M. Stanton has been thus deceiving the people while the fathers, husbands, sons and brothers of northern homes have been perishing by the thousand. How much better to disclose the truth."[26]

Drisko spoke with the confidence of one who already knew the outcomes of bloody repulses of Grant's army at Cold Harbor and Petersburg. Indeed, the Army of the Potomac's June 3, 1864, assault on Lee's entrenched divisions endures as the low moment of the campaign for the commanding general of the Union forces. Convinced that his determined ranks could drive the Rebels from the earthworks, Grant ordered a massive assault in the sultry dawn. After some initial success, the ranks of blue were shredded by brutal crossfire all along the line. By the time Grant called off the attack, its murderous folly was brutally clear to every general and every private.

With thousands of Union infantrymen lying dead and wounded between the two armies in a hellish no-man's-land, Dana and Stanton sought to summarize the fighting at Cold Harbor. Dispatches arrived at the War Department from Dana dated June 3, but they were not issued by Stanton until June 4 and were not run in newspapers such as the *Chicago Tribune* until June 6. When the reports finally reached the columns of northern journals, the nightmare of Cold Harbor failed to come home to readers in any meaningful way. Grant was quoted in the dispatch stating, "We assaulted at 4:30 this morning, driving the enemy within his entrenchments at all points, but without gaining a decided advantage." He went on to declare, "Our loss is not severe, nor do I suppose the enemy lost heavily."[27]

Sensing that the scope of the repulse was being underplayed, the *New York Times* came out the following Tuesday with an item that flatly stated, "The battle of Friday, last was a much more serious affair, both in its original conception, its actual character, and its final consequences than we had been led to believe from the brief dispatches heretofore given to the public." Although the overall tone of the article remained optimistic at the renewal of the campaign in the days to come, it represented some of the first significant questioning of Stanton's information and ability to be forthcoming in the face of mounting casualties.[28] Still, the support for Stanton and the Union cause was staunch, and the *Herald* called out the *Times* two days later, accusing its bitter rival of slandering Grant with its questioning of official accounts of the engagement. "We have no words adequate to express our reprobation of such dishonest and malicious political maneuvering as this," thundered the *Herald*. "For a paper professing to be loyal, it is simply abominable."[29]

By the afternoon of June 18, Grant's advance had brought him to yet another defining moment in the campaign before the enemy at Petersburg. Faced once more with strongly entrenched Confederate forces, Grant yet again ordered another ill-advised frontal assault. The results were predictable, and horrific casualties were sustained by such regiments as the First Maine Heavy Artillery, which lost more than 600 in killed and wounded in a matter of minutes.[30] As had been the case in the aftermath of the disaster at Cold Harbor, Dana's dispatches and Stanton's bulletins downplayed the cost at which Grant's forces pressed home the attack. Wired Stanton at 9:45 p.m. on June 19:

> This evening a dispatch from City Point, dated at 9 o'clock this morning, has reached the Department. It reports that our forces advanced yesterday to within a mile in front of Petersburg, where they found the enemy occupying a new line of entrenchments, which after successive assaults, we failed to carry, but hold and have entrenched our advanced position.[31]

The sketchy information was not inaccurate, but it did nothing to frame the bitter repulse in the true context of the massive casualties sustained by Union forces at Petersburg. Indeed, the failure to carry the Confederate works doomed Grant to a protracted siege of the city. In the absence of significant troop movements, Stanton's bulletins became intermittent and scarce as the summer wore on under the wilting Virginia sun. In their place, fantastic reports of a new Confederate threat began to creep into major metropolitan journals. During the first two weeks of July 1864, speculation ran wild on the intended objective of a Rebel raiding force under the command of Major General Jubal Early.

As Early's force advanced on Washington, Stanton suffered along with his special correspondent, Charles Dana, who was sitting idly in the lines outside Petersburg. With no ready source of information on the makeshift Union force assembled to meet the Rebel threat, Stanton's dispatches were notably absent from northern journals.[32] Finally, on the afternoon of July 9, Union Major General Lew Wallace made a stand against the gray-clad columns along the banks of the Monocacy River. Although his ragtag command was forced to give ground, it bought valuable time for reinforcements to be rushed from around Petersburg to help defend the capital. Wallace had saved the day. Although there would be some anxious moments ahead, the rebel threat was blunted, and Grant was able to renew his stranglehold on Lee and Petersburg.

With the Army of the Potomac locked in a vice-like siege at Petersburg, new information worthy of official war bulletins became a rare commodity. Absent the fluid movements that had characterized Grant's maneuvers from Spotsylvania to Cold Harbor, Stanton all but shut down his apparatus for issuing daily dispatches from the front. Northern newspapers, however, were not about to allow the secretary a painless exit from his commitment to provide information to the public. On August 3, 1864, the *New York Herald* queried, "Why do we get no more bulletins from Secretary Stanton? These reliable dispatches were of much service to the community, and had got to be anxiously expected, when all at once they were discontinued." The paper continued to apply pressure, adding, "The public have the right to know what is going on, and the War Department neglects its duty when it withholds intelligence which should at once be imparted." The *Herald* closed, "We want daily bulletins from the War Office. In the name of the people, we demand them."[33] Despite such pressures, there was to be no compliance from Stanton. Although occasional bulletins would continue to be issued until the end of the war, newspapers once again were forced to rely upon the accuracy and immediacy of reports from their own correspondents, signaling an end to the presence of consistent and official government information within their columns.

Although Stanton's official war bulletins may have sometimes confounded readers by being at odds with the reports of correspondents or out of sequence with more timely dispatches from the front, their influence on the presentation of war news in the daily newspapers cannot be underestimated. If Stanton's aim was for his bulletins or gazettes to preempt or supersede other sources, his initiative was an unqualified success. His judgment prompted him to seize an opportune moment at a pivotal juncture of the Civil War to institute a practice that simultaneously advanced the government agenda of prosecuting the war while steeling the resolve of the North to endure the cost of that effort.

The outcome succeeded Stanton's best expectations. Biographer Frank Abial Flower has summarized the impact of the bulletins as "verities supplanting all forms of newspaper and other unofficial information." Stanton's bulletins, he writes, "entirely suppressed fabricators of sensational rumors and peddlers of false reports, and wiped out the power of the hostile and quasi-disloyal papers to weaken the Government effort or harass the administration."[34] Beyond the preemptive and progressive censorship potential of the official war bulletins, Flower identified perhaps the most profound impact of Stanton's newswriting efforts, noting that the secretary had "accomplished more in the way of unifying and inspiring the people, re-electing Lincoln, destroying the news fakir, and hastening the end of hostilities than any other instrumentality of similar character."[35]

NOTES

1.   Benjamin P. Thomas and Harold M. Hyman, *Stanton: The Life and Times of Lincoln's Secretary of War* (New York: Alfred A. Kopf, 1962), 155.

2.   Emmet Crozier, *Yankee Reporters, 1861–1865* (New York: Oxford University Press, 1956), 386.

3.   Harry J. Maihafer, *The General and the Journalists: Ulysses S. Grant, Horace Greeley, and Charles Dana* (Washington: Brassey's, 1998), 168.

4.   Ibid.

5.   J. Cutler Andrews, *The North Reports the Civil War* (Pittsburgh: University of Pittsburgh Press, 1955), 544.

6.   Brayton Harris, *Blue and Gray in Black and White* (Dulles, VA: Brassy's, Inc., 1999), 141–142.

7.   Louis Morris Starr, *Bohemian Brigade* (New York: Knopf, 1954), 294.

8.   Ibid., 307.

9.   U.S. War Department, *The War of the Rebellion*, ser. 3, vol. 4/125, 277.

10. *New York Herald*, 8 May 1864.

11. Ibid.

12. Ibid.

13. *The Chicago Tribune*, 9 May 1864.

14. *Chicago Tribune*, 10 May 1864.

15. *Philadelphia Inquirer*, 10 May 1864.

16. William D. Matter, *If It Takes All Summer: The Battle of Spotsylvania* (Chapel Hill: University of North Carolina Press, 1988), 158, 161–167.

17. *Philadelphia Inquirer*, 12 May 1864.

18. Ibid.

19. *Chicago Tribune*, 9 May 1864.

20. *Chicago Tribune*, 11 May 1864.

21. *Chicago Tribune*, 17 May 1864.

22. *New York Times*, 12 May 1864.

23. *New York Times*, 24 May 1864.

24. *New York Herald*, 31 May 1864.

25. Andrews, 543.

26. *Machias (Maine) Union*, 21 June 1864.

27. *Chicago Tribune*, 6 June 1864.

28. *New York Times*, 7 June 1864.

29. *New York Herald*, 9 June 1864.

30. Donald W. Beattie, Rodney M. Cole, and Charles G. Waugh, eds., *A Distant War Comes Home: Maine in the Civil War Era* (Camden, ME: Downeast Books, 1996), 159.

31. *Boston Daily Advertiser*, 19 June 1864.

32. *Boston Daily Advertiser*, 7 July 1864.

33. *New York Herald*, 3 August 1864.

34. Frank Abial Flower, *Edwin McMasters Stanton* (Akron, OH: Saalfield, 1905), 214.

35. Ibid., 215.

"O the Sad, Sad Sights I See"

Walt Whitman's Civil War Journalism

— Roy Morris Jr. —

Walt Whitman went to Washington, D.C., in January 1863 from his home in Brooklyn, New York, intending to stay for a few weeks—he wound up staying for the next ten years. For the first three of those years he was a regular visitor to the various military hospitals in and around the nation's capital, where he devoted himself to bringing a little cheer and companionship to the thousands of suffering young soldiers confined to their beds with wounds, illness, or infection. By the end of the war, he estimated that he had personally made over six hundred visits to the hospitals and had spoken to some one hundred thousand soldiers during his rounds. His self-sacrificial service, which resulted in his own abrupt physical decline, transformed Whitman from a vaguely disreputable bohemian layabout into the "Good Gray Poet," a beloved, almost mystical figure who personally embodied for millions of Americans a democratic ideal of sharing and brotherhood that remains undimmed nearly a century and a half later.

An experienced if eccentric journalist, Whitman recounted his time in Washington in a series of articles for various Brooklyn and New York newspapers. In such articles as "The Great Army of the Sick," "Washington in the Hot Season," "Hospital Visits," "Life among Fifty Thousand Soldiers," "Return of a Brooklyn Veteran," "Our Wounded and Sick Soldiers," and "Fifty-First New York City Veterans," Whitman provided readers with vivid, impressionistic glimpses of what he termed—all too accurately—"war's hell scenes." In his own way, Whitman was a war correspondent—not on the front lines of the battlefields but in the rear, where the battles' true costs were hidden away and reckoned.[1]

Whitman famously predicted that "the real war will never get into the books," but his Civil War journalism went a long way toward bringing the war and its unprecedented costs home to a civilian public that—in the North, at least—was isolated from the day-to-day horrors of the battlefields and hospitals. Yet it was in those hospitals, Whitman said, that he found "the real precious and royal ones of this land," the common soldiers whose quite uncommon bravery and sacrifice moved him to a recommitment in both his life and art and prompted him to write a new style of poetry that was itself a kind of heightened journalism.[2]

The impetus for Whitman's journey to Washington was the wounding of his brother George at the Battle of Fredericksburg, Virginia, in late December 1862. George, unlike Walt, had enlisted in the Union Army at the very beginning of the war, marching down Broadway with his fellow soldiers in the 13th New York State Militia, each man equipped, Walt noted dryly, "with pieces of rope, conspicuously tied to their musket barrels, with which to bring back each man a prisoner from the audacious South, to be led on a noose, on our men's early and triumphant return."[3]

No one expected the war to last very long, least of all Whitman, who despite his own aversion to violence contributed a number of rousing patriotic poems to the Union cause. "Beat! beat! drums!—blow! bugles! blow!" one poem began. Another promised "no dainty rhymes or sentimental love verses" but instead depicted "a strong man erect, clothed in blue clothes, advancing, carrying a rifle on your shoulder, / With well-gristled body and sunburnt face and hands, with a knife in the belt at your side." Such poems were not up to Whitman's usual standards, but perhaps they were not meant to be. They did catch, however badly, the prevailing mood of the time, when even the mayor of Brooklyn could advise Whitman in all seriousness that "the Southern fire-eaters would be at once so effectively squelch'd, we would never hear of secession again." With the Union defeats at Bull Run, Ball's Bluff, and Fredericksburg and the even bloodier Union victories at Shiloh and Stones River, it became clear by the end of 1862 that the Civil War would not conclude so quickly or so easily.[4]

When the Whitman family read of George's wounding in a brief mention in the *New York Tribune*, Walt immediately threw together a few belongings and hurried south to Washington, where the main Union hospitals were located. For three days and nights he searched in vain for his brother, trudging from hospital to hospital through streets filled with dispirited Union soldiers and wild rumors of impending ruin. At last someone suggested that Walt go to Falmouth, outside Fredericksburg, where the Army of the Potomac was camped for the winter. There he found George only slightly wounded—a piece of Confederate shrapnel had pierced his cheek.

Walt spent the next ten days visiting with his brother and his fellow soldiers in the 51st New York Infantry, which George had joined after his initial enlistment ran out. The main topic of conversation, naturally enough, was the recent misbegotten Battle of Fredericksburg, which Whitman disgustedly termed "the most complete piece of mismanagement perhaps ever yet known in the earth's wars." Whitman was struck by how young many of the soldiers were. "The mass of our men in our army are young," he wrote later in an article published in the *New York Times*. "It is an impressive sight to me to see the countless numbers of youths and boys . . . poor lads, many of them already with the experiences of the oldest veterans."[5]

Of the original one thousand soldiers who had enlisted in George's regiment at the start of the war, only about two hundred still survived. Their patriotism, if not their numbers, remained high. "The men looked well to me," Whitman noted in his *Times* article, "not in the sense of a march down Broadway, but with the look of men who had long known what real war was, and taken many a hand in—held their own in seven engagements, about a score of skirmishes &c—a regiment that had been sifted by death." A civilian himself, Whitman marveled at the men's seeming matter-of-factness in the face of death. "Death is nothing here," he wrote. "As you step out in the morning from your tent to wash your face you see before you on a stretcher a shapeless extended object, and over it is thrown a dark grey blanket—it is the corpse of some wounded or sick soldier of the reg't who died in the hospital tent during the night—perhaps there is a row of three or four of these corpses lying covered over. No one makes an ado. There is a detail of men made to bury them; all useless ceremony is omitted. (The stern realities of the marches and many battles of a long campaign make the old etiquets [sic] a cumber and a nuisance.)"[6]

Whitman would later use such sights in the first artistically important poem he wrote about the war, "A Sight in Camp in the Daybreak Gray and Dim," in which he recounts "three forms I see on stretchers lying, brought out there untended lying." The first is an elderly man, "gaunt and grim, with well-gray'd hair." The second is a mere child, a "sweet boy with cheeks yet blooming." The third, neither old nor young, has "the face of Christ himself, / Dead and divine and brother to all." The poem, described by one modern critic as "gentle but lethal," derives much of its power from its understated tone. Here for the first time the famously expansive Whitman had begun to write with a soft-spoken plainness appropriate to the homely hush of the moment. One of the marks of any great writer is adaptability, and Whitman, after only a few short days in camp among the young Northern soldiers, had already begun to grasp that his old enthusiastic style of writing was sadly unsuited for capturing the grim realities of modern war. A new approach was needed, one that reflected more accurately the soldiers' homespun ways and quiet courage, and Whitman began to write poems that dealt with the war in the drawling voices of the men themselves. This was a new way of writing, not just for Whitman but for American literature in general, and its importance can scarcely be overstated.[7]

Whitman left Falmouth before sunrise on Sunday, December 28, 1862, to board a government steamer back to Washington. Traveling with him was a large contingent of badly wounded soldiers bound for the various military hospitals in the rear. During the three-hour trip by train and boat, Whitman went from man to man, collecting information to send to the folks back home. Those were the first faltering steps of a great humanitarian enterprise.

Back in Washington, Whitman looked up an old acquaintance, Boston novelist William D. O'Connor, who was working as a clerk at the Light-House Board. O'Connor and his wife invited Walt to stay with them, and with the help of other friends he managed to get part-time work as a copyist in the army paymaster's office. There he witnessed dozens of "poor sick, pale, tattered soldiers" climbing up five flights of stairs each day in search of pay that was not always forthcoming. Many of the men had been discharged from the army, but without money to get home they were stuck in the hospitals and convalescent camps, surrounded by sick and dying comrades. Some, even less lucky, were reduced to living on the streets and begging for pennies.[8]

Casually, with no particular plan or purpose, Whitman began to visit the hospitals. At first, it was merely to look in on the Brooklyn soldiers whom he knew from the old days, but soon it became a daily routine. Before the war Whitman had occasionally gone to visit injured friends at the Broadway Hospital in New York, but nothing in his far-from-sheltered life had prepared him for the sights, the sounds, and the smells of the army hospitals—they were literally a world unto themselves. At the end of 1862 there were approximately thirty-five hospitals in and around Washington, accommodating some thirteen thousand suffering soldiers. By the time they had made their way to Washington, the soldiers had already endured the disease-ridden squalor of camp life, the exhaustions of marching, the terrors of combat, the chills of fever, the hammering of bullets, the slicing of canister, and the dull grinding rasp of the field surgeon's saw. In many ways, however, their greatest trials were still ahead. Before they could return to their regiments or, better yet, walk through the gates of their peacetime homes, honorably discharged with an empty sleeve or a brace of crutches, they first had to survive the hospitals.

The hospitals, ranging in size and accommodations from such converted private mansions as the Douglas Hospital on Embassy Row to the filthy, mud-encrusted tents of the contraband camp, were places to be feared by any thinking person. The great European medical advances in bacteriology and antisepsis were still tragically a few years in the future, and the cause and prevention of disease remained unknown. Typhoid fever, malaria, and diarrhea, the three most prevalent and deadly killers in the Civil War, tore through every hospital and camp, spread by infected drinking water, contaminated food, and disease-carrying mosquitoes. Meanwhile, the overworked and understaffed physicians continued to ascribe the soldiers' ills to such ridiculous and fantastical causes as "malarial miasms," "mephitic effluvia," "crowd poisoning," "sewer emanations," "depressing mental agencies," "lack of nerve force," "night air," "sleeping in damp blankets," and "poisonous fungi in the atmosphere."[9]

Sick soldiers could expect little in the way of help from their doctors. Indeed, many of the physicians' favorite remedies made matters worse by violating the most basic of all medical tenets: first, do no harm. Civil War–era doctors were apt to prescribe a bewildering, if ineffective, array of drugs at the first sign of illness. Diarrhea, for example, was treated with laxatives, opium, Epsom salts, castor oil, ipecac, quinine, strychnine, turpentine, camphor oil, laudanum, blue mass, belladonna, lead acetate, silver nitrate, red pepper, and whiskey. Malaria called for large doses of quinine, whiskey, opium, Epsom salts, iodide of potassium, sulfuric acid, wild cherry syrup, morphine, ammonia, cod liver oil, spirits of niter, cream of tartar, barley water, and cinnamon. When all else failed, as it frequently did, doctors harkened back to more primitive methods of treatment: bleeding, cupping, blistering, leeching, binding, chafing, and even flannel belly bands.

Sharing hospital space with the ill were soldiers suffering from bullet wounds. Frequently, this meant that they were recuperating from amputations of their arms or legs and, more often than not, were also battling some sort of postoperative infection caused by the incredibly filthy conditions of Civil War surgery. Union surgeon W.W. Keen, a young Philadelphia physician who went through the war with the Army of the Potomac and later became one the nation's most respected neurologists, left behind a vivid description of the typical operating procedures at the time. "We operated in old blood-stained and often pus-stained coats," he wrote. "We used undisinfected instruments from undisinfected cases, and marine sponges which had been used in prior pus cases and had been only washed in tap water. If a sponge or an instrument fell on the floor it was washed and squeezed in a basin of tap water and used

as if it were clean. The silk with which we sewed up all wounds was undisinfected. If there was any difficulty in threading the needle we moistened it
with bacteria-laden saliva, and rolled it between bacteria-infected fingers. We
dressed the wounds with clean but undisinfected sheets, shirts, tablecloths,
or other old soft linen rescued from the family ragbag. We had no sterilized
gauze dressing, no gauze sponges. We knew nothing about antiseptics and
therefore used none."[10]

The predictable result of such hurried and horrific operations was postoperative infection, of which there was no shortage of dreadful candidates.
Pyemia, septicemia, erysipelas, osteomyelitis, tetanus, gangrene—the very
names of the so-called surgical fevers are terrifying, and with good reason.
Pyemia, literally "pus in the blood," was the most dreaded of all, with a mor-
tality rate of 97.4 percent, but the other surgical fevers claimed their fair share
of victims as well. It is little wonder that soldiers in the Civil War were four
times as likely to fall ill as civilians and five times as likely to die if they did.

Into this world of pain and death Walt Whitman freely advanced in January 1863, when it sometimes seemed, as he told Ralph Waldo Emerson, that
America herself had been "brought to Hospital in her fair youth—brought
and deposited here in this great, whited sepulchre of Washington." From the
start, Whitman's hospital visits were good therapy for him as well as the soldiers. The brave young men who were fighting and dying so uncomplainingly
for the Union cause restored his belief in the inherent strength and goodness
of the American people. Coming as they did on the heels of a half-decade of
personal drift and depression, Whitman's experiences in Washington were
nothing short of life altering. As he later told a friend, "There were years in my
life—years there in New York—when I wondered if all was not going to the
bad with America, but the war saved me: what I saw in the war set me up for
all time—the days in the hospitals."[11]

Whitman prepared for his daily visits—one might almost say his ministry—as carefully as a general prepares for a battle. He quickly discovered that
outward appearance counted greatly with the men, and he made it a point to
bathe, dress, and eat a good meal each afternoon before starting his rounds.
"In my visits to the Hospitals," he wrote, "I found it was in the simple matter
of Personal Presence, and emanating ordinary cheer and magneticism, that I
succeeded and help'd more than by medical nursing, or delicacies, or gifts of
money." He bought himself a good, sober suit, a pair of black Morocco boots,
and a wide-brimmed hat with a gold and black drawstring and gold acorns
at the bottom. He was, he boasted to his mother, "as much a beauty as ever. I
fancy the reason I am able to do some good in the hospitals among the poor
languishing and wounded boys, is, that I am so large and well—indeed like a

great wild buffalo, with much hair. Many of the soldiers are from the West, and far north, and they take to a man that has not the bleached shiny and shaved cut of the cities and the East."[12]

Whitman realized, of course, that the soldiers needed more than his mere presence to comfort and inspire them. He began bringing a knapsack full of little treats for the men—anything he could beg, borrow, or buy to make their stay in the hospital a little easier. Fruit, tobacco, candy, jelly, pickles, cookies, wine, brandy, shirts, handkerchiefs, and clean socks and underwear all went into his bag. During the hot weather he sometimes brought ice cream to the men as a special treat. All these gifts he distributed quietly and informally, knowing full well that the proud young soldiers would resist instinctively any hint of charity. He carefully kept track of his dispersals in small pocket notebooks he made by stitching together sheets of folded paper. Each day he jotted down whatever he could learn from the patients he visited—name, rank, company, regiment, bed number, ward, hospital, nature of wound, and names and addresses of parents and wives. He soon saw that what the men wanted most was writing materials, and he kept a ready supply of paper and pencils on hand for those wanting to write home. If a man was too weak to write for himself, Whitman took down dictation or simply wrote the letter for him.

An entry from Whitman's notebook reveals a typical morning in the hospital ward: "Bed 53 wants some licorice; bed 6 (erysipelas) bring some raspberry vinegar to make a cooling drink with water; bed 18 wants a good book—a romance; bed 25 (a manly, friendly young fellow, independent young soul) refuses money and eatables, so I will bring him a pipe and tobacco, for I see how much he enjoys a smoke; bed 45 (sore throat and cough) wants horehound candy; bed 11, when I come again, don't forget to write a letter for him. One poor German, dying—in the last stages of consumption—wished me to find him a German Lutheran clergyman. One patient will want nothing but a toothpick, another a comb, and so on."[13]

Whitman was not the only one visiting the hospitals. Indeed, a main characteristic of Civil War hospitals was their easy accessibility to the general public. At the time he began his visits there were 25 separate soldiers' aid groups already in operation—16 sponsored by the individual states—as well as regular visits by members of the United States Sanitary Commission and the Christian Commission. Whitman was always complimentary of the Christian Commission, a purely voluntary organization that he himself had briefly joined, but he did not think much of the Sanitary Commission, whose members were paid well for their work. Nor did the Sanitary Commission think much of Whitman. One commissioner, Harriet Hawley, told her husband, "Here comes that odious Walt Whitman to talk evil and unbelief to my boys. I think I would rather see the evil one himself—at least if he had horns and hooves."[14]

Union Colonel Richard Hinton, who met Whitman at Armory Square Hospital while recovering from a bullet wound suffered at Antietam, contrasted Whitman's easy-going style with that of the more formal Sanitary Commission. "When this old heathen came and gave me a pipe and tobacco," Hinton wrote, "it was about the most joyous moment of my life. Walt Whitman's funny stories, and his pipes and tobacco were worth more than all the preachers and tracts in Christendom. A wounded soldier don't like to be reminded of his God more than twenty times a day. Walt Whitman didn't bring any tracts or bibles; he didn't ask if you loved the Lord, and didn't seem to care whether you did nor not."[15]

To help finance his visits to the hospitals, Whitman fell back on his prewar training as a journalist. Like many American writers then and later, he had started working for newspapers as a boy, beginning as a printer's apprentice on the *Long Island Patriot* at the age of 12. By the time the Civil War began in 1861, he had worked for 14 different newspapers, mostly in Brooklyn and New York City but also including a brief stint as editor of the *New Orleans Crescent* in the late 1840s. As with his poetry, his lifestyle and his outward appearance, Whitman as a journalist was very much an individual. He did not particularly like working hard, and he generally set his own highly idiosyncratic hours. Nor did Whitman easily hew to the party line. He clashed frequently with his publishers, his fellow editors, and the general public, once kicking a local politician down the stairs and out the door of the *Brooklyn Daily Eagle*. Two years before the war, he had lost his most recent newspaper job, editor of the *Brooklyn Daily Times*, for writing editorials defending the right of women to enjoy premarital sex as freely and easily as unmarried men.

Despite his casual approach to journalism, Whitman was a trained observer and a gifted prose writer as well as poet. He counted among his friends a number of New York's most influential journalists, including John Swinton, managing editor of the *New York Times*, and Swinton's brother William, the *Times*'s Washington correspondent. It was in the *Times* that Whitman published his first Washington dispatch, "The Great Army of the Sick," on February 18, 1863. The article had a double purpose: to raise money for Whitman's continued hospital visits and to encourage others to join in the work. "A benevolent person, with the right qualities and tact," he wrote, "cannot make a better investment of himself, at present, anywhere upon the varied surface of the whole of this big world, than in these military hospitals, among such thousands of most interesting young men. Reader, how can I describe to you the mute appealing look that rolls and moves from many a manly eye, from many a sick cot, following you as you walk slowly down one of these wards? To see these, and to be incapable of responding to them, except in a few cases (so very few compared to the whole of the suffering men), is enough to make one's heart crack."[16]

The article told of Whitman's encounter with a young Bridgewater, Massachusetts, soldier named John Holmes, whom the poet found languishing at Campbell Hospital during one of his first visits. Holmes, a 21-year-old shoemaker by trade, was a member of the 29th Massachusetts Infantry. He had been brought to the hospital suffering from a severe case of diarrhea, which was epidemic during the Civil War. The disease, much more serious than modern versions of the complaint, affected some 54 percent of all Union soldiers and a staggering 99 percent of all Confederates and eventually claimed the lives of nearly one hundred thousand men during the course of the war. Holmes himself was near death when Whitman found him lying untended in Ward Six of the hospital. "He now lay, at times out of his head but quite silent," Whitman reported, "asking nothing of anyone, for some days, with death getting a closer and a surer grip upon him; he cared not, or rather he welcomed death. His heart was broken. He felt the struggle to keep up any longer to be useless. God, the world, humanity—all had abandoned him."[17]

Whitman happened to pass Holmes's bed on his way out of the ward and noticed "his glassy eyes, with a look of despair and hopelessness, sunk low in his thin, pallid-brown young face." Immediately recognizing the look of a dying man, Whitman stopped and made an encouraging remark; Holmes did not reply. "I saw as I looked that it was a case for ministering to the affection first, and other nourishment and medicines afterward," Whitman wrote. "I sat down by him without any fuss; talked a little; soon saw that it did him good; led him to talk a little himself; got him somewhat interested; wrote a letter for him to his folks in Massachusetts; soothed him down as I saw he was getting a little too much agitated, and tears in his eyes; gave him some small gifts and told him I should come again soon." When Holmes mentioned that he would like to buy a glass of milk from the old woman who peddled it in the wards, Whitman gave him some money. The young man immediately burst into tears.[18]

Whitman continued to look in on Holmes, who remained quite sick for several weeks before eventually recovering his health and rejoining his unit. "The other evening, passing through the ward," Whitman wrote, "he called me—he wanted to say a few words. I sat down by his side on the cot in the dimness of the long ward, with the wounded soldiers there in their beds, ranging up and down. Holmes told me I had saved his life. It was one of those things that repays a soldiers' hospital missionary a thousandfold—one of the hours he never forgets."[19]

"The Great Army of the Sick" was well received by readers and earned Whitman a congratulatory letter from managing editor John Swinton. *Times* publisher Henry Raymond liked the article so well that he sent Whitman an extra 50 dollars for his work. Three weeks later Whitman wrote a second article, "Life among Fifty Thousand Soldiers," for the *Brooklyn Daily Eagle*. Unlike the *Times* piece, this article was geared specifically to hometown readers, and Whitman took pains to mention by name as many of the local soldiers as he could. "At a rough guess," he wrote, "I should say I have met from one hundred fifty to two hundred young and middle-aged men whom I specifically found to be Brooklyn persons. Many of them I recognized as having seen their faces before, and very many of them knew me. Some said they had known me from boyhood. Some would call to me as I passed down a ward, and tell me they had seen me in Brooklyn. I have had this happen at night, and have been entreated to stop and sit down and take the hand of a sick and restless boy, and talk to him and comfort him awhile, for old Brooklyn's sake."[20]

Whitman concluded the article with an angry dig at a particularly annoying ward master he had encountered recently on his rounds. "Some pompous and every way improper persons, of course, get power in hospitals, have full spring over the helpless soldiers," he wrote. "An individual who probably has been [a] waiter somewhere for years past has got into the high and mighty position of sergeant-at-arms at this hospital; he is called 'Red Stripe' (for his artillery trimmings) by the patients, of whom he is at the same time the tyrant and the laughing-stock. Surely the Government would do better to send such able-bodied loafers down into service in front, where they could earn their rations, than keep them here in the idle and shallow sinecures of military guard over a collection of sick soldiers to give insolence to their visitors and friends."[21]

In August 1863, Whitman published another article in the *New York Times*, "Washington in the Hot Season." This long article appeared in the Sunday edition on August 16 and was reprinted the next Friday in the *Semi-Weekly Times*. It gave readers a good description of the nation's capital in the midst of civil war. "Soldiers you meet everywhere about the city," Whitman wrote, "often superb looking young men, though invalids dressed in worn uniforms, and carrying canes or, perhaps, crutches. I often have talks with them, occasionally quite long and interesting. I find it so refreshing to talk with these hardy, bright, intuitive, American young men (experienced soldiers with all their youth). There hangs something majestic about a man who has borne his part in battles, especially if he is very quiet regarding it when you desire him to unbosom. I now doubt whether one can get a fair idea of what this war practically is, or what genuine America is without some such experience as this I have had for the past seven or eight months in the hospitals."[22]

A longtime supporter of Abraham Lincoln, Whitman noted that he often caught a glimpse of the president passing through the city in an open carriage. "I saw the president in the face fully," he reported, "and his look, though abstracted, happened to be directed steadily in my eye. I noticed well the expression. None of the artists or pictures have caught the deep, though subtle and indirect expression of this man's face. They have only caught the surface. There is something else there."[23]

Whitman published two other articles in the *New York Times* that autumn, "Our National City" and "Letter from Washington," and the newly established *Brooklyn Union* printed a short letter from him detailing the capital's anxiety over the inconclusive campaigning. He also worked sporadically on a new collection of poems, to which he gave the evocative title *Drum-Taps*. These poems ranged from the early recruiting poem "Beat! Beat! Drums!" to the more reflective "Cavalry Crossing a Stream" and "By the Bivouac's Fitful Flame" and the poignant, semiautobiographical poem "The Wound-Dresser," in which he gave himself the imaginary role of hospital nurse to underscore his emotional connection to the patients. A little ruefully, he recalled his earlier bellicose writing: "Arous'd and angry, I'd thought to beat the alarum, and urge relentless war, / But soon my fingers fail'd me, my face droop'd and I resign'd myself, / To sit by the wounded and soothe them, or silently watch the dead."[24]

Whitman's once-robust health gave way in the face of repeated exposure to sick and dying soldiers, and he was forced to return home to Brooklyn in mid-1864 to recuperate. "O the sad, sad sights I see," he told his mother, "the noble young men with legs and arms taken off—the deaths—the sick weakness—sicker than death, that some endure, after amputations, just flickering alive, and O so deathly weak and sick." Still, he returned to Washington six months later to resume his hospital visits and reporting. His final newspaper articles summed up the wartime adventures of his brother George and his fellow 51st New York veterans. "The 51st," he reported in the *New York Times* on October 29, 1864, "has been in seven general engagements, and sixteen skirmishes—acquiring a reputation for endurance, perseverance, and daring, not excelled by any in the whole army of the U.S." His last wartime article, "Return of a Brooklyn Veteran," published in the *Brooklyn Daily Union* on March 16, 1865, recounted with pride George's return from a Confederate military prison in Richmond and his four years of dangerous service on the battlefields of Maryland, North Carolina, and Virginia. "Of the officers that went with the regiment, not a single one remains," Whitman wrote, "and not a dozen out [of] over a thousand of the rank and file. Most of his comrades have fallen by death. Wounds, imprisonment, exhaustion, &c., have done their work. His preservation and return alive seem a miracle. For three years and two months he has seen and been a part of war waged on a scale of amplitude, and with an intensity on both sides, that puts all past campaigning of the world into the second class." Whitman did not mention in the article that George was his brother; perhaps, given his audience, he did not feel the need.[25]

Of his own time as a witness to "war's hell scenes," Whitman always maintained an uncharacteristic modesty. "People used to say to me, Walt you are doing miracles for those fellows in the hospitals," he told his young disciple Horace Traubel many years later. "I wasn't. I was doing miracles for myself." To his own immense credit, he never regretted his wartime service or what it had cost him physically and emotionally. "I only gave myself," he said. "I got the boys." Half a decade before the war, in *Leaves of Grass*, he had written, "I am the man, I suffer'd, I was there." After the Civil War he could truly say that he had lived those words. More than that, he had lived his ideals. If he was not literally an angel—and he never claimed he was—he was a more than passable substitute.[26]

NOTES

1.   Whitman's Civil War journalism is reprinted in various works, including Richard M. Bucke, ed., *The Wound Dresser: A Series of Letters Written in Washington during the War of Rebellion* (Boston: Small, Maynard, 1898); Charles I. Glicksberg, *Walt Whitman and the Civil War* (Philadelphia: University of Pennsylvania Press, 1933); and Emory Holloway, ed., *The Uncollected Poetry and Prose of Walt Whitman*, 2 vols. (New York: Peter Smith Press, 1921).

2.   Floyd Stovall, ed., *Walt Whitman: Prose Works, 1892*, vol. 1 (New York: New York University Press, 1963–1964), 114–115. Edwin Haviland Miller, ed., *Walt Whitman: The Correspondence*, vol. 1 (New York: New York University Press, 1961–1977), 128–129.

3.   Walt Whitman, *Memoranda during the War* (Old Saybrook, Conn.: Globe Pequot Press, 1993), 60.

4.   Walt Whitman, *Leaves of Grass* (New York: W.W. Norton, 1973), 282–283. *Memoranda*, 60.

5.   *Correspondence*, vol. 1, 81. Glicksberg, *Walt Whitman*, 69.

6.   Glicksberg, *Walt Whitman*, 70, 73–74.

7.   *Leaves of Grass*, 306–307. The modern critic quoted is Robert B. Sweet, "A Writer Looks at Whitman's 'A Sight in Camp in the Daybreak Gray and Dim,'" *Walt Whitman Review* 17 (June 1971): 58.

8.   *Correspondence*, vol. 1, 61.

9.   For life in the hospitals, see George Worthington Adams, *Doctors in Blue: The Medical History of the Union Army in the Civil War* (Baton Rouge: Louisiana State University Press, 1971); Robert E. Denney, *Civil War Medicine: Care and Comfort of the Wounded* (New York: Sterling Publishers, 1995); or Frank R. Freemon, *Gangrene and Glory: Medical Care during the American Civil War* (Cranberry, N.J.: Associated University Presses, 1998).

10. W.W. Keen, "Military Surgery in 1861 and 1918," *Annals of the American Academy of Political and Social Science* 80 (1918): 14–15.

11. *Correspondence*, vol. 1, 69. Horace Traubel, *With Walt Whitman in Camden*, vol. 6 (New York: D. Appleton, 1908), 194.

12. *Memoranda*, 18. *Correspondence*, vol. 1, 89.

13. Walt Whitman, "Life among Fifty Thousand Soldiers," reprinted in Bucke, *The Wound Dresser*, 14–15.

14. Quoted in Justin Kaplan, *Walt Whitman: A Life* (New York: Simon and Schuster, 1980), 276.

15. Richard Hinton, "Washington Letter," *Cincinnati Commercial*, 26 August 1871.

16. Walt Whitman, "The Great Army of the Sick," reprinted in Bucke, *The Wound Dresser*, 8–9.

17. Ibid., 7.

18. Ibid., 7–8.

19. Ibid.

20. Whitman, "Life among Fifty Thousand Soldiers," 17.

21. Ibid., 17–18.

22. Walt Whitman, "Washington in the Hot Season," reprinted in Bucke, *The Wound Dresser*, 22.

23. *Correspondence*, vol. 1, 113.

24. *Leaves of Grass*, 309.

25. *Correspondence*, vol. 1, 205. Walt Whitman, "The Fifty-First New York City Veterans," reprinted in Holloway, *Uncollected Poetry and Prose*, vol. 2, 37–41. Walt Whitman, "Return of a Brooklyn Veteran," reprinted in Glicksberg, *Walt Whitman*, 88–89.

26. Traubel, *With Walt Whitman*, vol. 1, 332–333; vol. 3, 582. *Leaves of Grass*, 66.

Part IV

Continuing Conflict

Taking No Right for Granted

The Southern Press and the 15th Amendment

— Gregory Borchard —

The tumultuous events of the Civil War and Reconstruction eras were seen by writers and readers of the southern press as continued threats to their long-cherished way of life. Hundreds of thousands of Confederate soldiers and civilians had already died in the attempt to preserve those beliefs. Continued resistance to federal policies after the war proved an uphill battle as the tide of the nation's political structures and cultural beliefs turned toward a more expansive nationalism.

One such threat was the 15th Amendment to the United States Constitution, passed in early 1870, which stood as a milestone in the development of civil rights legislation. By allowing African American men the right to vote, the new Constitution acknowledged more fully that they had the same political rights guaranteed to white men before the Civil War. Three newspapers from leading centers of southern political and cultural thought in Atlanta, Georgia; Charleston, South Carolina; and Richmond, Virginia, reflected their readers' basic animosities toward the new federal legislation and the restored national government.

In the 1870s, the *Atlanta Constitution* had established some of the highest circulation counts in the nation. The *Constitution*'s masthead in 1869 proudly proclaimed, "The Largest City, County, and State Circulation."[1] A year later, it boasted the largest circulation numbers in the entire country. As the de facto capital of the New South, Atlanta held a critical position in southern politics and culture. Accordingly, the *Constitution*'s editorials provided a diversity of opinions on the 15th Amendment and other issues of the day, as well as a healthy level of debate for readers whose letters were published daily.

Isaac W. Avery, the editor of the *Constitution*, was widely rumored to be a member of the Ku Klux Klan, the terrorist organization that stormed through the South during Reconstruction. Three days before Christmas 1869, the editor lamented the compliance of Georgia's legislature with President Ulysses S. Grant's demand that they reconvene and ratify the 15th Amendment:

> To-day is seen the sad, piteous, shameful spectacle of her Executive conspiring with her enemies for the overthrow of her liberties. Plotting, scheming, bribing, truckling, maligning, toiling for her injury and abasement . . . the government of a million virtuous people is demolished by the act, and anarchy and their rule of ignorance substituted thereof. . . . Her rulers are against her, not for her; they are seeking personal aggrandizement, not the public weal.[2]

Georgia governor Rufus Bullock's refusal to resist the federal orders had won the praise of fellow Republicans, including Grant himself, but it cost him the support of the state's leading newspaper. On March 12, 1869, the *Constitution* published another alleged example of Bullock's capitulation to the North. Declaring that Bullock showed little reservation about emancipating African Americans, the newspaper quoted him as saying, "The Colored race is free all over this broad land. One more step was needed, and this amendment, if adopted by three-fourths of the States represented in the Union, completes it."[3] He was subsequently vilified by other editors—especially outside of Georgia—for caving in to the North.

Ultimately, the *Constitution* cast the former political goals of the Confederacy to the winds. Although it grumbled about the tactics of northern Republicans, it rarely went beyond the level of encouraging readers to pretend that the new amendments meant nothing more than mere words on paper. An April 3, 1870, editorial noted:

> The Amendment by the Federal Administration of the complete ratification of the 15th Amendment, and its official proclamation as the law of the land, have elicited a variety of comment. The Radicals are jubilant, the Democrats skeptical. . . . The President and Secretary know very well that the State has not legally acted upon the amendment; and they also knew that in placing her in the list of ratifying States, they publicly proclaim themselves liars . . . the 15th Amendment is no more a part of the Constitution today, than it was a month ago.[4]

For the most part, the *Constitution* played moderator between the interests of the Old and New Souths. Offenses against the South's traditional order were duly noted. An opinions piece written March 15, 1870, "Negro Equality," began by attacking Republicans for policies that promoted desegregation. Equality in political rights was interpreted as the misguided intentions of mad scientists bent on subverting the natural order of race relations. "The Radical Policy that destroys the theory of its republic, and gives the national government the improper control of the domestic concerns of the States, gives the power to make the country a homogenous mass of rascality and unnatural amalgamation," the *Constitution* complained. "Public degeneracy under it is inevitable. Nothing can be more fatal to morals or institutions than breaking down the nice distinctions of state character, the valuable differences of domestic polity."[5]

The *Constitution's* editor heralded his paper as having the largest readership in the New South, even rivaling claims of the most prominently read journals of the North. The diversity in its subject matter revealed his willingness to embrace the new capitalism, commercialism, and changed economic structures of the marketplace in the restored national economy. Atlanta's key role in serving as the center of economic activity in rebuilding the Old South lent a boom to the marketplace that the *Constitution* served. Its readership was, as advertised, wide and diverse, filled with businessmen of all types of cultural backgrounds and cultural sensitivities. Editor Avery neither sought to explicitly advance the arguments of states' rights nor to tear down the policies of the federal government. However, instead of calling for an observance of the restored Constitution as the law of the land, the publication offered a cool treatment of civil rights issues, nearly casting them aside.

The *Charleston Daily Courier* represented some of the most radical ideas of the Deep South, ideas that had been stirred up before the Civil War and perpetuated through the Reconstruction era. The newspaper felt called upon to respond to the imagined threat posed by the highest concentration of African Americans in any American city. After the war, the *Courier's* editorials remained unrepentant in their disgust with government under Radical Republican rule. Under editor Richard Yeardon's leadership, the *Courier* represented an unusual blend of literary flair, economic prudence, deeply institutionalized racism, and resistance to change.

On April 14, 1869, the *Courier* made the first of a long series of criticisms and condemnations of the federal government's new measures, arguing that the 15th Amendment was another attack made on the Constitution. Any federal measure aimed at curtailing the powers of the states, as outlined originally in the Constitution, should be rejected by all states, southern and northern alike, Yeardon wrote. The editorial described the proposed amendment as depriving the states "of all jurisdiction over suffrage within their limits. Its adoption will be, in fact, the consolidation of the government. For then the States will have lost, in the most vital sense, the control of their internal affairs."[6]

In a September 8, 1869, editorial, Yeardon stuck to his guns, maintaining that the 14th Amendment had left the right of determining suffrage the individual states. Had this provision been all that was required from the states, the editor argued, it would have been "stringent enough . . . But the 15th Amendment, goes still further. The great objection to it is that it takes from the States all control over the question of suffrage, and confers the supreme power in this respect upon Congress."[7] He then made a curious argument, not necessarily supported by historical accounts:

> Negro suffrage already exists in the Southern States. . . . And against it, upon a safe basis, there would probably be no dissent. The reason why the country is opposed to the amendment, and why it has not heretofore been ratified, is because its adoption makes the government one of consolidation. It takes away from every State all jurisdiction over suffrage within its respective limits.[8]

The suffrage issue allegedly had nothing to do with the emancipation of a race of people or the conclusion of the Civil War. It was, rather, according to the *Courier*, an issue of purely interpreting the Constitution that already existed. Elsewhere, the *Courier* hearkened back to the war, when law was decided at the end of the barrel of a gun. In an April 1, 1870, article, "The Rifle against the Ballot," the newspaper noted that power in the South was being regulated by northern guns. Although direct armed resistance to such alleged northern aggression was not advocated, the *Courier* loudly lamented injustices that it said paralleled those that had precipitated the Civil War. "The Radical party," the *Courier* continued, played "the same game in all of the Southern States. They are appealing to the military to aid and secure their succession to power at the fall elections."[9]

The *Courier* maintained that southerners sought reconciliation, with "no armed resistance, no uprising of the people, no outbreaks to disturb or hinder the full administration of civil law." It acknowledged that "[it] is true that murders and other atrocities have been committed," a veiled reference to Ku Klux Klan activities, but said such atrocities had not been confined "to any particular locality or any particular party."[10] The true enemy of the people of South Carolina, according to the newspaper, was Governor Robert K. Scott, who "represents to the President and to Congress that these acts are evidences of disloyalty, he is guilty of a willful libel upon a people whose rights he has sworn to protect."[11] The alleged atrocities of Scott and the Republicans heated up as the November elections approached. In a September 21, 1870, editorial, the *Courier* blasted the 15th Amendment for undermining the principles of a government designed to rule effectively and efficiently. "When we began the canvass," the *Courier* notes, "but few colored men in the State" had ever heard of the key issues at stake. However, Yankee abolitionists "had taught them to believe, in the first place, that they should not elect any but Northern or Eastern men to office, because they would be again enslaved if they trusted their own people." According to the *Courier*, southerners, not Congress, had set the record straight. "This falsehood has been exposed, and the provisions both of the Constitution of the United States and of the State of South Carolina have been read and explained in every part of the State."[12]

On March 3, 1870, the *Courier* ran another of its many arguments against the extension of civil rights to African Americans. The argument, which reappeared in different forms in the other newspapers, did not necessarily address the issue of suffrage rights per se. Instead of approaching the 15th Amendment from the perspective of new rights, the paper turned to the issue it saw as more important—the adherence to principles and social structures that existed before the war. In "The White Race of the Soil the Friend of the Colored Man," the *Courier* described the special bond between blacks and whites that northern readers could never fully understand and therefore should not have tried to legislate out of existence. "We have ever asserted, that the colored race in South Carolina have at heart, in truth, no better friends than the white race of our own soil," the writer claimed. "[They] are equal with the white, clothed with the elective franchise."[13]

The argument of preexisting racial harmony in the South, however, appeared to get sidetracked with the claim that "[in] order that they may intelligently exercise that right, the opportunity for education should, and under our Constitution, must be afforded them. This cannot, however, be accomplished by any system of mixed schools. Each race must be provided for separately."[14] Prophetically, the writer of the piece anticipated the segregationist response of the South as a whole to the new amendments before they were even fully put into effect.

The *Constitution* and the *Daily Courier* made the same argument: Only southerners knew what was best for former slaves. The sentiment was confirmed through a remarkable source in a September 29, 1870, news story, "Wise Words from a Colored Man," about an African American farmer who had sided with the Democratic party. The interviewee in this particular story explained to a white audience that he—if not many more African American voters—felt a certain disdain for the Republicans. Frankly, he explained, the

Republicans got the whole nation into more trouble than anyone bargained for. "He . . . declared himself as stoutly in favor of the amendments and universal suffrage," the writer claimed. The wise man was quoted, "If we do not forgive one another our Heavenly Father will not forgive us. For He enjoins on us to do unto others as we would have others do to us. I think the time has fully come when we can give the rebels the ballot in this State, and leave the result to take care of itself."[15]

The writer added additional interpretation, contextualizing the words for suspicious southern Democrats:

> We hail with joy the fact that the shallow pretenses by which bad men have obtained, and wish to retain, power are being exposed by colored men, and we hope that our people will profit by the teaching, and that they will, in October, condemn by their votes those who have not only outweighed the State down with debt and enriched themselves, but have also endeavored to stir up enmity between the two races, whose duty as well as whose interests is to live in harmony.[16]

The *Richmond Dispatch*, under one of the era's more celebrated editors, former Confederate captain Francis Warrington Dawson, toed the southern line with objections of its own to the issue of African American emancipation. One of the *Dispatch*'s earliest mentions of the 15th Amendment issue was also one of the more innovative references to the changes brought about by civil rights issues. On February 2, 1869, the *Dispatch* reran a column that had originally appeared two years prior, in order to illustrate how little discussion over rights for African Americans had progressed. "The Rights of Minorities" contemplated a question that was posed to readers before the 15th Amendment was ratified, asking rhetorically, "Should [we] not be better off if our fathers had left the country under British rule."[17] Although the *Dispatch* still sought to distance itself from "the Rebel element," the editor dared to consider the extremes in the implications of the new law. Especially troublesome were the yet unconsidered measures necessary in enforcing the federalist's new victory.

On April 22, 1870, the *Dispatch* laid out some of the issues that southerners might expect in the feverish constitutional debates, making the claim that "all of this is for the benefit of the colored people. The white man is still left without remedy." It complained that southerners and white northern agriculturists were being forced by intimidation to obey the new law. The specter of reverse discrimination was cast, "For the thousands intimidated by Northern manufacturers and made to vote in accordance with their wishes on threats of being discharged there is no protection. But the legislation of these times is all black."[18]

A May 5, 1869, article from a correspondent in Montgomery, Alabama, insisted that "Negro suffrage has not been fixed upon the South. It has been enacted into existence illegally by Congress, and must fall to the ground so soon as the character of Congress changes." The writer called on all southerners to resist the new legislation as null and void because it had been enacted by only half of the wishes of the restored country. "It has been temporarily forced upon us against the protests of the Democrats of the North—a vast party which at any moment may trip its opponent in the almost equally contested wrestle for power."[19] However, the *Dispatch* cautioned that such an extreme disregard for federal law was dangerous and potentially suicidal. "We have no strength to waste in this way," editor Dawson noted, concluding that a loss of votes in Congress because of such resistance would prove more harmful than any moral victory gained by white rule alone.[20]

With a touch of irony, the *Dispatch* portrayed the measures of Republicans as wrongheaded, opportunistic, and immoral demagoguery, measures taken at the expense of a weakened southern constituency. In almost the same breath, African American readers were reminded that the only sense of humanity they had ever known had been extended to them by the white race. A February 23, 1869, opinion piece addressed a symptom perceived by southerners in Republicans who acquiesced to the malicious agendas of abolitionists and suffragist radicals. The piece cited a "negro mania" referred to explicitly in the press as an affliction perpetrated on southern readers. The *Dispatch* claimed that the hysteria of northern reformers "has reached its culmination, and ever after this day [the adoption of the 15th Amendment] the negro will become less and less considered in the nation."[21]

The editor complained that southern whites were being sacrificed to the agendas of such "negro maniacs." The *Dispatch* argued:

> The amendment as it stands is negro, negro—and nothing else. Not a word in it relates to the white man, who is afflicted, oppressed, and paralyzed, and whose wisdom and experience are absolutely necessary to the welfare of the nation, and to its rapid progress to the destiny which a wise Government will most assuredly secure for it—an amendment which proposes to leave the white man where he is—disenfranchised, disqualified, and oppressed as he is—when everybody must see that there can be no peace and prosperity until he is made at least as free as the negro . . . [the Amendment] is a wrong, an outrage, growing out of a vulgar malice and fanatical madness which the people will not tolerate.[22]

Along these lines, the *Dispatch* offered other compelling arguments in which the heart of universal suffrage was criticized not only for its treatment of southern whites but also for its relatively shortsighted understanding of its implications on all Americans. A July 5, 1870, editorial insisted: "All we ask of the Radicals now is that they shall stand to their guns. Let them not faint or flinch in the hour of trial. It required no courage to force negro suffrage upon the South, the Northern States having no negroes worth speaking of." The nation can't afford to turn back, Dawson wrote, because everyone would soon have to face new rights for groups not even considered by the Republicans. He continued:

> [I]t will require a good deal of genuine courage to enable the Radicals to advocate . . . the right of the Chinese to immigrate to this country and . . . their right to the ballot . . . How can a Radical dare to intimate that any man of woman born, whether he be black, or yellow, or red, can be justly deprived of the right of suffrage?[23]

With a note of warning, the editor dared the true believers in universal suffrage to "hold the Radical doctrine that a Chinese or a negro is as good as a white man, and entitled to all the privileges and rights of white men," and "vote for the Radical candidate for President. We are willing to bide the result."[24] The possibility that Republicans might live to regret a diverse voting population—one with no particular loyalty to any particular party—was something the *Dispatch* looked forward to with serious skepticism.

A March 24, 1870, article illustrated, however, the level to which the 15th Amendment was accepted in at least some parts of the South. The article maintained that not all whites in the South were against the notion of blacks voting. "Previous to the meeting, a committee of twelve (six white and six colored) was appointed for the purpose of uniting, if possible, upon some candidate," the *Dispatch* reported. The story concluded with a happy ending, "The meeting . . . adjourned with the utmost good feeling existing between both parties."[25] This was one of the few signs of any kind of direct integration or cooperation between races in the South.

An October 14, 1870, article set a more sobering picture of race relations throughout the country. It used the words of northern opponents of African American suffrage in an attempt to undermine whatever progress might have been made in the South. The article, intending to strike fear in the hearts of paranoid whites of the South, announced that resolutions drawn up by Republicans in New York "were adopted to denounce the Democratic party as 'wholly undeserving the suffrages of colored voters either North or South.'" African Americans, both North and South, subsequently were criticized and condemned for the political resolutions of the New York Republicans. "If the colored people wish to be respected by the whites," the writer insisted, "they must first learn to respect themselves."[26]

Compared to the *Constitution* and the *Courier*, the *Dispatch*'s perspective on the political developments and procedures before, during, and after the passage of the 15th Amendment read as a critique of Washington's policies from an insider's angle. It contained the most comprehensive and race-centered details on the issue of the freedoms extended to former slaves. *Dispatch* reports on the daily affairs of Washington were more comprehensive than those of the *Courier* or the *Constitution*, suggesting that the proximity of the former Confederate capital to the nation's capital allowed it a unique angle on the development of the new Constitution.

All in all, the southern press during Reconstruction stood at a crossroads. Under the direction of editors caught in a whirlwind of an economic and constitutional revolution, the newspapers exposed their readers to the increasingly nationalized framework of American society. Not only did the newspapers of Atlanta, Charleston, and Richmond depict a tension in the values of the Old South and the New South, they also offered perspectives that juxtaposed the issues of suffrage for African Americans as irreconcilable with the South's traditional order. They would not—or could not—fully dismiss the issues as irrelevant, knowing full well the flow of history and the impact of the Civil War on the nation's consciousness. The restoration of the Union under a new Constitution created a choice for southern editors to reject or embrace: they could either choose to support a new country ruled by a Republican Party to which they had no allegiance, or they could retreat from the agreements made at the end of the war to advocate a more isolated position. The editors subsequently encouraged their leaders to rejoin the Union only because to do otherwise would prove too costly in political representation and the loss of future economic markets.

NOTES

1. *Atlanta Constitution,* 12 March 1869.
2. Ibid., 22 December 1869.
3. Ibid., 12 March 1869.
4. Ibid., 3 April 1870.
5. Ibid., 15 March 1870.
6. *Charleston Daily Courier,* 14 April 1869.
7. Ibid., 9 September 1869.
8. Ibid.
9. Ibid., 1 April 1870.
10. Ibid.
11. Ibid.
12. Ibid., 21 September 1870.

13. Ibid., 3 March 1870.
14. Ibid.
15. Ibid., 29 September 1870.
16. Ibid.
17. *Richmond Dispatch*, 2 February 1869.
18. Ibid., 22 April 1870.
19. Ibid., 5 May 1869.
20. Ibid.
21. Ibid., 23 February 1869.
22. Ibid., 5 July 1870.
23. Ibid.
24. Ibid.
25. Ibid., 24 March 1870.
26. Ibid., 14 October 1870.

"What Can We Say of Such a Hero?" Nathan Bedford Forrest and the Press

— Paul Ashdown and Edward Caudill —

Nathan Bedford Forrest was one of the great fighting generals of the Civil War. A slave trader, planter, and Memphis politician of humble origins, he enlisted in the Confederate Army as a private in 1861, raised his own cavalry unit, and rose to the rank of lieutenant general in the Army of Tennessee by the end of the war. He fought at Shiloh, Chickamauga, Brice's Cross Roads, Franklin, and many other major western battles, sustaining several severe injuries and personally killing some 30 men, often in hand-to-hand combat. On April 12, 1864, the great blot on his military career occurred during his successful assault on Fort Pillow in west Tennessee, where his troops allegedly slaughtered hundreds of black soldiers and Tennessee Unionists. Forrest was the subject of a congressional investigation and was widely condemned in the northern press, although his culpability in the so-called massacre has been debated ever since.

After the war, Forrest entered the railroad business and purportedly was a leading figure in the Ku Klux Klan, which he later attempted to disband. He was called to testify before a joint congressional committee probing the Klan in 1871. Fort Pillow and the Klan notwithstanding, Forrest emerged as one of the leading military figures of the war. Statues of Forrest abound in the South and give testimony to his legacy. In Tennessee, state and city parks are named for the controversial general, and his bronze bust is prominently displayed in the state capitol in Nashville. Indeed, there are more monuments to Forrest in Tennessee than there are monuments to Abraham Lincoln in Illinois. He is revered as a southern patriot and military genius by many students of the Civil War and is an icon to various neo-Confederate organizations. Accordingly, protesters call for removal of his image from public display, if not his excision from history altogether. He remains one of the most recognizable figures of the war.[1]

Forrest had more limited press exposure than other important figures in the Civil War for several reasons. First, he was in the western theater of operations, which meant he was farther removed from centers of communications in New York, Washington, D.C., and Richmond. Memphis was the nearest regional communications center with respect to Forrest's actions. Forrest's exploits were more remote and therefore less visible to a competitive, deadline-driven press and its audience. Second, Forrest's frontier character and lack of education limited his ability to initiate and sustain publicity about himself, had he even been inclined to do so. Accordingly, he left no substantial archive of personal papers. He did not write for publication and had to defer to others with more literary talent. Perhaps Forrest had his reputation in mind when he employed newspapermen as aides-de-camp at different times during the war.[2]

News of Forrest's exploits during the war ranged from detailed, factual accounts of his tactical brilliance to wild exaggerations and outright fabrications. In the North, the barbarian theme played well. The *Chicago Tribune* admitted that the stories got out of hand at times, for example reporting in March 1864 that a man arrested going aboard a steamer in Paducah had in his possession a scalp from a Federal soldier's head. The newspaper noted, "The wildest and most absurd rumors continually prevail. . . . At any time today a score of persons were willing to swear he had invaded our state with 20,000 cavalry, accompanied with eighteen pieces of artillery. It is very difficult to arrive at the truth among so many excited rumors."[3] Only a few days later, a *Tribune* writer reported Forrest and his men were scalping the enemy and using women as shields, promoting even further the image of Forrest as a savage barbarian. The report claimed that five female nurses had been placed in front of a charging column of Rebels, which kept the Union troops, who were apparently more chivalric than their Confederate counterparts, from firing.[4]

In Memphis, the general's hometown, Forrest's harshness was acknowledged, with the *Memphis Bulletin* reporting that the general had six of his soldiers shot for excessively celebrating news of General Joseph Johnston's surrender, which meant a speedy end to the war. The story also said that Forrest was shot the next day by his own men as revenge for the executions. The report was not true, of course, and the new day's edition admitted the error.

But the brief item also acknowledged Forrest's barbarity. "The report of his death seems to have been founded on the fact that his life was threatened by an old gentleman from Kentucky, two of whose sons, it is alleged, Forrest had caused to be shot without trial. Their offense was absence from their command without leave."[5]

The brutality and barbarism of the Forrest legend reached its zenith with the alleged Fort Pillow "massacre." Transcending the debate over the facts of the battle, Fort Pillow is critical to the interpretation of Forrest as either a racist killer or a good leader of men who didn't always have total control of events. One of the earliest press accounts of the battle, from the *Chicago Tribune*, headlined its story, "The Butcher Forrest and His Family / All of them slave drivers and women whippers." The story condemned the "cowardly butchery" at Fort Pillow and integrated Forrest's past as a slave trader with his growing reputation as an impenitent killer. Forrest was accounted "mean, vindictive, cruel and unscrupulous." His slave pen in Memphis was reported to be a "perfect horror," and he was said to have even whipped one slave to death.[6]

In creating and sustaining the Forrest legend, press coverage following the war was far more important than wartime reporting on his martial exploits, although it drew on battle reports to shape his legacy. In effect, the press reframed the picture of Forrest. For example, whereas before the war Forrest may have been looked down upon or snubbed in most quarters for being a slave trader, it was not generally proclaimed publicly that such a business was morally degenerate. After the war, slave trading became more than an unappealing enterprise—it was both illegal and immoral. And this issue had to be confronted in any account of Forrest's life and exploits. His connection with the Klan and Fort Pillow continued to haunt him and his legacy.[7]

The nature of the press itself shaped the image of Forrest, too. The war and postwar years were a period of transition as newspapers moved away from the traditional narrative-story form and into the inverted pyramid. Narrative demanded a story with coherent structure and purpose, but the facts of Forrest's life still begged for judgment, whether explicitly in the narrative tradition or implicitly by their inclusion in the news of the day. Editors used one another's words to launch debates over issues. Northern papers often portrayed southerners as bullies with whips and without honor. Eventually, this would have an impact on the portrayal of individuals like Forrest, who could be fitted easily into the one-dimensional stereotype of the slaveholding southerner, a hardened individual who seemed to relish the bloodletting of war. This was often the Forrest one read about in the northern press. The southern press saw a different individual and with the same set of facts would depict a man upholding the honor of the South, defending a way of life, demonstrating the bravery and ingenuity of southern men. The Memphis newspapers saw this individual in command of Confederate troops at Fort Pillow. New York papers saw a murderer who did not abide by the rules of war and thus was without honor.

Covering the 1868 congressional investigation of Fort Pillow, the strongly Republican *New York Times* recounted the details of the massacre and printed Forrest's version of the incident. National politics and the *Times*'s sympathies probably strongly colored the coverage because the story admitted that this coverage was provoked by the fact that Forrest had recently become a shining light of the Democratic Party and was a delegate to the recent national convention in New York. In revealing the depravity of that foremost Democrat, the *Times* claimed that even women and children were killed. The *Times* said "an official letter" from former Union General David Stanley, reprinted and signed in the *Times*, vouched for the truth of a statement that "throws some light upon Forrest's own exploits as a negro-killer." The *Times* also highlighted Fort Pillow in Forrest's obituary. The normally more reserved and responsible publication of the period reported that the attack was made while a truce flag was flying and that men, women, and children, as well as the sick and wounded in hospitals, were butchered.[8] The *Times* wanted Forrest's legacy to be based on Fort Pillow, a verbal shot at southern pretenses of chivalry.

Closer to Memphis, the *St. Louis Post-Dispatch* obituary was a marked contrast. "His name was unfortunately connected with the killing of some colored troops at Fort Pillow, after the place had been surrendered, which it was claimed he should have prevented, and did not," the newspaper observed. "It served to create a strong feeling throughout the North against him."[9] The lens through which Fort Pillow was viewed in the press could be predicted by geography. Southern newspapers tended to view it as a willful misrepresentation of the native son, an aberrant event, inevitably noting how the congressional investigation cleared him. Even after the turn of the century, Memphis papers continued to explain Fort Pillow. In a 1901 story describing Forrest's military career, the newspaper turned the blame around. It was the Union troops' fault, and Forrest was responsible and moral in his actions because he had urged surrender and had stopped the firing as soon as possible after the enemy ceased firing. A few years later, the *Commercial Appeal* called the capture of Fort Pillow "daring" but "minor" in Forrest's career and claimed that the investigation was unable to sustain the charge that Forrest gave black troops no quarter.[10]

Both the *New York Times* and the *Memphis Daily Appeal* carried an 1869 interview that was remarkable because of Forrest's observations about the critical role of black Americans in revitalizing the South. In the interview, a reporter said he was on his way down the Mississippi when he found that his company included Forrest. The conversation turned to the defeated, and when asked how the land could be repopulated, Forrest said "with negroes," whom he praised as hard workers. He contended that Europeans and northerners would not come to repopulate the South but that blacks would. The *Times* apparently was willing to give the general some latitude or was just at a loss for what to make of the comments. The remarks show that Forrest's attitude was not one-dimensional or static and that he was not a simple-minded hater of blacks. The *Daily Appeal* may well have picked up the interview for those very reasons, as well as to promote Forrest as a national figure. The *Times* responded similarly in 1875 when it reported on a Fourth of July speech by Forrest during which blacks applauded him and he was presented with a bouquet by one of the societies of black women.[11]

Press accounts promoted the Forrest myth, particularly in southern newspapers, but even northern newspapers could unintentionally contribute to it. For example, the *New York Times* probably meant no acclaim when, in its 1877 obituary, it gave Forrest credit for creating modern guerrilla warfare. At that time, it could well have been a muttered insult because guerilla warfare was contrary to the chivalric, romantic tradition of which the South was so enamored. On the other hand, it did recognize ingenuity and innovation in the conduct of war, noting his success as a cavalry leader, even though he had "never had a good officer sent against him, and only attacked when the numbers favored him."[12] The Memphis newspapers immediately saw it otherwise and across the decades promoted Forrest as a figure of national historical significance. According to the *Memphis Daily Appeal*, Forrest "was born a military hero, just as men and women are born poets. Though not familiar with history, he seemed to understand the methods of the Crusaders, and would adopt the tactics of Saladin or Coeur-de-Lion, as the exigency required."[13] The *St. Louis Post-Dispatch* had similar sympathies and, unlike the *New York Times*, saw Forrest's guerilla warfare as another way of showing genius and daring: "His name was at one period of the late war a very familiar one, and will rank among the most dashing and successful of Confederate cavalry officers. Like [John Hunt] Morgan, his greatest exploits were raids and independent expeditions, cutting off communications and capturing supply trains."[14]

In obituaries, Forrest had begun to emerge as an iconic figure for the South. Like the South as a whole, Forrest's forces were smaller than his foe's, in terms of numbers, materiel, and support. Stories of a youth defending and providing for family segue easily into those of a man defending his homeland. And he succeeds not because of material superiority but because he is innately superior, endowed by nature and environment with higher abilities. He is almost radically individualistic in the frontier tradition of self-reliance and tall tales.

The themes that emerge in the obituaries and other news about Forrest in the 1860s and 1870s are those that endure. Nearly four decades later, the *Commercial Appeal* deemed him the "South's Military Prodigy," one of "preeminent . . . genius. . . . among the great captains known to the world." And the theme of native intelligence remained: "[H]e showed an appreciation of the highest art of war even if he knew nothing of its science." The newspaper still insisted that "the world has been forced to recognize the abilities of the great cavalry leader. In the last few years . . . those who saw nothing specially brilliant in his record before are beginning to acknowledge him as one of the greatest generals that fought on either side."[15]

The Ku Klux Klan, like Fort Pillow, is problematic and unavoidable in dealing with the Forrest legacy, particularly if one were attempting to salvage or build a reputation for a man who becomes, for some, a symbol of southern ingenuity, toughness, patriotism, and devotion. In the 19th and early 20th centuries, southern newspapers often defended him and his role, or nonrole, in the founding of the Ku Klux Klan, whereas northern papers condemned the "butcher of Ft. Pillow" for the lawless vigilante Klan and noted the logical extension from massacring blacks during the war and helping create and lead the Klan after the war. Coverage of Forrest's testimony before Congress in 1871 often was surprisingly brief and without comment. The coverage in that period often could be characterized in the extremes—a heroic Forrest defending fellow citizens or a villain continuing his evil ways. The *Galveston Daily News,* for example, concluded: "Forrest knows whereof he speaks . . . it is about time to disbelieve the exploded story [of the Klan's existence]." The *New York Tribune* saw it otherwise, charging that "the hero of Fort Pillow" was seen in his "true colors" before the Congressional committee, with both admissions and contradictions in his testimony. The story recounted the same denial as other papers and charged that Forrest contradicted himself, while his memory seemed to conveniently fail him at times.[16]

With the turn of the century, a southern newspaper in a resurgent South of rekindled racism no longer needed to defend or even dodge the Klan issue. The *Memphis Commercial Appeal* celebrated the Klan and said Forrest took leadership to "prevent it from going to excesses" and in order to be in a position to disband it when it was no longer necessary. The congressional investigation, the paper said, justified the Klan during the gubernatorial term of Tennessee Unionist William G. "Parson" Brownlow.[17] In that period of American history, racism and lynchings reached new heights. This made the legend-building of Forrest easier. Myth makers could dismiss the issues of slave-holding, Fort Pillow, and the Klan, and focus anew on his supposed embodiment of American and Christian values. The newspaper gushed:

What can we say of such a hero whose meteoric dash across the firmament of life made both the North and South hold their breath in silent admiration? What words of praise are fitting for such a hero whose whole life was spent in loyalty and sacrifice for home, for loved ones and for his country? Praise is too weak, eulogies too shallow and words are too feeble to do his sacred ashes justice.[18]

The general's alleged infamy was not completely ignored in southern papers, but it was admitted in the context of heroism. The *St. Louis Post-Dispatch* said, with some understatement: "His name . . . will rank among the most dashing and successful of Confederate cavalry officers. . . . His name was unfortunately connected with the killing of some colored troops at Fort Pillow, after the place had been surrendered, which it was claimed he should have prevented, and did not." The *Memphis Daily Appeal's* response at that time to Fort Pillow was to reprint correspondence between Forrest and President Andrew Johnson, in which Forrest requested a pardon and claimed his reputation was unjustly demeaned, especially in connection with Fort Pillow. An accompanying editorial said that Johnson kept the letter as a model of how one should conduct reconciliation. The *Atlanta Constitution* praised Forrest's humble origins, devotion to family, and "some of the most daring and brilliant chapters of confederate war history." Fort Pillow was explained in the context of the pardon letters, citing one supporting letter from Frank Blair, who became a Democratic candidate for vice president, saying that "his courage, displayed in more than a hundred battlefields, ought to convince any man that he is incapable of the dastardly outrage alleged against him."[19]

The accounting in other papers, especially in New York, was less kind. In a bitter, sarcastic article headlined "In the Light of Conciliation," the *New York Times* derided Forrest's achievements and everyone defending his actions at Fort Pillow. The story noted that reconciliation had been imposed on the land and that justifying people like Forrest and his atrocities was no longer possible. In another obituary, the paper noted that Forrest was a "great guerilla" with a "stormy career" that included Fort Pillow. Seizing upon the same facts as the southern papers, the *Times* shows an individual who was antithetical in the worst way to the Virginia aristocracy and the romanticized South: "It was pointed out that while Virginia, and what might be called the 'old South,' produced gallant soldiers and dignified gentlemen, the Southwest, the rude border country, gave birth to men of reckless ruffianism and cutthroat daring. The type of the first was Gen. Robert E. Lee; that of the latter, Gen. Bedford Forrest."[20]

The 1905 unveiling of the Forrest monument in Memphis saw similar sentiments expressed and romanticized his frontier life, noting proudly that he was not "the polished cadet."[21]

But the dark side was undeniable, and some explaining was in order. The statue became a rallying point throughout the 20th century for those who would damn as well as enshrine him. Memphis newspapers in 1905 found the statue a point of civic and historic pride. The *News-Scimitar* devoted a whole section to the new monument, including a front-page photograph of veterans and citizens congregated at the unveiling ceremony. According to the story, a rebel yell from 15,000 to 20,000 people went up as "the parting flags revealed the heroic figure, the wizard of the saddle." The idea endured in the *Commercial Appeal* that the "South's great hero" was a man for the ages and "the great bronze statue of Gen. Forrest will stand for all times to come a vindication of a nation's hero." It was as though the war had just ended: "His career will always adorn one of the most romantic pages of history. There need be no apology for erecting this striking monument to commemorate his splendid deeds."[22]

The *News-Scimitar* was only slightly less effusive. At this time, the Klan affiliation was not an issue but a point of pride. The writer said the veil covering the statue reminded him Forrest's Klan robe, especially in the light of the moon, and found it an inspiring sight. Forrest was cast as something of a founding father of modern Memphis, with the *News-Scimitar* praising him for the city's glorious past, which would bode well for present and future. Nearly 20 years later, apparently small details about the statue could still provoke debate—such as the direction the statue faced, which was south. Some argued that this symbolized a retreat from Union troops, whereas others noted that the statue faced Union Avenue just outside the park. A *New York Times* article had pointed out in 1905 that some of the "dashing cavalryman's admirers" were unhappy with the positioning of the statue. And so it went in the early part of the century, with the Tennessee legislature in 1921 declaring July 13 a legal holiday to commemorate Forrest's birthday and getting press accolades for doing so.[23] Long after his death, Nathan Bedford Forrest was still making news.

NOTES

This article originally appeared in somewhat different form as a chapter in Paul Ashdown and Edward Caudill, *The Myth of Nathan Bedford Forrest* (Lanham, Md.: Rowman and Littlefield, 2005), 71–102.

1. Jack Hurst, *Nathan Bedford Forrest: A Biography* (New York: Vintage Books, 1994); Brian Steel Wills, *A Battle from the Start: The Life of Nathan Bedford Forrest* (New York: Harper Collins, 1992); James W. Loewen, *Lies Across America: What Our Historic Sites Get Wrong* (New York: Simon & Schuster, 1999), 258–261; Tony Horwitz, *Confederates in the Attic: Dispatches from the Unfinished Civil War* (New York: Random House, 1998), 294, 359–364.
2. Hurst, 369.
3. *Chicago Tribune*, 31 March 1864.

4. Ibid., 3 April 1864.

5. *Memphis Bulletin*, 18 May 1865.

6. *Chicago Tribune*, 4 May 1864.

7. Hurst, 363–366.

8. *New York Times*, 30 October 1877.

9. *St. Louis Post-Dispatch*, 11 November 1877.

10. *Memphis Commercial Appeal*, 30 May 1901, 17 May 1905.

11. *Memphis Daily Appeal*, 12 March 1869; *New York Times*, 15 March 1869, 9 July 1875. A similar report was run in the *Memphis Daily Appeal*, 6 July 1875.

12. *New York Times*, 30 October 1877.

13. *Memphis Daily Appeal*, 30 October 1877.

14. *St. Louis Post-Dispatch*, 1 November 1877.

15. *Memphis Commercial Appeal*, 30 May 1901; *Memphis Commercial Appeal*, 31 May 1901. See also, *Memphis Commercial Appeal*, 5 April 1905, which states, "Forrest is recognized by competent military men of Europe as being one of the greatest military geniuses of all time."

16. *Galveston Daily News*, 30 June 1871; *New York Tribune*, 28 June 1871.

17. *Memphis Commercial Appeal*, 30 May 1901. See also, Hurst, 297. On the resurgent South, see Joel Williamson, *The Crucible of Race* (New York: Oxford University Press, 1984).

18. *Memphis Commercial Appeal*, 14 May 1905.

19. *St. Louis Post-Dispatch*, 1 November 1877; *Memphis Daily Appeal*, 3 November 1877; *Atlanta Constitution*, 31 October 1877.

20. *New York Times*, 31 October 1877; *New York Times*, 30 October 1877.

21. *Memphis Commercial Appeal*, 14 May 1905.

22. *Memphis Commercial Appeal*, 17 May 1905.

23. *Memphis News-Scimitar*, 30 April 1905; 17 May 1905; 7 November 1931; *Memphis Commercial Appeal*, 13 July 1921.

Partners in Crime

Southern Newspaper Editors and the Ku Klux Klan

— G. Michael Bush —

In the aftermath of the Civil War, the only history most freedmen knew was the plantation, the cotton field, the overseer, the master, and the breakdown of everything else they had known before the war unfolded. Following the South's defeat, social safeguards were cast aside. Blacks were now free, but they were also unschooled, unsure of the future, and economically destitute. To make matters worse, darkness was taken over by hooded riders, men armed with ropes and rifles as they reined their steeds toward secret nocturnal rendezvous. These groups included, of course, the loosely knit dens of the Ku Klux Klan, which, Allen W. Trelease observes, "exemplified this kind of violence in the most spectacular way."[1] Other groups included the Knights of the White Camellia, the Black Cavalry, Men of Justice, and the Louisiana White League, some of which lost their individual club identities when the Ku Klux Klan emerged as *the* terrorist organization.[2]

All across the South, these and other gangs functioned as military arms of the Democratic Party, writes historian Brooks D. Simpson. They were most active just before elections, waging guerrilla warfare against Republican candidates and voters. President Ulysses S. Grant, after taking office in 1869, assured a delegation of black Tennesseans that he would do all in his power to protect them. But first he had to contend with a problem left over from the Andrew Johnson administration. Looking specifically at the scene in Georgia, Simpson describes it as "Democratic-supported political terrorism [that] targeted Republican voters, black and white."[3]

The Klansmen did not ride alone. They had sidekicks, fire-eating newspapermen who provided editorial backing and inspiration. These editors were as guilty as the night riders themselves and must share the blame for the carnage that gripped the former Confederacy in the wake of war. Smarting from defeat, these conservative Democrats chose words intended to alarm black fears and inflame the most racist of white passions. Their major electoral issue was black suffrage. In the postwar period, demoralized whites more than ever were afraid the black vote would lead to calls for equality and the undermining of the foundation of white superiority. This line of reasoning infected editorial viewpoints and spread like a contagion.

Editors and their readers also took umbrage at gun-toting freedmen, newly manifested but still rare black "insolence," black farm ownership, and—the ultimate threat—the perceived danger African American men might pose to white women should the rules of inequality be overturned. This was the supreme taboo, a fear that evoked white supremacy in its most virulent form. The only penalty sufficient to deter the tendency was violent and speedy death, lynching without the delay and dignity of formal trial. The *Fayetteville (Tennessee) Observer* echoed widespread opinion when it condoned the lynching of an alleged rapist in 1868: "The community said amen to the act—it was just and right. We know not who did it, whether Ku Klux or the immediate neighbors, but we feel that they were only the instruments of Divine vengeance in carrying out His holy and immutable decrees."[4]

These same editors also targeted carpetbaggers and scalawags as purveyors of Armageddon. As one North Carolinian put it, the sudden unleashing of the black hordes on the South and the attempt to elevate them to a level of political equality with their former masters would create a "spirit of exterminating violence toward the black race. The weaker race would be destroyed, and Negroes would become as rare in the South as Indians or buffaloes."[5] The *New Orleans Times* observed that northerners could scoff all they wanted over the notion of racial warfare, but to many white southerners it was a very real possibility.[6]

Trelease contends the Ku Klux Klan first adopted violence as a policy and strategy in the spring of 1868.[7] More likely, that was when the Klan, aided and abetted by racist newspaper editors, escalated such actions. "Continuing a long pattern of American, and particularly southern, behavior, many whites found an outlet for their frustration by attacking those deemed responsible for their suffering: white Republicans and blacks," Trelease writes. "The numerous 'outrages' reported by the Freedmen's Bureau and army officers and a bloody race riot at Memphis, Tennessee, in 1866 are symbolic of the tensions that boiled within the former Confederate states."[8] Sanctioned by the Democratic press, the Memphis riot ended with 46 blacks and one or two whites dead. African American homes, churches, and schools were primary targets of whites, whose numbers included civil officials who "justified their action by pointing to the blacks' earlier unruly behavior."[9] Carnage in New Orleans a few months later was similar: 34 blacks and four whites dead and another 199 African Americans and a far lower number of whites wounded. "The ratio of blacks to whites suggested who had come looking for a fight," Simpson concludes. "A dispassionate examination of the Memphis and New Orleans riots suggests that local authorities seized upon somewhat provocative behavior to deal brutal blows to their enemies on behalf of white supremacy."[10]

In Alabama, meanwhile, 1,400 cases of assaults on former slaves were brought before the Freedmen's Bureau between December 1865 and March 1966. Throughout the summer and fall of 1865, Republican newspapers carried reports of attacks on and murders of African Americans by white southerners. This was the turbulent soup from which the Ku Klux Klan sprang. It is extremely unlikely that it could have done so without the support of newspapers, by far the predominant medium of the day. Editors generally were community leaders, respected men whose words rang with authority.

Early in the 20th century, a whole school of writers took up the racist cause of their earlier editorial brethren, developing histories of Reconstruction that supported the Klan's notion of white supremacy. These writers were led by James Ford Rhodes and William A. Dunning, president of the American Historical Association and the American Political Science Association. Typical of Dunning's writings is this passage from a 1907 book on the disorder that attended Reconstruction elections:

> The whites ascribed the conditions to the insolence and ignorance of the blacks and the ambition and knavery of the carpet-baggers who led them; the negroes and their allies complained that they were victims of a brutal lust for that inhuman power which was lost when rebellion was subdued and slavery was abolished. The Union Leagues on the one hand, and the Ku-Klux Clans on the other, furnished secret and terrorizing elements to the conflict of the races. The radical state governments had no stomach for the task of maintaining order.[11]

Dunning followers such as Walter Lynwood Fleming not only adopted his antiblack tone but were equally hostile to Radical intervention in the South and eager to turn a blind eye to Klan outrages. They blamed the turmoil on the Republican-oriented and pro–black-rights Union League. Here is Fleming in an introduction to a 1905 history of the Ku Klux Klan:

The important work of the Klan was accomplished in regaining for the whites control over the social order and in putting them in a fair way to regain political control. In some States this occurred sooner than in others. When the order accomplished its work it passed away. It was formally disbanded before the evil results of carpet bag governments could be seen. When it went out of existence in 1869, there had been few outrages, but its name and prestige lived after it and served to hide the evil deeds of all sorts and conditions of outlaws. . . . In a wider and truer sense the phrase "Ku Klux Movement" means the attitude of Southern whites toward the various measures of Reconstruction lasting from 1865 until 1876, and, in some respects, almost to the present day.[12]

The far-reaching influence of Dunning and Fleming can be found in the works of subsequent writers such as Fred J. Cook, who, in a book chapter titled "An Accidental Birth" described the original Klansmen as merry pranksters,[13] whereas the Radical coalition that had "seized control of every branch of government . . . was composed of some unscrupulous Southerners—called derisively Scalawags—and adventurers from the North . . . a mixture of the lowest type of ward politicians, soldiers of fortune, and even some degenerates."[14] Even more surreal was a 1924 book on the Ku Klux Klan by Susan Lawrence Davis. Her stated purpose was "justification of the men and measures adopted which led to the redemption of the Southern States from Radical, Carpet-bag and Negro rule."[15] Davis, not surprisingly, found the Klan "unjustly misrepresented" by most historians.[16]

By the 1930s, historians had begun taking a more critical view of the early Klan and its knights and allies and their exploits. Depression-era socialists were also far less critical in their descriptions of the Union League. This more credible school started with W.E.B. Du Bois's 1935 classic, *Black Reconstruction: An Essay Toward a History of the Part which Black Folk Played in the Attempt to Reconstruct Democracy in America, 1860–1880*. Another important work by James S. Allen followed two years later, *Reconstruction: The Battle for Democracy, 1865–1876*. Speaking of Tennessee, Du Bois says flatly, "The attitude of the state toward Negroes was bad."[17] He then quotes the 1866 report of the Joint Committee on Reconstruction:

> The predominant feeling of those lately in rebellion is that of deep-seated hatred, amounting in many cases to a spirit of revenge towards the white Unionists of the State, and a haughty contempt for the Negro, whom they cannot treat as a freeman. The hatred for the white loyalist is intensified by the accusation that he deserted the South in her extremity, and is, therefore, a traitor, and by the setting up of a government of the minority. . . . The Negro is the Mordecai who constantly reminds them of their defeat, and of what they call a "just, but lost cause." And

the sight of him in the enjoyment of freedom is a constant source of irritation.[18]

Without the Union League, says Allen, "wholesale massacres would have resulted every time the Negroes attempted to vote or otherwise participate in political life."[19] He describes the Ku Klux Klan as a terror organization[20] and quotes Judge Albion W. Tourgee of North Carolina (a former Union soldier) to illustrate—presumably with a degree of rhetorical hyperbole—the extent of Klan outrages: "Of the slain there were enough to furnish forth a battlefield and all from these three classes, the Negro, the scalawag and the carpetbagger. . . . The wounded in this silent warfare were more thousands than those who groaned upon the slopes of Gettysburg.'"[21]

In the ashes of war, in every one the southern states conservative newspapers launched crusades for white supremacy and against conciliation. Some lauded the most violent excesses of the Klan. At the same time, vituperative and vindictive editorials in some northern papers contributed less to the carnage in the South, for no other reason than that they "rarely reached southerners, and mail facilities were woefully inadequate."[22] However, other newspapers, both North and South, editorialized against racism and called for calm reflection and fence-mending. Unfortunately, it was the more strident opinion that often carried the day.

Former slaves carrying guns had become a major concern of white conservatives, and all across the South editors warned of impending trouble. The *Macon (Georgia) Journal and Messenger* informed its readers of companies of armed blacks, privates and officers, training regularly in and around the city, a report picked up by the *Moulton Advertiser* on September 18, 1868.[23] Similarly, the *Alabama Beacon* reported exactly one year later that two companies of armed Negroes were preparing for Klan raids.[24] And on September 17, 1868, the *Athens Post* reported that a black regiment called the Warmouth Guards had organized and paraded in New Orleans.[25]

It can be argued that these accounts fell within the realm of responsible journalism. But consider the *Fairfield Herald's* April 29, 1868, editorial about the recent radical turn of events. The South Carolina paper "declared the Revolution 'the maddest, most unscrupulous and infamous revolution in history,' which 'has snatched the power from the hands of the race which settled the country . . . and transferred it to its former slaves, an ignorant and feeble race.'"[26] A few years later, on November 20, 1872, the *Herald* editorialized on a policy of the Reconstruction legislature:

A hell-born policy which has trampled the fairest and noblest of states
of our great sisterhood beneath the unholy hoofs of African savages and

shoulder-strapped brigands—the policy which has given up millions of our free-born, high-souled brothers and sisters, countrymen and countrywomen of Washington, Rutledge, Marion and Lee, to the rule of gibbering, louse-eaten, devil-worshipping barbarians, from the jungles of Dahomey, and peripatetic buccaneers from Cape Cod, Memphremagod, Hell and Boston.[27]

Such editorials, which numbered in the thousands, made it clear that in the minds of many white southerners, despite Lee's surrender at the Appomattox Court House, the war was not over. Planters, as a general rule, had adopted a wait-and-see posture in 1865. But with the emergence of the Union League as a political force, "most lost their composure. Alerted by widespread press coverage, planters immediately discerned a threat in League gatherings and many feared actual uprisings."[28] For various reasons, a considerable number of planters joined the League. But newspaper pressure on them to return to the white supremacist fold was great. "We will not trust those men who aver that they seek the companionship of Leaguers in order to see what they are about," said the *Tuscaloosa Monitor*. "The very same fellows are more apt to be spies against us than for us."[29] And the *Livingston (Alabama) Journal* said, "The brethren of weak nerves, who have gone into the Union Leagues to escape the dangers of confiscation, can now come out—shake off the unwholesome atmosphere of the Council Chambers and conduct themselves like white folks."[30] Some papers began printing the names of suspected leaguers.[31] At the same time, advertisers in Republican papers faced boycotts.[32]

The strongest economic pressure was brought to bear against freedmen who dared to vote. "Democrats relied mainly upon the economic leverage they held as employers over the freedmen," Fitzgerald says. "One paper advised that 'employers may prevent employees from voting by a firm judicious stand in their business relations,' and the Democratic press urged full utilization of this power. The Oxford (Mississippi) *Falcon*, for example, reported the names of all local blacks who voted, saying they should go to the Radicals for work or starve. The influential Montgomery *Mail* likewise recommended public disclosure and boycott of laborers joining the League."[33] These efforts, however, which included the refusal to hire freedmen, dismissal from their jobs, and even eviction from their homes, were largely unsuccessful. "The Vicksburg *Herald* complained that freedmen would 'talk fair, and scrape their feet and say yes, massa, but they will vote just as . . . the League bids them.'"[34] This tactical failure of economic intimidation "led directly to the emergence of the Ku Klux Klan"[35] and its "effective technique of intimidation."[36]

Throughout Alabama particularly, newspapers hailed the Klan. The *Selma Times and Messenger* called on citizens to "organize a Ku-Klux Klan whenever they organize a [Union] league." Similarly, the "Mobile Register urged: 'Organize! Organize! . . . even 'Ku Klux Clubs' if you choose." Ryland Randolph, editor of the *Tuscaloosa Monitor*, established and led a Klan of about 60 men. His paper denounced the Union League repeatedly, asked readers to forward the names of members, and listed several such members, describing them as worthy of Klan attention. Randolph even concocted and posted Klan death threats in his own hand.

In Mississippi, the *Forest Register* changed its name to the *Ku Klux* for a September 1871 election. "This kind of emphatic espousal of violence was common in the state."[37] Similarly, for brief periods, newspaper readers in Goldsboro, North Carolina, had the *Ku Klux Kaleidoscope*; in Jefferson, Texas, they could pick up the *Ultra Ku Klux*; and in Houston, there was the *Daily Kuklux Vedette*.[38] Pro-Klan messages were rampant. Some papers even printed direct Ku Klux Klan threats such as the following notice to Riley Kinman, the Jackson County, Arkansas, sheriff-elect:

> We have come! We are here! Beware! Take heed! When the black cat is gliding under the shadows of darkness, and the death watch ticks at the lone hour of night, then we, the pale riders, are abroad. Speak in whispers and we hear you. Dream as you sleep in the inmost recesses of your house, and, hovering over your beds, we gather your sleeping thoughts, while our daggers are at your throat. Ravisher of liberties of the people for whom we died and yet live, begone ere it is too late[.] Unholy blacks, cursed of God, take warning and fly. Twice has the Sacred Serpent hissed. When again his voice is heard your doom is sealed. Beware! Take heed! . . . To be executed by White Death and Rattling Skeleton, at 10 tonight. K.K.K.[39]

On May 31, 1870, Congress responded to the continuing Klan violence by passing the first of a series of laws known as the Enforcement Acts. The conservative editorial response was swift and furious. The *Rome (Georgia) Courier* intoned, "Every member of Congress who voted for the law 'was in his secret soul a perjured traitor.'" The *Jackson (Mississippi) Clarion* opined:

> The object of the "unconstitutional and hideously despotic" measure was "to supercede [sic] State authority with the government of the bayonet and of marshal [sic] law." It was "predicated on no other foundation than the malice and cowardly hatred of its authors for the white inhabitants of the South, and their desire to retain power at the cost of principle and honor."[40]

And so it went throughout the South, conservative Democratic newspaper editors unleashing an unending, vituperative torrent of hate against African Americans. They claimed to have God on their side, but there was nothing holy about their cause or their battles. It was, indeed, a dark hour for American journalism. Like the Ku Klux Klan and its terrorist ilk, from the very beginning these editors aimed for nothing good. They allied themselves with terror and saw to it that the war continued. And in that one area, they may finally have been correct—not right but correct—but for all the wrong reasons. The war *did* rage on. And so did the violence, hatred, and bigotry, well into the 20th century, a long legacy of wasted tears, wasted blood, and wasted lives. It is not difficult to find remnants of that legacy lingering to this day.

The editorial responsibility for the crimes committed by the Klan is clear. These newsmen were leaders of their communities. Unequivocally, the press helped set the agenda for the racial inequality and prejudice that troubles the South and the whole of the American nation to this day. The relentless racist advocacy of the southern press clearly influenced newspaper brethren in the North and West, with results as far afield as international relations and affairs. Rarely if ever in American history was the power of the pen mightier than it was following the Civil War—and never with more tragic consequences.

NOTES

1. Allen W. Trelease, *White Terror: The Ku Klux Klan Conspiracy and Southern Reconstruction* (Westport, Conn.: Greenwood Press, 1971), xvii.
2. Ibid., xlvi.
3. Brooks D. Simpson, *The Reconstruction Presidents* (Lawrence: University Press of Kansas, 1998), 142.
4. Trelease, xx, xxi.
5. Simpson, 23.
6. Ibid., quoting the *New Orleans Times*, 22 October 1866. See also Trelease, xliii.
7. Trelease, 419.
8. George C. Rable, *But There Was No Peace* (Athens: University of Georgia Press, 1984), xi.
9. Simpson, 105.
10. Ibid., 106, 107.
11. William Archibald Dunning, *Reconstruction: Political & Economic* (New York: Harper & Row, 1907), 182, 183.
12. Walter L. Fleming, introduction to *Ku Klux Klan: Its Origin, Growth, and Disbandment* by J.C. Lester and D.L. Wilson (New York: AMS Press, 1905), 35, 36.
13. Fred J. Cook, *The Ku Klux Klan: America's Recurring Nightmare* (New York: Julian Messner, Simon & Schuster, 1980), 17.
14. Ibid., 18.
15. Susan Lawrence Davis, *Authentic History of the Ku Klux Klan, 1865–1877* (New York: self published, 1924), v.
16. Ibid., vi. Davis concludes that the Union League "distributed leaflets to the negroes, instructing them to outrage the women and children, to force the Confederate soldiers to come home for their protection" (172), and brought free Negroes

to the South from places like Rhode Island "to do the crimes that the former faithful slaves would not do" (173). The Union League included "the lowest order of men on earth . . . spurious imitators of the uniforms and regalia of the Ku Klux Klan, who would kill, whip and otherwise punish negroes who refused to do their vile bidding, and report them as outrages done by the real Ku Klux Klan."

17. W.E.B. Du Bois, *Black Reconstruction: An Essay Toward a History of the Part which Black Folk Played in the Attempt to Reconstruct Democracy in America, 1860–1888* (New York: Russell & Russell, 1935), 574.

18. Ibid., quoting the *Report of Joint Committee on Reconstruction*, 1866, 91.

19. James S. Allen, *Reconstruction: The Battle for Democracy, 1865–1876* (New York: International Publishers, 1937), 95.

20. Ibid., 66.

21. Albion W. Tourgee, *A Fool's Errand* (Cambridge: Belknap Press of Harvard University Press, 1961), 226, quoted in Allen, 190.

22. Simpson, 81.

23. Allen, 99.

24. Ibid.

25. Ibid.

26. Du Bois, 400.

27. Ibid., 144.

28. Michael W. Fitzgerald, *The Union League Movement* (Baton Rouge: Louisiana State University Press, 1989), 201. See also Michael Perman, *Reunion without Compromise: The South and Reconstruction, 1865–1868* (Cambridge: Cambridge University Press, 1974), 229–265 passim.

29. Ibid., 204, 205, quoting the *Tuscaloosa Monitor*, 27 November 1867.

30. Ibid., 205, quoting the *Livingston (Alabama) Journal*, 21 September 1868.

31. Ibid. See the *Grove Hill (Alabama) Democrat*, 8 August 1867, quoting the *Mobile Times*.

32. Ibid. See the *Mobile Nationalist*, 30 April 1868.

33. Ibid., 208. See the *Tuscaloosa Monitor*, 28 January 1868; the *Montgomery Mail*, 18 August 1868; the *Montgomery Advertiser*, 9 November 1867; and the *Oxford (Mississippi) Falcon*, 28 June 1868. See also Trelease, xli.

34. Ibid., 211, quoting the *Forest (Mississippi) Register*, 10 December 1870 (quoting the *Vicksburg Herald*).

35. Ibid., 213.

36. Ibid., 215.

37. Ibid., 216, 217, quoting the *Selma Times and Messenger*, 31 July 1868, and the *Athens (Alabama) Post*, 6 August 1868 (quoting the *Mobile Register*).

38. Trelease, 60.

39. Ibid., 55.

40. Ibid., 390, quoting the *Rome (Georgia) Courier* and *Jackson (Mississippi) Clarion*.

AN IRRESPONSIBLE PRESS

Memphis Newspapers and the 1866 Riot

— MARIUS CARRIERE —

From May 1 to May 3, 1866, a riot sparked by a minor traffic accident between two hack drivers, one black and one white, raged in Memphis, Tennessee, leaving 48 people dead and more than 70 wounded. In addition, there were several rapes, hundreds of robberies, and damages to private homes, schools, churches, and government property totaling $130,981.[1] Contemporary observers and historians alike have sought to attribute blame and ascribe immediate and long-term causes for the unrest, the first full-scale race riot of the post–Civil War era, which ultimately enabled Radical Republicans in Congress to wrest control of Reconstruction from President Andrew Johnson, himself a transplanted Tennessean.

The first to place blame was Brigadier General Benjamin P. Runkle, superintendent of the Memphis District of the Freedmen's Bureau. A few weeks after the riot, Runkle listed the causes of the riot in a long communiqué to Major General Clinton B. Fisk, the bureau's assistant commissioner of Kentucky and Tennessee. Runkle noted that the garrison of black soldiers in the Third U.S. Heavy Artillery had for "a long time previous" engaged in a feud with the city's predominantly Irish police.[2] Runkle charged that Mayor John Park of Memphis had appointed policemen who, in Runkle's opinion, were so ignorant that "they were not aware that the laws governing slavery had been abolished." The Irish police, he said, were "not fit for any position." The

mayor, according to Runkle, had only appointed the men to protect his political power. Runkle also believed that many white laborers resented competing with blacks, whom they considered inferior.[3] Finally, the superintendent
blamed former Confederates, men who had served "in the Rebel army," for
encouraging the "low rowdies" to run riot through the city.[4]

Runkle reserved his harshest comments, however, for the Memphis
press. He advised Fisk that the "tone . . . of the articles published in certain
of the newspapers of Memphis, the *Avalanche* and *Argus*, particularly the
Avalanche, were incendiary." The articles in these newspapers, he said, were
biased against the African American population, "radicals," and "imported
people," and stirred up "evil passions and bitter prejudices of the lower classes
against the 'niggers' and 'yankees.'"[5]

Other contemporaries agreed with Runkle. A select committee of the
House of Representatives charged with investigating the riot likewise condemned the Memphis press. The majority report presented by Illinois Representative Elihu B. Washburne stated flatly that the "bloody massacre of the
colored people of Memphis, regardless of age, sex, or condition, was inspired
by the teachings of the press."[6] In more damning language, the select committee's majority report noted that "there can be no doubt that the feeling which
led to the terrible massacres at Memphis was stimulated by the disloyal press
of that city."[7] The *Memphis Daily Post*, a Republican newspaper, agreed. The
Post wrote that the city press was only interested in "the destruction of everything which may tend to improve the status of the freedmen."[8]

Traditional accounts of the May riot, on the other hand, have maintained that Memphis's newspapers "deplored the riots and . . . constantly
counseled moderation." In these accounts, Republican Governor William G.
"Parson" Brownlow, Radical Republicans, and the Freedmen's Bureau itself
were found to be at fault for carelessly and callously influencing and "manipulating the negroes," who received most of the blame for the riot. It was
equally alleged that the Radical press was responsible for fanning "the flames
of prejudice and hate."[9] This traditional view reflects what the Conservative
press believed at the time and what the Minority Report of the Special Committee of the House also maintained.[10] More recently, however, historians
have tended to agree with those contemporaries who argued that at least some
of the Memphis newspapers had contributed to the riot by needlessly inciting
white Memphians.[11]

Regardless of which account one reads, the chief fact on which all sources
agree is that the overwhelming number of the riot's victims were African
Americans. It is also inarguable that a large number of working-class whites
participated in attacks against black Memphians and that those in authority

intimidated and threatened white Republicans. More difficult to determine is the exact role of the Memphis press in the riot, and what part, if any, the press played in raising the level of racial, class, and political animosity in the city prior to and during the three-day riot.

The newspapers themselves began debating these questions even before the riot was over. On May 3, the last day of the riot, the *Memphis Daily Post* accused its fellow journalists at the *Avalanche* and the *Argus* of exacerbating the situation with what it called "inflammatory articles" that were "sensational, and in the highest degree, exaggerated."[12] In truth, these so-called inflammatory articles had begun long before May 1. All three of the Conservative papers, the *Avalanche*, the *Argus*, and the *Appeal*, were long-time critics of the Republican majority in Congress and the Republican-dominated Tennessee Legislature.[13] Republicans in both Washington, D.C., and Nashville were considered "Radical" and, as the *Avalanche* wrote in February 1866, the Radicals were "mean and cowardly" scoundrels who "are seeking to humiliate and disgrace the rebel soldier."[14] The Conservative newspapers were particularly worried that the legislature intended to "disfranchise the noblest men of the state, and to brand with disgrace all who aided the gallant struggle for independence."[15] Whereas the Tennessee Republican legislators were referred to as an oligarchy, Conservatives called Congress's 1866 Civil Rights Bill an encroachment "upon State Rights properly understood," and the Conservatives wrote that the Radicals intended to "elevate the negroes not only to a position of perfect political and social equality with white men, but . . . design to make them the aristocrats of the country!"[16]

Naturally, the likelihood of a Congressional Reconstruction did not appeal to the Conservatives, and the three Memphis newspapers supported President Andrew Johnson's more moderate approach. By January 1, 1866, when the *Avalanche* resumed publication, local Conservatives had grown equally tired of military rule, the disfranchisement of ex-Confederates, and the Radicals in Congress who were dragging out the resumption of normal relations between the states and the federal government. When Johnson in early April 1866 officially proclaimed the Civil War over, Conservative newspapers began their attack on congressional Radicals in earnest. Prominent lawmakers Thaddeus Stevens of Pennsylvania and Charles Sumner of Massachusetts were favorite targets of the Memphis papers, which claimed that Congress intended to strike "down all law and liberty that may stand in the way" of Radical Reconstruction.[17]

As the year progressed, the negative articles in the *Avalanche* and the *Argus* became numerous and violent. The targets essentially remained the same, but the Conservative press in particular abused African Americans, northern citizens residing in Memphis, and Unionists in no uncertain terms. In February, although the *Argus* called the Freedmen's Bureau unconstitutional, a view with which all of the Conservative papers agreed, it must have been its tone that stirred up the white population. That paper virtually predicted the May riot when it wrote that if the bureau, black suffrage, "and complete negro equality" were forced upon the South then "we may look for violations of peace to grow more frequent and serious." A few days later the same paper applauded Johnson's veto of the extension of the Freemen's Bureau Bill and called the bureau the Radicals' "attempt to rule the South with negro bayonets."[18]

As May 1 grew closer, the Conservative press became even more visceral. Less than two weeks before the outbreak of the riot, the paper wrote that the "Radical Rebellion" must be stopped. The *Argus* said the Radicals in Congress were

> willfully and confessedly trampling upon the Constitution and the rights of the states in their efforts to enslave the South, to degrade white people, and elevate the negroes to a position of political and social superiority. In giving the ballot to four millions of black barbarians . . . is a revolution . . . and will prove more disastrous to civil and religious liberty on this continent . . . than a half dozen civil wars.[19]

Even the more temperate *Daily Appeal* was not free from heightening the tension between the races and sections. Announcing that African Americans were "utterly incapable of self-civilization," the *Appeal* believed that southern people needed to "take in their own hands the education of this class of our population." It would be a "grave error to allow persons brought from other States and sections with their peculiar notions" to educate African Americans.[20] With the exception of the *Daily Post* and perhaps one other Memphis paper, the *Daily Bulletin*,[21] the newspapers of the city were united in their belief that the United States had been created by whites, for whites, and that nothing should be allowed to change the status quo. The Civil Rights Bill, for example, even received a fair share of abuse from the more moderate *Appeal* when it reported the bill "allows blacks to sit in Congress, intermarry with our daughters, represents us as (foreign) ministers, permits a black to be president, allows blacks to own firearms, and makes blacks five times better than a white."[22] Naturally, to these papers, particularly the *Avalanche* and the *Argus*, African Americans were better off under "wholesome, personal control" and the papers believed the "negro's present condition" illustrated the "justice and wisdom of the institution [slavery]."[23]

The *Avalanche*, as many contemporaries noted at the time, was in a league of its own when it came to intemperance and vitriolic press coverage. To the *Avalanche*, radicals were "violent, aggressive, unreasonable, vindicate, and destructive"; they were, in short, "insane fanatics."[24] African Americans, however, received much of the paper's harshest criticism. African American troops stationed in Memphis were bad enough, thought the *Avalanche*, but the paper likewise despised blacks in general. Months before the riot, the paper wrote how Memphis was "to have the black flesh of the negro crammed down our throats . . . to have the black soldier, the black magistrate, the black man's government."[25] Throughout the spring of 1866, the *Avalanche*'s tone grew more incendiary. Critical of both northerners and African Americans, the paper noted how northern abolitionists believed the "nigger is their equal." The *Avalanche* would have none of this and proclaimed "we insist that he [the African American] is not the equal of *Southern* men."[26]

A particularly disturbing tactic of the *Avalanche*, which caught the attention of the Republican and Freedmen's Bureau personnel, was the listing in the *Avalanche*'s columns of the names of Radicals and those who associated with Radicals. The paper demanded its readers boycott the businesses of these men. To the *Avalanche* these "Radicals seem to forget that violence begets violence . . . and persecution engenders resistance."[27] L.M. Wolcott, a grocer on Front Street, because of his alleged Radical tendencies became one target of the paper. The *Avalanche* promoted a boycott of his store because "it is only done in exchange for the political fanaticism he would mete out to us." The paper also labeled Wolcott's business associate, A.M. Smith, and a Tennessee legislator, an "unprincipled small-fry demagogue." Another target, Frederick Katzenbach, a music dealer, was "a marked man from this time, and may as well hang up a sign, 'small pox,' before his door." The *Avalanche* announced that it "will hold up to public scorn and contempt" all those who are "Radical negro-worshipping" and who support "the degradation of whites to the standard of the negro."[28]

On the first day of the riot, the *Avalanche* appeared with as much, if not more, venom than in the last days of April. The paper called the Radicals "a race of small men—a filthy scum" and said that those in the Tennessee Legislature were "consummate blockheads, destitute of brains." Its firebrand rival, the *Argus*, reserved its criticism on May 1 for the new Metropolitan Police Bill. Radicals, nonetheless, were the culprits in this, too. The *Argus* saw the bill as a way the "entire police machinery of Memphis and Shelby County will be worked by ultra Radicals, who will make it serve Radical ends."[29]

By the time these and other similar inflammatory articles had appeared, the riot was already raging. The day after the fateful traffic accident, two Irish policemen had attempted to arrest the black hack driver. The man had retreated to the comparative safety of the red-light district in south Memphis around Grady's Hill. There he joined a crowd of newly discharged black soldiers from the notorious Third U.S. Heavy Artillery who were idly waiting for their mustering-out pay. The soldiers and the police had a long-standing mutual antipathy, based in part on the traditional social and economic rivalry between African Americans and Irish immigrants. That antipathy had been heightened by the burgeoning political power of the Irish in the vacuum provided by the large-scale disfranchisement of former Confederates after the Civil War. The mayor, 9 of 16 aldermen, and 67 percent of all elective and appointed local offices were Irish, as was an astounding 90 percent of the police force.

Economic competition between the two groups worsened following the war because freed slaves competed with Irish laborers for scarce jobs on the waterfront and in the brickyards. The Reverend Ewing O. Tade, a transplanted Iowan, soon took note of the festering competition. As he later testified before Congress:

> The Irish have an intense hatred for the negroes, because they are afraid they will take away their work. They have combinations here now to drive out colored draymen and hackmen. The Irish and others, I know, are in league now having regular organizations for the purpose of suppressing colored labor.[30]

Underscoring Tade's point was the minor collision between the black and the white dray drivers. When the Irish police arrived at Grady's Hill to arrest the black driver involved, a bitter shouting match arose between them and the recently discharged black soldiers from the Third Heavy Artillery, which even district commander Major General George Stoneman conceded was "probably the worst regiment of colored troops which had been stationed in the city. . . . There was a direct relation between the stationing of these troops and the rising crime rate in Memphis."[31] The *Avalanche* underscored the regiment's parlous reputation:

> For months past, acts of violence, bloodshed and murder have been too common on our streets; but they have almost always had some direct connection with the negro troops stationed here. Time and again stores have been broken open and plundered, and white men shot down in our city by drunken, brutal negro soldiers; and we have yet to hear of the first instance where punishment followed the crime.[32]

In this powder-keg environment, racial violence was virtually inevitable. After a crowd of blacks began following the policemen and their prisoner back down Causey Street toward the city jail, pistol shots suddenly rang out. A white policeman and a white onlooker were wounded, and the riot soon gathered irresistible momentum. The county sheriff's office joined forces with the city police to form a 100-man posse and headed back to the scene of the initial confrontation in south Memphis. Encountering a crowd of black soldiers, the sheriff demanded that they surrender; they refused. More shots rang out, and scattered fighting erupted in the shantytown. A popular white fireman named Henry Dunn was shot and killed near the South Street bridge, and two black prisoners were shot down in cold blood in retaliation. Posse members cried out that they were going to "kill the last damned one of the nigger race, and burn up the cradle, God damn them."[33]

For the next two days, anarchy reigned in the streets of Memphis. The situation was made worse by the refusal of General Stoneman to send army troops to restore order. By the time he had reversed himself and declared martial law, dozens of blacks had been killed and numerous homes, churches, and schools destroyed. Meanwhile, the newspapers kept their readers informed— or misinformed—about the fighting. On May 2, the *Appeal* lost whatever moderation it had possessed. It reported that "we have had too much of this lawless aggression on the part of the vicious negroes infesting South Memphis, and it is high time more stringent measures were adopted to either force them to behave themselves or leave the city."[34] The *Argus* called it "the negro riot" and condemned "the bulk of the colored population in the evil causes upon which they have entered."[35] As to be expected, it was left to the *Avalanche* to throw more oil on the fire. Under the headline "The Law Outraged by Negroes," the paper wrote that armed blacks "began an unprovoked assault on the police. . . . Blacks began firing at every white person they saw."[36] The entire Conservative press blamed the African American soldiers for beginning "an unlicensed foray upon law and order."[37]

The reliability of the Conservative press is doubtful in view of the conflicting stories that appeared in the three newspapers. The *Avalanche*, for example, reported that a large number of grown blacks (presumably discharged soldiers) began the riot with an unprovoked attack on police officers who were attempting to stop a disturbance between a white man and a black man. The *Argus*, on the other hand, wrote that African Americans had attacked the police when they traveled into south Memphis to arrest a man who sold liquor.[38] Although the *Daily Appeal* heaped its share of abuse on the African American community, it did note in an article on the last day of the riot that "wild rumors prevailed yesterday without any foundation in fact."[39]

The wildest rumor, and perhaps the most damaging one, appeared in both the *Avalanche* and the *Appeal*. Both papers claimed that they had received reports "from reliable sources, that it has been the intention of the negroes, for some days, to make a descent upon the municipal authorities and citizens, as soon as they were mustered out of the U.S. service."[40] Other unfounded rumors included how bullets "came from it [Fort Pickering] thick and fast" and later how the African American former soldiers came out of the fort "in line of battle."[41] Considering the disproportionate deaths of African Americans over those of white Memphians and the testimony of two white federal officers on how they kept African Americans in the fort for protection against the white mob, the credibility of the Conservative press evaporates.[42]

Numerous witnesses before the special congressional committee, General Stoneman, Freedmen's Bureau officials, and the *Daily Post* all agreed that the articles in the Conservative press, particularly the *Avalanche* and the *Argus*, had been

> characterized by a bitter hostility to the government, and by appeals to the lowest and basest prejudices against the colored population, by bitter personal attacks upon northern people residing in Memphis; . . . the whole tenor of the disloyal press was a constant incitation to violence and ill-feeling.[43]

Even a cursory glance at the pages of the Conservative press during the last weeks of 1865 and the first four months of 1866 demonstrates the accuracy of the *Daily Post*'s comment that the *Argus* and the *Avalanche* had exacerbated the situation with inflammatory articles, articles that were "sensational, and in the highest degree, exaggerated."[44]

Following the riot, the managing editors of both the *Argus* and the *Avalanche* testified before the special committee of the House investigating the riot, and both minimized their responsibility in the affair. David A. Brower of the *Argus* told the committee that another editor had written an inflammatory article in the newspaper and that had he, Brower, read it before publication, he would not have permitted such "language embodying such sentiments to be published in the paper." He did not, however, offer any explanation for the inclusion of dozens of other incendiary articles in the paper.[45] Matthew C. Galloway, the managing editor of the *Avalanche*, seemed to think that because he opposed mobbing the *Daily Post*'s editorial office during the riot he had acted with restraint. Another editor of the *Avalanche* appeared before the special committee and unwittingly offered incriminating evidence of Galloway's complicity in stirring up the mob. Michael W. Clusky testified that he "saw several men take hold of Mr. Galloway, evidently with a desire to receive his encouragement."[46]

In fact, before the special congressional committee, the editors of both the *Argus* and the *Avalanche* readily admitted that they were responsible for various articles that blamed "the poor ignorant deluded blacks" for the riots and the Radical press for "churches, school-houses, and shanties burned by the mob."[47] Galloway of the *Avalanche*, however, had to retract one of the statements that appeared in his columns during the riot. In it he claimed "life has been taken, the result of the incendiary impressions of the radicals upon the public and too willing intellect of the negroes." When asked to "state the names of any persons referred to as radicals . . . who instigated or encouraged the recent riots," he could furnish none.[48] The Memphis police chief, Benjamin G. Garrett, also contradicted another of Galloway's statements during the riot, an assertion that the chief had an affidavit from an African American woman claiming that before the riot broke out blacks had "contemplated rising, sacking the city, and robbing the banks" of Memphis.[49]

The articles in the Conservative press before and during the May riots of 1866 were clearly biased at best and inflammatory at worst. The evidence is more than ample to sustain the view of Shelby County Criminal Court Judge William Hunter that "he has no doubt but the mob was stimulated by the newspapers."[50] As far as just how much those newspapers affected public opinion, General Stoneman testified before the special committee that the "papers receive the countenance and support of the community."[51] Galloway, during his testimony, confirmed Stoneman's testimony and incriminated himself and the Conservative press in general, when he affirmed Michael Clusky's earlier testimony that the "crowd came to where I was, shouting for the *Avalanche.* Some . . . in the crowd seized hold of me to raise me on their shoulders."[52]

Although Galloway testified he knew no one in the crowd and they "appeared to be a low class of community,"[53] Reverend Tade appears to have accurately captured just what Galloway and other Conservative newspapermen had done. For Tade, the "effect of the press was to incite the riotous proceedings; and . . . the Irish have been used as mere cats'-paws . . . the papers . . . had every day incited them to the deeds of violence."[54] Without a doubt, the Conservative press of Memphis had been guilty of unreasonableness at best and irresponsibility at worst. Ironically, the federal government, which these papers criticized unsparingly, treated those who rioted, burned, looted, raped, and murdered, along with the Conservative press, with judicial and military fairness. No individual was ever indicted, much less brought to trial, for any of the crimes committed between May 1 and May 3, 1866.

NOTES

This essay first appeared in the *Tennessee Historical Quarterly* 60 (Spring 2001).

1. *Memphis Riots and Massacres*, Report, the Special Committee of the House Charged with an Investigation into All Matters Connected with the Riots at Memphis, which Took Place on the First Days of May, 1866, Elihu B. Washburne, Chairman (repr., Miami: Mnemosyne Publishing Co., Inc.,) 1969, 35–36. Hereafter cited as *Riots and Massacres.*

2. B.P. Runkle to General C.B. Fisk, Selected Records of the Assistant Commissioner, May 23, 1866. Bureau of Refugees, Freedmen and Abandoned Lands (Washington: National Archives). Hereafter cited as Selected Records, Freedmen's Bureau Papers.

3. Ibid.

4. Ibid.

5. Ibid.

6. *Riots and Massacres*, 5.

7. Ibid., 31.

8. *Memphis Daily Post*, 20 May 1866. All references to newspapers are to the Memphis press. Therefore, hereafter, Memphis will be omitted from the citations.

9. Gerald M. Capers Jr., *The Biography of a River Town: Memphis; Its Heroic Age* (repr., New Orleans: Hauser-American, 1966), 178; Stanley J. Folmsbee, Robert E. Corlew, and Enoch L. Mitchell, *History of Tennessee*, 2 vols., (New York: Lewis Historical Publishing Co., Inc., 1960), 108, 114. Jack D.L. Holmes, "The Underlying Causes of the Memphis Riot of 1866," *Tennessee Historical Quarterly* 17 (September 1958): 201. The Folmsbee, Corlew, and Mitchell book, despite its 1960 publication date, is a caricature of Reconstruction with its stock characters: venal blacks, greedy northerners, and manipulated native, southern whites.

10. *Riots and Massacres*, 43–44. Congressman G.S. Shanklin of Kentucky, in his minority report, wrote he did not "think any fair or legitimate inference or opinion as to the sentiments of the people among whom the papers are published can be drawn or proven from mere extracts." Mr. Shanklin, while in Memphis from May 22 to June 6, 1866, obviously either did not read any of the Conservative papers or sympathized with the Conservative press because the *Avalanche*, *Argus*, and even the *Appeal* continued their rather strong anti–African American, Freedmen's Bureau, "Yankee," and Radical polemics the entire time the Special Committee remained in the city.

11. James Ryan, "The Memphis Riots of 1866: Terror in a Black Community During Reconstruction," *Journal of Negro History* 62 (1977): 245; Bobby Lovett, "Memphis Riot: Reaction to Blacks in Memphis, May 1865–July 1866," *Tennessee Historical Quarterly* 38 (Spring 1979): 9–30; Bobby Lovett, "The Negro in Tennessee, 1861–1866: A Socio-Military History of the Civil War Era" (PhD diss., 1982), 221–222. A recent historical account of the Memphis riot is "Community, Class, and Race in the Memphis Riot of 1866," *Journal of Social History* 18 (1984): 233–246, by Altina L. Waller. Waller does not ignore race, the Civil War experience of the rioters, or even the traditional view that the Irish working class resented having to compete for the ever declining jobs with newly arrived African Americans. She nonetheless argues that the riot was a "social conflict within one discrete neighborhood" in response to a perceived "economic and social collapse of their [the middle-class] community." Waller briefly addresses the role of the press but only as, in her view, a part of how elites manipulated what she calls the middle class.

12. *Daily Post*, 3 May 1866.

13. Because the Democratic Party had been associated with secession and rebellion, many native white southerners eschewed the name *Democrat*, instead favoring the name *Conservative*. These old Democrats and conservative Whigs made up the

bulk of the opposition to Republican rule and found support in these "unrepentant" newspapers—the *Avalanche* and *Argus* and, to a lesser extent, the *Appeal*.

14. *Avalanche*, 9 February 1866.

15. Ibid., 28 February 1866.

16. *Argus*, 17 April 1866.

17. *Avalanche*, 1 January 1866; *Argus*, 6 April 1866. In the January issue of the *Avalanche*, the editorial writer said that he, and presumably his readership in the city, accepted defeat and would submit to only "what the war had properly decided." Simply put, that was the restoration of the Union and the end of slavery. Federal authorities in Memphis may have believed the future would be difficult because the *Avalanche* forcefully stated that it would oppose black equality and black suffrage and would continue to support state rights and the "orthodoxy of the Democratic party."

18. *Argus*, 17 February 1866, 21 February 1866.

19. *Argus*, 21 April 1866.

20. *Daily Appeal*, 12 April 1866.

21. The *Memphis Daily Bulletin* from time-to-time supported the Republicans in Washington and Nashville, as well as the Freedmen's Bureau and its activity among African Americans.

22. *Appeal*, 4 April 1866.

23. *Avalanche*, 3 March 1866.

24. Ibid., 9 March 1866, 14 March 1866.

25. Ibid., 4 January 1866.

26. Ibid., 13 April 1866.

27. Ibid., 15 April 1866.

28. Ibid., 13 April 1866, 14 April 1866, 4 May 1866. Wolcott and Smith owned the grocery firm of Wolcott, Smith & Co. on Front Street. The *Avalanche* apparently was unconcerned that its rhetoric might reignite the rioting because the last attack against Smith came the morning of the first day of calm. Whereas these two men were apparently newly arrived to Memphis, Katzenbach had lived in Memphis since at least 1859. Tanner, Halpin and Co., comp., *Memphis City Directory for 1859* (Memphis: Hutton and Clark Publishers, 1859), 27.

29. *Avalanche*, 1 May 1866; *Argus*, 1 May 1866.

30. Testimony of Rev. Ewing O. Tade, quoted in *Memphis Riots and Massacres*, 90.

31. Official Report, Stoneman to General U.S. Grant, in *American Cyclopaedia*, 1866, 730.

32. *Avalanche*, 5 May 1866.

33. Lovett, "Memphis Riots," 21–23.

34. *Appeal*, 2 May 1866.

35. *Argus*, 2 May 1866.

36. *Avalanche*, 2 May 1866.

37. Ibid., 2 May 1866; *Appeal*, 2 May 1866; *Argus*, 2 May 1866.

38. *Avalanche*, 2 May 1866; *Argus*, 2 May 1866.

39. *Appeal*, 3 May 1866.

40. *Argus*, 3 May 1866. The quote is from the *Argus*; the *Avalanche* published an article that spoke of a "well organized scheme to bring on a collision." The *Avalanche*

even wrote of how the police reported a black woman signed an affidavit confirming an African American plot. None of the official investigations ever confirmed or even hinted at such a possibility.

41. *Avalanche*, 2 May 1866.

42. *Riots and Massacres*, 11.

43. Ibid., 31.

44. *Daily Post*, 3 May 1866.

45. *Riots and Massacres*, 328. The article to which Brower's testimony applied included such statements as the assertion that African Americans' "idleness and profligacy . . . is such that they are a perfect nuisance, and forfeit all regard that humanity can offer them in their present condition." Brower and Benjamin Harnwell were the publishers of the *Argus*. Before the Civil War, Brower had been editor and proprietor of the *Evening Argus*.

46. *Riots and Massacres*, 21, 328. Galloway's name is at times spelled Gallaway, but the correct spelling is with an *o*.

47. Ibid., 333.

48. Ibid., 333–334.

49. Ibid., 333–334.

50. Ibid., 31.

51. Ibid., 58.

52. Ibid., 325.

53. Ibid.

54. Ibid., 31.

Race, Reconciliation, and Historical Memory in American Newspapers During the Centennial Year

⸺ Robert Rabe ⸺

It is difficult to blame Americans for feeling apprehensive as they set out to celebrate their glorious centennial in July 1876. "The mood of self-congratulation seemed somewhat incongruous," notes historian Eric Foner. "[It] was only achieved by ignoring some less than admirable features of contemporary American life."[1] As one newspaper remarked, the past year "was in many ways an exceedingly disastrous year, and no amount of rejoicing over its close can conceal the fact."[2] With the economy only slowly recovering from recession, a scandal-plagued administration in the White House, and violent, unresolved issues of reconstruction clouding the horizon, few could have expected to greet the centennial year with unalloyed optimism. Feelings of pride in the accomplishments of America's first century seemed to be no match for the long shadow cast by the previous two decades.

Although the memory of the Civil War lived fresh in their everyday experience, many Americans took advantage of the signal anniversary to look back to the Revolutionary period for inspiration. As they attempted to reimagine the national spirit, they called forth the memory of the founding generation and the Constitution it had drafted for guidance on how to reunify the nation and establish equality for all citizens before the law. At stake was not just the right to be included in the celebration; the public debate over historical

351

memory touched on the very idea of national identity. Was the United States to be a "white man's country," or was there room somewhere for black Revolutionary War hero Crispus Attucks and those who would write him into the national memory?

Newspapers played a vital role in the memory discourse as Americans examined their collective past. In a society still dominated by the printed word, it was only natural that groups vying for political rights and legitimacy would turn to the press to stake their claims to the nation's heritage. Moreover, readers in the nineteenth century were accustomed to taking political cues from their newspapers—journalism in the 1870s remained for the most part a partisan affair. As Mark Wahlgren Summers has pointed out, the modern newspaper was "fresh out of the eggshell," only slowly emerging as an independent political institution no longer controlled by the political party apparatus.[3] Increasingly, newspapers sought to assert their political ideology and interpret news events of the centennial year according to the often brutal calculus of Reconstruction-era politics.

By the centennial year, the decade-long process of Reconstruction had frustrated attempts to achieve peace or justice, led to the impeachment of a president, and exhausted the resolve of northern Republicans. Moreover, the northern public had been swept up in what historian Nina Silber has called the "romance of reunion," nostalgia for a more peaceful time based on antebellum stereotypes and rooted in deep discontent with the present.[4] As David Blight has noted in *Race and Reunion*, by 1876 white northerners and southerners alike were anxious to put the Civil War behind them. This "general feeling of amity and fraternity" necessarily excluded the black population, who were often viewed as the source of the nation's ills, and African Americans were acutely aware of the receding promise of rights and equality seemingly won in the "second American Revolution."[5]

The centennial naturally drew people's attention to the revolutionary past and called upon them to reach some agreement on a usable meaning of the experience. Michael Kammen has argued that most white Americans "perceived the Revolution—or wanted to—as a mutually shared memory, a common core of national tradition that could end the old bitterness."[6] White Americans on both sides of the Mason-Dixon line imagined a common heritage that allowed them to forget the "recent unpleasantness" of the Civil War by reaching back to a deeper and more profound historical memory of unity.[7] The exclusion of African Americans from this constructed identity eventually resulted in the articulation of "the Un-American Negro," to use Heather Cox Richardson's evocative phrase.[8] With black Americans effectively written out of national history and identity, it became politically viable for party leaders to negotiate away Reconstruction, already on its last legs, without alienating any significant core of the voting public.

Every nation is based at least loosely around a central core of historical events and figures, often shrouded in myth for many citizens, which serve as a foundation and source of unity. Memory "adds perspective and authenticity" to this process but is "selectively retrieved" along lines that mirror divisions in society over questions of power.[9] Among the uses of memory listed by Barbie Zelizer are instances in which "political traditions are validated through some sense of a stable past" that can be projected through cultural institutions, commemorative activities, or the mass media.[10] Because memory is linked to power, it is always, as John Gillis makes clear, "fiercely contested from the very beginning."[11] Collective memory used in the formation of national identity lends authority and legitimacy to those groups that associate themselves most convincingly with the accepted past or assert an alternative vision that becomes widely accepted, a process that is often, though not always, carried out in the political arena.

The Fourth of July, 1876, symbolized for many the lingering politicization of the past. The white elite in many parts of the South did not celebrate the Fourth at all. It was, in their eyes, a holiday for the Republicans, both northern and southern, who seemed to control the political system. The holiday was also racialized; it was a memorable day for African Americans, who had a new reason to celebrate political freedom. As the historian Carolyn Sue Weddington has noted, the slave owners equated their struggle for freedom with that of the colonists and argued that the history of the Revolutionary period demonstrated that direct action was sometimes necessary in order to achieve freedom.[12] The Civil War had been a failed attempt to reclaim the "true" heritage of the Revolution, and in the postbellum period, many white southerners held on to this interpretation of the past and used it to justify continued opposition to Reconstruction.

The "New South," only slowly taking form in 1876, would be based on these principles. Newspapers were foremost among those who "defended racial subordination, fought Republican and Yankee aggressors, attacked centralizers in Washington, called for Southern economic independence . . . while celebrating the superiority of a southern way of life."[13] The *Atlanta Constitution* summed up this attitude in an editorial marking the Fourth, writing that in the South

> the celebrations of the 4th are not now much in vogue. But it is quite natural that we should not feel very enthusiastic over the Fourth or the Centennial, so long as we're politically proscribed and a great political party constantly seeks to deny to us the equality of citizenship. We can

never take that deep interest in these patriotic days and occasions 'till the selection of a national democratic administration by the people assures of a full and free share in the rights, privileges and glories purchased by the common forefathers.[14]

Atlanta had turned its eyes to the past instead on April 27 to mark Memorial Day for the Southern dead of past wars. To good southerners, "there is not another day in the year's calendar which finds a heartier, deeper sympathy and calls out the devotion and patriotism" in the same way.[15] Memory served to pay tribute to the ultimate sacrifice of those who had died defending southern honor in the Civil War and, by definition, fighting for a southern memory of the Revolution. Occasions for public commemoration of these men's sacrifice naturally drew on the meaning of the Revolution. While describing the ceremonies and processions of the day, the *Constitution* promoted the day as a southern holiday. Orations delivered, and reprinted in the paper, fully played on this memory. When the Fourth of July arrived, the paper told its readers, "it is not that we are less true to the principles and memories connected with this day, but because we feel persecuted, that we do not enter heartily into the patriotic observances so dear to us in the past."[16] Northern Democratic newspapers echoed this sentiment. As the *Chicago Times* told its readers, the white southerner had no reason to celebrate the day because "people who are obliged to submit in some cases to Negro rule and in others to Negro equality are not in the humor of celebrating an event in which the utterances are all in the interest of an independence, a freedom, which—for them—has no real existence."[17]

So intense was the anti-Fourth sentiment in Charleston that the city celebrated an alternate Fourth of July during the centennial year. During the Revolutionary War, the Battle of Fort Sullivan had been South Carolina's greatest military contribution to the rebellion and the colony's most heroic hour. The battle's centennial fell on June 27, 1876, just a week before the Fourth. With the memory of the "stern dark hours of the Confederate War fresh in their memory," troops of the state and local militia paraded through the streets to the celebrated fort, where they were greeted with decorations, applause, and a series of history lessons in the form of orations by local notables.[18] Newspaper accounts, as well as many of the speakers, described the battle as the key contribution by the South to the Revolution and a glorious victory over tyranny. No mention was made of the nation's centennial.

In many other parts of the nation, however, the Fourth of July, 1876, was celebrated with as much merriment and patriotism as the public could muster. Many northern cities and towns essentially closed down government and business operations for several days and dedicated themselves wholly to the centennial. In addition to reporting broadly on local and nationwide festivities, newspapers published a wide variety of columns and essays on Revolutionary history. The *New York Times,* noting the centrality of the Declaration of Independence to the meaning of the day, ran a lengthy history of the debate and deliberation that produced the document and its philosophy.[19] The *Louisville Courier-Journal* gave up most of a page in its centennial edition to a facsimile of the Declaration and described the massive outpouring of sentiment evident in the city as "purely patriotic and not partisan," even though a few hearty souls had sewn patches lettered "Tilden and Hendricks" on their flags in honor of the Democratic presidential ticket of Samuel Tilden and Thomas Hendricks.[20] Boston newspapers filled multiple pages with news and commentary, describing the lights and parades and fireworks and militia processions in vivid detail. This "patriotic outburst" included a recitation of the Declaration by Brooks Adams and an "able and worthy" speech by Charles Francis Adams in which he lionized the nation's forefathers (and his own) and offered a hopeful vision of a unified future based on a solid nonpartisan foundation.[21]

In Colorado, which had just ratified a state constitution and would soon be admitted as the "Centennial State," eager throngs welcomed the day with gunshots. Fourth of July activities in Dubuque, Iowa, were so vibrant that only the tornado that struck south of town, killing at least two dozen people, could distract the revelers' attention from the gala patriotic mood.

Every newspaper, even those in southern cities, reported on the day's extensive celebration in Philadelphia. Special events were held at the Centennial Exhibition, and crowds filled the streets all around Independence Hall to shoot firecrackers, listen to oratory, and partake of copious "liquid patriotism," as the *Chicago Tribune* put it. As the *New York World* described it, "the nucleus of this great rejoicing is at Independence Hall in Philadelphia, but it is a festival from ocean to ocean."[22] Rejoicing would likely have been even more extensive except for fragmentary news of the unhappy fate of General George Armstrong Custer and his troops at the Little Bighorn River in Montana a few days earlier. First reports of the shocking massacre of Custer and his men were trickling east via telegraph, putting a damper on the afterglow of the Fourth and pushing continued coverage of the centennial celebration from the front pages of most newspapers.

The vision of the past articulated in news columns and editorials was more than just a reflection of the glory of bygone days. Although much of the news material promoted a noncontroversial and idealized past and showed the Revolutionary leaders in the best possible light, the reports also carried a political subtext. The spirit of the American people and the lessons apparent in the magnificent story of the nation's founding and first century of existence demanded unity and reconciliation. "There is something sublime," noted the *New York Tribune*, "in the spectacle of a Republic of more than forty million people, covering the broad breast of a Continent and fronting the two great oceans of the globe." Unity rather than sectionalism, said the *Tribune*, must emerge from any reflection on the meaning of the centennial.[23] Other newspapers were more explicit in their call: "The arrival of the centennial of American independence will be best celebrated by reviving the patriotic memories and renewing the pledges of common brotherhood and citizenship . . . of a century ago," opined the *Baltimore Sun*.[24]

This common brotherhood could only be achieved if the seemingly intractable problems of racial inequality and violence were minimized or forgotten entirely and the reemergence of white rule in most former Confederate states overlooked. The rhetoric of many northern newspapers did just this by claiming that the abolition of slavery had solved the nation's problems. The *Chicago Tribune*, one of Abraham Lincoln's staunchest supporters during the Civil War, editorialized that the North had

> struck the fetters from the negro and abolished human slavery. It secured every man in the United States in his rights to the enjoyment of life, liberty, and the pursuit of happiness. . . . It forever secured every man the right to enjoy the fruits of his labor. It made every man, without regard to race, color, or previous condition of servitude, a citizen having equal rights with every other citizen, which is the foundation core of the Declaration of Independence. It has reconstructed the southern states and brought order out of chaos.[25]

This proclamation would have surprised any black person living in the South in 1876—or in the North, for that matter. In the same vein, the *Boston Globe* reported that, although

> there have been times within the last quarter of a century when the future was clouded with doubt and we could not have entered upon such a celebration without misgivings . . . the clouds have passed with their storms and dark portents, and we hail a brighter day. The causes of danger and discord have been removed.[26]

Other papers minimized the severity of the racial crisis. The *Milwaukee Sentinel* listed a series of problems that the nation would have to solve in its second hundred years but made no mention of race. The *New York Times* more realistically included "race-differences in the southern states" among the current woes but described them as "neither ineradicable, nor increasing, nor relatively threatening. It is, in a sense, local."[27]

Mark Summers has argued that most northern newspapers had been hostile to the idea of Reconstruction all along and had distorted the "larger truths" by focusing only on corruption and mismanagement in the administration of the various programs. Moreover, most northern newspaper reporters and editors shared racist assumptions about blacks that led them to rely on white sources and belittle the black perspective.[28] The overall effect of this unconscious racism was to almost completely marginalize the place of the black American in the Fourth of July celebrations taking place across the nation. No mention was made of festivities in minority neighborhoods. The black public was effectively written out of the parades and other public events, although they participated just like their white neighbors. In both news and opinion columns of the white newspapers, the black population was effectively excluded from the centennial, which was constructed both implicitly and explicitly as a white celebration.

Some journalists publishing in the black community used their newspapers to demand inclusion in the Revolutionary heritage and remind readers that the nation belonged to all citizens, regardless of race. The *Pacific Appeal* revived the memory of Crispus Attucks and other heroes of the Revolution, describing Attucks as the "leader and first martyr" of the cause for independence at the Boston Massacre. "It was through the act of one of our race that its [the Declaration of Independence] promulgation was effected . . . yet, again, it was in the blood of the Massachusetts Negro that the foundation stone of this American Temple of Liberty was laid."[29]

The *Southwestern Advocate* gave an even more expansive view of American history. In its construction, there was no practical difference between the races, only one history, white and black. Most black Americans celebrated the centennial as full citizens, proud of their past and hopeful for a bright future. As the paper noted:

> No heart, we trust, is so dull as to fail to respond with patriotic impulse to the memories of our country's struggles and victories, her progress and prosperity that come crowding about these commemorative times. Certainly no people have greater occasion for rejoicing and thanksgiving than the large number of colored people of the Southern states, and we may certainly expect that for their part especially, there will be the liveliest expressions of appreciation of the great feast day.[30]

The same message comes through in the editorial "Our Centennial," published in the *People's Advocate*. The date was "celebrated . . . with a becoming unanimity of patriotism" and a "self-sacrificing patriotism" that would lead to prosperity and greatness.[31] The July issue of the *Southern Workman* contained a woodcut engraving of a group of children, both black and white, marching through the street with an American flag. Rather than celebrating largely unremembered black heroes, this assertion of memory staked a claim on the heroes common to all. George Washington, for example, was portrayed as "a man dear to every American heart."[32] Black citizens in many cities took part in the public celebrations and parades that were held on the Fourth. In San Francisco they were "treated fairly" by their white counterparts and were "able to mingle freely" among the crowds watching fireworks and listening to music and orations. Blacks were also included in a mile-long procession parading through the streets of New Orleans.[33]

It would be wrong to view these responses to the Fourth of July, even in the face of white hostility and continuing inequality, as naïve. Instead, black newspapers used the different appeals to historical memory to press the demand for greater political and social equality and wider access to educational opportunity. This hope for a better future and demand for the realization of the promise of citizenship, described by Frankie Hutton as "democratic idealism," was a goal that could only be achieved if African Americans were able to attain an equal place in the historical memory of the nation.[34] The common history celebrated on the holiday, wrote one editor, "behooves us to sink as much as possible the partisan feeling and endeavor to grasp with firmness . . . and with clear convictions of political duty, foresight, and sagacity, boldly and fearlessly apply whatever remedy justice and sound policy alike dictate."[35] The *Pacific Appeal*, urging readers to prepare to use the coming centennial Fourth as the means to equality, reminded that even though

> the end of the first century of the nation's existence ends with the great curse of slavery abolished, and the constitution and Declaration of Independence are in union on the principles of freedom, full civil rights to colored citizens is yet grudgingly conceded, but must come to full culmination ere long. When the great bell of Independence Hall tolls the 4th of July, 1876, it is to be hoped that it will be the signal to wipe out all color proscription and discrimination between American citizens in the new era of the second century.[36]

The promise of equality, of course, was not to be attained in the wake of the centennial or at any time during the lifetimes of those readers who read these stirring words. The voice of the black press was no match for the larger historical forces at work that would continue to deny their vision. As the nation basked in the glory of its one-hundredth birthday, sectional divisions, race hatred, and political scandals drew attention away from the more positive accomplishments of the century. Many observers used the occasion to envision a remembered past that brought honor to the nation's heritage and motivated Americans to bridge their divisions. The vigorous celebration of the Fourth of July, in particular, seemed to tell white Americans that their ultimate strength was in unity and that all parts of the country shared the same basic history.

Newspapers in the North mirrored public opinion that was moving firmly toward reconciliation. This message was not lost on southerners. Newspapers in the South, reporting on the Fourth of July festivities in Philadelphia and all across the nation, were struck by the power of the occasion and the celebration of a past that they too could imagine. Writing about the general tone of northern celebrations, the *Atlanta Constitution* struck a positive tone. Reports coming over the telegraph "read like leaves from the history of a score of years ago . . . the evidences of the present are quite enough to prove that there is a new national spirit animating the whole American people which cannot be extinguished" and the reemergence of celebration in the South was "one of the most auspicious signs of the times." Not only that, but the holiday could once again be embraced because

> the best glories of the fourth of July belong to the south . . . we are entitled to all of the honors attaching to the labors of so grand an ancestry as is represented by the southern signatures upon that Declaration of Independence which marks an era in the world's progress. It is ours in full measure and while we reap its present harvest, we will also teach our children . . . and leave them to ever cherish its glories.[37]

This recovered inheritance provided the historical foundation for the New South. Many forces at work in American political and cultural life in the 1870s were drawing the two sections together, but the reconciliatory sentiments manifest in the centennial Fourth of July celebrations undoubtedly played a part in creating the mindset that would result in the end of Reconstruction. In the great debate over the true heritage of the Revolution that took place in 1876, newspapers in the North and South ultimately projected and supported a vision of the past that excluded the bitterness of the Civil War era and sought to move on, leaving the hard questions unanswered. The construction of historical memory, as John Gillis has observed, is marked as much by forgetting as remembering.[38] Forgotten in the spirit of progress and the assertion of a simplified white past were vital questions of racial equality and the fundamental meaning of "life, liberty, and the pursuit of happiness." This sentiment was made clear by the *New York Tribune*, editorializing on the meaning of the first one hundred years. Although the column reminded readers of "aims not yet realized in our national life," the final verdict of this newspaper, and evidently most Americans in the centennial year, was that "we can be made most swiftly whole by forgetting its bitterness."[39] The cost of this forgetting was steep and was paid for first by blacks of the South but ultimately by all Americans.

Notes

1. Eric Foner, *Reconstruction: America's Unfinished Revolution, 1863–1876* (New York: Harper and Row, 1988), 565. See also John D. Bergamini, *The Hundredth Year: The United States in 1876* (New York: Putnam, 1976), and Dee Brown, *The Year of the Century: 1876* (New York: Scribner's, 1976), for background on economic weakness and political corruption in the period.

2. "A Happy New Year," *Detroit Free Press*, 1 January 1876.

3. Mark Wahlgren Summers, *The Press Gang: Newspapers and Politics, 1865–1878* (Chapel Hill: University of North Carolina Press, 1994), 2. On the decline of party-sponsored journalism, see Gerald J. Baldasty, *The Commercialization of the News in the Nineteenth Century* (Madison: University of Wisconsin Press, 1992), 36–58.

4. Nina Silber, *The Romance of Reunion: Northerners and the South, 1865–1900* (Chapel Hill: University of North Carolina Press, 1993), 4–6.

5. David W. Blight, *Race and Reunion: The Civil War in American Memory* (Cambridge: Harvard University Press, 2001), 132–134. See also James M. McPherson, *Abraham Lincoln and the Second American Revolution* (New York: Oxford University Press, 1990), 23–42.

6. Michael Kammen, *Season of Youth: The American Revolution and the Historical Imagination* (Ithaca, N.Y.: Cornell University Press, 1988), 61.

7. Ibid., 15. Kammen would probably prefer that he had written "after 1876" instead of "by 1876" because this would make the statement more accurate.

8. Heather Cox Richardson, *The Death of Reconstruction: Race, Labor, and Politics in the Post-Civil War North, 1865–1901* (Cambridge: Harvard University Press, 2001), 183–184.

9. John Bodnar, *Remaking America: Public Memory, Commemoration, and Patriotism in the Twentieth Century* (Princeton: Princeton University Press, 1992), 15.

10. Barbie Zelizer, "Reading the Past against the Grain: The Shape of Memory Studies," *Critical Studies in Mass Communication* 12, no. 2 (June 1995): 226–227.

11. John R. Gillis, *Commemorations: The Politics of National Identity* (Princeton, N.J.: Princeton University Press, 1994), 8.

12. Carolyn Sue Weddington, "The Image of the American Revolution in the United States, 1815–1860" (PhD dissertation, Louisiana State University, 1972), 95–97.

13. Carl R. Osthaus, *Partisans of the Southern Press: Editorial Spokesmen of the Nineteenth Century* (Lexington: University Press of Kentucky, 1994), 148.

14. "1776–1876," *Atlanta Daily Constitution*, 4 July 1876.

15. On the rise of Memorial Day in the South and its relationship to the "lost cause," see Blight, *Race and Reunion*, 64–76; "Our Southern Dead," *Atlanta Daily Constitution*, 27 April 1876.

16. "1776–1876," *Atlanta Constitution*, 4 July 1876.

17. "The Section with No Fourth of July," *Chicago Times*, 6 July 1876.

18. "The Day We Celebrate," *Charleston News and Courier*, 27 June 1876.

19. "The Work of a Hundred Years Ago," *New York Times*, 3 July 1876.

20. "Centennial Salutations," *Louisville Courier-Journal*, 4 July 1876.

21. "The Centennial Fourth: The Celebration in Boston," *Boston Evening Transcript*, 5 July 1876.

22. "The Century We Celebrate," *New York World*, 4 July 1876.

23. "A Hundred Years," *New York Daily Tribune*, 4 July 1876.

24. "The Centennial Fourth of July," *Baltimore Sun*, 4 July 1876.

25. "The Republican Party's Fourth of July," *Chicago Tribune*, 4 July 1876.

26. "The Centennial Fourth," *Boston Daily Globe*, 3 July 1876.

27. Editorial, *New York Times*, 4 July 1876.

28. Summers, *The Press Gang*, 194–198.

29. *Pacific Appeal*, 15 July 1876.

30. "Our National Birthday," *Southwestern Advocate*, 15 June 1876.

31. *People's Advocate*, 8 July 1876.

32. "The Fourth of July," *Pacific Appeal*, 1 July 1876.

33. "The Fourth of July," *Pacific Appeal*, 8 July 1876; "The Fourth of July in New Orleans," *Southwestern Advocate*, 15 July 1876.

34. Frankie Hutton, "Democratic Idealism in the Black Press," in *Outsiders in Nineteenth Century Press History: Multicultural Perspectives*, ed. Frankie Hutton and Barbara S. Reed (Bowling Green: Bowling Green University Press, 1995), 7.

35. "Our Centennial," *Southern Workman*, 8 July 1876.

36. *Pacific Appeal*, 6 May 1876.

37. "A Recovered Inheritance," *Atlanta Daily Constitution*, 7 July 1876.

38. John R. Gillis, "Memory and Identity: The History of a Relationship," in *Commemorations: The Politics of National Identity*, ed. John R. Gillis, 3–26 (Princeton: Princeton University Press, 1994), 6.

39. "A Hundred Years," *New York Daily Tribune*, 4 July 1876.

God of Wrath, God of Peace

Popular Religion, Popular Press, and the Meaning of the Civil War during Reconstruction

─ Edward J. Blum ─

Historians have often stressed the influence of popular literature and the popular press on the northern mind, particularly during the years immediately following the Civil War. Paul Buck and Nina Silber, for example, have shown convincingly the importance of postbellum journalism and fiction on northern attitudes toward regional reconciliation and reunion.[1] Such scholars, however, have largely ignored one of the most powerful and persuasive voices in secular print—the sermon.[2] In the nineteenth century, some pastors attained widespread popularity and press coverage not because of their theological expertise but because of their ability to spin a good tale.[3] Printed sermons functioned as compelling short stories and religious social commentaries that reflected and shaped northern popular opinion.[4]

This phenomenon is evident at two critical moments in Reconstruction when the northern press paid an inordinate amount of attention to religious voices. The first occurred after Abraham Lincoln's assassination, when confused and sullen northerners turned to their clergy to interpret the seemingly senseless tragedy. The second took place a decade later, when the evangelist Dwight Lyman Moody set the North aflame with the fires of a great religious awakening. In both cases, popular press coverage of the ways in which Protestants remembered the Civil War and narrated its meanings in their sermons helped form northern opinions regarding issues of social reform and attitudes toward the defeated South.[5]

As Civil War rifles fell silent during the spring of 1865, a single-shot, brass derringer pistol in the hands of assassin John Wilkes Booth dashed any hopes for a quick and easy reunion between North and South. Few events in American history have appeared to have such divine touches; the savior of the Union and the savior of humanity martyred on the same day—Good Friday. The *Chicago Tribune* noted the sad similarity: "The most horrid crime ever committed on this globe, since the wicked Jews crucified the Savior of mankind, was perpetrated by rebel emissaries in the assassination of the great, wise, and good Abraham Lincoln."[6]

Because Lincoln perished on Good Friday, northern clerics had their first opportunity to console their parishioners and interpret the tragedy during the subsequent Easter Sunday services. The popular press recognized that most northerners would seek explanations in their houses of worship. "Churches of every persuasion," the *New York Herald* reported, "were thrown open to the faithful to enter, in order to offer up prayers for the departed statesmen . . . and for the orphaned nation. Every pew was crowded, and every member of the numerous congregations seemed actuated by genuine sorrow and unaffected piety."[7] For a week after the president's death, secular papers often afforded several pages more than usual to sermons and religious services.[8]

These printed sermons were remarkably similar in that ministers sought to transform the nonreligious Lincoln from a respected political leader into a transcendent saint. The dead president, reported the *New York Herald*, was "a man simple in habits, child-like in humor, truthful in intercourse, earnest in purpose, meek in spirit, pure in heart, illustrious in deeds, and christian in all his ways."[9] Like the fictional Little Eva of Harriet Beecher Stowe's influential prewar novel, *Uncle Tom's Cabin*, Lincoln represented the deceased embodiment of Christ's Sermon on the Mount. Surveying the national mood a week after the tragedy and the ministerial responses, one pastor commented that the assassination "has been not the destruction, but the immortalizing of the venerated and beloved" president.[10] The clergy did a great deal to create and solidify Lincoln's apotheosis in the northern mind.[11]

Along with lauding Lincoln's virtues, pastors contended—somewhat disingenuously—that the commander-in-chief during the nation's only civil war had in reality been a "prince of peace" who embraced a lenient policy of forgiveness and reconciliation with the rebel states. Preaching on "Our Treatment of the Conquered," the Reverend Dr. Stephen Tyng of St. George's Church employed a biblical typology to explain Lincoln's supposed peaceful inclinations:

The resulting treatment of the captives in the Lord's example—"Thou shall not smite them—set water and bread before them, that they may eat and drink and let them go." The carrying out of this resuscitating plan seemed eminently adapted to the mind and heart of President Lincoln.[12]

The northern clergy divined a cosmic meaning in Lincoln's death that obliterated the impulse to "forgive and forget all the past."[13] The assassination was a sign from above. "One of the great lessons which this war had taught us," articulated a New York pastor, "was to recognize the hand of God" in human affairs.[14] The people of the North "must not be astonished so much at the death of our late President as at the lessons which, through that event are taught the nation."[15]

And what were these sacred instructions? The lessons were very clear: "The blow which struck down our respected President was one aimed at all of us . . . and was not the blow of an individual; no, it was the premeditated blow of Treason and Rebellion, against the lawful legitimate authority of the country."[16] The tragic death demonstrated that God demanded vengeance, not mercy, for the entire South. The *New York Tribune*'s summation of Emma Hardinge's sermon at the Cooper Institute epitomized the arguments of most other clerics:

> [T]he entire war was a work of Providence . . . Abraham Lincoln's special mission being accomplished in the triumph of the national arms, Providence saw that his kind heart would not permit him to hang quite so many traitors as would secure our country against future Rebellions, and so disposed of him through the instrument of the Rebellion itself . . . for the place of a sterner, less merciful successor.[17]

According to such a view, God had removed the peace-loving Lincoln as a divine message to the North that the war was not over. The religious response clearly shaped cultural understandings of the war and Reconstruction. In his ode to Lincoln, "The Martyr," written one year after the event, Herman Melville lamented:

> They have killed him, the Forgiver—
> The Avenger takes his place . . .
> Who in righteousness shall do
>   What the heavens call him to.[18]

These types of arguments, as historian Paul Buck contends, did a great deal to provoke tension between northern and southern whites.[19]

Divine retribution, however, did not constitute the only lesson. Many took the slaying as a holy call to build a new society in the postbellum South. Preaching in place of Henry Ward Beecher at Plymouth Church, the Reverend

N.G. Burton employed much of the same wording from Lincoln's Gettysburg Address to urge his crowd to complete the destruction of the "slavocracy":

> [We] the American people rededicate [ourselves] to the great work in which he [Lincoln] with myriads of our brave brethren have died, and swear that this dying Rebellion shall be laid out stone dead, that the ferocious Slave system . . . shall have no mercy at our hands, but shall die like a malefactor before the eyes of the nation.[20]

Other pastors sought to use Lincoln's death to push for racial equality. The Reverend George Cheever saw fit to "pray that the colored race might live as we lived."[21] In this milieu, some northern Protestants envisioned and set forth to create a reconstructed South that, by the standards of a generation before, might have seemed to border on the utopian. The *New York Independent*, a radical religious newspaper, hoped that southern whites would "learn to respect the rights of their fellow men, without regard to color." The freedmen could be "redeemed from ignorance and other evils fastened on them by slavery." These hopes for a born-again South were supported by huge donations to various freedmen's aid societies, most notably the Freedmen's Bureau and the American Missionary Society.[22]

All in all, the ways in which these preachers narrated Lincoln's life and interpreted his assassination suggest that the Reconstruction of the South began in the minds of northern ministers and their followers with a sacred grant not merely to bring vengeance on the old South but also to build a new society below the Mason-Dixon line.[23] The northern clergy thus interpreted Lincoln's death not as a sign that they should follow his presumed wishes but as a holy call to arms.

The pastoral response may help to explain the intense opposition toward Lincoln's successor, Andrew Johnson, and his lenient Reconstruction policies. Eric McKitrick finds anti-Johnson passions stemming from a "solidarity and moral certainty" committed to punishing the South and forcibly instituting reform, but he is unable to locate the genesis of such moral certainty. In many ways, Johnson's pacific policies toward southern whites and his opposition to radical Republicanism challenged the religious environment, and he lost. Droves of northerners responded by anathematizing the president for his moderate course of action. The clerical arguments and the evangelical temper of northern Republicans help to explain why many northerners leveled the epithet of "Judas Iscariot" at Johnson. In their view, Johnson had transgressed not merely against the Republic but also against the wishes of God.[24]

After the Lincoln assassination, the secular press paid little attention to religious voices for nearly a decade.[25] When it did, it revealed northern Protestant views strongly at odds with the sermons of 1865. On August 15, 1875,

Dwight Moody returned home from a triumphant revival tour of Great Britain to the cheers of over five thousand New Yorkers. Over the next two years, Moody would ascend to the height of American popularity, "set[ting]the people of their cities religious crazy," as poet Walt Whitman wrote.[26] Moody preached to literally millions of northerners in Brooklyn, Philadelphia, New York, Chicago, and Boston. Observing the national response, the *Cleveland Leader* insisted, "the United States is now in the midst of the throes of the third of [its] great Religious Awakening[s]."[27]

During the revivals, the press hardly missed a chance to highlight Moody's accomplishments. The *New York Times, New York Herald, Chicago Tribune, Boston Evening Transcript, Boston Daily Globe*, and a host of other papers carried extensive coverage of the evangelist's work; both *Harper's Weekly* and *Leslie's Illustrated* saw fit to make Moody a cover star. Along with newspaper coverage and illustrations, a profusion of Moody biographies flooded the North. Between 1875 and 1877, nearly thirty full-length biographical sketches found their way into print, many in excess of four hundred pages.[28] In short, Moody and his revivals were ubiquitous.

Moody and the press had a mutually beneficial relationship. Secular periodicals did a great deal to publicize the revivals and disseminate the evangelist's teachings. For his part, Moody quickly recognized the importance of good press coverage and constructed special seating areas for reporters near his podium, complete with candles and writing desks included. "It is amazing to note how the subject of religion was handled by the secular press, whose readers numbered millions," one follower of Moody proclaimed.[29] Many who could not attend the revivals avidly followed them through newspaper reports. One Bostonian, although thoroughly displeased with Moody, indicated the importance of newspaper coverage noting that he had "read the reports of your meetings . . . quite carefully."[30] The press, too, found Moody's tour a blessing, as the popularity of the revivalist helped many papers weather the stormy economy of the 1870s. For example, the *Boston Daily Globe* tripled its readership by covering the revivals and thus thwarted financial ruin.[31]

Religious historians have tended to portray the revivals as part of a Protestant reaction to changes in industrial America, and Reconstruction scholars have thoroughly ignored the revival. All have failed to recognize that Moody's meetings played a crucial role in ending Reconstruction in the northern mind.[32] In many ways, this new Great Awakening provided a religious impetus to regional reconciliation and authorized the abandonment of the southern freedmen. In stark contrast to the clerics of 1865, Moody found little meaning in political affairs. "If the President should die to-night," he preached to a Philadelphia audience, "that would make an outcry here. But perhaps even so great an event would not be mentioned in heaven at all."[33] Extending this logic, the revivalist railed against religious involvement in secular affairs, especially politics and reform. Peace and happiness could not be found in "business, in honor, in pleasure, [or] in politics," he maintained. "Don't flatter yourselves that the world is going to get any better," Moody instructed. "The world is on the rocks."[34]

Along with championing a retreat from secular affairs, Moody preached a theology centered on forgiveness and reconciliation. "Let me tell everyone in this hall tonight that I bring good news . . . it is the Gospel of Reconciliation," he thundered. Generally, Moody directed his message of reunion toward warring denominations, but he also implicated regional palliation as well. "I think if I know my own heart," he proudly announced to a crowd of over ten thousand in New York, "I love the South as well as I do the North." The most popular preacher in all America, in short, both sanctified regional reconciliation and discouraged interest in reform.[35]

Moody's popularity, however, did not hinge on his theology. E.L. Godkin's *Nation* magazine noted that "little dogmatic theology or biblical exegesis" appeared in his sermons.[36] Although no scholar, Moody was the nation's best teller of tales. *Scribner's Monthly* commented that he exercised a "power over the popular mind" through his stories that few other public figures enjoyed.[37] The *Boston Sunday Times* put it this way: "On an average, [Moody] relates four anecdotes in every address, and three addresses per day—that's about six dozen first-class stories a week."[38] Walt Whitman best described the evangelist as a "magnet of religion, inventor of legends miraculous and mythical, the boss story-teller of this year 101 of the States."[39]

Most attendees were enthralled by Moody's stories, especially those of the Civil War.[40] He preached a sentimentalized and romanticized version of the struggle that diminished differences between the warring regions:

> When I was in Nashville during our late war I was closing the noon prayer meeting one day and a great strong man come up to me, trembling from head to foot. He took a letter out of his pocket and wanted to have me read it. It was from his sister. The sister stated in that letter that every night as the sun went down she went down on her knees to pray for him. The sister was six hundred miles away, and said the soldier, "I never thought about my soul until last night. I have stood before the cannon's mouth and it never made me tremble, but, Sir, I haven't slept a wink since I got that letter."[41]

In most of his Civil War stories, Moody obfuscated the notion that the conflict had actually been a battle between the regions. Instead, he honored the struggle in which "we had to give up our young men, both North and

South, to death." Furthermore, Moody regularly prefaced these stories with conciliatory remarks, noting, "I hope if there are any Southern people here they will not think, in this allusion, I am trying to wound their feelings."[42] The evangelist's biographers and newspaper publishers played up these themes of regional reconciliation when recounting anecdotes of Moody's own Civil War and Reconstruction experiences. Most extolled him for his ministry to imprisoned Confederates and praised him for treating them "as brethren of Christ." One account even applauded the evangelist for deceiving Union officials so that he could preach to captured Confederates.[43] One of Moody's 1876 biographers put it best when he commented that the evangelist "seemed to hold the Union men by one hand and the ex-Confederates by the other, thus constituting himself a tie of Christian brotherhood between them."[44]

While downplaying regional differences, Moody lauded the North in his Civil War stories. Preaching in New York, he favorably recalled the northern response to the war, observing, "All Abraham Lincoln had to do, was to call for men, and how speedily they came. When he called for 600,000 men how quick they sprang up all over the nation. Are not souls worth more than this republic?" The *New York Tribune* specifically noted that as Moody narrated the northern response, "the attention of the audience was very close."[45] This may have been the history New Yorkers wanted to believe, but it was anything but accurate. After Lincoln called for men, many "sprang up" not to defend the Union but to assault African Americans living in their midst. Moody conveniently effaced the 1863 New York Draft Riot and a host of other such embarrassing episodes. Perhaps due to tales like this, avid Union patriot Walt Whitman raged: "I do not believe in him. Nor his God . . . nor his stories which sound like lies."[46]

Between 1875 and 1877, a revival of national pomp, reconciliation, and reunion squared well with the domestic mood, as most northerners celebrated America's centennial. *Scribner's Monthly* hoped that the Spirit of '76 was one that would "heal all the old wounds, reconcile all the old differences."[47] In this milieu, as neoabolitionist historian Eric Foner points out dyspeptically, white northerners cheered ex-Confederate soldiers parading in Boston and New York.[48] Moody's revivals also paraded some noteworthy southerners. One telling example occurred while the evangelist preached in Philadelphia on New Year's Eve, 1875. During the eleven o'clock worship service, Moody invited the Reverend Dr. William Plumer of South Carolina to share the podium with him. The evangelist then asked the "venerable doctor" several theological questions, using him as an exemplar of the Christian faith. As the service neared midnight, Moody and Plumer closed the meeting together, wishing all a "Happy New Year."[49]

An examination of Plumer's career reveals that his participation at the revival was a particularly significant act of regional reconciliation. Plumer held southern pastorates for most of his career and was a conservative old-school Presbyterian leader throughout the denominational schism of the 1830s. During that dispute, Plumer not only defended slavery both biblically and morally but also advocated political disunion.[50] In the 1860s, when the nation divided, Plumer found himself on the wrong side of both the Mason-Dixon line and the domestic temper. After he refused to publicly pray for the Union flag, members of his Pennsylvania congregation accused him of perfidy and dismissed him.[51] When Plumer later preached at a revival in New England, many locals avoided the meeting specifically because of his dubious allegiance.[52] In the 1870s, he accepted a position in South Carolina, and by 1885, Virginia's Washington and Lee University was pronouncing Plumer a southern hero alongside Robert E. Lee and Stonewall Jackson.[53]

Moody's position as a regional unifier stood out during a trip he took between his New York and Chicago revivals in 1876. Few northerners could have garnered the acceptance and popularity that Moody did in the 1870s when thousands of southerners flocked to his meetings. Once again, Moody's message consisted of denunciations of reform and entreaties for reunion. On Decoration Day, a new holiday honoring dead Confederate soldiers, Moody prayed for "broken-hearted ones, both North and South . . . who were mourning for friends lost in the late war." Later, the evangelist commented that he "wished especially to say that he had no sympathy at all with men in any section of the country who were continually seeking to stir up strife and embitter the people against each other." Writing in 1876, one biographer assured northerners and southerners that the evangelist had absolutely no "interest in Northern radicals."[54]

Moody's emphasis on social reunion, similar to the growing desire of many whites for political reconciliation, had disastrous consequences for African Americans. Both the *Atlanta Constitution* and the *New York Times* reported that some local whites became so enraged at the sight of African Americans mingling with other whites at a revival in Augusta, Georgia, that they constructed a dividing fence to segregate the races. Moody seemed surprised and expressed faint disapproval over the separation to one of the local pastors. The minister promptly retorted, "I am proud of my rebellious feelings, and will rebel until the day I die." Quickly and quietly, the matter was dropped; the meetings continued segregated.[55] Moody's desire for unity trumped any impulse for equality; he thus acquiesced to the demands of southern whites.

The revivals' reconciliatory nature may help to explain why Reconstruction, which had begun with a sacred blessing, now quietly faded into history. Along with economic depression, the loss of radical leadership, and the demoralizing effects of political scandal, popular Protestantism and the desire for Christian forgiveness also lent a hand to the waning of northern support for Radical Reconstruction.

In the 1880s, regional and racial issues once again flared up during Moody's revivals. Before he held meetings in Richmond, Virginia, some newspapers implied that during the war Moody had preached against the South, especially Generals Lee and Jackson. The evangelist quickly defended himself to the public, telling a reporter from the *Washington Post* that during the national strife, "I entertained the highest respect for Gens. Lee and Jackson. They lived and died Christian gentlemen, and were friends of mine."[56] Moody was further vindicated when Mrs. Stonewall Jackson made several highly publicized visits to the revival.

In addition to associating himself with the heroes and heroines of the Lost Cause, Moody continued to permit segregated revivals. This led to a thorough denunciation by many in the African American community. A black delegate to the African Methodist Episcopal Church's Annual Conference blasted the evangelist, fulminating that "His conduct toward the Negroes during his Southern tour has been shameless, and I would not have him preach in a barroom, let alone a church. In Charleston he refused to give the Negro churches representation at his evangelical meetings and placed caste above Christianity."[57] Frederick Douglass expressed the combination of dejection and fury felt by many African Americans toward the evangelist and his followers:

> Infidel though Mr. Ingersoll may be called, he never turned his back upon his colored brothers, as did the evangelical Christians of this city on the occasion of the late visit of Mr. Moody. Of all the forms of negro hate in this world, save me from that one which clothes itself with the name of the loving Jesus. . . . The negro can go into the circus, the theatre, and can be admitted to the lectures of Mr. Ingersoll, but he cannot go into an evangelical Christian meeting.[58]

Between Lincoln's assassination and Moody's revivals, a great reversal had taken place in the northern mind, and popular religion, as disseminated through the secular press, both reflected and shaped that transformation. After Lincoln's death, the northern clergy created a religious impetus for a vengeful Reconstruction and a social revolution in the South. With Moody, a gospel of reconciliation replaced biblical interpretations of divine vengeance and reform. Moody's revivals constructed a religious bulwark that authorized southern and northern reunion at the expense of social and racial change. In the span of only a decade, Protestant clergy and their narration of the Civil War helped transform their supposedly immutable deity from a God of wrath to a God of peace.

NOTES

Part of this chapter was previously published in Edward J. Blum's book *Reforging the White Republic: Race, Religion, and American Nationalism, 1865–1898* (Baton Rouge: Louisiana State University Press, 2005).

1. See Paul Buck, *The Road to Reunion, 1865–1900* (Boston and Toronto: Little, Brown and Company, 1937); Nina Silber, *The Romance of Reunion: Northerners and the South, 1865–1900* (Chapel Hill & London: University of North Carolina Press, 1993). For more on religion during the Civil War and Reconstruction, see Edward J. Blum, *Reforging the White Republic: Race, Religion, and American Nationalism, 1865–1898* (Baton Rouge: Louisiana State University Press, 2005).

2. Several examples of this phenomenon include: Eric Foner, *Reconstruction: America's Unfinished Revolution, 1863–1877* (New York: Harper & Row, 1993); James M. McPherson, *Ordeal by Fire: The Civil War and Reconstruction* (New York: McGraw-Hill, 1992); Kenneth M. Stampp, *The Era of Reconstruction, 1865–1877* (New York: Alfred A. Knopf, 1965).

3. For a discussion of the rise of pulpit storytelling, see David S. Reynolds, *American Quarterly* 35, no. 5 (Winter 1980): 479–498.

4. We should remember that Harriet Beecher Stowe's momentous work, *Uncle Tom's Cabin*, was really a novel–sermon hybrid, one that, she believed, bore the inspiration of God. Writing in 1888, Boston pastor Joseph Cook contended that in essence Stowe had done little more than "preach in print." See Frances E. Willard, *Women in the Pulpit* (Boston: D. Lothrop Company, 1888), 12.

5. For an account of the northern clergy during the Civil War and the first years of Reconstruction, see James Moorhead, *American Apocalypse: Yankee Protestants and the Civil War, 1860–1869* (New Haven and London: Yale University Press, 1978). For a more recent account of religion and Reconstruction, see Daniel W. Stowell, *Rebuilding Zion: The Religious Reconstruction of the South, 1863–1877* (New York and Oxford: Oxford University Press, 1998).

6. *Chicago Tribune*, 15 April 1865. For another example of the connection between Christ's and Lincoln's death see *New York Herald*, 17 April 1865.

7. *New York Herald*, 20 April 1865.

8. For the purposes of this paper, I have used primarily sermons from New York papers, especially the *Herald* and the *Tribune*. Other sermons of the same flavor could be found all over the nation. See Moorhead, 178–182.

9. *New York Herald*, 18 April 1865.

10. *New York Herald*, 21 April 1865.

11. For more on Lincoln in the northern mind, see Merrill D. Peterson, *Lincoln in American Memory* (New York: Oxford University Press, 1994). As Carl Sandburg maintained, Lincoln became a mirror by which northerners understood themselves and their institutions.

12. *New York Herald*, 21 April 1865.

13. *New York Herald*, 17 April 1865.

14. Ibid.

15. *New York Herald*, 20 April 1865.

16. *New York Tribune*, 18 April 1865; for another example, see *New York Tribune*, 17 April 1865.
17. Ibid.
18. Herman Melville, "The Martyr," from *Battle-Pieces and Aspects of the War* (New York: Harper & Brothers, 1866).
19. Buck, 58–66.
20. *New York Tribune*, 17 April 1865.
21. *New York Herald*, 17 April 1865.
22. David M. Remies, *White Protestantism and the Negro* (New York: Oxford University Press, 1965), 761; Richard B. Drake, "Freedmen's Aid Societies and Sectional Compromise," *Journal of Southern History* 20, no. 2 (May 1963), 175–186.
23. For a similar discussion, see Moorhead, 175–185; David B. Chesebrough, *"No Sorrow Like Our Sorrow": Northern Protestant Ministers and the Assassination of Lincoln* (Kent, Ohio: Kent State University Press, 1994); though Moorhead and Chesebrough find many of the same phenomena, they primarily examine religious periodicals and printed sermons; neither recognizes the importance of how secular periodicals portrayed these sermons, nor do they connect the ministerial response to larger cultural trends.
24. Eric McKitrick, *Andrew Johnson and Reconstruction* (New York: Oxford University Press, 1960), 440–445.
25. One could argue that the press paid a great deal of attention to the Reverend Henry Ward Beecher during his supposed scandalous relationship with Mrs. Theodore Tilton. In this case, however, the press was not paying attention to religious interpretations of society but was interested in religious scandal and corruption.
26. I.A.M. Cumming (pseudonym), *Tabernacle Sketches* (Boston: The Times Publishing Company, 1877), 33–34.
27. Dwight Lyman Moody, *The Great Redemption; or, Gospel Light, under the Labors of Moody and Sankey* (Cleveland: C.C. Wick & Co., 1880), 9. For the most recent biography of Moody, see Lyle Dorsett, *A Passion for Souls: The Life of D.L. Moody* (Chicago: Moody Press, 1997); for the best scholarly appraisal, see James F. Findlay Jr. *Dwight L. Moody: American Evangelist, 1837–1899* (Chicago & London: University of Chicago Press, 1969).
28. See Wilbur M. Smith, *An Annotated Bibliography of D.L. Moody* (Chicago: Moody Press, 1948).
29. Robert Boyd, *The Wonderful Career of Moody and Sankey in Great Britain and America Together with the Trials and Triumphs of Faith* (New York: Henry S. Goodspeed & Company, 1875), 606.
30. "The Coming Revival." *Boston Daily Globe*, 22 January 1877. For another example of this, see "Should Honest Criticism Be Prohibited?" *Boston Daily Globe*, 2 February 1877.
31. See Bruce Evensen, "It Is a Marvel to Many People: Dwight L. Moody, Mass Media, and the New England Revival of 1877," *New England Quarterly* 72, no. 2 (June 1999): 251–274.
32. William G. McLoughlin, *Modern Revivalism: Charles Grandison Finney to Billy Graham* (New York: The Ronald Press Company, 1959), 167; Sidney Ahlstrom,

A Religious History of the American People (New Haven and London: Yale University Press), 743–746; Sidney E. Mead, *The Lively Experiment: The Shaping of Christianity in America* (New York: Harper & Row Publishers, 1963), 134–189; Martin Marty, *Righteous Empire: The Protestant Experience in America* (New York: Dial Press, 1970); Bernard Weisberger, *They Gathered at the River: The Story of the Great Revivalists and Their Impact upon Religion in America* (Boston: Little, Brown and Company, 1959).

33. Boyd, 581.
34. For the above quotes and similar arguments, see the *Boston Daily Globe*, 30 April 1877; Dwight Moody, *New Sermons, Addresses, and Prayers* (Chicago: J.W. Goodspeed, Publisher, 1877), 504, 359; Dwight Moody, *Glad Tidings, Compromising Sermons and Prayer-Meeting Talks, Delivered at the N.Y. Hippodrome* (New York: E.B. Treat, 1876), 318. Books with Moody as the author are merely collections of Moody's sermons as printed by the local press during the revival campaigns.
35. Moody, *New Sermons*, 370 and 40; Moody, *Glad Tidings*, 335.
36. *New York Nation*, 9 March 1876.
37. "Topics of the Time," *Scribner's Monthly*, June 1875, 241–243.
38. Cumming, 12.
39. Cumming, 33–34.
40. Ibid.
41. Moody, *Glad Tidings*, 27; Moody, *New Sermons*, 36.
42. Ibid., 485 and 321.
43. For a few examples of this, see E.J. Goodspeed, *A Full History of the Wonderful Career of Moody and Sankey in Great Britain and America* (St. Louis and Chicago: N.D. Thompson & Co., Publishing, 1876), 29; Dwight Lyman Moody and Ira David Sankey, *Moody and Sankey in Hartford* (Hartford, Conn.: W.H. Goodrich, 1878), x–xi; W.H. Daniels, *D.L. Moody and His Work* (Hartford: American Publishing Company, 1876), 99–100.
44. Daniels, 172.
45. Moody, *Glad Tidings*, 38; *New York Tribune*, 10 February 1876.
46. Quoted in Cumming, 34.
47. See Buck, 121 and 134; Foner, 525.
48. Eric Foner, *Reconstruction: America's Unfinished Revolution, 1863–1877* (New York: Harper & Row, Publishers, 1988), 525.
49. Goodspeed, 351–357.
50. See C.C. Goen, *Broken Churches, Broken Nation: Denominational Schisms and the Coming of the Civil War* (Macon, Georgia: Mercer University Press, 1988), 74.
51. Board of Trustees to W.S. Plumer, 12 November 1861; for Plumer's response, see W.S. Plumer, "My Fidelity to the Government." William S. Plumer Collection, Princeton Theological Seminary Special Collections.
52. Henry Glarly to W.S. Plumer, 31 January 1865. William S. Plumer Collection, Princeton Theological Seminary Special Collections.
53. Margaret J. Preston, *Centennial Poem for Washington and Lee University* (New York & London: G.P. Putnam's Sons, 1885), 11.
54. Goodspeed, 615–619.

55. *Atlanta Constitution*, 4 May 1876; *New York Times*, 10 May 1876. I have not found any indication of racism in Moody's writings or personal letters. Though he would continue to segregate meetings in the 1880s, he had a change of heart in the 1890s. During one of his last revival meetings, five years before his death, Moody became so upset with physical barriers separating the races that he physically thrust his 270-pound frame against the wooden railings. Though he could not pull them down with brute force, they were removed the following day. See "Race Prejudice—Is It Waning?" *American Missionary*, July 1895, 220–221; *Atlanta Constitution*, 4 May 1876; *New York Times*, 10 May 1876.

56. *Washington Post*, 16 January 1885; *Washington Post*, 6 January 1885.

57. *Louisville Courier-Journal*, 13 February 1888; *New York Times*, 11 June 1887; Findlay, 280.

58. *American Missionary*, June 1885, 164.

"Draw Him Up, Boys"

A Historical Review of Lynching Coverage in Select Virginia Newspapers, 1880–1900

— James E. Hall —

When a white man named Captain Yancey walked into a bar in Keysville, Virginia, in 1890, he saw two black men playing cards and quarrelling over five cents. Yancey told them that five cents was too small an amount to argue over, and he offered the wronged man a nickel. One of the card players, Thaddeus Fowlkes, became upset and rushed at Yancey. "I don't allow no damn white man to interfere with me," he said, plunging a knife into Yancey's belly and spilling his blood onto the barroom floor. Yancey died the next day, and Fowlkes was arrested and charged with murder. Residents probably would have lynched him then, but a judge ordered the sheriff to take him to Danville, 60 miles away. Later, when the sheriff brought Fowlkes back to town for the trial, a mob stopped them on the road from the train station. The mob dragged Fowlkes to a pine tree 150 yards from the road, and when the leader cried, "Draw him up, boys," they hanged him.

The *Richmond Dispatch,* the regional daily, reported on the lynching the next day, noting that the only cause for regret in Keysville was that with Fowlkes dead, the prosecuting attorney would not be collecting his fee. "The colored people concurred in the action of the lynchers," the paper added.[1] The coverage of Fowlkes's death by what was then the largest-circulation newspaper in the state illustrates the attitude toward lynching of many of Virginia's white-owned newspapers of the late 19th century. These newspapers excused lynching and, at times, even encouraged it. They voiced contempt for blacks and support for their harsh treatment.

During the "killing years" from 1880 to 1900, when more blacks were lynched in the United States than at any other time, Virginia's mainstream white newspapers joined in the mania. White-owned newspapers, sometimes without intending it, articulated the harsh reality of race relations in late 19th-century Virginia. During this period, blacks were subjected to systematic statewide campaigns of segregation, discrimination, and disenfranchisement. The mainstream publications helped uphold this treatment and mold public opinion; their support of lynching helped perpetuate the practice.

Lynching in the late 19th century was but the latest chapter in the troubled relationship between whites and blacks in Virginia. The first cargo of slaves in America landed in Virginia in 1619, bringing 20 Africans to Jamestown. Soon after, Virginia planters began earnestly to import blacks as slaves. On the eve of the American Revolution, 40 percent of all Virginians were slaves.[2] After the Revolution, Virginia and its neighbor Maryland were home to more than half the nation's slaves.[3] The growth of the slave population in Virginia gave rise to a body of laws meant to ensure white dominance. In this era with its slave codes can be seen a preview of the lynching era. In both periods, whites and blacks lived together in uneasy peace, and whites demonstrated a willingness to use violence to maintain control. "Before the end of the colonial period, Virginia, like her neighbors, had become an armed camp in which masters figuratively kept their guns cocked and trained on the slaves in order to keep them docile and tractable," says historian John Hope Franklin.[4]

This harsh relationship continued until the 1860s, when the conclusion of the Civil War and the emancipation of the Southern slaves brought a better era for blacks. During the ensuing period of Reconstruction, blacks enjoyed unprecedented opportunities, both politically and socially. In Virginia, blacks won 27 of the 181 seats in the first postwar legislature. Blacks were elected to office in Norfolk, Lynchburg, Danville, Alexandria, Hampton, and Richmond. In Petersburg in 1883, three blacks were elected to the city council, and blacks also served on that city's school board and police force.[5] Race relations were often better in Virginia than in other parts of the South, mainly because of the presence of a large number of free blacks and the absence of the great cotton plantations, which, of necessity, were run by overseers rather than owners.[6]

Race relations in Virginia deteriorated between 1870 and 1900. This is not to imply that relations were ever good, but such as they were, they got worse.[7] This deterioration was apparent in Danville in 1883, when a tense racial climate finally erupted in a melee, and five blacks were shot and killed after a black man bumped into a white man on the sidewalk. "The immediate cause: Negro insolence," concluded the *Richmond Dispatch*.[8] Over the years, blacks were excluded from or segregated in hotels, restaurants, bars, theaters, and hospitals. State law in 1879 prohibited mixed marriages. In 1900 it required separate seating on the railroads, and in 1906 on the streetcars. Legislation in 1894 began to exclude blacks from the electoral process, and a change in the state constitution in 1902 completed the task. With these changes, Virginia blacks lost most of what they had gained since the Civil War except their legal freedom and the right to a minimal public education.

It was against this backdrop that whites began to lynch blacks in great numbers in Virginia and the South. Lynching occurred in all parts of the United States during its early history, but no time or place matched the ferocity of the South in the late 19th century. Stewart E. Tolnay and E.M. Beck, in their study *A Festival of Violence,* list 1,193 black lynch victims in 10 southern states from 1882 to 1900.[9] Lynchings occurred, on average, almost three times a week. Estimates vary on exactly how many people were lynched in Virginia. The National Association for the Advancement of Colored People, one of the first to document lynching deaths, put the number of black deaths in Virginia from 1889 to 1900 at 43.[10] Later historians, such as W. Fitzhugh Brundage, using the NAACP's list and newspaper archives, published what they believed were more accurate numbers. Brundage counted 49 black lynch deaths in Virginia for 1880–1900, or about one every six months.[11]

Only a third of Virginia's 100 counties experienced a lynching, and no county experienced more than two incidents in the years 1880 to 1900. When a lynching did occur, the event was newsworthy. During this period, most cities in Virginia had competing dailies, and smaller papers could be found in all the county seats. It is impossible to know if the lynch accounts in these papers are accurate. Ida B. Wells, a newspaper editor and antilynch crusader, labeled white press reports on lynching "unreliable and doctored."[12] She also pointed out that newspaper editors might have been a part of the mob or friends of those who were. "News agencies in the South often deliberately suppress these reports and in nearly all cases are vague as to names, places, and details," W.E.B. Du Bois said.[13] It is clear, however, that reporters did not spare their readers. Thomas D. Clark noted in his study of rural southern papers that reading stories about lynchings was like "walking through a chamber of horrors." The papers reported lynchings in full, including the lurid details.[14]

These gruesome details can be found in the stories in Virginia papers, which recounted cries for mercy from lynch victims and how mob members swung from victims' legs to hasten strangulation. A front-page story in the

Richmond Times told how William Shorter tried to save himself while being lynched outside Winchester in 1893: "He grasped with his hands the rope above his head. The man on the limb kicked them loose, saying 'God d—n you, take your hands down.' Then a regular fusillade of shots were aimed at the swinging form, only a few taking effect. He died instantly."[15]

One of the most gruesome accounts followed the lynching of Thomas Smith, who was accused of assault in Roanoke in 1893. After the lynching, the mob cut down Smith's body, loaded it on a coal cart and headed for the river. The *Richmond Times* reported:

> Arriving at the river near the palatial estate of R.H. Woodrum a halt was called. Immediately plank fences were torn down to built a funeral pyre. Planks were piled up, there covered with dry cedar boughs, and on the whole several gallons of kerosene were poured. Preparations were completed and the body was dragged to the pile and laid upon it. A lighted match was applied, and the body was soon enveloped in flames. When the fire burned low, more plank was thrown on and around it. When a member of the body became separated from the rest, it was pushed back with a pole. This performance was kept up until all that remained of Thomas Smith was a small pile of ashes.[16]

Lynch stories often followed a familiar pattern, beginning with a summary lead that flashed the news quickly before the reader, followed by a transition sentence and a chronological retelling of the lynch death. The *Richmond Dispatch* story of February 6, 1894, is an example.[17] It begins with the headlines: "Hanged to a Horse-Rack. Judge Lynch's Quiet Performance at King William Courthouse." The story, by an unnamed reporter, was filed from King William on February 5:

> About 2 o'clock yesterday morning a party of armed men entered the jail at this place, took therefrom Peter Bland, a negro under sentence of fourteen years in the penitentiary for beating Mr. S.G. Littlepage nearly to death, shot him, and hung him to a horse-rack in the rear of the clerk's office. The lynchers were well organized, and the affair was conducted with the utmost secrecy and deliberation.[18]

The story quotes the jailer as saying that a man disguised as a policeman from the nearby town of West Point knocked at the jail door and told him that he had a prisoner. When the jailer opened the door, a gang of about 15 men armed with pistols and double-barrel shotguns took the keys from him. They removed Bland from the jail and took him into the adjacent yard, where they shot him, hanged him, and "fired fourteen buckshot into his body."

Many of the stories, especially the eyewitness ones, were written in a spare, staccato style. It was as if the reporter understood that the details themselves, told in simple sentences with few adjectives and adverbs, were powerful enough to engage the reader. When William Lavender was lynched in Roanoke in 1892, a reporter for the Roanoke *Times* described the incident this way:

> The party hurried the negro to the bank of the river near the ore washer and just within the city limits on the north bank of the river. A long rope was found at the washer, a hangman's noose quickly tied and the noose thrown over the quaking wretch's neck. "Now say your prayers." Down on his knees in the light snow went Lavender. His prayer was an almost incoherent jumble of denial. He was given a quick taste of the tightened rope. It quickened his memory. He acknowledged that he was the man Alice Perry had identified. Still he denied touching her. Again the rope was tightened and he went three feet from the ground. When he came down again, he owned up. It was still a rambling confession, but he admitted being drunk and knocking the girl down. "Are you satisfied?" the party was asked. "Yes," came the answer from deep throats. "It is enough. Time!" The execution took place at 1:30 a.m.[19]

It is possible that these accounts are exaggerated, created by their authors for dramatic effect. Yet sometimes reporters from competing papers were at the scene of a lynching, and their stories, published on the same day, generally agree on the important details. In addition to this attention to detail, lynch stories shared a common language that revealed much about the newspapers themselves and the communities they served. First, the stories assumed that the black lynch victim was guilty. For example, after John C. Wilson was lynched in 1886, The *Richmond Dispatch* did not describe Wilson as an "alleged" or "accused" thief. Instead, it reported that he "stole two mules" from a farmer in Patrick County, then fled to North Carolina. A lynch mob seized him from the sheriff on the return to Patrick.[20]

As for mob members, reporters never identified them or appeared to make any attempt to learn their identities. In fact, their accounts often tried to justify the lynchings by pointing out the seriousness of the alleged crimes of the person lynched. When John Henry James was lynched for an alleged assault on Miss Julia Hotopp in Albemarle County in 1898, the *Richmond Times* reporter interviewed the local Commonwealth's attorney:

> He said it was one of the most atrocious cases of assault ever committed, the circumstances being of such a character and so revolting that he was unwilling to state them in detail. They were, he said, of a character to stir any community to its deepest depths.[21]

Sometimes the reporters tried to make heroes of the executioners, as in an 1893 report in the *Roanoke Times* on a lynching in Tazewell County that claimed more victims than any other in state history:

This makes five negroes who have been lynched, and a more orderly and brave set of men hardly ever got together. No disturbance of any kind occurred, and a pistol shot was not heard. They worked quietly and with determination, giving each of the negroes time to confess.[22]

Occasionally a measure of doubt seeped into newspaper stories. John Forbes denied to the last that he raped Mrs. John Moran at Crewe in 1889, and the *Richmond Times*'s story about the incident carried the headline: "A Negro Lynched. Some Doubts as to Whether He Was the Right Man."[23] When the *Richmond Dispatch* reported on the lynching of Isaac Brandon in Providence Forge in 1892, it quoted Brandon's son, who was with him in the cell when the mob arrived:

> The boy says that the men entered the jail with pistols in hand and told Brandon to cross his hands behind him. He asked them if they were going to hang him. They told him they were. He said, Well you are going to hang an innocent man. Whether he confessed afterwards, of course, is not known. His body was found hanging the next morning.[24]

But doubt was the exception. Many accounts conveyed a sense of certainty, a belief in the rightness of the deed. These stories reported that the white victim had positively identified the attacker and that the accused had confessed to his crime. The stories also said that local blacks saw the punishment as just and frequently refused to claim the lynch victim's body. As the *Richmond Times* reported in 1893 after the lynching of Abner Anthony in Hot Springs, "There was no uncertainty about the crime, none about the identity of the man, and none about the completeness of the lynching."[25]

In this and other ways, the news stories in white papers were a measure of the community support that distinguishes lynching from other murders. By publishing detailed accounts of the incidents, including the method of seizure, place of death, behavior of the mob, and the inevitable conclusion of the coroner's jury, newspapers revealed an official indifference toward lynching and its acceptance as a brutal form of popular justice. Most jailers, for example, surrendered their prisoners without a struggle, and newspaper stories defended them, noting that it was the only sensible thing to do. When 60 masked men showed up at the Petersburg jail in 1880 and demanded the keys to James Black's cell, the jailer complied.

Another form of official indifference can be seen in the work of the coroner's jury. Summoned to the scene after a lynch death, these groups of citizen volunteers were charged with determining the cause and manner of death. Reporters frequently used the jury's official verdict to end their stories, as the *Wytheville Dispatch* did in 1885:

The jury reviewed the body and returned the following verdict: "That on the night of the 4th of February, 1885, Alvy Jackson was forcibly taken from the jail of this county by persons unknown to the jailer and by these persons tied to a fence post with a rope and shot, from which wounds he died.[26]

Published accounts also showed how lynchers wore masks and worked at night. But they chose public locations for their executions. Lynchings did not occur in remote, wooded sites. Instead, they were done beside busy roads, on street corners, and as in Bland's case, in the symbolic heart of the community, at the courthouse. In 1893 outside Winchester, a mob seized William Shorter from the sheriff on a crowded train and lynched him beside the track in view of all the passengers. In this and other cases, the lynchers sent a clear, public message of intimidation to blacks, and in doing so, did not fear legal sanction or the disapproval of their neighbors.

Another measure of community support can be seen in the fact that many Virginia lynchings were neither spontaneous nor private. Instead, they were planned in advance and done by and before large groups of people. A story in the *Petersburg Index-Appeal* in 1880 said of James Black's lynchers, "They came from different directions and from different portions of the county, as though in accordance with a preconcerted arrangement."[27] Other stories described how local residents were "agitated" or "outraged," and how groups of people were standing on street corners discussing the need for "swift, sure and certain justice." Stories in both the *Norfolk Virginian* and the *Norfolk Landmark* in November 1885 predicted the lynching of suspected child murderer Noah Cherry in Princess Anne County. Even with these warnings, authorities did not stop the seizure of Cherry, and a follow-up story the next day in the *Landmark* said, "As we predicted in our last issue, the murderer paid the penalty of his crime Sunday night at the hands of Judge Lynch."[28] The papers estimated the size of the crowd at Cherry's lynching at 200 to 300. Published mob sizes at other black lynchings ranged from six in the case of George Towler, lynched in Pittsylvania County in 1892, to 3,000 at Benjamin Thomas's lynching in downtown Alexandria in 1899. When five blacks were lynched in Buchanan County in 1893, the *Roanoke Times* reported that the crowd of men, women, and children was so large, at least 500 people, that they climbed onto rooftops to see.

Further evidence of community support can be seen in the papers' reports of souvenir hunters. Mob members sought mementos of the lynchings and proudly displayed them. The *Norfolk Landmark* reported that residents of Norfolk visited the scene of Noah Cherry's hanging and brought back pieces of the tree and the rope. "One man secured the hat and shoes of the fiend and they can now be seen at his place of business on Market square," the paper reported.[29] Hundreds of Charlottesville-area citizens plucked relics from the tree on which John Henry James was lynched. And the *Roanoke Times* reported that residents of that city stripped branches from the tree and clothing from the body of Thomas Smith after his lynching there in 1893.

By examining details such as these in lynch stories, it can be seen that white papers in the late 1800s mirrored the majority attitude in their communities. The language used to describe the lynch victim, the seizure, the size of the mob and its advance planning, the lynch location, and the collection of souvenirs all are indications that white residents of Virginia did not consider blacks equals and did not regard lynching as a crime. Given this attitude, it is not surprising that many editorial writers for Virginia's daily and weekly papers supported lynching. Some, like Herbert J. Browne, even participated. Browne was the owner and editor of the *Roanoke Times* in 1892 when he led a mob that stormed the city jail and tried to lynch an accused child-molester. The local militia stopped the mob before it could seize the prisoner. Browne was arrested, convicted of rioting, fined $100, and sentenced to one hour in jail.

Lynching editorials, published in white-owned Virginia newspapers from 1880 to 1900, fell into three broad categories: support, ambivalence, and criticism. The majority of editorials supported lynching. The *Richmond Dispatch,* for example, believed that lynching was a sensible, even preferred, way of dealing with black "beasts." The paper blamed the black victims when lynchings occurred. "So far as Virginia is concerned nearly all of the lynchings that occur are the result of one specially heinous crime," it said. This was the crime of rape. When R.T. Barton, president of the Virginia Bar Association, described lynching as "murder" and a "barbarism," the paper disagreed:

> This is what we all feel and what many of us say—until we are brought
> face to face with a case where one of our own women has been the victim
> of the man who is to be punished. Then we either join the mob and string
> the man up or rejoice when others have done it.[30]

To the *Dispatch*, lynching was suitable because it was certain, speedy, and terrible. Without it, "young white women living in lonely country places would be ever at the mercy of lustful blacks," it said. Critics, such as Frederick Douglass, who denounced lynching, missed the point, the paper said: "Stop the crime and lynchings will stop—not before." [31]

The *Alexandria Gazette* shared these views. After a mob hanged accused rapist Joseph McCoy from a lamppost in downtown Alexandria in 1897, the *Gazette* called the punishment "well-deserved" and blamed the victim for the mob's action: "When the negroes shall cease to commit such monstrous crimes, lynchings in the South will cease, but not before."[32] Two years later, the events of the McCoy lynching were repeated when another mob stormed the Alexandria jail and lynched Benjamin Thomas. This time the *Gazette* said, "The public lynching here last night was only another glaring instance of the fact that law or no law, Southern men will wreak vengeance upon negroes who outrage their women and girls."[33] The paper again blamed the lynching on "negro rowdies" in the community "who had roamed the streets the night before, threatening attacks upon the white people" if Thomas was lynched.

After the McCoy lynching, the *Fredericksburg Daily Star* said the citizens of Alexandria deserved a "well-done." The paper said the lynching was justifiable and added:

> The action was not in accordance with our statute law, but it was with the higher law of self-preservation. It was the same justifiable instinct that prompts us to shoot the mad dog or crush the serpent.... It was merely the preservation of society against the attacks of the noxious beasts.[34]

Other papers excused lynching as the will of the majority. After the lynching of five blacks in Tazewell County in 1893, the *Roanoke Times* said, "It is useless to hold up the hands in horror at lynching. Under certain circumstances the sentiment of a large majority of the community upholds it, and a majority of the people can neither be indicted nor punished for their opinions."[35] To some editorial writers, lynching was understandable, given the inefficiencies of the criminal-justice system. To them, lynching sprung from a belief that the law's delay was worse for the community than the lynching. The *Roanoke Times* was in this group. The *Times* called lynching "the court of last resort," and said, "When the people come to believe that the machinery which they have erected for the carrying out of justice has lost its power to right wrongs, they create new machinery."[36]

Other white newspapers seemed less certain about lynching, their editorials including both criticism and acceptance. Frequently, a "however" sentence, or one with a "but" in it, signaled their ambivalence. The *Abingdon Weekly Virginian* had mixed feelings about the lynching of Martin Rollins in Russell County in 1889: "The lynching was a horrible deed, but the provocation also was horrible."[37] After a mob lynched Benjamin Thomas in Alexandria in 1899, the *Washington Post* described the incident as hideous, deplorable, and unnecessary. "We have never advocated or defended [lynching], and we never expect to," it said. Then the paper added:

> When our people become convinced of the necessity of extraordinary measures for the protection of their homes, their families and their personal honor and self-respect, they will set aside the text-books and the

codifications and return for one brief and bloody moment to the prime-
val instincts of humanity. Nothing can restrain that frightful frenzy.[38]

A minority of other white-owned papers were neither ambivalent nor
supportive in their editorial pages. They rejected lynching. As the *Richmond
Times* said, "There is no real excuse in public opinion for such a violation of the
law."[39] Its opposition to lynching would eventually become the norm among
Virginia's white-owned newspapers, but at the turn of the century, it was in
the minority. Public indignation ran so high after some crimes that "men of
all classes" approved of lynching, the paper said. Still, the *Times* preferred law
and order to popular approval. Besides, lynching was unnecessary, the paper
said. Courts would punish the guilty. But the *Times*'s respect for the majesty
of the law had its limits. It did not recognize blacks as equals, and its racism
could be found on both its editorial and news pages. In 1889, the *Times* noted
that when blacks were "under the kindly control of Christian civilization,"
they were good citizens and workers. When the black man was in a majority
and took control of the political process, "he becomes a savage," it said. The
South without white civilization was "another Haiti," the paper added. "The
worst thing for the negro would be negro control, and the only thing to save
and civilize him was white control."[40]

Readers of much of Virginia's white-owned press at the turn of the century learned that they needn't worry about the anarchy in their midst. The
black lynching victims were guilty as charged, the stories said, and the dangerous "brute" got what he deserved. In the editorial columns, readers frequently
found excuses for what was depicted on the news pages. The mob's fury was
understandable, editors argued, given the inefficiencies of the criminal-justice
system and the enormity of the offense. When editors criticized the barbarity,
it was because it reflected poorly on the community. Still, they argued, people
outside the region didn't live with blacks and didn't understand their true
nature. Virginia's white-owned newspapers documented the full horror of
lynching in the late 19th century. In the process, they revealed much about the
editors and publishers who ran the papers and the communities they served.
The view was not a pleasant one.

NOTES

1. *Richmond Dispatch*, 3 December 1890.
2. David Brion Davis, *Slavery in the Colonial Chesapeake* (Williamsburg: The Colo-
    nial Williamsburg Foundation, 1986), 1.
3. Ibid.
4. John Hope Franklin, *From Slavery to Freedom: A History of Negro Americans*
    (New York: Alfred A. Knopf, 1967), 74.

5. William E. Katz, ed., *The Negro in Virginia* (New York: Arno Press, 1969), 233.

6. Charles E. Wynes, *Race Relations in Virginia, 1870–1902* (Charlottesville: University of Virginia Press, 1961), 97.

7. Ibid., 144.

8. *Richmond Dispatch*, 4 November 1983.

9. Stewart E. Tolnay and E.M. Beck, *A Festival of Violence* (Urbana: University of Illinois Press, 1995), 271.

10. *Thirty Years of Lynching in the United States, 1889–1918* (New York: National Association for the Advancement of Colored People, 1919), 99.

11. W. Fitzhugh Brundage, *Lynching in the New South: Georgia and Virginia, 1880–1930* (Urbana: University of Illinois Press, 1993), 281.

12. Jacqueline Jones Royster, ed., *Southern Horrors and Other Writings: The Anti-Lynching Campaign of Ida B. Wells, 1892–1900* (Boston: Bedford Books, 1997), 70.

13. W.E.B. Du Bois, "Lynching," *Crisis*, March 1914, 239.

14. Thomas D. Clark, *The Southern Country Editor* (Indianapolis: Bobbs-Merrill, 1948), 228.

15. *Richmond Times*, 14 June 1893.

16. *Richmond Times*, 22 September 1893.

17. During the time period examined here, the Richmond papers had various names, including the *Daily Dispatch*, the *Richmond Dispatch*, the *Times*, and the *Daily Times*. For consistency's sake, the names *Richmond Dispatch* and *Richmond Times* will be used in this paper.

18. *Richmond Dispatch*, 6 February 1884.

19. *Roanoke Times*, 12 February 1892.

20. *Richmond Dispatch*, February 1886.

21. *Richmond Times*, 13 July 1898.

22. *Roanoke Times*, 3 February 1893.

23. *Richmond Times*, 9 June 1889.

24. *Richmond Dispatch*, 9 April 1892.

25. *Richmond Times*, 28 February 1893.

26. *Wytheville Dispatch*, 12 February 1885.

27. *Petersburg Index-Appeal*, 14 April 1880.

28. *Norfolk Landmark*, 17 November 1885.

29. Ibid.

30. *Richmond Dispatch*, 3 August 1893.

31. *Richmond Dispatch*, 14 and 15 May 1893.

32. *Alexandria Gazette*, 23 April 1897.

33. *Alexandria Gazette*, 9 August 1899.

34. *Fredericksburg Daily Star*, 23 April 1897.

35. *Roanoke Times*, 3 February 1893.

36. *Roanoke Times*, 12 February 1892.

37. *Abingdon Weekly Virginian*, 11 April 1889.

38. *Washington Post*, 10 August 1899.

39. *Richmond Times*, 4 December 1890.

40. *Richmond Times*, 14 September 1889.

Index

Calhoun, John C., 2, 26, 27, 32, 33, 39, 44, 47n11, 48n16, 63, 67; opposition of to the Wilmot Proviso, 34
Camden Journal and Southern Whig, 26
Cameron, Simon, 133, 284
Campbell, Archibald, Jr., 75, 81n11
Campbell, John, 186n7
Carolina Gazette, 26
Carolina Spartan, 144
Carriere, Marius, 8, 394
Carrington, Henry B., 230
Carter, Hodding, 145, 173n4
Cash, E.B.C., 26
Cass, Lewis, 72, 73, 75, 77, 81n11
Caudill, Edward, 8, 14, 23
Charleston, 13, 14, 26, 27, 106, 110, 112, 114, 121n67, 135, 137, 138, 149, 153, 155, 157, 309, 371; anti–July Fourth sentiment in, 354
Charleston Daily Courier, 8, 58n8, 110, 116, 118n5, 119n25, 119n30, 119n38, 120n41, 120n58, 121n68, 121n73, 121n74, 140, 143, 145, 147n15, 147n23, 162n13, 164n24, 164n39, 176n50, 176n51, 360n18; coverage of the Vallandigham case, 190, 191, 198, 201n41, 201n44, 201n45; response of to the 15th Amendment, 311–314, 317, 317n6
Charleston Mercury, 27, 33, 111, 116, 137, 138, 142, 143, 151, 161n10; coverage of the Vallandigham case, 190, 191; editorial of concerning abolitionists, 117, 118n11; money owed to by subscribers and advertisers, 144, 146n3, 146n6, 146n8, 147n29
Charlotte Bulletin (North Carolina), 112
Chase, Salmon P., 114, 120n42, 217n29, 264, 277, 282
Cheathem, Mark R., 3, 395
Cheever, George, 366
Cherokee Nation v. Georgia (1830), 39
Chicago Daily Tribune, 89, 92, 96n10, 285, 287–288, 289, 355, 367; on the accomplishments of the North, 356; coverage of Nathan Bedford Forrest, 320, 321; coverage of the Vallandigham case, 191, 192, 194, 199; on Lincoln's assassination, 364; reports of congressional violence in, 93; and the state Democratic

platforms of Georgia and South Carolina, 96n17
Chicago Times, 7, 159, 191, 261, 262, 267, 268, 269n5, 354, 360n17
Chiles, Jim, 175n33
Chomsky, Carol, 236, 245n2, 245n3, 245n10, 247n32, 247n37
Christian Recorder, 7; as a forum for African American experiences in the Civil War, 249–250; position of concerning African American colonization, 252–253; reaction of to African American military participation in the Civil War, 255–259, 258n3, 258n4, 259n9; reaction of to the Emancipation Proclamation, 253–255
Cincinnati Commercial, 264, 267, 305n15
Cincinnati Enquirer, 192
Cinquez, Jose (Joseph), 52, 54, 55, 57, 60n33
Civil Rights Bill (1866), 341, 342
Civil War, 1, 13, 214–215n1, 229, 231n10, 352; as an attempt to reclaim the "true" heritage of the American Revolution, 353; conditions found in hospitals during, 297–301; medical procedures during, 297–298; and the mobilization of human will, 204; role of communications in, 203, 211–214; slavery as the cause of, 250–251. *See also* Civil War, battles of
Civil War, battles of: Allatoona, 158–159; Antietam, 152; Atlanta, 158; Chancellorsville, 155, 163n25, 287; Chickamauga, 157; Cold Harbor, 289–290; First Manassas, 140–141, 181; Fishing Creek, 140; Fredericksburg, 295; Petersburg, 289, 290; Second Manassas, 142, 151–152; Spotsylvania, 205, 286–287; Vicksburg, 155, 264–265; Wilderness Tavern, 286
Civil War, press coverage of. *See* newspapers
Clark, Thomas D., 379, 387n14
Clark, W.G., 153
Clay, Henry, 66, 72
Cleveland Leader, 90, 367
Clisby, Joseph, 153

About the Editors

David B. Sachsman holds the George R. West Jr. Chair of Excellence in Communication and Public Affairs at the rank of professor. He came to the University of Tennessee at Chattanooga in August 1991 from California State University, Fullerton, where he had served as dean and professor of the School of Communications. Previously, he was chair of the Department of Journalism and Mass Media at Rutgers University. Dr. Sachsman is the director of the annual Symposium on the 19th Century Press, the Civil War, and Free Expression, which he and S. Kittrell Rushing founded in 1993. Dr. Sachsman is an editor of *The Civil War and the Press,* a book of readings drawn from the first five conferences, published by Transaction Publishers in 2000. Dr. Sachsman also is known for his research and scholarly activities in environmental communication and environmental risk reporting and for the three editions of *Media: An Introductory Analysis of American Mass Communications,* for which he wrote the history chapter. A journalist by trade, Dr. Sachsman also has written about the suburban press. Three of his books and a series of articles have won statewide awards from the Society of Professional Journalists. In 2005 Dr. Sachsman headed the team appointed to evaluate the U.S. Agency for International Development's environmental education and communication efforts in more than thirty countries across twelve years.

S. Kittrell Rushing is Frank McDonald Professor and the former head of the Communication Department at the University of Tennessee at Chattanooga. Before joining the UTC faculty more than twenty years ago, Rushing taught for several years at the University of Mississippi. Dr. Rushing's most recent publication is the rerelease by the University of Tennessee Press of Eliza Frances Andrews's (1840–1931) first novel, *A Family Secret* (University of Tennessee Press, 2005). The work is a fictionalized account of Andrews's experiences during the last year of the Civil War. The novel was in 1876 the top-selling work of fiction in the United States. Rushing's interest in the works of Fanny Andrews began with his 1998 discovery in the University of Tennessee at Chattanooga Library Archives Andrews's 1870–1872 diary. The diary with notes and an introduction was published in 2002 by the University of Tennessee Press.

Roy Morris Jr. is the editor of *Military Heritage* magazine and the author of four well-received books on the Civil War and post–Civil War eras: *Fraud of the Century: Rutherford B. Hayes, Samuel Tilden, and the Stolen Election of 1876* (Simon and Schuster, 2003); *The Better Angel: Walt Whitman in the Civil War* (Oxford University Press, 2000); *Ambrose Bierce: Alone in Bad Company* (Crown, 1996); and *Sheridan: The Life and Wars of General Phil Sheridan* (Crown, 1992). He also edited and wrote the introduction for a popular new edition of Ambrose Bierce's *The Devil's Dictionary* (Oxford University Press, 1999). A former newspaper reporter and political correspondent for the *Chattanooga News-Free Press* and the *Chattanooga Times*, he was founding editor of *America's Civil War* magazine, which he edited for 14 years.

CONTRIBUTORS

LINUS ABRAHAM

Linus Abraham is the dean of the College of Communication at the African University of Communications in Ghana. He has a B.A. and M.A. from the University of Minnesota and a Ph.D. from the University of Pennsylvania. His research interests are in the area of visual persuasion and minorities in the media.

T. HARRELL ALLEN

T. Harrell Allen is a professor in the School of Communication at East Carolina University. His B.A. in journalism is from the University of Texas, his M.A. from West Virginia University, and his Ph.D. in communication from The Ohio State University. His research interests include journalism history and civil war newspapers.

PAUL ASHDOWN

Paul Ashdown is a professor of journalism and electronic media at the University of Tennessee, Knoxville. He is the author, with Edward Caudill, of *The Mosby Myth: A Confederate Hero in Life and Legend* and *The Myth of Nathan Bedford Forrest*. He is also the author of *A Cold Mountain Companion* and *James Agee: Selected Journalism*.

MENAHEM BLONDHEIM

Menahem Blondheim teaches in the departments of American history and communication at the Hebrew University of Jerusalem and serves as director of the university's Smart Family Institute of Communication. His most recent publication on the ACW is *Copperhead Gore: Ben Wood's Fort Lafayette and Civil War America* (Indiana University Press, 2006).

EDWARD J. BLUM

Edward J. Blum is an assistant professor of history at San Diego State University. He is the author of *W.E.B. Du Bois, American Prophet* (2007).

GREGORY BORCHARD

Gregory A. Borchard is an assistant professor at the University of Nevada, Las Vegas, in the Hank Greenspun School of Journalism and Media Studies. This paper, which he originally presented at the symposium in 1999, was based on research for his master's thesis at the University of Minnesota.

DAVID W. BULLA

A professor at Iowa State University, David W. Bulla focuses his research on the history of the U.S. news media, examining limitations on press performance, especially in wartime. Bulla earned a Ph.D. in mass communication from the University of Florida, an M.A. in journalism from Indiana University, and a B.A. in English from the University of North Carolina at Greensboro. He worked as a sports writer in North Carolina from 1977 to 1987.

CROMPTON BURTON

Crompton Burton is the associate vice president of Alumni and College Relations at Marietta College. He earned his B.A. from the University of Arizona and his M.A. from Ohio University. It was while pursuing his graduate work in journalism that he first encountered the record of Marcellus Emery and his trials in the summer of 1861. Burton's research in the field of journalism history and the Civil War also includes the study of the public relations strategies employed by General George B. McClellan and Secretary of War Edwin M. Stanton and their efforts to influence coverage of the Union war effort.

G. MICHAEL BUSH

Gerald Michael Bush is a retired journalism professor and newspaper journalist. He received his Ph.D. in mass communications from the University of North Carolina at Chapel Hill. He taught at Long Island University and before that at Cal State Long Beach and Long Beach City College. He has reported for the *Los Angeles Times*, the *Long Beach (California) Press-Telegram* and the Los Angeles legal newspaper, the *Daily Journal*. He was also the *Journal*'s city editor.

MARIUS CARRIERE

Marius Carriere received his doctorate from Louisiana State University and is currently the dean of the School of Arts and professor of history at Christian Brothers University in Memphis, Tennessee. He has published several articles on antebellum politics, nativism, and slavery, as well as articles and essays on Reconstruction.

EDWARD CAUDILL

Dr. Edward Caudill is a professor of journalism and electronic media at the University of Tennessee. His research has focused on the history of ideas in the press, and his publications include *Darwinian Myths: The Legends and*

Misuses of the Theory (University of Tennessee Press, 1997), and *The Mosby Myth: A Confederate Hero in Life and Legend*, coauthored with Paul Ashdown (Scholarly Resources, 2002).

MARK CHEATHEM

Mark R. Cheathem is an associate professor of history at Cumberland University in Lebanon, Tennessee.

DOUGLAS W. CUPPLES

Douglas W. Cupples teaches American history courses at the University of Memphis. His major area of study is the American Civil War and Reconstruction with a focus on the Confederate home front along with the history of the South. In addition to the Ph.D. in history he holds a B.A. in political science and an M.A. in international relations.

GIOVANNA DELL'ORTO

Giovanna Dell'Orto earned her Ph.D. from the University of Minnesota, focusing on the historical and international aspects of mass communication. She is the author of *Giving Meanings to the World: The First U.S. Foreign Correspondents, 1838–1859* (Greenwood Press, 2002). She is an assistant professor at the University of Minnesota.

HAZEL DICKEN-GARCIA

Hazel Dicken-Garcia, professor of journalism and mass communication at the University of Minnesota, is best known as the author of *Journalistic Standards in Nineteenth-Century America*.

BRIAN GABRIAL

Brian Gabrial is an assistant professor of journalism at Concordia University in Montréal, Québec. He earned his M.A. and Ph.D. from the University of Minnesota. His research looks at discourses found in 19th-century newspapers regarding race and gender. His work also examines how the mainstream press contributes to "moral panics."

JAMES E. HALL

James Hall is a long-time reporter and editor at newspapers in Virginia. Currently he works for the *Free Lance-Star*, the daily newspaper in Fredericksburg, Virginia. This article is based on the research he did for his master's degree in mass communications at Virginia Commonwealth University in Richmond, Virginia.

WILLIAM E. HUNTZICKER

William E. Huntzicker, assistant professor of mass communications at St. Cloud State University in Minnesota, is the author of *The Popular Press, 1833–1865* (Greenwood Press, 1999) and several articles on nineteenth-century journalism. He contributed three chapters to *Memory and Myth: The Civil War in Fiction and Film from Uncle Tom's Cabin to Cold Mountain* (Purdue University Press, 2007) edited by David B. Sachsman, S. Kittrell Rushing, and Roy Morris Jr.

CALVIN M. LOGUE

Calvin M. Logue is Josiah Meigs Professor Emeritus of Speech Communication, the University of Georgia, specializing in the history and criticism of southern public address. He has written on Ralph McGill, Eugene Talmadge, Richard Russell Jr., and communicative initiatives during slavery, Civil War, and Reconstruction. He coedited *Representative American Speeches* from 1995 to 2006.

GREGG MACDONALD

Gregg A. MacDonald has a journalism degree from Georgia State University. He has worked in Savannah, Georgia, and New Orleans, Louisiana, and was a founding member and managing editor of the *Volunteer Times* in LaFollette, Tennessee. He is currently working just outside Washington, D.C., and writing a book about Appalachia.

DIANA KNOTT MARTINELLI

Diana Knott Martinelli is the Widmeyer Communications Professor in Public Relations at the P.I. Reed School of Journalism at West Virginia University. She was a Roy H. Park Fellow at the University of North Carolina at Chapel Hill, where she received her doctorate under Donald Shaw in 2001.

PATRICIA MCNEELY

Patricia G. McNeely is the Eleanor M. and R. Frank Mundy Distinguished Professor Emerita in the School of Journalism and Mass Communications at the University of South Carolina. She has been chair of the print journalism sequence since 1977 and head of the newspaper, magazine, and history divisions of the Association for Education in Journalism and Mass Communication. In 2001, she was named the National Distinguished Educator of the Year by the Newspaper Division.

EUGENE MILLER

Eugene F. Miller is professor emeritus of political science at the University of Georgia. His areas of research include the history of political philosophy,

American political thought, and semiotics. He has published widely in professional journals in these areas. He is editor of *David Hume's Essays, Moral, Political, and Literary* (revised edition, Liberty Press, 1987).

ROY MORRIS JR.

Chattanooga, Tennessee, native Roy Morris Jr. has long had an interest in the Civil War and the literature it inspired. Among his many works, he is the author of *The Better Angel: Walt Whitman in the Civil War* (Oxford University Press, 2000), and he is now at work on a new biography of Stephen Crane for Oxford University Press.

GENE MURRAY

Gene Murray, Ph.D., a professor of mass communication, joined the Grambling State University faculty in 1992. He holds degrees from Murray State University, Ohio University, and Texas A&M. Murray authored *Covering Sex, Race, and Gender in the American Military Services* (Edwin Mellen Press, 2004).

RANDALL PATNODE

Randall Patnode is an associate professor of communication at Xavier University in Cincinnati. He earned his Ph.D. from the University of North Carolina at Chapel Hill. His interests include the history of communication technologies.

KATHERINE A. PIERCE

Dr. Katherine A. Pierce is assistant professor of history at Sam Houston State University. She specializes in politics and print media in antebellum America. She is currently working on *Networks of Disunion: Politics and Print Media and the Coming of the Civil War*.

ROBERT RABE

Robert A. Rabe is an assistant professor in the W. Page Pitt School of Journalism and Mass Communication at Marshall University, where he teaches journalism history, reporting, and news writing.

FORD RISLEY

Ford Risley is the head of the Department of Journalism at Penn State. He has published articles on the 19th-century press in *American Journalism, Civil War History, Georgia Historical Quarterly*, and *Journalism History*.

CHRISTOPHER J. SCHROLL

Chris Schroll earned his Ph.D. in speech communication from the University of Georgia in 1996. He held teaching positions at the University of North Dakota and Wayne State University and managed the Office of Instructional Programs at Wayne State. His essays have appeared in *Communication Theory*, *Critical Studies in Mass Communication*, and *Journal of Mass Media Ethics*. Chris currently is employed in the private sector.

Donald L. ... m and
Mass Con ... l Hill,
teaching m ... recipi-
ent of the ... duca-
tion in Jour

Bernell E. T ... y of
Florida. Her ... en-
tury African ... ted
from her rese ... the
African Amer

Debra Reddin ... y
and Philosophy ... n
Press in the Civi ... d
America's Wars.

DATE DUE	RETURNED